# The Renaissance *Hamlet*

# The Renaissance HAMLET

## Issues and Responses in 1600

Roland Mushat Frye

PRINCETON UNIVERSITY

PRESS

Copyright © 1984 by Princeton University Press
Published by Princeton University Press, 41 William Street, Princeton, New Jersey 08540
In the United Kingdom: Princeton University Press, Guildford, Surrey
All Rights Reserved

Library of Congress Cataloging in Publication Data will be found on the last
printed page of this book
ISBN 0-691-06579-9

Publication of this book has been aided by a grant from the Whitney Darrow Fund of
Princeton University Press

This book has been composed in Linotron Sabon type
Clothbound editions of Princeton University Press books are printed on acid-free paper,
and binding materials are chosen for strength and durability. Paperbacks, although
satisfactory for personal collections, are not usually suitable for library rebinding

Printed in the United States of America by Princeton
University Press, Princeton, New Jersey

# DEDICATION

To my friends and colleagues at The Institute for Advanced Study in Princeton and at the Henry E. Huntington Library in San Marino, California, in whose stimulating company this book was written.

# Contents

# Illustrations

Illustrations are listed by Roman and Arabic numerals,
referring to chapter and figure numbers respectively.

# Acknowledgments

A SCHOLARLY life, among its various joys, offers the pleasure of consultation with others along the way, and it is always a source of satisfaction to acknowledge the assistance one has received. Although no investigator can shift the responsibility for work done, the sum total of scholarly contribution would be far less were it not for the sharing of knowledge and insight through conversation and correspondence as well as through publication. My footnote references will record many of the obligations I have incurred in developing these thoughts about *Hamlet*, primarily through reading what others have written in a wide variety of fields, but there are other debts which should also be recognized here.

I have been much assisted at various points in the development of historical background by the suggestions of Professors John Elliott of the Institute for Advanced Study, Franklin L. Ford of Harvard University, Ralph E. Giesey of the University of Iowa, Robert M. Kingdon of the University of Wisconsin, Albert J. Loomie, S.J., of Fordham University, and J. Russell Major of Emory University. Each of these scholars, in their different ways, offered highly valuable insights into the varied attitudes toward resistance and rebellion (as well as other historical issues) in my period of interest. At a much earlier stage of the consideration of the Ghost (over twenty years ago), I was saved from later embarrassment by the kindly intervention and advice of Professor Robert H. West of the University of Georgia. Charles R. Forker of Indiana University was helpful in discussing with me some of the issues and problems encountered along the way, especially for Chapter Three. Camille Wells Slights and the Princeton University Press kindly permitted me to see a pre-publication copy of *The Casuistical Tradition in Shakespeare, Donne, Herbert, and Milton* while I was putting my analysis of casuistry into final form. Terence R. Murphy of American University has corresponded with me at great and useful length about a whole range of matters associated with suicide. Elizabeth Read Foster of Bryn Mawr has offered wise insight on a wide range of issues, and her doctoral student Myra Rifkin was invaluable in the consideration of funeral practices. John H. Leith of Union Theological Seminary and Hugh T. Kerr of Princeton Theological Seminary offered valuable suggestions and support at various points.

Hallett Smith of the Henry E. Huntington Library has helped me, as he has so many others, in innumerable ways.

The staffs of many libraries have made my research more pleasant as well as more efficient: especially to be mentioned here are the staff of the University of Pennsylvania Libraries, along with those at the Folger Shakespeare Library and the Henry E. Huntington Library. The visual resources of the Paul Mellon Centre for Studies in British Art, in London, along with the Yale Center for British Art, as well as the Witt Library of the Courtauld Institute in London, proved highly useful. Sir Oliver Millar, Keeper of the Queen's Pictures, has assisted me by providing access to the Royal Collection, and many museums have helped in providing illustrations, as acknowledged in the captions for my reproductions here. As always, it is a pleasure to work with the Princeton University Press, and I wish especially to thank my editor, Mrs. Arthur Sherwood, who has been most helpful at every point, and Mrs. Carolyn MacKinnon for her meticulous work with a very difficult set of proofs.

My secretary, Mrs. Eileen Cooper, has been an invaluable coadjutor in the process of bringing this book from the inchoate stage of preparatory notes, through many preliminary drafts, to its final form. Graduate students in my classes and seminars, as well as research assistants, have been very helpful, as have the audiences before whom I have presented papers on different parts of this study. Friends, academic and nonacademic, have been generous in expressing interest and support. Abbreviated versions of some portions of earlier stages in the development of this book have appeared as articles in *Shakespeare Quarterly*, *The Huntington Library Quarterly*, and *Theology Today*.

Membership in the Institute for Advanced Study in 1979, and an NEH-Huntington Library Fellowship in 1981, made possible the writing of the book, while research grants from the American Philosophical Society assisted me in carrying out preparatory research in England. The University of Pennsylvania has been both understanding and generous in giving me leaves for this work.

My wife Jean has been constant in her interest and support at every point along the way.

The dedication acknowledges other debts, both professional and personal, which are more deeply felt than a dedication can show.

University of Pennsylvania                                    Roland Mushat Frye
Philadelphia, Pennsylvania

# The Renaissance *Hamlet*

# ONE

# The Form and Pressure
# of the Time

Suit the action to the word, the word to the action, with this special observation, that you o'erstep not the modesty of nature. For anything so overdone
is from the purpose of playing, whose end, both at the first and now, was
and is, to hold, as 'twere, the mirror up to nature, to show virtue her own
feature, scorn her own image, and the very age and body of the time his
form and pressure.[1]

THE TRAGEDY OF HAMLET poses challenges to every intelligent person,
challenges that vary depending upon the points of view from which we
see it. My purpose here is to examine the play afresh in the light of the
audiences for which it was initially written, and to see it in the ambience of
Elizabethan attitudes. In this context, much can now be seen which has been
missed in the past. Continuing advances in historical knowledge, made by many
different scholars in many different fields of investigation, make it possible now
for us to reestablish more fully, more accurately, and more sensitively the
audience responses upon which Shakespeare played. We can thus see that his
*Hamlet* was so constructed as to evoke very different understandings in 1600
from those which have become typical of modern times. To recover the Elizabethan understandings to which Shakespeare appealed, I shall document relevant Elizabethan frames of reference Globe audiences would have brought to
the play. In this way, we shall see *Hamlet* in a fresh light: we shall discover in
its familiar text a play which in many ways is surprisingly unlike what we are
ordinarily accustomed to expect, and we shall discover a different set of cer-
tainties and an equally different (and equally important) set of mysteries from
those we may assume. My purpose throughout will be to examine the play in
terms of the form and pressure of its own time, approached in the light of
rigorous historical scholarship.

The most profound and seminal definition of drama as a representation or imitation of life comes in the forty lines of Hamlet's advice to the players, from which the headnote to this chapter quotes the central passage. Containing Shakespeare's most extensive comments on drama, these words are primarily applied to the play-within-the-play, but they can also serve as a highly useful commentary upon the more general relations between life and art, and they provide the basis for my method of interpretation here.

In this definition of dramatic art, Shakespeare unites the universal with the particular by showing "virtue her own feature, scorn her own image, and the very age and body of the time his form and pressure." The derivation of the universal from the particular is the essence of the poetic, as Goethe saw it, and his words are directly pertinent to Hamlet:

> It matters a great deal whether the poet is seeking the particular for the universal, or seeing the universal in the particular. The former process gives rise to allegory, in which the particular serves only as an instance or example of the universal; the latter, on the other hand, is the true nature of poetry . . . . And he who vividly grasps the particular will at the same time also grasp the universal, and will either not become aware of it at all, or will only do so long afterward.[2]

It is in some such way that Shakespeare's genius operated. By holding up a mirror to reflect the age and body of the time he knew best, he transmuted the problems, attitudes, and concerns of his own age into something rich, fresh, and marvelous, transcending any one cultural epoch. It is this successful combination of effects that sets him apart. Even the most highly regarded writers of any age begin to appear oddly old-fashioned or even out of date after a few decades and their most serious concerns often seem irrelevant to later generations. But the words Shakespeare's characters speak still voice our concerns, and their problems merge into our problems. Whether they are dressed in Roman togas or medieval armor or Elizabethan doublets, they are perennially our contemporaries.

Marvelously universal though they are, however, Shakespeare's plays originate in his own time and place. It could not be otherwise, because even a great genius must begin by perceiving, reflecting upon, and transmuting what is immediately before him. Hamlet's description of the players as "the abstract and brief chronicles of the time" underscores that point (2.2.512). What Shake-

speare knew that is relevant to all men and to every society was learned in his
own period and place, and was timelessly expressed in the language of his own
age. If we are to understand his universality, we can scarcely better begin than
with his particularity.

When viewed in its original milieu, *Hamlet* takes on unexpected freshness.
Some things which are problems to us would not have appeared to be problems
in 1600, and different sets of questions would have arisen in Elizabethan minds,
which often do not occur to us at all. Furthermore, certain discontinuities and
discrepancies in the play when approached in twentieth-century terms simply
would not have appeared in its original context. The Elizabethans for whom
Shakespeare wrote would have found in *Hamlet* different excitements and
challenges from those we today generally recognize. They would also have
found a more pervasive unity, and an even more profound resolution to the
play.[3] Viewing *Hamlet* against the background of the time and the people for
whom it was written yields a number of fresh perceptions, but this "novelty
of interpretation" is not really new: it results from a systematic reconstruction
of Elizabethan conceptions the words of the dramatist would have evoked in
the minds of his original audiences. Playing upon the interests and concerns,
the convictions and the doubts of his English contemporaries, Shakespeare has
indeed held a "mirror up to nature, to show virtue her own feature, scorn her
own image."

But caution and balance are necessary, for that "mirror" to which Hamlet
refers is a more complicated image than modern experience automatically prepares us to recognize. Thinking of large modern mirrors which can cover as
much as an entire wall and reflect sweeping panoramas of nature with perfect
fidelity, some readers in recent generations have assumed that Shakespeare's
definition of art stipulated an absolute, virtually photographic or naturalistic
reproduction of nature. Thus even so great a scholar as C. H. Herford maintained that for Shakespeare "the height of art is reached by a copy of nature
exactly like the original" and that his criterion for art is "the elementary one
(invariable in Shakespeare) of being *like*," and the even greater Edmond Malone
had earlier interpreted Hamlet's mirror as requiring a play to "delineate exactly
the manners of the age and the particular humor of the days."[4] The problems
and meanings of Hamlet's mirror are treated in considerable detail in Appendix
A, but it is important to observe here that neither for Shakespeare nor for his

earlier audiences would the "mirror up to nature" have evoked the kinds of mirror Malone, Herford, and others have apparently had in mind in their interpretation of Hamlet's words.

As artifacts, Elizabethan mirrors were small instruments, and as often as not represented a flawed or changed image of what they reflected. More importantly, mirrors were familiar metaphors for knowledge and understanding, beginning of course with the self-reflection which comes from looking into even a small glass: put in terms familiar to twentieth-century analysis, the "vehicle" was the small Elizabethan mirror, the "tenor" was the understanding and knowledge it conveyed. Furthermore, the mirror as a symbol for art and drama had a long history before Hamlet gave it its finest expression, and it did not suggest naturalistic or one-for-one reproduction of the reality it conveyed. No Elizabethan would have understood Hamlet's mirror metaphor as promising a literal or isomorphic reproduction of events and persons in their society or in any other society. What they would have understood was that the "mirror up to nature" excluded a non-representational world removed from the world they and all men know. In short, it was not a self-contained and self-reflexive artifact. Such art as Hamlet postulates represents or imitates human reality, a reality Shakespeare's audiences could recognize as evoking concerns familiar to them and with which they could therefore identify, even while elevating this reality into a broader and more profound understanding of human existence. Shakespeare's "mirror" indicated his intent to present the breadth and depth of human nature as he understood it, but not a precise, reproductive picture of any historical events.

Our task in this book will thus not be to find one-for-one sources in the world of Shakespeare's time for the events, persons, and ideas in *Hamlet*. Indeed, we are not seeking sources at all, but rather resources Shakespeare could employ as stimuli to evoke audience response in his creation of a great work of art. If we identify historical situations comparable to those Shakespeare dramatized and if we establish the reactions of Shakespeare's contemporaries to those comparable situations, we will be in a better position to postulate the kinds of reactions Shakespeare's dramatization would have evoked, through an understanding of the human concerns he appealed to in his audiences. By reconstructing and entering into the pertinent contexts of the sixteenth-century world, we can better appreciate what he was doing and what he achieved in

*Hamlet*. We will not achieve a perfect appreciation, of course, because there are no perfect parallels and even if there were we should not assume that exactly the same reaction would occur to a dramatized event in the theater as to a similar event in historical reality. But we will at least have established working approximations and qualified probabilities for what *Hamlet* meant to its author and to his Elizabethan contemporaries in the Globe Theater.

This does not mean that we can or will find an historical person who served as the original model for Hamlet, or for Polonius, or for Gertrude. If there were such, and I doubt that there were, we are not likely to be able to identify them across the intervening centuries and through the shadows of aesthetic distance.[5] Nor should we expect to uncover many passing and topical allusions to famous persons and events in Elizabethan England: there are only a few such allusions in all of Shakespeare, the best-known being perhaps the reference to the expedition into Ireland in *Henry V* and the glance at the "wars of the theaters" in *Hamlet*, and neither of these is very significant. On another plane of allusion, our understanding of *Measure for Measure* may be enriched if we recognize the play's complimentary treatment of the ideas of King James, but what can be an aid to understanding becomes an obstacle if we substitute James Stuart's ideas for William Shakespeare's poetry. Furthermore, Shakespeare did not write his plays to advise crown, court, parliament or people as to what should be done about this, that, or another problem of state. If we expect such "timeliness" in Shakespeare we will miss the point of his peculiar greatness, and if we never go beyond Elizabethan frames of reference in interpreting him, we shall miss his universality. Shakespeare neither can nor should be confined within a straight jacket of Elizabethan opinions, nor should we reduce the majesty of his words to the commonplaces and clichés of his time. Here balance and moderation are as important to the interpreting scholar as to the interpreting actor: Hamlet's advice to the one should also apply to the other, "that you o'erstep not the modesty of nature." Or, as one distinguished historian of drama has put it, knowledge and tradition "must be used with all the skill and caution with which one handles edged tools."[6]

But if we are to appreciate Shakespeare's plays fully, we should not omit any practicable means for seeing them in their own nascent environment. Thanks to generations of careful scholarship, we know a great deal about that environment, and Shakespearean interpretation has greatly profited from research into Elizabethan stage and theatrical practices, literary forms and genres, the transmission of texts, and the history of ideas. With such contributions taken for granted, my concern in this study is to explore the broader cultural milieu of Shakespeare's time, and my purpose is to reconstruct relevant aspects of the Elizabethan context so that modern readers may be able to see *Hamlet* more nearly as it would have been seen by the original audiences for whom Shakespeare wrote it. The achievements of historical research, especially since the Second World War, have provided insights into Elizabethan attitudes and customs which can assist, revitalize, and in important ways change our understanding of *Hamlet*.

To attain that understanding, at least in some measure, is easier than to express it in writing. A cultural milieu is an encompassing phenomenon and is thus best conceived as circular or even global, whereas historical criticism requires a linear presentation. To convey the complex and sophisticated concerns of Elizabethan minds demands organization and clarity. Yet the very organization and clarity which will make the subject accessible and intelligible in twentieth-century terms can lead to oversimplification, on the part either of the writer or of the reader, or both. In writing this book, I have been pervasively aware of a tension between the sixteenth and the twentieth centuries, a tension which cannot be entirely dispelled but which I hope as a literary historian to mediate and make fruitful.

Such an historical approach can provide safeguards against the precarious subjectivisms of individual critics and the provincialisms of critical schools. The most dangerous type of critic, according to T. S. Eliot, is "the critic with a mind which is naturally of the creative order, but which through some weakness in creative power exercises itself in criticism instead. These minds often find in Hamlet a vicarious existence for their own artistic realization."[7] Historical reconstruction can give some protection against that danger.

But while protecting us from that danger, historical approaches typically expose us to others. Scholars can be betrayed by historical reductivism as readily as by any other form of oversimplification. While studying historical backgrounds, we must remind ourselves that a great creative writer like Shakespeare used the materials his culture made available to him, but that he refused to be used by those materials. Instead, he transcended and transmuted them. Wilbur Sanders has wisely observed that "historical criticism, if it is to be useful, needs to know the difference between the greatness which is unique, and the competence for which one can find adequate parallels elsewhere."[8]

What I attempt to do here is to present a sufficiently broad cross-section of relevant Elizabethan attitudes so that we who are each other's contemporaries in the twentieth century can also feel ourselves at home with the responses of Shakespeare's contemporaries. At points this entails the re-establishment of Elizabethan uncertainties, ambiguities, doubts, and disagreements in such a way that we in our time can understand them and see their implications. At other points, Elizabethan agreements and consensuses are treated in the same way and to the same end. In some cases, these sixteenth-century attitudes are broadly interesting and significant in themselves and in other cases they would be only marginally so were it not for their pertinence to *Hamlet*. Throughout, the pertinence to *Hamlet* is our overriding concern.

When that concern requires information on Elizabethan burial and mourning practices, that subject will be explored: even though scarcely a lively subject in itself, Shakespeare has vitalized it by his dramatic treatment. In the same way, incest is seen in Elizabethan terms by recapturing typical reactions to actual unions such as that of Claudius and Gertrude. Similarly, Hamlet's agonizing debates over resistance to the monarch and tyrannicide are placed in frames of reference familiar to the playwright and to those before whom the play was originally presented. In sum, I am drawing assistance from a number of historical fields (political, social, intellectual, religious, artistic, and so on) in order to draw modern readers into the cultural ambience of the Globe Theater audiences. Throughout, the particular is surveyed as an avenue for approaching the universal. In all these ways, I hope we can better understand and in good measure participate in the responses Shakespeare could have expected from the original audiences for whom he wrote *Hamlet*, thereby enriching our own responses today.

But it cannot be overemphasized, particularly in a study which combines practical criticism with history in the broadest sense, that Shakespeare never becomes a servant of the topicalities of his own culture. I have tried to make that point sufficiently clear in this introduction, because to repeat it throughout this book would be tedious. For the remainder of this study, our primary concern will be with *Hamlet* as designed to appeal to Shakespeare's original audiences, and that concern should deepen our understanding by enabling us to encounter the play in terms which made it so intensely exciting to the Globe audiences in 1600. Shakespeare transcends the merely timely by the magic of insight and style, and elevates it to perennial interest and significance, but he did so by manipulating predictable patterns of stimulus and response in his Elizabethan audience.

# TWO

# Problems, Challenges, and Ambiguities

## 1. The Challenge

TWO MAJOR commands are given to Hamlet by the Ghost: "If thou didst ever thy dear father love/ —Revenge his foul and most unnatural murder," and "Let not the royal bed of Denmark be/ A couch for luxury and damnèd incest" (1.5.23-25 and 82-83). In the face of these imperatives, interpreters of the play have too often simplified Hamlet's problems far beyond the complexity Shakespeare presented to his Globe audience. On the one hand we may be told that the usual moral laws forbidding revenge and murder applied to Hamlet as to other men, and that the Prince would be condemned, even damned, for acting against Claudius. On the contrary we may also be assured that Hamlet must discharge the supernatural command of revenge, and that failure or even delay in doing so would earn him the condemnation of an Elizabethan audience. These opposing interpretations seem to assume that there was one universal or at least pervasive sixteenth-century attitude toward such matters, but historically this is not the case. Actual responses to such problems as Hamlet faces were far less unified and considerably more ambiguous in 1600 than some literary historians and critics have recognized.

Even when the Ghost's report on the murder has been validated, the right course of action for the Prince would still not have seemed entirely clear to an Elizabethan audience, for reasons which would have contributed to the great dramatic intensity of the play. Hamlet surely has an obligation, but an obligation which would have been subject to diametrically opposite interpretations. Some Elizabethans would have held that he is morally bound to accept Claudius as *de facto* king, despite the fact that he is an evil and tyrannous ruler, whereas others would have seen it as his duty to purge the realm of a tyrannous usurper and establish himself as rightful king in succession to his father. That uncertainty of position, especially when joined with the questionable nature and purpose of the Ghost, makes Hamlet's problem intensely challenging, and perhaps even insoluble. Shakespeare has created for his protagonist a predicament which can generate the most blatantly melodramatic and at the same time the most subtly philosophical suspense, appealing equally to the "unskillful" and to the "judicious," as he has done for almost four centuries. To understand the range and depth of the play's explorations, as they would have been understood by the audiences for whom Shakespeare wrote, we need to examine attitudes actually existing among Shakespeare's contemporaries, attitudes toward retribution, rebellion and even tyrannicide—issues as important in sixteenth-century Europe as they are in the play itself.

"The Elizabethan World Picture" which E.M.W. Tillyard so ably and helpfully portrayed for us several decades ago is admittedly pertinent here, and it neither can nor should be ignored, even though it presents only one part of the actual historical picture.[1] Insurrection and violence cannot be taken lightly by any stable society, and certainly were not so taken in Tudor England. To understand the abhorrence sixteenth-century Englishmen felt for willful rebellion, we need only remind ourselves of the Wars of the Roses in the previous century, which reduced the country to the near anarchy and pervasive violence dramatized by Shakespeare in his two great cycles of English history plays. Those experiences were alive in the minds of Englishmen throughout the Tudor dynasty, and help to explain the abhorrence of anything approaching a militant assault upon the English monarch—an abhorrence both widespread and official. *The Book of Homilies* appointed to be read in churches contains several sermons commending obedience and condemning strife and willful rebellion.[2] In the opening paragraph of "The Homily against Disobedience and Willful Rebellion," the instigator of all such rebellion is identified as Satan, who led the fallen angels against God and who throughout the ages has inspired many subsequent assaults upon authority. The same homily goes on to teach that "a rebel is worse than the worst prince, and rebellion worse than the worst government of the worst prince that hitherto hath been."[3]

The conception of rebellion as the service of Satan helps (along with other more basic factors) to explain Hamlet's acute anxiety that the Ghost may be a devil who will betray his soul, or as he puts it at the very end of act two; "abuses me to damn me." That prolific Anglican apologist Thomas Becon warned that the devil may "put in thy head, that the magistrates and high powers do not their duty in the right government of a commonweal, but too much cruelly oppress their subjects, and that therefore thou mayest justly rise and rebel against them, and take upon thee of thine own private authority to redress things that are amiss in the commonweal; take heed that thou by no means consentest to his most subtle and wicked temptation, whereby he goeth about to throw thee into everlasting damnation, both of body and soul, beside the shameful death that thou shalt have in this world."[4] Similar statements were made by persons as dissimilar as Bishop Latimer, King James I, and Sir Thomas Browne, as we shall shortly see. We may be sure that such suspicions of demonic solicitation would already have occurred to members of the Globe audience even before Hamlet spells out his own particular fear of the Ghost.

Had Hamlet accepted that position expressed in the *Homilies*, he would have had no problem of decision, and had the Globe audience regarded that position as the only acceptable response to a murderous and usurping king, Shakespeare could not have written a popular and successful play in which a rebellious prince emerges as a sympathetic and even approved hero. But the *Homilies* did not express the only judgment on such matters—nor even the only responsible judgment. The Pope thought and pronounced differently, and prominent Jesuits wrote powerfully to a different effect. So too in Protestantism: in Scotland, France, Holland, and Geneva there were persuasive, intelligent, and authoritative voices justifying the use of force against an unjust monarch. The Wars of Religion which began in 1562 in France, and largely preoccupied that country for the remainder of the century, forced Protestants and Catholics alike to re-examine and reassess the whole question of passive submission to a *de facto* king. At first this reassessment came within the Protestant camp, as the Huguenot nobility persuaded themselves to take arms against an antagonistic Catholic government. "As there were princes of the blood among them, and even crowned heads, resistance to the authority of the day was not thought to be seditious." In those words, Lord Acton summarized much of the rationale with which we will be dealing.[5]

The London audiences for whom Shakespeare wrote would not have brought with them to the theater a single and unvarying view of the proper response to such problems as those with which Hamlet is confronted. Viewing his situation, some in those early audiences would have thought that he should accept passively the rotten state of Denmark, and take no action against Claudius— "No, not for a king,/ Upon whose property and most dear life/ A damned

made," as Hamlet himself says (2.2.554-56). Others would have
~onsibility differently and would have held that he was indeed
a' fatted all the region kites/ With this slave's offal," as he also
(2.2.564-65). In his soliloquies and elsewhere, Hamlet analyzes virtually
every alternative which would have occurred to a thoughtful Elizabethan in
the circumstances of the story, and does so with a pyrotechnic display of
intellectual and poetic power. By the end of the play, Hamlet would have
earned the dramatic admiration of most members of an Elizabethan audience,
whether or not they agreed with his particular views and his course of action.
In this chapter, our purpose will be to understand the complexity of the challenges facing Hamlet, within the broad cultural context of Shakespeare's time.
Hamlet's words deal with real problems and possible solutions which were
current in Shakespeare's Europe, but those words transcend any merely topical
or commonplace reference. Although we lay our basis for understanding *Hamlet*
by beginning with Shakespeare's own time, the reason for our interest is that
both the plot and his prince are not for an age but for all time.

## II. The "Questionable" Ghost

### A. *The Range of Possibilities*

*Hamlet* begins with the Ghost, and it is here too that we must begin if we
are to understand the range of audience responses Shakespeare manipulated in
developing the play. The Ghost not only launches the action of the tragedy,
but in doing so he confronts the Prince with a dangerous task and also with
uncertainty and enigma. By the use of no other device could Shakespeare have
told Hamlet of the murder of his father so as to raise so many doubts and
inspire so many questions, in his own mind and in the minds of the Globe
audience.

Shakespeare constructed the story so that we are never perfectly certain
as to just who or what the Ghost is. Dubiety about the Ghost would have been
far greater for Shakespeare's original audience than for us, and that difference
in attitude entails major consequences for understanding the play. For most
modern audiences, ghosts exist only in literature and folklore, so this Ghost
seems little more than a theatrical device for beginning the play and for commanding Hamlet to discharge the revenge incumbent upon him. By virtue of
that convention, typical modern readers accept the Ghost for literary purposes

14

as the authoritative spirit of the murdered king,[6] and if the Ghost is so perceived as a literary convention to trigger action, then the Prince is perceived to be at best dilatory and perhaps even madly indecisive in his responses to the Ghost's commands.

But the problem would have seemed far more complicated to the Elizabethans for whom Shakespeare wrote the play. They would have recognized the Ghost as a stage device, just as we do, but Shakespeare's very choice of a ghost, and particularly of this ghost, to launch the action would have introduced elements of uncertainty, suspicion, and mistrust which we today can recapture only by an act of historical and imaginative reconstruction. It is only through understanding the enigmatic character of this ghost, as Shakespeare presented it to the contemporaries for whom he wrote, that we in the twentieth century can appreciate Hamlet's inescapable doubts and painful deliberation about dispatching his uncle. Other and different problems arise as the play progresses, but it is here that we must begin.

The text of *Hamlet* introduces four attitudes toward ghosts, and of these the play itself excludes only one as impossible. That excluded explanation is the one which Shakespeare presents initially, namely that the Ghost is only a figment of the imagination. Horatio is introduced in the first scene as a skeptic who refuses to believe the report of the two officers of the guard, maintaining that the Ghost existed only in their "fantasy." As the play opens, Marcellus has persuaded Horatio to join the midnight watch so that "if again this apparition come,/ He may approve our eyes and speak to it" (1.1.23-29). It was theatrically important that this test be made explicit, and that it be made at the very beginning of the play—the first test to which the Ghost is exposed. The result is conclusive for Horatio, who is entirely convinced of the reality of "this thing." In all, the Ghost appears four times to Marcellus, three to Bernardo, and two each to Hamlet and Horatio, for a total of eleven sightings.

The appearance of the Ghost only to Hamlet but not to Gertrude in act three would not have suggested to Elizabethans that it had by that point become merely a figment of Hamlet's imagination. Spirits were able to make themselves visible to as many or as few observers as they might choose. As Lewes Levater wrote in his book on apparitions, "it cometh oftentimes to pass that some one man doth hear or see some thing most plainly, when another which standeth by him or walketh with him neither seeth nor heareth any such matter."[7] Similarly, Thomas Lodge declared that spirits "appear in assumed bodies, appropriate to their intents: and . . . they appear to none but to those to whom the vision appertaineth."[8] The modern stage practice of enacting the Ghost as heartbroken because Gertrude could not see it would have struck Elizabethans as the height of sentimental nonsense: had the Ghost wished to be visible to Gertrude, it could have made itself so. Shakespeare established the reality of the Ghost as an objective presence by the total of eleven sightings by four different characters. That would have been proof enough for Elizabethans who believed in the possibility of such specters, and it should be so for us, at least literarily, even though most moderns do not otherwise accept the possibility or have frames of reference within which to explore it.[9]

In addition to the first possibility, which Shakespeare so carefully excluded, three principal frames of reference for ghosts were known to the Elizabethans: Greek and Latin literature furnished precedents for wraiths returning from the dead to visit the living; Protestant doctrine did not deny the appearance of ghosts, but typically regarded them as devils in masquerade; Roman Catholic doctrine also warned that many ghosts were devils, but at the same time maintained that others might be spirits of the dead temporarily returned from purgatory. Shakespeare introduces each of these theories into *Hamlet*, but he has been careful not to weight his dramatic evidence decisively in favor of any one. The result is that Hamlet is given a mandate he cannot ignore, but from a source which remains mysterious and dubious from first to last—even after the truth of the Ghost's accusation against Claudius has been confirmed. The ambiguity of the Ghost needs to be affirmed once again,[10] in the light of evidence both new and old from Shakespeare's time.

The pagan view of ghosts is introduced in a long speech of classical recollection by Horatio, who describes how "A little ere the mightiest Julius fell,/ The graves stood tenantless and the sheeted dead/ Did squeak and gibber in the Roman streets/ . . . As harbingers preceding still the fates" of Caesar's assassination (*Ham.* 1.1.113-20; see also *Caes.* 2.2.17-24). Elizabethans could have accepted for literary purposes this view of the Ghost as a shade returned from some Virgilian underworld, but there is nothing in the play which either affirms or rejects this as a final explanation.[11] After Horatio's speech, no more is made of it in the play, either pro or con, whereas the two other remaining possibilities continue to receive attention.

As for the Christian interpretations, no major denomination has ever placed primary doctrinal weight on the question of ghosts, but certain central doctrines did bear upon that question in ways which would have been clear even for the simplest believers. The spiritual indoctrination to which Shakespeare's original audiences were most consistently exposed came from the established Church of England, and was heavily Protestant in emphasis. Protestant beliefs affirmed only three worlds—the earth on which we live the present life, and after death either heaven or hell. It was generally agreed among Protestants that the souls of the human departed could not return to earth either from heaven or hell, and that there was no intermediate state such as purgatory from which return would be possible.[12] Obviously, then, basic Protestant doctrine did not accept the possibility of legitimate ghosts of departed men or women. It was not denied that angels could appear like the dead, but it was not thought that they would wish or need to do so.

Protestants therefore typically interpreted lifelike specters as demons in disguise who assumed human form in order to achieve a devilish purpose.[13] Thomas Cranmer, the first Protestant Archbishop of Canterbury, approvingly quoted Lactantius about "the deceits of them that lurking under the names of the dead intend to plague them that be alive."[14] James Calfhill complained of wicked spirits which "appear to men in divers shapes, disquiet them when they are awake, trouble them in their sleeps."[15] The influential Henry Bullinger expressed the standard teaching when he declared that apparitions "are neither sent by God, neither can they enter in unto men to instruct and warn them either of things present or of things to come. Whereupon it followeth, that appearing of souls, that revelations and oracles, are mere delusions of Satan, ordained contrary to the sincerity and pureness of true religion."[16] The familiar Biblical account of the raising of the ghost of Samuel by the witch of Endor was explained in exactly those demonic terms.[17] The marginal gloss appended to I Samuel 28:14 in the most popular translation of Shakespeare's time, the 1560 Geneva Bible (and to similar effect in the Bishop's Bible), explained that it was not actually Samuel who appeared to Saul but "Satan, who to blinde his eyes tooke upon him the forme of Samuel, as he can do of an angel of light."[18]

All this is clear enough in terms of standard Protestant doctrine, but in actual practice interpretation might not be so simple, and staunch Protestants could be uncertain in their response to numenous appearances. A case in point was James Pilkington, Bishop of Durham, who frankly declared himself non-plused by an apparition which had appeared on several occasions to several

17

witnesses within his own diocese. Reporting to Archbishop Parker on the parishes within his see, he gives a special note to events in Blackburn where

> there is a fantastical (and as some think a lunatic) young man [the rector], which says he has spoken with one of his neighbors that died four years since or more. Divers times he says he has seen him, and talked with him, and took with him the curate, the schoolmaster, and other neighbors, which all affirm that they see him too. These things be so common here, and none of authority that will gainsay it, but rather believe and confirm it, that everyone believes it. If I had known how to have examined it with authority, I would have done it.[19]

Unfortunately, we do not know what (if anything) was finally concluded in this case, but it is nonetheless instructive, for several reasons. The actuality of the ghost was confirmed by several witnesses who had known the living man, as in *Hamlet*, even though the principal observer (the young clergyman) was thought by some at least to be lunatic, as also in *Hamlet*. But most significant of all is the perplexity of the bishop, who does not dismiss the matter out of hand on doctrinal grounds but even admits that he does not know how to proceed: "If I had known how to have examined it with authority, I would have done it"—which neatly states the problem Hamlet has to face and furthermore indicates that even a doctrinally Protestant theologian such as Bishop Pilkington was just as perplexed as was the Prince of Denmark when it came to dealing with a ghostly apparition.

There are a number of comments in *Hamlet* which assume that the Ghost either is or very well may be an evil spirit—most notably Hamlet's own concern that "The spirit I have seen/ May be a devil [who] ... / Abuses me to damn me" (2.2.584-89). But there are also contrary indications. It is difficult to argue that the Ghost, if it were a devil, would wish to save Gertrude, and yet the Ghost commands the Prince to "taint not thy mind, nor let thy soul contrive/ Against thy mother aught. Leave her to heaven" (1.5.85-86).[20] Hamlet's own references to the Ghost show ambivalence; he invariably prays for heavenly protection when the Ghost appears (1.4.39 and 3.4.104-05), thus taking the wise precaution in dealing with a spirit which is or may be demonic, but in his mother's closet he unequivocally identifies the Ghost as "my father, in his habit as he lived" (3.4.136). For these and other reasons, the evidence of the play does not allow us to assert a simple explanation of the Ghost as a devil.

Whereas Protestant doctrine logically provided only one interpretation of ghost (while in practice admitting of possible uncertainty), Roman Catholicism allowed for two interpretations. Catholics recognized that ghosts could be devils in disguise, come from hell to tempt and destroy on earth, and were therefore highly suspicious of spectral visitors. At the same time, the doctrine of purgatory provided an intermediate state between earth and heaven from which a human soul could conceivably return, so it was possible to grant legitimacy to ghosts who for some reasons were granted temporary release from purgatory. It is in this role that the Ghost appears to cast himself when he says to Hamlet:

> I am thy father's spirit,
> Doomed for a certain term to walk the night,
> And for the day confined to fast in fires,
> Till the foul crimes done in my days of nature
> Are burnt and purged away. (1.5.9-13)

The flames referred to here are said to be purifying, rather than punitive, and they also represent a temporary sentence rather than a permanent fate, which accords with Roman Catholic belief about purgatory as distinguished from hell. Equally Catholic doctrine appears to come in the Ghost's statement that at death it was "cut off even in the blossom of my sin,/ Unhouseled, disappointed, unaneled,/ No reck'ning made," so that the Ghost seems to be introducing itself within distinctly Roman Catholic frames of reference (1.5.76-78).[21]

All this, obviously, would have been impressive to the Globe audience, as it was to Hamlet. Although the Prince was moved by the Ghost's story about its purgation, at no point does he affirm his own belief in the truth of that story. Having been educated at the first and most famous of Protestant universities, Martin Luther's own Wittenberg, Hamlet never even refers to purgatory although there are references aplenty to heaven and hell, as when he speaks to Claudius only of heaven and "th' other place" where the King will go (4.3.33-34). Protestants typically assumed that ghostly affirmations of purgatory were deceits of the devil, as we can see from Bishop Latimer's reference to the devil working "miracles" in "the preaching of purgatory"[22] and from Henry Bullinger's warning that "appearing of souls" were "mere delusions of Satan . . . to prove unto us that there is purgatory."[23] The Prince affirms the afterlife, but it remains for him "the undiscovered country from whose bourn/ No traveller returns"—which in principle flatly denies the Ghost's claim to be a returned spirit (3.1.79-80). Furthermore, if he were convinced that the Ghost was indeed his father temporarily released from purgatorial flames, he would not say about his father "And how his audit stands, who knows save heaven?" (3.3.82)—a remark made well after the Ghost had reported explicitly upon how the audit stood and immediately after the Mousetrap play has verified the Ghost's story of regicide. So again Shakespeare leaves us unsure as to the true identity of the Ghost.

That the Ghost told the truth at least about the regicide does not resolve the mysteries which surround him in other regards. After the Mousetrap play, Hamlet says "I'll take the Ghost's word for a thousand pound," but everyone knew that specters could tell the truth for their own spectral purposes, whether they were pagan, purgatorial, or demonic (3.2.277). As for Roman history, the ghost of Julius Caesar visited Brutus with an ominous but veracious prediction of the Battle of Philippi (*Caes.*, 4.3.275ff). As for demonic agents, Banquo warns Macbeth that

> oftentimes, to win us to our harm,
> The instruments of darkness tell us truths.
> Win us with honest trifles, to betray 's
> In deepest consequence,

and Macbeth himself eventually recognizes "th' equivocation of the fiend/ That lies like truth" (*Macb.*, 1.3.123-26 and 5.5.43-44). Christians of all persuasions would have agreed that the truth of the accusation against Claudius was no guarantee of the Ghost's good faith. Catholics and Protestants alike recognized that "the devil sometimes uttereth the truth, that his words may have the more credit, and that he may the more easily beguile."[24] Similarly, Thomas Becon has a Christian knight tell the devil that in "speaking the truth thou liest also," for "thou dost allege, and with tooth and nail set forward, that which maketh for thee, and serveth thy turn to destroy men."[25]

Of the three principal interpretations of ghosts which we find in this play and which were current in Shakespeare's England, only a Catholic spirit who was known to have returned from purgatory might be implicitly trusted, but we should not therefore assume that the considerable number among Shakespeare's contemporary audience who were of Catholic conviction or sympathy would automatically credit the Ghost as being just what it claims to be. Although affirming the legitimacy of some ghosts, Roman Catholics were taught to be highly skeptical of any spectral visitors. After all, they no less than Protestants took seriously the Biblical admonitions in Deuteronomy 18:10-11 and Isaiah 8:19 that the living should not seek information or guidance from the dead, and also the counsel of 1 John 4:1: "Beloved, believe not every spirit, but try the spirits whether they are of God." In the fourth century, St. Chrysostom warned those credulous believers who claimed to have "heard dead men's souls many times cry, 'I am the soul of such a one.' Yea, but these words proceed out of the fraud and deceit of the devil. For it is not the dead man's soul that saith this, but the devil that feigneth this, that he may deceive the hearers."[26] Even recognizable identity of appearance between a spirit and a dead person (recall Horatio's "These hands are not more like"—1.2.212) was inconclusive. It was not only the Protestant spokesman Lewes Lavater who wrote that "we need not doubt at all" that "the devil can represent the likeness of some faithful man deceased," but Lavater's Roman adversary Father Noel Taillepied similarly affirmed that "we should always bear in mind that the devil can take the shape of someone who is dead, even a good and holy person of eminent sanctity."[27] The Roman Catholic lawyer and authority on visitant spirits, Pierre Le Loyer, wrote in 1586 to the same effect that "since the souls do not appear so often as do angels and demons, it is necessary to examine diligently the souls which appear, to discern if they are truly souls or if it is an ambush of the enemy of the human race."[28] It is a mistake to assume (as is too often done) that Hamlet voices a uniquely Protestant attitude when he declares that

> The spirit that I have seen
> May be a devil, for the devil hath power
> T' assume a pleasing shape, yea, and perhaps
> Out of my weakness and my melancholy,
> As he is very potent with such spirits,
> Abuses me to damn me.                                    (2.2.584-89)

Those words express a caution which in 1600 would have seemed no less laudable to Catholics than to Protestants.

Even from a strictly Romanist point of view, there would have been anomalies about the claims and comments of this Ghost, because what one would normally expect a soul from purgatory to ask, this spirit does not, and what souls in purgatory would not be expected to request, it does. Horatio as a scholar addresses the expected need of one returned to earth from purifying fires when he says:

> If there be any good to be done
> That may to thee do ease and grace to me,
> Speak to me.                                                    (1.1.130-32)

That question goes to the heart of the sixteenth-century Roman Catholic system of mortuary endowments, indulgences, masses and prayers, all directed to alleviating the pains of souls in purgatory and to lessening the time which they must spend before passing on to the unmixed bliss of heaven. It must have seemed strange indeed to Shakespeare's original audience that one who appears to make an orthodox Catholic claim to be "confined to fast in fires,/ Till the foul crimes done in my days of nature/ Are burnt and purged away" should never make even the least hint of an appeal for the kinds of relief established so that the living could "do ease" to the dead (1.5.11-13).[29]

Shakespeare's presentation of this Ghost raises one final problem, and this concerns its call to vengeance. This issue of vengeance is complex enough to require extensive treatment in the following section of this chapter, for it goes beyond the identity of the Ghost and involves the whole course of Hamlet's action throughout the play. Still, the ambiguities of the Ghost cannot be fully understood apart from that command, which would in itself have created grave suspicion. The major authority on ghost lore, Robert H. West, writes that orthodox pneumatology in Shakespeare's time, whether Catholic or Protestant, hardly "gives any account of an apparition that demands revenge, unless it is a devil usurping the likeness of the dead."[30] This is not to say that the Ghost would necessarily have been regarded as a disguised devil, but only that his appearance and his words would have seemed "questionable" to all elements of Shakespeare's audience, as well as to his protagonist.

The instigation of private persons to achieve revenge by taking the law into their own hands was a major concern of Satan. Upon this Catholics and Protestants agreed, but as Elizabethan ethical teachings were largely Protestant it is to the Protestant statements that I shall primarily turn. Bishop Latimer preached that the devil would repeatedly tempt us to take private vengeance, and he postulated an example: "There is a man that hath done me wrong, taken away my living, or hurt me of my good name: the devil stirreth me against him, to requite him, to do him another foul term, to avenge myself upon him. Now, when there riseth up such motions in my heart, I must resist; I must strive. I must consider what God saith *Mihi vindicta*, 'Let me have the vengeance': *Ego retribuam*, 'I will punish him for his ill doings.' "[31] Ghosts were regarded as especially dangerous instigators of revenge, as various comments show. Sir Thomas Browne wrote that "those apparitions and ghosts of departed persons are not the wandring souls of men, but the unquiet walks of Devils, prompting and suggesting us unto mischief, blood, and villainy."[32] King James I also "pictured the Devil as leading his victim on to guilt through desire of revenge, as appearing in the likeness of one dear to the victim in order to secure his attention, as taking advantage of his victim's despair to entice him to his own destruction."[33]

One further example should be cited, because it parallels Hamlet's problem—and places it in its full complexity. A popular book of instructions on family life, written by William Gouge and first published in 1622, contains the following analysis under a heading entitled "Of the Unlawfulness of Children's Seeking to Revenge their Parents' Wrongs":

> That which *Heathen* add is that children after their parents' death, revenge such wrongs as have been done to them in their lifetime. And they press this so far upon children as they affright them with their parent's *Ghost*, saying, that if they neglect to revenge their parent's wrongs, their Ghost will follow them, and not suffer them to live in quiet, but molest them continually. This concept ariseth from the corruption of nature, which is exceeding prone to revenge: but it is expressly forbidden in Scripture, in these and such prohibitions, "resist not evil" (Matt:5.39), "recompense to no man evil for evil" (Rom:12.17), "avenge not yourselves" (Rom:12.19).

All of which seems clear enough, but if we leave the matter there we would be guilty of settling for a dangerous half-truth in reestablishing the Elizabethan responses upon which Shakespeare was playing in his construction of this drama. Private revenge is patently evil, but some children are born to be public executors of justice, or are at some point in their lives properly ordained as such, and for them the situation is different. Here Gouge makes a major qualification of what he has said before, and he cites an Old Testament precedent. When very close to death, King David charged Solomon, his son and appointed heir, to execute Joab because of his earlier murder of Abner and Amasa, and after David's death King Solomon carried out that command of retribution.[34] Having recalled that story, Gouge goes on to make the standard observation that this "was no matter of private revenge, but only a lawful execution of justice, which children may and ought to do."[35]

Hamlet's dilemma is illuminated by Gouge's remarks, but his problem is further complicated by two important factors. In the first place, David's charge to his son was unambiguous, directly delivered on his deathbed and not through a dubious ghost. In the second place, Solomon's public status was unambiguous, where Hamlet's is not: when Solomon executed Joab, it was as the reigning king and not as the heir apparent. Hamlet, on the other hand, is the crown prince, a public figure to be sure and at least a subordinate magnate within the kingdom, but withal he is not the crowned king. In view of all this, we cannot jump to the conclusion that it is Hamlet's duty to obey the Ghost's command and execute vengeance or that it is his duty not to do so. Elizabethan attitudes were too sophisticated, too qualified, too carefully balanced to allow of any unilateral judgment on this issue, as will become apparent when we discuss Hamlet's duty, and we must be fully conscious of such ambiguities if we are to understand the reactions toward the Ghost which Shakespeare has so carefully elicited from his audience in his sequential treatment of that Ghost.

## B. The Dramatic Sequence

The play opens upon a midnight changing of the guard, and we are at once plunged into an atmosphere of challenges and questions, as each entrant upon the stage is demanded to "stand and unfold" himself—establishing a process of disclosure which will be required of every major character hereafter throughout the play. We feel suspicion in the air, and some impending unresolved mystery. The questioning turns from the identity of those who keep the watch, to that of some other unspecified force or presence. Horatio asks, "What, has this thing appeared again tonight?" Reference to "this thing" is significantly vague, as are the references to "this dreaded sight" and "this apparition" "twice seen" by Bernardo and Marcellus and yet doubted by Horatio (1.1.21-29). Then the Ghost enters as a "fair and warlike form," majestic in its presence and bearing, and yet "it harrows me with fear and wonder." It is "like the king that's dead," "most like," "as thou art to thyself," and yet in this opening scene no one calls it the king (1.1.40-65). And when Horatio addresses it, he uses the same degrading *thou* which is applied to the witches in *Macbeth*, never the courtly and respectful *you* which was proper for a subject speaking to a king.[36] Throughout this opening scene, the Ghost is called a "thing," "image," "illusion," or "spirit," and referred to by the neuter pronoun *it* rather than the personal pronoun *he*. Upon the crowing of the cock "it" departed—a suspicious sign, because then "th' extravagant and erring spirit hies/ To his confine," a general observation which Horatio finds confirmed in the fact that the Ghost "started, like a guilty thing/ Upon a fearful summons" (1.1.147-56).

Mysterious and perhaps even sinister though the Ghost appears to be, it has an impressive quality which will not allow anyone to dismiss it as merely evil or patently fraudulent. This Ghost conveys a dignity never before seen in a specter on the Elizabethan stage, where typically

> a filthy whining ghost,
> Lapt in some foul sheet or a leather pilch,
> Comes screaming like a pig half-stickt,
> And cries "Vindicta! revenge, revenge!"[37]

Those lines come from *A Warning for Fair Women*, a play belonging to Shake-speare's company which dates from about 1599 and so provides evidence of the standard ghost of the London stage just before *Hamlet*.[38] The only picture of a ghost I have been able to find from Elizabethan England dates from 1581 (Fig. II.1), and although it has no stage connection it does convey a lack of dignity which accords with that "filthy whining ghost" of theatrical tradition, as it stands clothed only in foul sheet or pilch and summons a man to leave his bed and follow it wherever it may lead him.[39]

How very different from such ghosts is the Ghost we encounter in *Hamlet*. The dialogue in scene one affirms the convincing majesty of the Ghost as he twice passes across the Globe stage, and scene two contains Horatio's detailed description. There is terror in this description to be sure, for the watchers were "distilled/ Almost to jelly with the act of fear," but withal there is also awe and a kind of wondering respect for the regal figure which "with solemn march/ Goes slow and stately by them." This is no common specter clad in a foul winding sheet or coarse pilch, but an heroic presence "armed at point exactly, cap-a-pe," with a commanding countenance, not threatening, but "more in sorrow than in anger." And in this scene the Ghost is referred to by the personal pronoun *he* as often as by *it* (1.2.199-242).

When Hamlet encounters the Ghost in scene four both he and Horatio

FIG. II.I. "A Ghost Appearing," from
Stephen Batman, *Doom Warning to
Judgment*, 1581

revert to calling it by the neuter pronoun, and Horatio's distrust is manifest:
"do not go with it."

> What if it tempt you toward the flood, my lord,
> Or to the dreadful summit of the cliff
> That beetles o'er his base into the sea,
> And there assume some other horrible form
> Which might deprive your sovereignty of reason
> And draw you into madness? Think of it.          (1.4.69-74)

Here we have a nearly explicit reference to the possible demonism of the Ghost,
but expressed as a question rather than as a flat affirmation. Demons did draw
men into "madness or outrage," as Bullinger observed, and we hear of "cliff
demons" who would lead people to a precipice from which to topple into the
sea as Edgar described the "fiend" who supposedly enticed his father at Dover.
Also relevant is Archbishop Cranmer's story of a devil disguised as Moses who
led certain Jews into the sea, where many were drowned.[40] Accounts of such

26

satanic deceptions were to be found in general as well as theological literature, and in folklore and gossip. Conditioned by such attitudes, an Elizabethan audience would have taken Hamlet's resolute following of the Ghost as the act of an extraordinarily bold and decisive character—as far removed as any could imagine from a timid and inactive dreamer.

No Elizabethan could have been ignorant of the dangers inherent in a ghostly visitation, and Hamlet certainly is not. On the contrary, he acts in full awareness of the perils involved, as his words make clear when he determines to meet the Ghost:

> If it assume my noble father's person,
> I'll speak to it though hell itself should gape
> And bid me hold my peace.                    (1.2.244-46)

On both occasions when he encounters the Ghost, he invokes divine protection. In the first instance he prays "angels and ministers of grace defend us," for as William Tyndale wrote in summarizing the universal Christian understanding, "the angels of heaven are also our brethren, and very servants for Christ's sake, to defend us from the power of the devils."[41] Hamlet then goes on to demand

> Be thou a spirit of health or goblin damned,
> Bring with thee airs from heaven or blasts from hell,
> Be thy intents wicked or charitable?

Here the problem is phrased as a question, not as an allegation, and there is no answer. With no reply forthcoming, Hamlet combines boldness with prudence to declare, "I'll call thee Hamlet,/ King, father, royal Dane" (1.4.39-45 and see also 3.4.104-05). To have addressed a demon directly by a demonic name would have resulted in "blasting," which was described as rather like being struck by lightning, although a somewhat more unpleasant experience. Kittredge's interpretation clarifies the situation:

> Hamlet, like Horatio, is a scholar and knows how an apparition should be addressed. He understands the danger of speaking to a spirit. . . . Accordingly he begins by invoking the angels and all good spirits (the ministers or agents of God's grace) to protect him, and then, calling the apparition by his father's name, he adjures it to tell its errand. By using this form of words he avoids to some extent the

danger involved in accosting it if it should be a demon; for in that case he has not, strictly speaking, addressed it at all.[42]

So if the Ghost is a devil in masquerade, Hamlet is addressing him in the most circumspect way. On the other hand, if it is legitimately the spirit of his dead father, he has shown the filial respect appropriate to his own feelings. Throughout his encounter with the Ghost, Hamlet's behavior would have struck the Globe audience as admirable. Again we may profit from Kittredge's analysis:

> From his first sight of the Ghost "he is fully alive to the possibility that this may be a demon in his father's shape," and calls on heavenly agents to guard him. When the Ghost beckons, he follows it without hesitation, though the danger is so great that his friends "actually lay hands on the Prince." When alone with the Ghost, however, he heeds Horatio's warning, halts, and refuses to go further. Here surely is that union of boldness and prudence which in Aristotle's ethics constitutes the truest courage.[43]

When the Ghost departs at the first sign of dawn, Hamlet's friends rejoin him. His comments about the Ghost are now clouded by the need not to reveal what he has heard, but in other ways as well there is pervasive ambiguity. "Look you, I'll go pray" would be appropriate under any interpretation of the Ghost (1.5.132). Lavater counseled such a response "for otherwise the devil may delude and deceive us,"[44] but surely prayer would be equally in order if this Ghost were indeed his father, so the line tells us nothing decisive. Hamlet's wild and whirling words when the Ghost moves about under the stage, in what theatrical people called "hell" (1.5.149-82), imply disrespect for the "old mole," and at this point his use of *thou* is unmistakably condescending, even demeaning, whereas his use of *thee* and *thou* when alone with the Ghost suggested filial affection and respect.[45] Hamlet here declares that "it is an honest ghost," but in the next act he expresses the urgent need to test it in order to confirm or reject what it reveals about his father's death (1.5.138, and 2.2.584-91).

It is all very confusing, and any effort to eliminate the confusion would be counterproductive, because Shakespeare requires us to be confused. In thirty-six plays he demonstrated an unrivalled ability to write as clearly as his dramatic needs required—or as opaquely. His provision of so much conflicting evidence about this ghost, yielding such deep ambiguity, indicates that ambiguity was both necessary and desirable. Neither clearly an emissary of divine justice, nor of demonic cunning, nor of pagan shades, this ghost is and will remain a "questionable shape." If it were not so, Hamlet's task would have been simpler, and his struggles less profound.

Just as the source of Hamlet's mandate is questionable, so too is that mandate. Hamlet expresses the dilemma in typically Elizabethan idiom, as being "prompted to my revenge by heaven and hell" (2.2.570). We now need to consider Elizabethan attitudes toward retribution, resistance to tyranny, and tyrannicide.

## III. Retribution in Doctrine and Fact: The Darnley Murder

The *lex talionis* or law of retaliation in the Old Testament attempted to establish the just bounds of retribution and to avoid the escalation of vengeance which characterized the vendetta. Throughout human history victims have sought revenge which would not merely repay the original evil but multiply it upon the heads of their enemies, an attitude summarized by Claudius when he declares to Laertes that "revenge should have no bounds" (4.7.127). In contrast, the Mosaic law is stark and uncompromising, but it is equitable and precise in its balance of the scales of justice: Exodus 21:23-25 has it, "you shall give life for life, eye for eye, tooth for tooth, hand for hand, foot for foot, burn for burn, wound for wound, stripe for stripe"—but no more.

A concise summary of the Old Testament attitudes is provided by *The Interpreter's Dictionary of the Bible*:

> Seldom does 'vengeance' in the Bible carry the connotation of 'vindictiveness' or 'revenge'. . . . Vengeance was understood to be a necessary means for the healing of the breach made in the solidarity of the family or the community as a result of manslaughter. The avenger of blood was considered to be acting, not only in behalf of family or community, but in God's stead (Gen. 9:5-6). . . . The cries to Yahweh for vengeance, therefore, are cries for redemption, restoration, health, and healing, even though such redemption and healing may involve Yahweh's retributive justice. (Jer. 15:15; 20:12)[46]

The avenger of blood, or the redeemer of blood as a more strict translation of the Hebrew would have it, was the brother, son, or closest relative who was bound to take upon him the sacred obligation of performing justice within the carefully prescribed code. All of this was considered part of a covenantal relationship with God who had forbidden hatred and the vendetta. The Old Testament thus carefully circumscribed the retribution which could be achieved by the avenger of blood, under the governing conception that ultimately God is the only judge. The *lex talionis* was after all a *law*, a restriction of unlimited and unregulated vindictiveness.[47]

The Old Testament statement by God that "Vengeance is mine, I will repay" forms the basis for all treatments of revenge in the New Testament.[48] This conception was closely linked to a respect for the positive laws governing particular societies. As St. Paul wrote, "Let every person be subject to the governing authorities. For there is no authority except from God," and he went on to declare of the ruler that "he does not bear the sword in vain; he is the servant of God to execute his wrath on the wrongdoer."[49]

Christ's absolute commandment against vengeance, obliterating the *lex talionis*, was interpreted within this context. The key passage here comes from the Sermon on the Mount, translated by Tyndale as follows: "Ye have heard, how it is said, an eye for an eye, a tooth for a tooth. But I say unto you, that ye withstand not wrong. But if a man give thee a blow on the right cheek, turn to him the other also."[50] Tyndale distinguishes between the application of this commandment to the private citizen and to the ruler or magistrate. As a private person, one is "never to think it lawful to avenge, how great soever the injury be."[51] At the same time, the magistrate or prince is not disabled from administering retributive justice, because "Christ here intended not to disannul the temporal regiment, and to forbid rulers to punish evil doers."[52] Addressing the prince or magistrate, Tyndale declares that "where thou art no private man, but a person in respect of other [i.e., one set apart and in authority], thou not only mayest, but also must, and art bound under pain of damnation to execute thine office."[53] Tyndale's comment is directly pertinent to our consideration of Hamlet, for under the ancient interpretation Tyndale has here defined, it is possible to argue that Hamlet, as the crown prince, is morally obligated to take action against Claudius as a usurper and murderer. Although Tyndale's devotion to passive obedience precluded him from making such an argument, his position on the magistrate's obligation to dispense retributive justice was universally held and others, as we shall later see, would have argued that a prince could and should judge a vicious king.

The distinction between the private person and the official or ruler had long been established. In the thirteenth century, Vincent of Beauvais gave the ancient definition in his encyclopedia of Christian and pagan learning: "private persons are those who are not constituted in some dignity."[54] Such a private person had no right to "plot the death of rulers even when they were tyrannical," according to Thomas Aquinas, who taught that whenever "a man takes vengeance outside the order of divine appointment, he usurps what is God's and therefore sins." But for one in authority, the situation was different, as Aquinas expressed the orthodox understanding: "He who takes vengeance on the wicked *in keeping with his rank and position* [emphasis added] does not usurp what belongs to God, but makes use of the power granted him by God. For it is written (Rom:13:4) of the earthly prince that 'he is God's minister, an avenger to execute wrath upon him that doeth evil.' "[55] The expression of the orthodox Catholic attitude by Aquinas, and the Protestant attitude by Tyndale, indicates the substantial convergence between the two: although retribution was forbidden to a private person, it was required of rulers. To understand what all this means for *Hamlet*, we should turn to what was the most notorious scandal in Shakespeare's Britain.

Some thirty years before Shakespeare dramatized the responsibility laid upon Prince Hamlet to avenge his father's "foul and most unnatural murder" (1.5.25), a similar responsibility of revenge was laid upon an actual prince who was also told in effect that he was born to set it right. That prince was James VI of Scotland, destined within some three years after the appearance of Shakespeare's *Hamlet* to succeed Elizabeth on the English throne. The historical events in Scotland involved James' mother, Mary Queen of Scots, and the assassination in 1567 of his father, Lord Henry Darnley, who after his marriage to Queen Mary was known as King Henry. King Henry's dead body was discovered lying in the orchard. The assassin was certainly the Earl of Bothwell, who shortly after committing the crime of regicide married the widowed queen and moved toward the crown. The story will be considered in greater detail later, but here our concern is only with the responsibility for vengeance imposed upon a royal son.

James' paternal grandparents the Earl and Countess of Lennox laid the challenge of revenge squarely upon their infant grandson King James, and did so in one of the most remarkable testaments to come down to us from that time. They arranged for a memorial painting to be executed by Livinus de

FIG. II.2. Livinus de Vogelaare, *The Darnley Memorial*

Vogelaare between October, 1567, and January, 1568, within a year of the assassination. Known as *The Darnley Memorial*, this oil was carefully planned and prepared as a complete visual record of the whole scandalous history (Fig. II.2). Due to the age of that painting, and the grime and abrasions from which it has suffered in the course of over four hundred years, the action and message can best be followed by studying the copy engraved by George Vertue in the eighteenth century[56] (Fig. II.3). As the wall plaque in the right background states, the work was commissioned by the Earl and Countess of Lennox so that "if they, who are already old, should be deprived of this life before the majority of their descendent, the King of Scots, he may have a memorial from them in order that he shut not out of his memory the recent atrocious murder of the King his father, until God should avenge it through him."[57] In effect, the parents of the murdered King Henry were attempting to inspire in their grandson King James the response which Hamlet gave to the Ghost:

FIG. II.3. George Vertue, engraving of *The Darnley Memorial*

> Remember thee?
> Ay, thou poor Ghost, while memory holds a seat
> In this distracted glove. Remember thee?
> Yea, from the table of my memory
> I'll wipe away all trivial fond records,
> . . . .
> And thy commandment all alone shall live
> Within the book and volume of my brain. . . .        (1.5.95-103)

Every effort was made during the reign of James to secure the return to Scotland and execution of the regicide Bothwell, but to no avail. Bothwell died in April, 1578, apparently insane, in a dungeon in Denmark, where he was imprisoned for crimes committed in Scandinavia.[58] Bothwell's confession (apparently in anticipation of death) declared that Mary was innocent and that she had no connection with the murder plot or its execution. The authenticity of the statement may be questioned, as well as its value even if authentic, considering Bothwell's late insanity and lifelong mendacity. However that may be, the exoneration was reported to Mary in June, 1576, while she was under guard in England, and to the ten-and-a-half-year-old James VI in Scotland the following January. James accepted the statement as clearing his mother, to the great relief of his own mind.[59] In June, 1581, the Earl of Morton was convicted and executed for complicity in the regicide, thereby officially implying Mary's innocence of that crime.[60] King James was only twelve years old when Bothwell died, and fifteen when Morton was put to death. Thereafter there was no more vengeance to enact, and for the rest of his life James remained convinced that his mother had not been involved in the initial murder.[61]

*The Darnley Memorial* documents one sixteenth-century conviction of the duty of a prince to exact retribution for the murder of a royal father. The painting includes several figures, but it centers upon two—the murdered father and his son. The father is laid out in full armor on a royal tomb, while the infant son kneels just in front of the sarcophagus, in the regalia of a king. A label issuing from his mouth contains the following prayer: "Arise, O Lord, and avenge the innocent blood of the King my father and, I beseech thee, defend me with thy right hand."[62] The scroll issuing from the heads of the earl and countess (to the right of the young James) contains their prayer beseeching God to hear their cries and revenge the innocent blood of the murdered King Henry, their beloved son, while just behind them the King's younger brother Charles makes a similar petition. On the front of the sarcophagus is a bas-relief showing the King's dead body lying where it was found in the orchard. Inscriptions on the wall spell out the whole sordid story, condemning both Bothwell and Queen Mary.

In the lower left-hand corner there is an inserted view of the Battle Array at Carberry, the final confrontation between Mary and the Scottish nobles who were incensed by the assassination of the King and the hasty remarriage of the Queen to the man responsible for that assassination (Fig. II.4). With the Confederate Scottish Lords on the one side, and Mary and Bothwell on the other, this vignette represents the surrender of the Queen to her alienated nobles, while the bridegroom-regicide flies from the scene to the right. The most interesting detail here is the conspicuous banner carried by the lords, and flaunted before Mary's eyes (Fig. II.5). During her house arrest in Edinburgh, this large

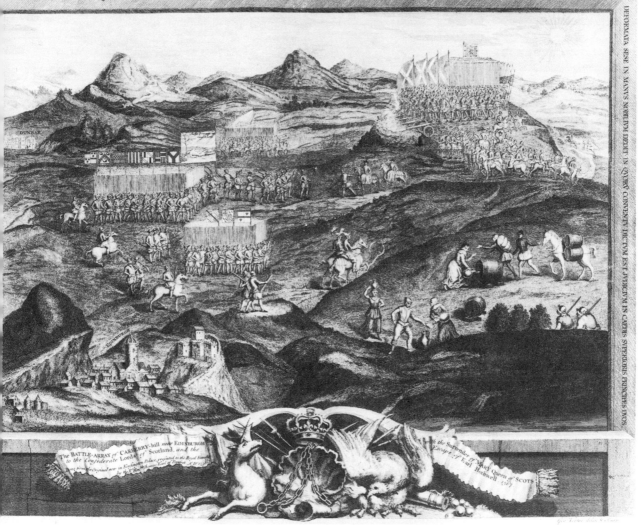

FIG. 11.4. George Vertue, engraving of *The Battle Array at Carberry*

FIG. 11.5. Revenge Banner, detail from
George Vertue, *The Battle Array at
Carberry*

35

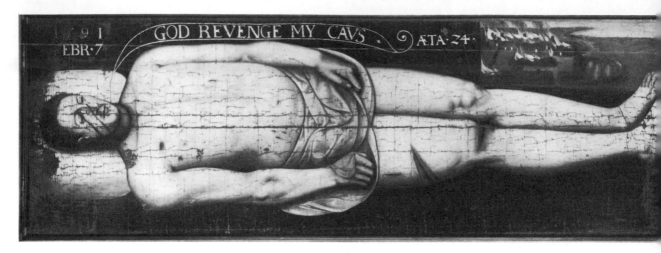

FIG. II.6. *Memorial of James Stewart, Second Earl of Moray*

canvas was hung directly outside her window where she could not fail to see the painted corpse of her "precedent lord" with the inscription "Judge and avenge my cause, O Lord."[63]

That banner achieved considerable fame, and indeed inspired a kind of minor genre in Scotland—the painting of mangled bodies accompanied by calls for vengeance. One such commemorated the young Earl of Moray who was killed in Scotland almost twenty-five years to the day after King Henry. On the night of February 7, 1592, the Earl of Huntley set fire to Donibristle House near Aberdour, "so that the Earl of Moray was forced to come forth . . . and so was killed and cruelly demained." Subsequently, Moray's mother had a painting (Fig. II.6) made of "her son's picture, as he was demained, and presented it to the King in a fine lain cloth, with lamentations, and earnest suit for justice." From the mouth of Moray's corpse a label contains the prayer, "God revenge my cause." Three years later, and only five years before the appearance of *Hamlet*, a follower of the Earl of Mar named Forester was killed in another feud, and his master had carried in the funeral procession "the picture of the defunct on a fine canvas, painted with the number of the shots and wounds, to appear the more horrible and ruthful to the beholders."[64]

Returning now to the dénouement at Carberry of the sequence of events triggered by the assassination of King James' father, we should examine a letter written by one of the Protestant bishops in England, for what it implies of Elizabethan attitudes. Six weeks after the surrender and capture of Mary Queen of Scots, John Parkhurst, Bishop of Norwich, wrote to the influential Swiss theologian Henry Bullinger in Zurich to recount the scandalous happenings in Scotland, which understandably kept the international mails hot with reports and rumors. Parkhurst's letter presents a responsible account which basically accords with what we can learn elsewhere. His description of the banner displaying the dead body does, however, differ from what we find in *The Darnley Memorial* on two relatively inconsequential details: Parkhurst's banner combines features of Vogelaare's memorial painting with those of his inset view of Carberry, and Parkhurst says that there were many such banners, whereas Vogelaare represented only one. For our purposes, the most significant point is the bishop's tacit acceptance of the call for vengeance. Of the rebellious Scottish nobility, Parkhurst wrote:

> The nobles of Scotland have at their command some regiments, and in all their colors or standards they bear this painted representation. There is depicted a green and beautiful tree, under which is lying a tall man, naked, and strangled with a rope [King Henry]; near him is a young man [King Henry's servant], also naked, and pierced with many wounds; next is painted a little boy [the infant James] with a crown of gold upon his head, with bended knees and uplifted hands, and these words written as proceeding from his mouth, "Lord, have mercy on me, and avenge my father's blood." Hereby are represented the King, his attendant, and his son.[65]

Even in its complete form, of which I have quoted only a few sentences, this account by an Anglican bishop conveys not the slightest hint of criticism for that appeal to vengeance. The attitude of Bishop Parkhurst, the charge laid upon the infant James by his grandparents, and the armed revolt of the Scottish lords do not represent the only Elizabethan viewpoint on royal retribution, but we do find in all these events the closest historical parallel to the circumstances of the fictive Hamlet. The notorious developments in Scotland in 1567 do not provide a "source" for *Hamlet*, at least in my judgment, but they do provide some pertinent guidance to us in our search for Elizabethan responses to the kinds of conflicts and problems Shakespeare dramatized on the Globe stage, and we shall recur to them at later points in this study (especially Chapter Three, Part IV).[66]

## IV. Tyrants, Tyrannicide, and the Monarchomachs

*A. Tyrants and Tyranny*

The obligation laid upon James was simpler than that laid upon Hamlet, for James was the King of Scotland and the murderer only a ruffianly nobleman. Hamlet, however, is prince and presumed heir (we do not learn until the final scene of the play that the Danish monarchy is elective), and the assassin wears the crown of Denmark. That difference vastly complicates the already complex problem facing the Prince, for in *Hamlet* the fault lies with that very king who was expected to correct such faults as he himself had committed.[67] In this circumstance, would anyone in the sixteenth century regard it as permissible to strike directly against the monarch? The answer is that a considerable number of highly responsible people regarded it not only as permissible, but even as obligatory. The issues must be explored in considerable detail.

Tyrants were fundamentally and radically distinguished from kings,[68] and tyrannicide from regicide. Regicide was universally decried as the murder of a just and rightful ruler. Tyrannicide, on the other hand, was directed against (and sought deliverance from) an unjust oppressor of his subjects and abuser of his office. George Buchanan, one of the most influential political theorists of the later sixteenth century, gave a fine Renaissance definition: "tyrants, cherishing the false appearance of a kingdom, when by fair means or foul they have once obtained it, cannot hold it without crime, nor can they give it up without destroying it."[69] The reign of Claudius in Denmark is summarized in that brief general description, but he is also characterized by the more particular marks of the tyrant, as we shall see.

Mercenary guards, brought from abroad, were one of the most universally noted signs of the tyrant, and would have been among the simplest to dramatize on stage. The first entrance of Claudius attended by his "Switzers"—among the most notorious mercenaries of sixteenth-century Europe—would have aroused immediate suspicions of him.[70] Erasmus said that "the tyrant guarantees safety for himself by means of foreign attendants and hired brigands. The king deems himself safe through his kindness to his subjects and their love for him in return."[71] Such comments were general in the Renaissance, as when the Scottish Lords of the Congregation complained loudly about the two hundred mercenaries kept by Bothwell.[72] Claudius' twice-stated recognition of Hamlet's popularity—"he's loved of the distracted multitude" and "the great love the general gender bear him" (4.3.4 and 4.7.18)—indicates the tyrant's fear of being supplanted, however Claudius may disguise it by his aspersions on Hamlet. Claudius displays the tyrant's desperate need for security: "the guards of a king are citizens, but of a tyrant mercenaries," as Aristotle put it.[73]

Also typical of the tyrant is Claudius' choice of advisors such as Polonius, Rosencrantz, and Guildenstern: the conception could be traced as far back as Aristotle that the "tyrant has his humble companions who flatter him."[74] Such assistants to Claudius conform to Erasmus' statement that a tyrant chooses as advisors "stupid dolts, on whom he imposes," and in such perilous service "stupid dolts" do not long survive, as Claudius' flatterers discover.[75] But because the tyrant's concern is only for himself, he could scarcely be expected to show much downward loyalty. So Du Mornay writes in 1579 that when a tyrant gives prominence and favor to certain subjects, and allows them "like sponges to gather some moisture, it is but to squeeze them out afterwards to his own use." That analogy goes back at least as far as Suetonius, and it was repeated again and again until Shakespeare introduced it in Hamlet's confrontation with Rosencrantz:

> HAMLET. Besides, to be demanded of a sponge, what replication should
> be made by the son of a king?
> ROSENCRANTZ. Take you me for a sponge, my lord?
> HAMLET. Ay, sir, that soaks up the king's countenance, his rewards,
> his authorities. But such officers do the king best service in the end.
> He keeps them, like an ape, in the corner of his jaw, first mouthed,
> to be at last swallowed. When he needs what you have gleaned, it
> is but squeezing you and, sponge, you shall be dry again.
>
> (4.2.12-20)

A visualization of the tyrant and sponge motif was published in Jeffrey Whitney's *A Choice of Emblems* in 1586 where we see the sponge being wrung out in the foreground by a king who is quite unconcerned about the fate of his former servants in the background (Fig. II.7).[76]

Such hangers-on and tools to a tyrant not only inflate his self-regard and cater to his whims, but they also serve him as spies. "A tyrant," Aristotle wrote, "should also endeavor to know what each of his subjects says and does, and should employ spies, like the 'female detectives' of Syracuse, and the eaves-

FIG. II.7. King and Sponge Emblem,
Jeffrey Whitney, *A Choice of Emblems*,
1586

droppers whom Hiero was in the habit of sending to any place of resort or meeting."[77] In *Hamlet*, Rosencrantz and Guildenstern serve as spies sent to observe what the Prince says and does, Ophelia is cast as a "female detective," and Polonius as an eavesdropper.[78]

Just as Claudius conforms to each of these particular characteristics of a tyrant, so does he conform to the overall conception. When Johannes Althusius published his influential and representative treaties *The Politics* in 1603, he gave this summary definition:

> A tyrant is therefore one who, violating both word and oath, begins to shake the foundations and unloosen the bonds of the associated body of the commonwealth. A tyrant may be either a monarch or a polyarch that through avarice, pride, or perfidy cruelly overthrows and destroys the most important goods of the commonwealth, such as its peace, virtue, order, law, and nobility.... [He is one who] having accepted and then neglected the just rule of administration, acts contrary to the fundamentals and essence of human association, and destroys civil and social life.... [and who thus] violates the bonds and shatters the restraints by which human society has been maintained.[79]

Hamlet could have accepted that assessment of the tyrant as describing Claudius.

Granted that Claudius is a tyrant according to these criteria, what could and should have been done about him? When that question is answered solely by reference to the well-publicized (and often oversimplified) Anglican doctrine of passive resistance, some very odd results ensue: we can be told in effect that Hamlet is the villain of the piece, and Claudius virtually the hero, so that we may be invited to regard the Prince as the destroyer of peace and civility in the urbane Denmark of King Claudius. But that kind of reading turns the play very much on its head. There seem to be two possible responses: we may argue that Elizabethan attitudes really do not matter for interpreting Shakespeare's plays, but such an avenue of escape will only lead us into other interpretive cul-de-sacs.[80] Another approach is to reassess the original cultural milieu itself, to determine whether the attitudes toward resistance held by Shakespeare's contemporaries were in fact quite so unilateral as we have too often been led to believe.[81]

We surely cannot and should not ignore the historic Anglican emphasis on non-resistance and passive obedience, and we shall give that doctrine due attention, but it must be placed in a broader perspective. In the Tudor context, the passivity advocated by the formative Anglican spokesmen allowed for diametrically different applications, as we shall see in the opposite responses of Archbishop Cranmer and Bishop Hooper in 1553 to the question of who was the legitimate successor to the throne of King Edward VI. Equally important is the broader context which embraced not only an insular Anglican view but also the development of resistance theory among Calvinists and Roman Catholics on the continent of Europe and in Scotland—all of which directly or indirectly influenced and involved England. Furthermore, Queen Elizabeth herself commissioned from Bishop Thomas Bilson a major modification of the traditional Tudor doctrine, published in 1585.

Between the mid-sixteenth and -seventeenth centuries, people throughout Europe were forced to consider anew how to deal with rulers who were perceived to be unjust, oppressive, or illegitimate. That span of approximately one hundred years was one of the revolutionary periods in history which saw kings and queens repudiated, overthrown, assassinated, and executed. These developments were marked not only by violent action but equally by the most intense debate, along with the gradual development of various intellectual justifications for action against a monarch. The introduction of Shakespeare's *Hamlet* on the stage in 1600 was utterly timely, and its timeliness was due not to topical references to any particular historical events, but rather to the climate of the times and the general concerns of the play. It is surely significant that it was also in 1600 that a new word, "monarchomachist," was coined to identify militant and aggressive opposition to a monarch.

The monarchomachs addressed themselves to what they regarded as the extreme abuse of power. They were a diverse lot, including Protestants and Catholics alike, who were often influenced by each other despite their religious differences. All monarchomachs justified armed resistance where necessary to curb the abuses of royal power. As for the actual killing of a tyrant, some argued for it as a noble act, while others were more reticent, but few would have denied it as a possibility under extreme circumstances.

"Tyrannicide is locked into the political and religious mentalities of the age," as Orest Ranum declares in his recent "The French Ritual of Tyrannicide in the Late Sixteenth Century,"[82] and he regards this understanding as having been admirably developed by Shakespeare and other dramatists on both sides of the Channel. Hamlet was surely the greatest of the fictitious monarchomachs, and we can understand him better if we set him against the background of these historical developments in Shakespeare's time.

The classical precedents were obvious and widely recognized. As John Milton wrote in *The Tenure of Kings and Magistrates*, "The Greeks and Romans, as their prime authors witness, held it not only lawful but a glorious and heroic deed, rewarded publicly with statues and garlands, to kill an infamous tyrant at any time without trial."[83] That classical tradition had been firmly rejected by Christians throughout the early centuries of the church, when even the most extreme persecutions were borne passively and with patience. Sometime after the patristic period, however, attitudes changed, or perhaps it would be more accurate to say that they diversified, and some Christian thinkers defended tyrannicide while others forbade it.[84] Probably the most famous medieval advocacy of tyrannicide was made by the eminent John of Salisbury in the twelfth century. His position may be summarized in the words of C.C.J. Webb: "The tyrant is the devil's image as the true prince is God's; he may be slain while the true prince should be reverenced. . . . The overthrow of the laws by the tyrant is the supreme treason and may be avenged by any citizen. Any citizen indeed who fails to avenge it when he can is thereby proved false to himself and to the commonwealth.[85]

Thomas Aquinas perhaps evaded, and certainly modified, John's acceptance of tyrannicide, if he did not reject it altogether. As we have seen, he denied the right of resistance which John had approved for private citizens. But Aquinas also recognized that "tyrannical government is unjust government because it is directed not to the common welfare but to the private benefit of the ruler"— a definition which may call to our minds Claudius' confession that his actions were designed to protect his crown, his ambition, and his queen (3.3.54-55). Under such circumstances, according to St. Thomas, "the overthrowing of such government is not strictly sedition," but with typical balance he qualifies again by adding: "except perhaps in the case that it is accompanied by such disorder that the community suffers greater harm from the subsequent disturbances than it would from a continuance of the former rule."[86] Gerson, Chancellor of the University of Paris after 1395, argued strenuously against tyrannicide without ever quite repudiating the possibility altogether, so that he still acknowledged "that under certain conditions the doctrine might be defensible."[87] John D. Lewis has summarized medieval theory as follows: "the resister or slayer of the law-defying tyrant could be said to act not for the protection of his own private values but for the protection of values common to the whole community." Jászi and Lewis also point out that medieval considerations were almost always theoretical: "actual tyranny usually remained outside the direct experience of those scholars who discussed tyranny and tyrannicide."[88] Thus the practical problem remains: how can one be sure what to do in a particular and concrete situation? That question indeed puzzles the will, and the Middle Ages provided no single or simple answer. Neither did the sixteenth century.

Sir Thomas More rejected not only tyrannicide but also every other form of active monarchomachic resistance to the crown.[89] When he found himself and his fellow Catholics oppressed by Henry VIII in ways which appeared to him to be both unjust and tyrannical, he never once even hinted at the possibility of resisting in any way and certainly not by a direct blow against the king. His attitude was the same as that of the early Christians under Roman persecution. On this point he and his great Protestant antagonist William Tyndale were in entire agreement, and both died as martyrs to the oppressive intolerance of the other's party, thus exemplifying the virtue of patience and the passive endurance of injustice. Hamlet, in his careful appraisal of all the options open to him, describes that position as bearing "the whips and scorns of time,/ Th' oppressor's wrong, the proud man's contumely," but it was not the alternative which he eventually chose (3.1.79f.).

## B. Tudor Anglicanism

It was, however, the response recommended by the Tudor establishment until the last two decades of the sixteenth century. When Henry VIII broke with Rome in the early fifteen-thirties, he inaugurated a system in which the head of the English state was also head of the English church. For over a hundred years thereafter, adherents fully dedicated to Anglicanism as a religion found themselves in the fortunate situation where conflicts between their religious and political commitments were minimized, because all Anglicans were subject to a secular ruler who was also the chief power in the church. This coincidence of leadership was broken for only five years under the reign of Henry's Roman Catholic daughter, Queen Mary, but for more than a century it provided a franchisement to Anglican Christians which was denied in Europe to many other Reformed and Roman Catholic Christians alike. It was as close an approximation as Western Europe ever attained to the Caesaro-papism of the Byzantine Empire. Under these circumstances, adherents of the protestant episcopal Church of England in Shakespeare's lifetime were able to avoid many of the struggles between ethical-spiritual commitments and political commitments to which their Reformed contemporaries were subjected for a time in Scotland and very generally on the Continent, and to similar conflicts experienced by their Roman Catholic contemporaries in England. As Richard Hooker put the Anglican position, "with us one society is both the Church and commonwealth."[90]

When Shakespeare's John of Gaunt refused to act against King Richard II despite that king's record of assassination and incompetence, his words are sometimes understood as the only conceivable sixteenth-century reaction to an evil but legitimate king:

> since correction lieth in those hands [i.e., the king's]
> Which made the fault that we cannot correct,
> Put we our quarrel to the will of heaven,

Who, when they see the hours ripe on earth,
Will rain hot vengeance on offenders' heads (*RII*, 1.2.4-8)

These words do indeed represent a very important part of the frame of ideas within which Shakespeare could expect his audiences to react, but it is not the only part. There has been a widespread tendency among literary historians to accept and use passive resistance as the panacea for too many problems and ills, historical and critical, in Shakespeare's lifetime. Here the influence of E.M.W. Tillyard and Lily B. Campbell has very largely dominated interpretation.[91] Both have contributed much of lasting value to our understanding, but under their influence literary historians have assumed an almost unilateral applicability of Gaunt's words (or others like them) to the judgment of action and character in Shakespeare.[92] Ulysses' famous speech on order and degree (*Troilus* 1.3.75-137) was taken by Tillyard as his touchstone, and we should continue to recognize its importance, but developments in the history of political thought have made such major advances since the time of Tillyard that reassessments and qualifications can and must now be made. We now know that Ulysses' eloquent words summarize an older view, that of the earlier sixteenth century, rather than that of the late Elizabethan and Jacobean periods.[93] Our task here is not to determine Shakespeare's own convictions on these matters (and I do not know how we could do that in the present state of our evidence), but is rather to reestablish the range of audience reactions upon which his dramatic creations played. Although it is not safe to assume that we can define Shakespeare's personal beliefs, it is beyond question that he wrote for particular audiences at a particular period in history, and I assume that he had a sophisticated awareness of the convictions and conflicting convictions of those audiences, so as to elicit audience responses to his stage characters and actions.

Our task here is to reconstruct, as fully as we now can, what the Globe audiences would have found to interest and excite them in *Hamlet*. We will miss much of the initial excitement generated by the play if we assume that Shakespeare's contemporaries would have rejected all resistance to authority in any singleminded way.[94] Within the Church of England itself there were differences of view directly pertinent to Hamlet's problem. These first came to the fore during the two short reigns which separated the long reigns of Henry VIII and Elizabeth I, and especially at the time when the pronounced Protestant Edward VI was succeeded by the equally pronounced Catholic Mary. The reactions to these events by two prominent Reformation churchmen, Archbishop Thomas Cranmer and Bishop John Hooper, illustrate the complexity possible within the Anglican insistence upon accepting a *de facto* monarch.

The first Reformed churchman to serve as Archbishop of Canterbury and primate of the Church of England, Thomas Cranmer was a fundamental influence in establishing the Anglican acceptance of passive obedience, and there can be little doubt that he sincerely believed in it. But Cranmer's case illustrates the complications which could arise in applying what superficially appears to have been a principle allowing of no exceptions. In June, 1553, King Edward VI knew that he was dying, and as he had no children he was faced with the question of his successor. His father Henry VIII had specified in his will that if Edward were to die without issue, the throne should pass directly to his elder sister Princess Mary, despite the fact that she had been publicly proclaimed illegitimate both by her father and by Parliament and that royal bastards were normally excluded from succession. Under that Henrician will, the succession was clearly established, but if one king could by legal testament establish one succession, another could establish a different one. On the basis of precedent, then, a will was prepared for Edward which excluded his sister Mary (King Henry VII's "illegitimate" granddaughter) and bequeathed the crown to his cousin Lady Jane Grey (Henry VII's legitimate great granddaughter). The arguments for this action were sufficiently plausible that the principal judges of the realm, although at first reluctant, agreed to the new succession, with only Sir James Hales dissenting. The whole Council also agreed, with the initial exception of Archbishop Cranmer, who alone attempted to dissuade Edward from this course of action. The young king was adamant, however, and insisted that Cranmer not be the sole dissenter in the Council. Cranmer recounted the rationale which led him to change his mind: recognizing "the sentence of the Judges and others his learned counsel in the laws of this realm (as both he and his Council informed me), methought it became not me, being unlearned in the law, to stand against my Prince therein." On the assumption that the king was supreme, Cranmer signed, later explaining that "I will never, God willing, be author of sedition to move subjects from the obedience of their heads and rulers, which is an offence most detestable," a position he uniformly maintained both under the Protestant Edward and the Catholic Mary.[95] On July 6, 1553, Edward died, and on the tenth of the same month Jane Grey was duly proclaimed Queen to begin a "reign" which lasted only a few days and was brought to an end when Mary with widespread support declared her own succession and decisively took over the realm.

Here an historical question may be raised which, although it may at first appear unrelated to our literary concerns, will bring us back to the situation dramatized in *Hamlet*. Should Jane or Mary have succeeded to the throne? Mary was the eldest child of Henry VIII, although she was born of a marriage later abrogated and declared to have been illegal. Jane Grey was further removed by one generation from the Tudor progenitor, but her descent did not bear the legally imposed stigma of a bar sinister and she was duly recognized by another Tudor king. Jane had, furthermore, the virtually unanimous support of the judges of the realm and the unanimous acceptance of the royal Council, all of whom can be said to "have freely gone/ With this affair along," to apply here Claudius' words about support for his own succession to the throne (1.2.15f). At least as strong arguments could be advanced for the succession of "Queen Jane" in England as for King Claudius in *Hamlet*—but in England they did not prevail.

The majority of Englishmen in 1553 did not regard Jane as their true queen, and when Mary entered London on August 3 to assume the throne of her father she was greeted by a great wave of popular support. Like Prince Hamlet, she was "loved by the distracted multitude," at least for the time, and even more importantly she had powerful support from leaders both of the state and the church, which Hamlet obviously lacked (4.3.4). Even the leaders of the English Reformation predominantly supported her, with only a few important exceptions (Ridley and Sandys in addition to Cranmer and those cited elsewhere here).[96] Of the justices called upon by Edward to support Jane and thus assure the continuance of Protestantism, the staunchest Protestant was Judge James Hales, and he was the only one who stood resolutely for Mary's right, despite the possibility that he would himself be persecuted under her, as eventually he was.

So it was also with John Hooper, the Protestant Bishop of Gloucester and Worcester. Shortly before Mary executed him as a heretic in 1555, Hooper wrote an account of his behavior during the crisis over the succession, an account which demonstrated his unwavering support of Mary's right to the throne and therefore established that he died as a martyr rather than a traitor:

> As for my truth and loyalty to the Queen's highness, the time of her
> most dangerous estate can testify with me, that when there was both
> commandments and commissions out against her, whereby she was,
> to the sight of the world, the more in danger, and less like to come
> to the crown; yet, when she was at the worst, I rode myself from
> place to place (as it is well known), to win and stay the people for
> her party: and whereas another was proclaimed [Jane Grey], I pre-
> ferred her [Mary], notwithstanding the proclamations.[97]

As Hooper's biographer and editor Charles Nevinson notes, his support for
Mary was "true to the principles which he had always professed."[98] That is
correct, but it is equally pertinent to observe that Cranmer's support of Lady
Jane was true to his principles, and that these two Anglican prelates had very
similar views of the right of kings and the duty of subjects, if not always of
other issues. Both acknowledged the obligation to support the legitimate monarch, but in the critical months of June and July, 1553, they disagreed as to
who that monarch might be. Surely the Anglican doctrine of passive obedience
to the throne was not so simple as we have sometimes been led to assume.

After Mary had successfully claimed and held the throne, Tudor orthodoxy
defended her right to reign even when under Elizabeth her "bloody" image as
persecutor was also developed, but if Mary had lost and "Queen Jane" had
won, there would doubtless have been a different interpretation, all within the
same basic conception of royal right. While the whole issue was in question,
and individual decisions were being made, accepted and shared understandings
of royal prerogative and the obedience of subjects did not obviate differences
of opinion even to the point of bloodshed. Alternative positions had to be
weighed, and were weighed in many minds, although we rarely have records
preserved as to just how various individuals came to their resolution.

If we go back before that crisis developed in the summer of 1553, we will
find the same Bishop Hooper making a public statement which will warn us
against assuming an automatic English acquiescence to whoever might be *de
facto* king. In a sermon preached during Edward VI's reign, the bishop developed a very significant analysis whose pertinence to *Hamlet* will be indicated
by my bracketed comments:

> Like as the king's majesty, that now is [Edward VI], immediately
> after the death of his father [Henry VIII], was the true and legitimate

king of England, right heir unto the crown, and received his coronation, not to make himself thereby king, but to manifest that the kingdom appertained unto him before. He taketh the crown to confirm his right and title. [On the same principle, would not many members of the Elizabethan audience have made the same assumption about Prince Hamlet as Hooper made about Edward?] Had all England said nay, and by force, contrary unto God's laws and man's laws, with an exterior ceremony and pomp, crowned any other man, he should have been an adulterous and wrong king, with all his solemnities and coronation. [Here Hooper's attitude towards his hypothetical interloper accords with Hamlet's view of Claudius.] Though this ceremony confirm and manifest a king in his kingdom, yet it maketh not a king, but the laws of God and of the land, that giveth by succession the right of the kingdom to the old king's first heir male in England and other realms. [Typically, Englishmen regarded regality as primogenitive and we should recall that Shakespeare gives no hint until the very last scene of the play that the Danish monarch was elective.] And the babe in the cradle hath as good right and claim, and is as true a king in his cradle uncrowned, as his father was, though he reigned a crowned king forty years. And this right of the babe should be defended and manifested, not only by the ceremony of coronation, but with all obedience and true subjection.[99]

The principles outlined here are directly pertinent to the conflicting claims of Hamlet and Claudius, as Hooper has developed his revealing hypothesis: it is neither the coronation nor the crown which makes the king, but rather the right of succession. Hooper continues, maintaining that even if a usurper had ascended the throne and excluded Edward VI from his right (as Claudius did with Hamlet). Edward would nonetheless still be truly king:

As the king's majesty may not attribute his right unto the crown, but unto God and unto his father, who hath not only given him grace to be born into the world, but also to govern as a king in the world; whose right and title the crown confirmeth, and sheweth the same unto all the world. Whereas this right by God and natural succession precedeth, not the coronation, the ceremony availeth nothing. A traitor may receive the crown, and yet [be a] true king nothing the rather.

> So an hypocrite and [an] infidel may receive the external sign of baptism, and yet no christian man nothing the rather; as Simon Magus and other.[100]

Hooper did not go on to specify what the rightful son and heir should do if a usurper had in fact "popped in between" the crown and his hopes, but when that hypothetical case was actualized in 1553, he supported and applauded the decisive and militant action of Mary as the first-born heir to claim the throne from an already proclaimed monarch.

As the examples of Cranmer and Hooper show, cases of conscience involving obedience and disobedience were not always easy to resolve even among those who held to the official Anglican doctrine of nonresistance to the crown, and even the general acceptance among Englishmen of the Tudor monarchy and of the established church did not obviate the need to consider such issues. When Hamlet appeared on the Globe stage to debate "whether 'tis nobler in the mind to suffer/ The slings and arrows of outrageous fortune/ Or to take arms against a sea of troubles/ And by opposing end them" (3.1.57-60), Shakespeare was dramatizing one of the most profound and disruptive political problems of the sixteenth century.

### C. Calvinist and Catholic Agreements

When we move beyond the confines of official Anglicanism to consider other points of view we find that Calvinist and Catholic attitudes toward an oppressive state and king were often very similar. This sometimes overlooked fact should not surprise us, since both groups regarded themselves as carrying on the authentic Christian tradition, and both sometimes found themselves facing very similar problems in different countries. Elliott Rose has studied the circumstances of Puritans and Catholic recusants in Shakespeare's time, and has concluded that "certain aspects of their predicaments were similar, and furnish grounds for comparison, but both would have been horrified to think so."[101] He points out also just how widespread was the dilemma of "conscientious objectors" in this period of English history: "If we include absolutely silent sympathizers with each group and add the two together they may well have been a majority of the English nation."[102] Whatever may have been the actual proportions of the population involved, the problems posed by "unjust" government were widely faced by Englishmen in the time of Shakespeare, and by other Europeans as well.

In France, for example, Protestants under the Catholic Valois monarchy developed sophisticated justification for violent rebellion, while their Catholic opponents advanced elaborate arguments for passive obedience, but when the Protestant Henry of Navarre succeeded to the French throne, the circumstances were reversed, and each group began to take over and advocate the arguments drawn up by their opponents.[103] All the terms which we use descriptively of this period—Calvinist, Anglican, Catholic—covered a wider spectrum of attitudes toward resisting authority than modern readers sometimes recognize when considering political problems in Shakespeare. Professor Arnold Pritchard's analysis may help us to avoid oversimplification:

> Calvinism and Catholicism both had radical and conservative political potential, but the strength of radicalism or conservatism in either tradition at any given time depended largely on circumstances, both on the course of events within the group involved or its relationship with the state and society. The differences over the relationship between religious belief and the political and social order were fought out within confessional groups, as well as between them.[104]

The point is that different responses had to be "fought out," both within groups and in the individual conscience, and a great many people in Europe of the time were engaged in just such debates, whether public or private. An anonymous versifier referred to the antimonarchial militance advocated alike by the Scots Presbyterian Buchanan and the Jesuit Mariana as the anomalous alliance of "A Scot and Jesuit, hand in hand" to crush the growing power of monarchs.[105]

The significance of that striking conjunction is explained by Quentin Skinner: "The Jesuit Mariana may thus be said to link hands with the Protestant Buchanan in stating a theory of popular sovereignty which, while scholastic in its origins and Calvinist in its later development, was in essence independent of either religious creed, and was thus available to be used by all parties in the coming constitutional struggles of the seventeenth century."[106] That this position runs counter to the strong and predominantly absolutist claims for the ruler in this period is obvious, but it should also be obvious that the right of tyrannicide was well known, eloquently and logically defended, and widely debated from the time of the Greeks through the Middle Ages. Resistance theory was not the primal creation of Calvinism, although Calvinists did much to develop its popularity, beginning with highly influential statements made by Calvin himself at the end of the *Institutes* to which we shall turn later.[107] Skinner thus summarizes the developments: "In the course of the 1580's, as the result of a sudden shift of fortune in the French religious wars, a number of Catholic theologians began to adopt a very similar and no less radical justification of political resistance" to that which had been made by Calvinists, especially Buchanan. When Henry of Navarre became the direct heir to the French throne, the Catholic League "proceeded to put a demand for a general insurrection against the Valois monarchy directly to the whole body of the people."[108] For our purposes, these developments among Catholics and Protestants alike will repay more detailed analysis.

## D. Catholicism at Home and Abroad

In these years, the spectrum of attitudes toward violent resistance and even tyrannicide produced many cases of conscience which, although certainly not identical with Hamlet's, were in important ways instructively similar. The inner debates of the fictitious Prince of Denmark would have struck a familiar chord with many of Shakespeare's contemporaries, whatever their religion. Take for example that substantial minority of Englishmen who continued to be Roman Catholic despite the Elizabethan settlement of a national church whose Protestantism was inimical to their religion, both in doctrine and in practice. When considered from the papal viewpoint the Protestant sovereigns of England were not only dangerous heretics but also unjust tyrants who excluded the true church and oppressed its faithful adherents. This judgment applied especially to Elizabeth, but the Holy See maintained toward her that combination of charity and prudence which has distinguished it over the centuries and it was not until she had been on the English throne for a dozen years that she was formally excommunicated. In the bull *Regnans in Excelsis* of 1570, Pope Pius V declared that "she has forfeited her pretended title to the aforesaid kingdom and is deprived of all dominion, dignity, and privilege." Consequently, Pius continued, "we declare that nobles, subjects, and people are free from any oath to her and we forbid obedience to her monitions, mandates, and laws. Those who do otherwise incur the same anathema."[109] At one stroke, believing English Catholics (who along with strong sympathizers may have numbered as much as a third of the population at the time) were freed from all allegiance to the English queen.

The implications of that bull need to be spelled out, if we are to understand the problems which it raised for individual Catholics in England. In the words of R. B. Wernham,

> Pope Pius V's bull had excommunicated not only Elizabeth but also all who continued to obey her and recognize her as their sovereign. It thus commanded resistance and legalized rebellion. The Explanation, which Pope Gregory XIII (1572-85) authorized Campion and Parsons to publish in 1580, did release the English Catholics from this anathema and these obligations, but only until the 'Enterprise of England' could be launched and the invader was ready to hurl Elizabeth from her throne. Then they would still be expected to play their parts.[110]

That statement summarizes the intended effect to the bull upon the *status quo* in England, but for its effect upon individual consciences, we need to observe the comments of Arnold O. Meyer:

> By his bull, Pius V had placed English Catholics in a desperate position between conflicting duties. Whoever acknowledged Elizabeth, or even merely obeyed her laws and orders, was guilty of disobedience to the Pope, and, according to the letter of the bull, incurred excommunication. Obedience to the pope was high treason against the queen— the choice lay between faith and country.[111]

The dilemma was not theoretical but painfully existential.

Most Catholics remained loyal to their queen, as did for example Sir Thomas Tresham. For the Catholic recusant Tresham, any resistance to the sovereign, and especially violent resistance, was a mortal sin, and he declared in 1585 for himself and his co-religionists in England that "we for our parts utterly deny that either pope or cardinal hath power or authority to command or license any man to consent to mortal sin." Later, after Elizabeth's death, he himself initiated the proclamation at Northampton of the succession of James. In public discussions after that action, a Puritan minister interposed some qualification that the "king prove sound in religion," and Tresham gave the man a lecture on the duty of subjects toward kings. The preacher then raised the issue of papal excommunications, to which Tresham's response is especially interesting: "The pope, he implies angrily in his reply to the preacher's question, has nothing to do with it. It is purely a matter for Tresham, his king, and his God." Tresham illustrates one Catholic attitude, that of passive obedience and loyal acceptance of the sovereign, and the missionary priest Thomas Hill, even as he awaited execution at the hands of the Anglican establishment, wrote that he regarded Tresham as perhaps the most worthy of the professing Catholic laity. On the other hand, a Jesuit professor in the English seminaries at Rome and Seville, Henry Tichborne, wrote that Tresham "is holden among us for an atheist, and all others of his humor either so or worse."[112]

The Roman Catholic community, although often supposed to be monolithic, was in fact not so.[113] John Gerard, the missionary priest and martyr, "was loath to forbid one of his penitents to serve on the queen's side in the Irish wars," in apparent violation of the 1570 bull excommunicating Elizabeth. Other Catholics, on the contrary, declared that it was a grievous sin for Catholics to fight against the Catholic Irish in their rebellion, and the papacy surely endorsed the rebel cause.[114] The obvious unwillingness of Catholic princes on the Continent to heed the Pope's deposition of Elizabeth and to mount an invasion to depose her from the English throne seemed "truly terrible" to some faithful recusants at home.[115] As we shall soon note, the unwillingness of English Protestant nobles to rise up and depose Elizabeth's Catholic sister "Bloody Mary" from the English throne had seemed equally reprehensible to John Knox, but for the moment our concentration should remain on the diverse Catholic views of forceful resistance to authority.

There were numerous plots to assassinate Queen Elizabeth, and most of these were the work of conscientious recusants who felt called to remove the monarch whom other equally conscientious Catholics felt called to defend. When Dr. William Parry was tried for his 1585 "Parry Plot," a letter addressed to him from the Cardinal of Como, the papal Secretary of State, was produced as evidence and later printed by Holinshed in a copy which accords with the draft kept in the Vatican archives. As for the plot, the cardinal encouraged Parry on behalf of the pope: "his Holiness doth exhort you to persevere, and to bring to effect that which you have promised." More than that encouragement, Cardinal Como added:

> And to the end you may be so much the more holpen by that good Spirit which hath moved you thereunto, he granteth unto you his blessing, plenary indulgence, and remission of all your sins, according

to your request. Assuring you, that beside the merit that you shall receive therefore in heaven, his holiness will further make himself debtor, to acknowledge your deservings in the best manner he can. . . . Put therefore your most holy and honourable purposes in execution, and attend your safety.[116]

Although it is not entirely clear what Parry was really plotting, and whether he actually sought to kill the queen, popular English opinion at the time assumed that he did and that the pope approved the action.

The pope involved here was Gregory XIII, who had praised and celebrated the St. Bartholomew's Massacre of French Protestants. According to A. O. Meyer, "he alone among the popes of the Counter-Reformation regarded assassination, when employed in the church's service, as a work well-pleasing to God."[117] That he did so regard it had long been charged in England, and Meyer lists four cases of attempts against Elizabeth's life which were thought in England to have had the papal blessing. But the conclusive evidence came to light only in this century. As it is tremendously revealing of late sixteenth-century attitudes toward cases of conscience involving violence against a crowned sovereign, I shall recount the evidence in some detail, relying upon Meyer's discoveries and analysis.

In 1580, an Englishman named Humphrey Ely (later ordained to the Roman priesthood) approached the papal nuncio in Madrid, Filippo Sega, on behalf of an unidentified group of English nobles who were considering the murder of Queen Elizabeth, but who "were willing to attempt it only on condition that the pope assured them, at least verbally, that they would not thereby incur sin." Sega pointed out at once that the 1570 excommunication gave subjects the right to take arms against Elizabeth, and he urged the conspirators to act speedily on the assurance that even though the Pope might not approve the assassination beforehand, he could be expected to grant absolution afterwards. In addition, Sega wrote on November 14 to Como, the papal Secretary of State, reporting everything and asking for the response of the Supreme Pontiff. He also asked that he himself be absolved for his involvement in the matter.[118] On December 12, the Cardinal of Como replied from Rome on behalf of the pope:

Since that guilty woman of England rules over two such noble kingdoms of Christendom and is the cause of so much injury to the Catholic faith, and loss of so many million souls, there is no doubt that whosoever sends her out of the world with the pious intention of doing God service, not only does not sin but gains merit, especially having regard to the sentence pronounced against her by Pius V, of holy memory. And so, if those English nobles decide actually to undertake so glorious a work, your Lordship can assure them that they do not commit any sin. We trust in God also that they will escape danger. As far as concerns your Lordship, in case you have incurred any irregularity, the pope bestows upon you his holy benediction.[119]

From a twentieth-century point of view, this all looks quite ghastly, but it would be hasty of us to brand Pope Gregory XIII, Sega, and Como as bloodthirsty and unscrupulous men. For our purposes here, it is important to recognize how men conscientious enough to reach the highest offices in Roman Catholicism were able to maintain and endorse an assassination which they regarded as justifiable tyrannicide. "Assassination is not merely tolerated, it is distinctly encouraged, and that, not in passing, but on principle," at least as regards the assassination of Queen Elizabeth, as Meyer has put it. The circumstances were exceptional, and the Vatican response certainly was, going "far beyond what canon law permits to be done to excommunicate persons. Excommunication in canon law corresponds to outlawry in civil; to kill an excommunicate person is not regarded as murder by canon law, but rather as a deed which calls for penance, 'lest the discipline of the church suffer harm,' and because impure motives can easily prompt the deed."[120] But in this case, Gregory and other princes of the church were so convinced of the ignominy of Elizabeth that they not only overruled the established canon law but even declared that this tyrannicide would be no sin, would do God service, and would gain merit for the assassins.[121] The papacy's approval of the assassination of Elizabeth was at least morphologically similar to Hamlet's decision to kill Claudius in "perfect conscience" because to allow that "canker" to grow to further evil would be to invite damnation (5.2.67-70).

Eight years after the Vatican's endorsement of that particular plot to assassinate Elizabeth in 1580, a massive Catholic invasion effort was launched, and the Spanish Armada set out to conquer England. The Pope declared the invasion a crusade and blessed it as such. The most formidable of Catholic exiles, Cardinal William Allen, wrote *An Admonition to the Nobility and People of England* reminding his fellow countrymen that two popes had pronounced on Elizabeth "concerning her illegitimation and usurpation and inability to the Crown of England, as for excommunication and deprivation in respect of her heresy, sacrilege and abominable life." The Cardinal's exhortation is summarized by Garrett Mattingly as follows:

> The rest of the pamphlet was devoted to a proof that the deposition of Elizabeth was right by natural law because she was a tyrant, and by divine law because she was a heretic, that it was the duty of all Englishmen to help purge their country of the iniquity of her reign, and that by doing so they would help save their own and their children's souls, as by any other course they would surely damn them.[122]

Other English Catholics disagreed, at home and abroad. During the invasion crisis at home, most Roman Catholic subjects continued to support Elizabeth as their lawful queen, just as most Protestants had earlier acknowledged her Catholic elder sister Mary Tudor. When word of the defeat of the Grand Armada reached the theological college in Rome, "the English students . . . cheered aloud at the news."[123] Such evidence should help us to understand a point of some importance: the experience and exposure of sixteenth-century Englishmen forced them to realize that questions of obligation and obedience were not so simple as the words of the *Book of Homilies* and of Shakespeare's John of Gaunt in *Richard II* have led some literary critics to assume. Both among those Catholics who took violent action, and among those who did not, there must have been much soul-searching and many an inner debate. If one rebelled, was one a villain, inviting the anarchy which would make everything worse? If one did nothing, was one a coward? Whatever course was followed would have involved severe conflicts in mind and conscience—inner conflicts very similar to those Hamlet eloquently debated on the Globe stage.

After Elizabeth's death, there was only one more significant Catholic plot to assassinate an English Protestant monarch during Shakespeare's lifetime. This was, of course, the notorious Gunpowder Plot of 1605, in which Guy Fawkes and a group of recusant colleagues conspired to blow up King James and both houses of parliament at the same time. The incessant vigilance of Cecil apparently allowed that plot to develop so far as to create a huge popular sensation, and then stepped in at what was apparently the eleventh hour to save the nation from disaster. All Protestants, and most Catholics as well, rejoiced in the deliverance Cecil had so carefully stage-managed. Those events are so well known that they need merely be mentioned here as further evidence of divided attitudes toward regicide within the community of English Catholics.

Although attempts to murder Elizabeth and James were uniformly unsuccessful, the situation just a few leagues across the Channel was markedly different. Within about ten years before and also after the appearance of Shakespeare's *Hamlet*, two successive French monarchs were assassinated by Catholic zealots. In 1589 a Dominican named Jacques Clément stabbed and killed King Henry III with a poisoned dagger, in retaliation for the king's earlier assassination of the leaders of the Catholic League, the Duke de Guise and his brother Cardinal Guise. The successor of Henry III was Henry IV, the former Protestant champion against Catholic occupants of the French throne which he himself occupied after 1589. Despite his *politique* conversion to Rome in 1593, he remained suspect to many Catholics, and over twenty attempts were made to kill him.[124] In 1610 he was assassinated by a schoolmaster named François Ravaillac. In each case, the unsuccessful plans to kill Elizabeth and James and the successful assaults upon Henry III and Henry IV, the advocates of such actions defended them as morally justifiable tyrannicides.

Directly pertinent to these issues was a major study of political history and theory published in 1599 by the eminent Jesuit scholar Juan de Mariana— the *De Rege et Regis Institutione*. This book was a balanced and learned analysis of kingship, intended to limit the absolutist tendencies of the time, and anyone who reads it today will be impressed by its rational and judicious approach. It became a cause célèbre because of a single chapter, which considered whether it is morally justifiable to kill a tyrant, and concluded (as had so many others) that it is.[125]

Mariana himself regarded the assassination of Henry III as a just act, and the young regicide as a hero. His account of those events in 1589 is highly instructive:

> Jacques Clément . . . was studying theology in the Dominican college of his order. He was told by the theologians, whom he had consulted, that a tyrant may be killed legally. . . . [He then gained admission to the King's presence by a ruse.] He went in as the King was arising and was not yet fully dressed. They had some conversation.

As he approached under color of handing over some letter into his hands, he inflicted a deep wound above the bladder with a knife treated with poison which he was concealing in his hand—a deed of remarkable resolution and an exploit to be remembered. Grievously wounded, the King struck back at the murderer, wounding him in the eye and breast with the same knife, crying out against the traitor and king-killer.

The courtiers break in, aroused by this unusual occurrence. Though Clément is prostrate and senseless, they inflict many wounds on him in their wildness and savagery. He says nothing, rather is glad, as appears from his countenance, because with the deed accomplished he missed the other tortures which he feared would be due him.[126]

The king died without the administration of the sacraments, the assassin's work being so effective that, as in *Hamlet*, no shriving time was allowed, a fact which appears not to have concerned the assassin although he was himself a Dominican priest. Nor did it concern his admirers. As for the mortally wounded king, he declared as he lay dying, "Behold I was shapen in iniquity, and in sin did my mother conceive me"—and Mariana commented of his reign that he had "turned everything into a mockery." On the other side, Mariana regarded the young assassin as a hero, and in this view he was not alone. Oscar Jászi and John D. Lewis have written, Clément "was promptly honored by the League preachers and by his Order as a martyr. He was proclaimed from the pulpits of Paris as 'the holy martyr of Jesus Christ,' who had delivered France from 'that dog of a Henry of Valois.' Even the pope, Sixtus V, regarded the event as a sign that God still watched over the kingdom of France. Jean Boucher and Rossaeus [William Rainolds] were among those who found in Clément's deed an example of the proper method for dealing with tyrants."[127]

Mariana expressed one responsible and widely-held judgment when he described the murder of Henry III as just retribution for blood that the king himself had spilled:

A killing expiated by a killing, and at [Clément's] hand the betrayal and death of the Duke of Guise were avenged with the royal blood.

Thus Clément died, an eternal honor to France, as it has seemed to very many, twenty-four years of age, a young man of simple tem-

perament and not strong of body; but a greater power strengthened his normal powers and spirit.

But Mariana acknowledged that there were different judgments of the act and of the regicide:

> There was no unanimity of opinion about the deed of the monk. While many praised him and deemed him worthy of immortality, others, eminent in their reputations for wisdom and learning, condemned him, denying that it is right for anyone on his own private authority to kill a king . . . even though he be profligate in his morals and also has degenerated into tyranny.[128]

Mariana gave a scrupulously fair consideration of those who denied any justification for tyrannicide, but concluded that it must be allowed when justice can be obtained by no other means. His analysis, the fullest to be written up until that time, illustrates the topicality of the debate over tyrannicide within a year of the appearance of Shakespeare's play.

About a decade later, regicide overtook another and more famous French king. In 1610, King Henry IV was killed by François Ravaillac who had convinced himself that he was the chosen instrument of God to eliminate the continuing threats to the papacy from that formerly Protestant rebel. Although Ravaillac was influenced by a general familiarity with the theories of tyrannicide circulating at the time, there is no evidence that he knew Mariana's work and he appears to have acted entirely on his own initiative.[129] Nonetheless, Mariana and the Jesuits were widely suspected of direct or indirect involvement, and renewed attacks on the doctrine of tyrannicide placed the Jesuits under great pressure. Aquaviva, the able General of the Society of Jesus, responded by forbidding any member of the Society either to write or teach "that it is allowed for anyone whosoever, under any pretext of tyranny whatsoever, to kill kings or princes or to plan their murder."[130] But within three years the brilliant Francisco Suarez, himself a Jesuit, had included in his *Defense of the Catholic Faith* "one of the most systematic expositions of the rightfulness of tyrannicide ever written." That section earned his book, in addition to its acknowledged intellectual merits, the notable distinction of being burned by the common hangman both in Protestant London and in Catholic Paris.[131] But Suarez was responding against the rising tide of divine right absolutism, and his teachings were praised and defended by Pope Pius V.[132]

## E. International Calvinism and Resistance

Protestant leaders in the early stages of the Reformation, both on the Continent and in England, were almost unanimously committed to a policy of passive resistance, their weapons restricted to persuasion and debate, but under changing conditions that attitude also changed. What was perhaps the first modification may be observed in the Lutheran city of Magdeburg. Placed under the ban of the Holy Roman Empire, the city was threatened from all sides, and in 1550 a group of clergymen issued the first orthodox Protestant defense of using force to resist force.[133] A few years later, the death of the Protestant King Edward VI and succession of his Catholic sister Mary placed English Protestants under a severe strain; some three hundred were burned, and many others were forced to seek refuge abroad. Among those émigrés were three of the more aggressive exponents of Edwardian Reform, of whom John Knox was the most famous because of his later leadership of the Reformation in Scotland. Having served as chaplain to the recently deceased English king, Knox now attacked Mary Tudor in a number of militant publications, calling upon the English nobility to rise up against her and even punish her "to the death."[134] Yet the instruments of retribution, he declared, were ignoring their obligation:

> But this part of their duty, I fear, do a small number of the nobility of this age rightly consider; neither yet will they understand that for that purpose God hath promoted them. For now the common song of all men is, we must obey our Kings, be they good or be they bad; for God hath so commanded. But horrible shall the vengeance be, that shall be poured forth upon such blasphemers of God.... For it is no less blasphemy to say that God hath commanded Kings to be obeyed when they command iniquity, than to say that God by his precept is author and maintainer of all iniquity.[135]

Christopher Goodman propagated almost exactly the same view as Knox, and although the exiled Anglican Bishop of Rochester and of Winchester John Ponet differed from them at various important points, he came to essentially the same conclusion. As J. W. Allen puts it, "even the assassination of a 'tyrant' by a private individual would, it seemed to him, be justified under some not clearly specified circumstances."[136] That was always a difficulty with tyrannicide: how to define conditions which would justify it.

The issue was considered and debated in Protestant as in Catholic circles.

Although I know of no Protestant defense so extensive as those by the Jesuits Mariana and Suarez, Protestant leaders after the fifteen-fifties on the Continent at least were unwilling to dismiss tyrannicide out of hand. There were Old Testament precedents, and these were often cited, as when Henry Bullinger wrote that

> sometime he [God] stirreth up noble captains and valiant men to displace tyrants, and set God's people at liberty; as we see many examples thereof in the books of Judges and Kings. But lest any man do fall to abuse those examples, let him consider their calling by God: which calling if he have not, or else do prevent [that is, assume a calling from God which he does not have], he is so far from doing good in killing the tyrant, that it is to be feared lest he do make the evil double so much as it was before.[137]

The dispatch of a Biblical tyrant could be commanded by God and executed by men who were themselves notably evil, as was the case with Jehu who killed Queen Jezebel and King Joram. Of Jehu, the Geneva Bible provides the following gloss at 1 Kings 10:30: "Thus God approveth and rewardeth his zeal in executing judgment, albeit his wickedness was afterward punished." Translated into the terms Hamlet uses, this means that Jehu was both scourge and minister.[138]

Calvin's successor in the leadership of the Reformed Church at Geneva, Théodore de Bèze, never either theoretically or actually endorsed tyrannicide, but he left the possibility open:

> I cannot accept the opinion of those who, without exception or distinction, would condemn all slayers of tyrants, to whom, indeed, the Greeks of old gave honors and rewards. Nor do I share the view that finds the liberations mentioned in the Book of Judges [e.g., 3.15-25] to be so special and extraordinary that no general implications may be drawn from them.[139]

On the positive side of the issue, Queen Elizabeth and certain members of her council, when debating the future of Mary Queen of Scots, inclined at one point to the thought that assassination would be preferable to judicial trial and execution, and wrote to sound out the willingness of Sir Amias Paulet, to whose custody Mary had been committed. Although Paulet had earlier favored assassinating Mary, he now vacillated, and then returned this answer: "God forbid that I should make so foul a shipwreak of my conscience," a reply Elizabeth regarded as hypocritical. To her mind, conscience was making cowards of such people who thought "too precisely" on the event (here recall Hamlet's reflections on himself) and Sir John Neale comments on her caustic reaction to the " 'niceness of these precise fellows' who had taken an oath to lynch Mary and were clamouring for her death, but must thrust the odium of it on their Queen, who did not desire it."[140] Yet the problem was complex, and Elizabeth herself vacillated more than anyone else.

Whereas Amias Paulet refused to assassinate Mary Stuart, even though he regarded her as an undoubted former tyrant in Scotland plotting to assume tyrannical power over England, the leading British classicist of the generation defended any action against tyranny, up to and even including assassination. George Buchanan was widely recognized as one of Europe's most distinguished scholars when he left France to return to his native Scotland under the newly inaugurated Reformation there. His arguments were primarily based upon Greek and Roman precedents which justified attacking tyrants by all available means, and in developing the larger arguments Buchanan defended assassination. Whenever a King misuses his powers, he must be regarded as a tyrant. "Now a tyrant," he wrote, "is an enemy of the people. War against an enemy on account of grave and unendurable injuries is a just war," indeed it is "the most just of wars," in which "not only the whole people but also individuals have the right to kill the enemy."[141] Buchanan acknowledged that this principle was subject to abuse, but he argued that the potential abuse of a just principle did not negate its validity.

Buchanan advanced these and other related arguments in his *De Jure Regni apud Scotos*, which was composed shortly after the Protestant Lords of the Congregation in Scotland had taken arms against Mary in 1567, captured her, and deposed her from the throne. Although not printed until 1578, it was a major theoretical defense for the aggressive form taken by Protestantism in the northern kingdom, and was both intended and recognized as such. But its influence ranged far beyond the bounds of Scotland, and Harold Laski regarded it as perhaps "the most influential political essay of the century."[142] The English knew and widely discussed it, as did the French, the Dutch, and the Germans.

In citing the importance of Buchanan for the development of resistance theory among Calvinists, we should not overlook the prior and seminal contributions of John Calvin himself. In a few carefully constructed sentences near the end of the *Institutes*, Calvin affirmed the right and even the duty of "lesser magistrates" (that is, officers of state below the king) to resist a tyrannous ruler. Citing as precedents the ephors and demarchs in Greece, the tribunes in Rome, and in Europe the three estates in their assemblies, he pronounced a right which was to prove of great historical importance over the next two and a half centuries in Europe and America:

> I do not so forbid them according to their office to withstand the outraging licentiousness of kings: that I affirm that if they wink at kings wilfully raging over and treading down the poor communality, their dissembling is not without wicked breach of faith, because they deceitfully betray the liberty of the people, whereof they know themselves to be appointed protectors by the ordinance of God.[143]

Influential though this doctrine became, it did not spell out specific programs of action such as were later developed by Scottish, French, and Dutch followers of Calvin.

As for armed disobedience against a monarch, Protestants on the continent of Europe propagated no detailed analyses and theoretical arguments prior to 1572. This is not to say that there had previously been no resorts to arms, for there had been. The French Wars of Religion had been underway for some years, but they had not yet generated a systematic reconsideration of the earlier Protestant attitudes. Even John Calvin had consistently urged restraint and patience as the proper response to persecution and violence under the Catholic monarchs of France, and he advised strongly against the Conspiracy of Amboise, a futile uprising which eventually cost many Protestant lives. One of the arguments he advanced against armed resistance by the Huguenots was that they lacked leadership by a prince of the blood royal, even though the House of Bourbon had already publicly converted to Protestantism. In 1562, however, Louis Bourbon, Prince de Condé, assumed active leadership of the Huguenots and raised the standard of armed revolt. Thereafter, Calvin "supported the Huguenot cause without a murmur of protest," although he had staunchly opposed any such action on earlier occasions.[144] Calvin's rationale has been ably summarized by Michael Walzer: "A rebellion of the nobles against the Guise would only be justified, he wrote shortly before the Conspiracy of Amboise, if it were led by a prince of the blood; but if only one prince were to take part, then it would have to be the leading one, nearest by birth to the royal house."[145]

That a prince of the blood royal could legitimatize resistance was recognized in both Calvinist and Jesuit positions. Like Calvin, the Jesuit theorist Suarez affirmed the right of princes of the blood to act against tyrannical misuses of the royal power. As Clancy has summarized the views of Suarez, "if the pope did not specify who was to execute the sentence on the tyrant, this duty was to be performed by the tyrant's legitimate successor."[146] Although Suarez would have repudiated Calvin's authority, as Calvin renounced that of the pope, they concur in assigning responsibility to princes of the blood who were, as Hamlet correctly said, "born to set it right."[147] This consensus developed across religious lines, and may be summarized in the words of Roland Mousnier: "contemporary political theory permitted princes of the blood to share in governing the country and to lead a revolt if the king ever turned into a tyrant."[148]

The spelling out of crown-princely prerogative was largely developed among French Protestants only after the bloody slaughter of thousands of Huguenots in the famous St. Bartholomew's Massacre of 1572.[149] During the religious wars of the latter quarter of the sixteenth century, a large proportion of the French nobility were Huguenots.[150] And it was that group of upper-class Huguenots who developed within Protestantism an extensive ethical theory of disobedience and armed resistance to an abusive king. These theories were far more militantly applied by Protestants against a Catholic monarchy in France than were the comparable Catholic attitudes against the Protestant regime by recusants within England. Elizabethan England supported those Huguenot activities abroad, with attitudes ranging from reluctance to enthusiasm.

There can be no doubt that both Huguenot resistance and resistance theory were well known in England. In *The French Religious Wars in English Political Thought*, J.H.M. Salmon observes that participants in English political discussions and debates proceeded "as if they expected their readers to grasp the significance of French example from an established knowledge of the French background. The French conflicts had become part of the English historical consciousness, and the ideas which accompanied them had already crossed the threshold of English political thinking."[151] Not only were these French events and ideas part of an international lingua franca in England as on the Continent, but there were many connections between the Huguenot resistance theorists and the principal English statesmen under Elizabeth.[152]

The first of the major Huguenot theorists was François Hotman, one of the leading jurists of the time whose scholarly reputation was international. He was well connected and well known in England: among his friends were Sir John Cheke, Archbishop Edmund Grindal, and Archbishop Edwin Sandys, as well as Sir William Cecil, and his son was a close friend of Sir Philip Sidney and Secretary to the Earl of Leicester.[153] His *Francogallia* of 1573 argued from historical precedents going back to classical times that a king's misbehavior justified subjects in withdrawing their consent to his rule and in deposing him from the throne, by force if necessary. As "a virtuoso feat of scholarship," this treatise "caused an immediate sensation" and established a rationale in law and conscience for aggressive Protestant resistance to an evil ruler.[154]

Whereas Hotman was a jurist, the next major Huguenot theoretician was the eminent theologian Théodore de Bèze. Born into a prosperous family of French nobility, Bèze led the Calvinist community from its headquarters in Geneva after the death of Calvin in 1564. His *Right of Magistrates*, appearing in 1574, further developed Calvin's argument that princes, nobles, and officials of cities and provinces were vested with an "ephoral" authority to correct such abuses as might come from the king. These classes were known collectively as the lesser magistrates, and although they were subordinate in status to the crown, Bèze and others maintained that they had the power to oppose a monarch: "If the king, hereditary or elective, clearly goes back on the conditions without which he would not have been recognized and acknowledged, can there be any doubt that the lesser magistrates of the kingdom, of the cities, and of the provinces, the administration of which they have received from the sovereignty itself [rather than from the king], are free of their oath [to the king], at least to the extent that they are entitled to resist flagrant oppression of the realm which they swore to defend and protect according to their office and their particular jurisdiction."[155]

In 1579, the third of the great Huguenot treatises appeared, the *Defense of Liberty Against Tyrants*. Sometimes attributed to Hubert Languet (who as advisor and friend deeply influenced Sir Philip Sidney), this work is now thought to have been composed largely or entirely by Philippe du Plessis-Mornay, a prominent nobleman closely associated with the struggles of Henry de Bourbon,

King of Navarre, against the French throne he eventually assumed. As soldier, statesman, and diplomat, Mornay served the Huguenot prince in many capacities and on at least two occasions was sent as his envoy to the English court of Queen Elizabeth, also developing over the years a considerable reputation as a writer and propagandist, all of which activities earned him the popular title of Huguenot pope. His *Contra tyrannos* went beyond the treatises of Hotman and Bèze by being a call to military struggle, "an exhortation to rebel," with a major reliance upon nobles and princes to curtail and even depose tyrannous kings.[156]

In so arguing, Mornay built upon a distinction of considerable importance both historically and for our interest in *Hamlet*. As Skinner summarizes, Mornay "begins by distinguishing 'the officers of the kingdom' from 'the officers of the king.' He then argues that while the latter are merely 'domestics of the king established only to obey him,' the former are 'associates in the royal power' amongst whom the king is merely a 'president,' while 'all of them are bound, just like the king, to look after the welfare of the commonwealth.' "[157] In this sense, Hamlet is clearly an officer of the kingdom, rather than of the king, because he is not a domestic established only by the king but in his own right represents independent power and responsibility.

It is clear that these arguments were not distinctively "Calvinist," despite the fact that they were largely advanced by and on behalf of the Huguenot magnates. Their sources may be traced to pre-Reformation scholastics and so on back to the classical and Biblical writers. Furthermore, these later followers of Calvin increasingly universalized the rationale of their appeals beyond the limits of their own religious position. A growing emphasis on natural law "enabled them to present their demand for resistance as a purely political and non-sectarian argument, so performing the vital ideological task of appealing not merely to their own followers, but to the broadest possible spectrum of Catholic moderates and malcontents."[158] These developments were patently among the most important changes in the history of European thought, and they were taking place in the decades immediately before the appearance of Shakespeare's *Hamlet*. It was in these years, as Quentin Skinner summarizes, that the Huguenot nobles and princes were able "to make the epoch-making move from a purely religious theory of resistance, depending on the idea of a covenant to uphold the laws of God, to a genuinely political theory of revolution, based on the idea of a contract which gives rise to a moral right (and not merely a religious duty) to resist any ruler who fails in his corresponding obligation to pursue the welfare of the people in all his public acts."[159]

The justification of resistance to the crowned monarch by magistrates and princes of the blood was extraordinarily important historically, and eventually led to certain modifications in Anglican doctrine under Elizabeth to which we shall turn in the last section of this chapter. But before we leave the tangled subject of developments in France during the Wars of Religion, there is another striking series of events there which has at least coincidental relevance to the political situation which Shakespeare dramatized in *Hamlet*. This involves the effort of the Catholic League to interpose the Catholic uncle of Henry of Navarre ahead of Henry in the direct line of succession to the French throne, thereby assuring the continuation of a Catholic monarchy in France. That attempt eventually failed, and Navarre succeeded to the throne as Henry IV, but the whole story is so fascinating that, even though I do not regard it as a source or direct inspiration for Claudius' "popping" into the throne ahead of his nephew Hamlet, I should at least sketch in the sequence of events.

The Catholic League knew that it could expect no heir to the throne from the last of the Valois line of kings, Henry III, who was impotent. The major hope for continuing a Catholic succession thus lay with the younger brother of Henry III, the Duke of Anjou, but Anjou died without issue in 1584. This left Henry de Bourbon, the Huguenot King of Navarre, as the primogenitive heir to the French throne, an eventuality the Catholic League in France was unwilling to accept. As a result, some Catholic leaders attempted to insert Henry de Bourbon's uncle, Cardinal Charles de Bourbon (Fig. II.8), ahead of him as direct successor to the throne, and in March, 1585, the League declared the Cardinal to be the legitimate heir.[160] King Philip II of Spain, the most active royal proponent of Catholicism, had already endorsed and promised to support this substitution.[161] The primogenitive basis for such a move was at best highly dubious, but even an aging Roman Catholic cardinal was perceived by the Catholic faction as highly preferable to a militant young Protestant.

The eminent Huguenot jurist and monarchomach theorist François Hotman entered the fray, this time maintaining the inviolability of primogenitive successions. In his pamphlet of 1585 entitled *Disputation on the Controversy over Royal Succession between an Uncle and his late Brother's Son* (*Disputatio de controversia successionis regiae inter patruum et fratris praemortui filium*), he argued in favor of the time-sanctioned right of a son rather than a brother

FIG. 11.8. Cardinal Charles de Bourbon, engraving by Jean Gourmount

or uncle to inherit, thus defending the succession of his Huguenot chieftain. In his *Francogallia* of twelve years earlier, Hotman had argued that the French monarchy was originally elective, and should still be so, for on that basis he hoped to secure the peaceful succession to the throne of Henry de Bourbon, but his *volte-face* here was in keeping with the tendency of French Protestant and Catholic factions alike to adopt each other's positions as circumstances changed.[162] The ensuing arguments on both sides of the succession debate are so Byzantine as to make the mind boggle, but eventually the issue was decided by direct action rather than by logic.[163]

Issues were further complicated by the fact that Henry III, despite his Catholicism, was intensely unpopular with the Catholic League, so unpopular in fact that he was assassinated in 1589 by the Dominican Jacques Clément, as we have already seen. Cardinal Charles de Bourbon was thereupon hailed as King Charles X by members of the League,[164] but they had failed to secure him from capture by the irate Huguenots. The Cardinal had been under the custody of Monsieur de Chavigny, the Governor of Chinon, where he had been assigned by Henry III for safekeeping. As soon as Henry of Navarre heard of the death of the Catholic Henry III, he charged his faithful du Mornay "to find a way to get the Cardinal de Bourbon out of Chinon and away from M. de Chavigny at whatever cost, even to all he had, because if once the Cardinal regained his freedom he would proclaim himself king," as Lady Mornay put it.[165] Thereupon, Mornay went directly to Chinon, arranged to secure the Cardinal by the payment of large sums of money, and spirited him away before the nearby forces of the Catholic League could secure his person and place him on the throne.[166] The Cardinal was then kept safe in the Abbey of Mailezais in Poitou, unharmed but also uncrowned. The attempt to pop an uncle between Henry of Navarre and the French crown was aborted, whereas under comparable circumstances the efforts of the fictive Claudius succeeds.

That story indicates in yet another way the topicality of *Hamlet* late in the sixteenth century. This rivalry between a royal nephew and uncle for possession of the French throne would have been known to many well-placed Elizabethan Englishmen, but I do not argue that the majority of the Globe audiences would have been familiar with it. What we can assume with confidence, on the other hand, is that resistance both in fact and theory was very much in the air in 1600, among Protestants and Catholics alike.

## v. Born to Set it Right: Hamlet and Others

Assertions of the right of officials, nobles, and princes to resist and even depose a tyrant were so widely known on the Continent and in Scotland as to be inescapable in England as well. While Queen Elizabeth, as head of both church and state, was maintaining the Anglican insistence upon the obedience of subjects at home, she was giving diplomatic, financial, and even military support to Protestant rebels abroad. Indeed, Queen Elizabeth's favorite, the Earl of Leicester, led a large English army against King Philip II in the wars of independence in the Netherlands. Ben Jonson fought there, and Sir Philip Sidney died there, as we should recall.

During and after the very years when Hotman, Bèze, and Mornay were developing the grounds for conscientious disobedience, "Elizabeth's foreign policy was largely devoted to the business of feeding fires in their neighbors' houses," as Conyers Read has put it. Whether she liked it or not (and she did not), Elizabeth and her kingdom were actively committed to the support of armed and aggressive assaults against duly constituted sovereigns on the continent of Europe. And everyone knew it.[167]

Elizabeth's support of Protestant warfare against the Valois monarchs in France and even more aggressively against Philip II in the Netherlands required explanation and if possible justification at home and abroad. She assigned the difficult task of bringing the traditional Tudor doctrine of non-resistance into line with the new realities of the fifteen-eighties to Thomas Bilson, whom she later made bishop of Worcester and then of Winchester and who still later served as a member of the privy council under James I. This new statement of Anglican policy was published at Oxford in 1585, and dedicated to the Queen herself. Entitled *The True Difference between Christian Subjection and Unchristian Rebellion*, it met the late-sixteenth-century need to maintain and uphold both the doctrine of passive obedience to the crown at home in England and also active rebellion under different circumstances against monarchs abroad. At the time Bilson appeared to have succeeded in this very difficult balancing act, but in the long run his persuasive efforts contributed to rather different results from those he originally had in mind, and were found to have contributed to monarchomach theory and practice. The *Dictionary of National Biography* notes that although Bilson's book at first unquestionably "served the queen's present purpose, it contributed more than any other to the humiliation, ruin, and death of Charles I."[168] What interests us here is not the execution of that unfortunate king in 1649, but rather the legitimatizing of monarchomach views within the Elizabethan settlement. Although he never went so far as to endorse tyrannicide as such, Bilson gave wide scope to virtually every other kind of armed resistance against tyranny under the conditions existing on the Continent toward the end of Elizabeth's reign.

Anthony à Wood supplies a fine summary of the intent, and the contrast between the immediate and the more lasting impact of Bilson's *True Difference*:

> It must be now noted that whereas in England the interest of the state had a great influence upon the doctrine of obedience, Queen Elizabeth therefore, conceiving it convenient for her worldly designs to take on her the protection of the Low-Countries against the king of Spain, did employ our author Bilson to write the said book of *Christian Subjection*. In which, to justify the revolt of Holland, he gave strange liberty in many cases, especially concerning religion, for subjects to cast off their obedience. But this book which served her designs for the present, did contribute much to the ruin of her successor King Charles I (which one calls 'a just judgment of God'). For there is not any book that the presbyterians have made more dangerous use of against their prince (Charles I) than that which his predecessor commanded to be written to justify her against the king of Spain.[169]

In effect, then, Bilson's justification of Elizabeth's intervention in support of Protestant militancy against monarchs on the Continent brought Anglicanism more nearly in line with the monarchomach tendencies developed by international Calvinists and others.

Bilson's arguments were intricate and broad-ranging. He offers a wide variety of examples of the use of force by Protestant princes and nobles against kings or emperors in Germany, the Low Countries, France, and Scotland, and in each case he justifies the monarchomachs. For Scotland, his arguments are similar to those we have already noted; for the Netherlands he maintains that Philip II is not a legitimate king but only the Count of Flanders. "In France, the King of Navarre and the Prince of Condé might lawfully defend themselves from injustice and violence"—an argument very similar in principle to that which Hamlet makes in act five for action against a king who has killed his father and "thrown out his angle for my proper life" (5.2.63-70)—and he suggests that "the laws of the land do permit them means to save the state from open tyranny."[170]

In England, however, there are two absolutely critical distinctions, in his view. In the first place, he argues that there has been no tyranny under Elizabeth. But in the second place, and even more fundamentally, he asserts that the English monarchy is hereditary and primogenitive. Even if a tyrant were to occupy the throne—any throne in any nation—by virtue of such direct descent and not election "he must be endured," according to Bilson, and "may not be deposed."[171] Thus Bilson manages to justify both the Anglican doctrine of passive resistance at home with the Elizabethan practice of supporting armed and violent resistance abroad.

Relevant as all this is to the climate of ideas in which *Hamlet* appeared in 1600, there is another equally pertinent argument advanced by Bilson: elective monarchies are set radically apart from succession by primogeniture. In countries where the king or emperor is elected to the throne, princes and nobles "may lawfully resist him . . . or else repel him as a tyrant, and set another in his place by the right and freedom of their country." Here he cites and endorses the view of the Swiss Reformer Zwingli, and he defends without quite endorsing the similar position taken by John Knox: "they which choose one governor, have the same right to choose another if he be unfit," as Bilson phrases it. And he adds that if an elected monarch "show himself unworthy of the regiment," he may be deposed by those who elected him.[172] Always excepting those rulers who properly inherited a crown, he cites the case of Protestants who took up armed resistance to the Holy Roman emperor. "The German lawyers made evident demonstration" of the right of electors to resist the emperor himself by arms. He supports the view of the princes and nobles who maintained against the emperor that "unjust violence is not God's ordinance, neither are we bound to him by any other reason, than if he keeps the conditions on which he was created emperor."[173] The German princes, he maintains, bear the sword "as lawful magistrates to defend their liberties and prohibit injury against all oppressors, the emperor himself not excepted."[174] These formulations by Bishop Bilson of the final position of Elizabethan Anglicanism toward the use of armed force against a tyrant may help us to understand the double announcement in the final scene of *Hamlet* that the Danish monarchy is elective rather than hereditary, information which Shakespeare did not earlier provide. But about that point I shall have more to say in my concluding chapter.

Let us now return to the actual process of deciding whether militant action is necessary. The Huguenot leaders in France disliked rebellion almost as much as Elizabeth did. When they felt themselves forced into it, they circumscribed it by the most careful and conscientious safeguards. Magistrates and magnates were not to act against the monarch except in extreme cases. As Mornay wrote, "we should not look for perfect princes but consider ourselves fortunate, indeed, if we have men of middling virtue as our rulers." But in cases of flagrant violations of justice and law, the officials, nobles, and princes "are permitted to use force against a tyrant. And they are not only permitted but obliged, as part of the duty of their office, and they have no excuse if they should fail to act." Indeed, "if they fail to suppress tyranny or to prevent it," Mornay held, they thereby share the tyrant's guilt.[175] That duty should not be lightly accepted however, but only after the most scrupulous analysis of the national situation and the individual conscience. As for private citizens, they had no such obligation to act, apart from following their leaders, as Mornay makes clear: "But is anyone, no matter how menial his station, permitted to resist? . . . Not in the slightest. . . . Private persons . . . have not been presented with the sword, either by God or by the people. Hence if they draw the sword they are seditious, no matter how just the cause may be."[176] Even when "the time is out of joint," assault upon the monarch must be left in the hands of those who are "born to set it right"—men like Henry of Navarre, the Prince de Condé, and Prince Hamlet—and then only on the basis of the most conscientious probing of the self and examination of the challenge (1.5.188-89).[177] When understood in terms of these sixteenth-century attitudes, Hamlet's relentless self-examination of his own "case of conscience" would not have appeared either weak or dilatory, but rather an exemplary application of wisdom and justice in the face of a desperate crisis.

When Hamlet in the last scene of the play summarizes the tyrannous and bloody actions of Claudius—his assassination of the former king, whoring of Gertrude, seizing the crown, and plotting against the life of the Prince—he is arguing as did the Huguenot nobles who saw themselves forced into a life-or-death struggle. Like Hamlet, the Huguenots claimed that their only recourse was self-defense "against the designs of those who wished to ruin them" and who had already "violated every right" of civilized society, so that "they had no other recourse than to take to arms."[178] Like many of the historical princes and magnates of the sixteenth century, Hamlet was forced by the circumstances of his time to agonizing struggles with his conscience, and the manner in which he resolved his case of conscience was similar to that of the Huguenot nobles:

> is't not perfect conscience
> To quit him with this arm? And is't not to be damned
> To let this canker of our nature come
> In further evil?                                    (5.2.67-70)

# THREE

# The Court and the Prince

## 1. Multiple Scandals

THE GHOST in the first scene of *Hamlet* introduces mysteries which are never fully resolved, as we have seen. The second scene brings forward most of the other characters with whom the play will deal, while focusing upon those mighty opposites Claudius and Hamlet. The first speech belongs to Claudius, but the visual scene introduced at the outset is dominated by the Prince. This is the only play in which Shakespeare tells us exactly how the protagonist was costumed. The visual contrast between the Prince and the rest of the court is striking, and stands as an outward symbol of moral contrasts which underlie the entire scene.

The opening address from the throne is highly impressive as a piece of rhetoric, and by it the King establishes himself as an imposing figure, but even as his regality is presented it is also rendered suspicious. His long and beautifully phrased opening sentence discloses two things, both of which would have shocked an Elizabethan audience: his recent marriage has followed with great speed upon the death of his brother, and he has married his sister-in-law. As this scene develops, this initial information is considerably developed, and in later scenes we learn in addition that the live brother murdered the dead one, and then took possession both of his throne and of his wife.

Hamlet's reactions (in whole or in part) to these disclosures have often been interpreted as extreme beyond measure. To many readers, the Prince's words, whether spoken in dialogue or in soliloquy, have seemed excessive, unbalanced, irrational, or even mad. Diverse critical arguments have been advanced in favor of such views. Few of these arguments would have convinced audiences at the Globe Theater in 1600, but they have influenced many modern responses to the play and have thus oversimplified criticism of it. These views cannot be conflated or amalgamized, but they may for our purpose be epitomized in T. S. Eliot's judgment of the play. As Eliot saw it, Hamlet's reactions to the actions of others in the play were exorbitant; or, put differently, nothing in the play was sufficient to justify the Prince's responses; or, in yet another expression, Hamlet was dominated by a state of mind "in excess of the facts as they appear," without an "objective correlative" for his eloquently expressed feelings. My concern here is not to express yet another twentieth-century response to such views, but is rather to present evidence of what Shakespeare could have expected his original audiences to think about them and about the Prince.[1]

Three primary issues are involved, issues which overlap but for purposes of convenience should be considered separately. First is the marriage of brother-in-law and sister-in-law, which was regarded as incest and treated with intense moral revulsion in Elizabethan times. Second is the speedy remarriage of a widow, without observing the sanctions of decent mourning, which would have been regarded not only as a minor or ordinary social impropriety but as a major indecency, not only for the Queen but for the whole court, in ways which costuming and speech make clear. Third is the union of a widow with the assassin of her deceased husband, compounded by the fact that the murdered spouse had been king and the widow was queen. To these we shall turn in order.

## II. Marriage Feasts and Incestuous Sheets

Claudius' first speech begins with the graceful and dignified assertion that "though yet of Hamlet our dear brother's death/ The memory be green," and continues with fitting references to grief and woe. Then comes the quiet but explosive introduction of his consort as "our sometime sister, now our queen"— a callously imperturbable admission of royal incest. The marriage of brothers- and sisters-in-law had been branded shameful over hundreds of years of moral teaching since Old Testament times, and was prohibited both in England and on the Continent. It was only in 1907, some three hundred years after the appearance of Shakespeare's *Hamlet*, that the last of such laws was repealed by the British parliament.[2]

The incest taboo is one of the strongest to which people are subject, and in 1600 it would have condemned any union such as that of Claudius and Gertrude. The basis is found in the Mosaic Law. Leviticus 18:16 and 20:21 emphatically prohibited marriage or other sexual relationship between a brother and a deceased sibling's widow, classing such unions not only as incest but grouping them with bestiality and other revolting practices.[3] The sole exception to this taboo in the Old Testament could not have applied in *Hamlet*, for it took effect only if the previous marriage had been without issue, leaving that deceased brother with no heir to carry on his name and line. Under those circumstances, and only under them, the oldest surviving brother was required to marry the widow and provide an heir for the dead brother. That was the so-called Levirate (for brother-in-law) provision of Deuteronomy 25:5-10. Under these Mosaic conceptions, still in legal effect in England, the marriage of Claudius and Gertrude could be justified only on the assumption that young Hamlet either did not exist, or that he was not actually the child of the dead king but merely the bastard child of Gertrude—neither being a particularly happy alternative for the Prince.[4] Circumstances which would have justified the marriage of a brother and sister-in-law simply do not exist in this play.

A famous case in Tudor England should be considered in this connection. When King Henry VII arranged a marriage between his eldest son Prince Arthur and Catherine of Aragon, he was signalizing an important alliance between the royal families of England and Spain. Because of Arthur's youth, the marriage was not physically consummated, so that when he died Catherine was left as both widow and virgin. Henry VII wished to preserve the advantages of the alliance with Spain, and so application was made to the Pope to obtain sanction for Catherine to marry the future Henry VIII. On the basis that her virginity was intact, it was possible to argue that this subsequent marriage would not involve incest and so would be allowable. Furthermore, the fact that Prince Arthur had no heir by the marriage seemingly placed it under the Levirate provision, so the marriage seemed to be both permissible by the general law in Leviticus and mandated by the exceptional provision in Deuteronomy. Pope Julius II thus allowed it, and Henry and Catherine were wed in 1509. It is important for us to note that the ameliorating circumstances which made it possible for the pope, as well as the kings of England and Spain, to approve the marriage of Henry and Catherine do not apply even remotely to the marriage of Claudius and Gertrude. Nonetheless, that royal Tudor marriage in 1509 was subjected to terrible strains due directly or indirectly to the Mosaic prohibitions in Leviticus and to ingrained European attitudes directly attributable to them. In over two decades of marriage, Henry and Catherine were unable to produce a living male heir to the English throne, although Henry had bastard sons. Considering the state of knowledge and opinion in the sixteenth century, it is not surprising that the failure of the royal couple to produce a Prince of Wales was attributed to a curse laid upon the marriage as an incestuous union between brother- and sister-in-law. After twenty-two years of marriage, Henry VIII became convinced that the "failure" of his marriage in its primary mission was the result of its having been incestuous. Eminent scholars on university faculties agreed, as did an English ecclesiastical court under Archbishop Thomas Cranmer as well as the English parliament, and consequently Henry and Catherine were divorced. Henry married Anne Boleyn, from which union issued the great Queen Elizabeth. None of this served to lessen that deep-seated antipathy the average Englishman showed toward marriages between brothers- and sisters-in-law, and it is certain that Elizabeth was born with what may be called a legitimate interest in preserving that antipathy. But Elizabeth had to exert no personal influence in that direction, because such attitudes were pervasive in Shakespeare's time, and long thereafter.

In Tudor sermons and theological tracts, marriages such as that of Gertrude and Claudius are invariably classified as adultery, even if whitewashed by a marriage ceremony.[5] Thomas Becon placed under adultery "the unlawful company of man and woman, as is the marriage with the mother, sister, aunt, brother's wife, and such other wherein Moses treateth."[6] William Tyndale was even more emphatic: "Wherefore, to be so forgetful of natural honesty that I should defile my brother's wife unto mine own shame and all my kin is more grievous and heinous (as they say) and springeth of greater lewdness or malice than to take my neighbor's wife which is not of my kin."[7] Tyndale does not here speak specifically of married incest, but of the thing itself, to indicate scorn for any such physical union as that of Hamlet's mother and uncle. The official book of *Homilies* turns to the specific issue of such marriage in the case of King Herod who had married his brother's divorced wife, and to the fact that John the Baptist had lost his head for rebuking this marriage:

> If whoredom had not been sin, surely St. John Baptist would never have rebuked King Herod for taking his brother's wife, but he told him plainly that it was not lawful. . . . He would rather suffer death . . . than to suffer whoredom to be unrebuked, even in a king. . . . Truly John had been more than twice mad if he would have had the displeasure of a king . . . and lost his head for a trifle.

Claudius has, of course, out-Heroded Herod by first killing his brother (which even Herod did not do in this instance) and then wedding his widow.[8]

In the light of such Tudor attitudes, J. Dover Wilson has properly insisted that Shakespeare would have expected his audience to respond to the marriage in this play with as much abhorrence as the Athenians felt for the union of Oedipus and his mother Jocasta in Sophocles. As Wilson put it, "the incest-business is so important that it is scarcely possible to make too much of it." The analysis of incest as fundamental in this play has been so convincingly developed by Wilson and in a later study by Jason Rosenblatt that no more needs to be said in defining the issue, but it is possible to increase our sensitivity to Hamlet's emotional revulsion by noting certain actual treatments of brothers- and sisters-in-law like Gertrude and Claudius.[9]

The criminal punishment of incest between brother-in-law and sister-in-law was the same as for blood brother and sister and a marriage ceremony was considered a mere subterfuge. Pertinent records are not easily accessible and have not often been printed, but there is sufficient evidence to make the patterns unmistakably clear. Incest, as a flagrant sin, carried with it a conspicuous punishment and penance, designed both to impress the public and to humiliate the offenders. The injunctions of Archbishop Edmund Grindal required exposure on an elevated place or platform in front of a church or in the market, but it is apparent that such exposure could also take place in the front part of a church during service, within full view of the whole congregation. A distinctive robe of penitence was imposed so that the offender appeared "bare-legged and bare-headed, in a white sheet," and also had to "make an open confession of his crime in a prescribed form of words."[10] I have been unable to discover such "a prescribed form of words," and suspect that expressions of this sort were prepared individually or extemporized as a case might arise. In 1575 a brother- and sister-in-law who married each other in Essex were convicted of incest, and it was adjudged that "hereafter they do not cohabit and keep company together under pain of the law" and that they perform the standard penance by exposure in the local parish church on Sunday. Some couples were able to avoid public penance by paying a sizable fine (for the use of the poor) but some were subject both to fine and public exposure. Thus in Essex in 1572 one woman guilty of marrying her brother-in-law was ordered "to stand in the parish church of All Saints in a white sheet over her uppermost garments . . . all the service time, penitently before the congregation there assembled, and to give to the poor people of Maldon forty shillings, and the poor scholars of the University either Oxford or Cambridge twenty shillings.''[11] In London the public exposure was also geared to public humiliation, but arranged in a different style appropriate to a large city: brothers and sisters guilty of incest were ridden about the streets in a cart, open to the jeers and missiles of the populace, and exactly the same punishment was applied to a brother- and sister-in-law who had married as to blood siblings who had cohabited, as is clear from Henry Machyn's London diaries for 1559-60.[12] In Buckinghamshire in 1662 sentence was passed upon "John Tilbie and his wife for unlawful marriage, she marrying [successively, not bigamously] two brothers": he was ordered to do penance in the church and at the marketplace and when he failed to comply he was excommunicated.[13] For the same offense of marriage between brother- and sister-in-law, the familiar humiliation of public exposure in a sheet was still being imposed in Essex as late as 1717.[14] Printed records of these cases being scarce, I have had to rely here on examples over a century and a half, but the patterns are entirely consistent: popular revulsion against the offense and humiliation of the offenders. We would not of course expect to find a king and queen punished in the same way as ordinary citizens, by public exposure in a sheet of penance, and by receiving the abuses of their neighbors. That is not the point of citing these cases of public response and indignation. What is significant about these responses to marriages like that of Claudius and Gertrude is that they demonstrate the revulsion people felt toward such unions: Eliot and others may argue that Hamlet responds in excess of the facts, but the Elizabethans for whom Shakespeare wrote the play would not have agreed.

That is the context for the intense shame Hamlet and the Ghost express over Gertrude's marriage.[15] According to the Ghost, the royal bed has been made "a couch for luxury and damned incest," while the once "seeming-virtuous Queen" has abandoned herself to "shameful lust" to "prey on garbage (1.5.45-46, 57, and 82-83). If anything, the recent marriage may have made the whole business even more shameful, for it is a mere whitewash of corruption, evidencing hypocrisy, and the Prince wishes "I had met my dearest foe in heaven/ Or ever I had seen that day" (1.2.182-83). Nothing can obliterate the son's shame over those "incestuous sheets" and over the fact that Claudius has "whored my mother"[16]—nothing, that is, save Gertrude's repentance (1.2.157, and 5.2.64). But now we must turn from the moral indignity of the incest to the social indignity of the impetuous rush from burial to bridal.

### III. Most Wicked Speed

"A beast that wants discourse of reason/ Would have mourned longer" (1.2.150-51): thus Hamlet assessed his mother's animal-like dash from the grave of one husband into bed with another. Just as the rejection of incest is distinctively human (animals are not known to have such taboos), so formal mourning also separates men from beasts. The first distinction represents man's ethereal nature or morality; the second reflects his organization of social conventions or mores. Both are important, and they overlap in this play as in life. In the Renaissance, ceremonies were not regarded as merely superficial observances, but rather as contributing to and even in some sense insuring the good health of society. So here: properly observed forms and protocols of funeral and mourning were necessary to the health of surviving family and friends and, especially within the royal family, necessary to the wellbeing of society as a whole. Then as now, of course, hypocrisy might be displayed in such activities, for as Hamlet said, "they are actions that a man might play," but there was no doubt in the minds of most Elizabethans that such actions, when properly carried out, were of massive and inherent significance—satisfying "that within which passeth show," as Hamlet put it (1.2.84-86).

Claudius refers in general terms to the speed of these events, with the marriage following rapidly after the funeral. But it is Hamlet in his first soliloquy who gives us a specific accounting of the time—indeed the most fully documented report of recent pre-dramatic time we have in any Shakespearean tragedy (1.2.137-59). He consistently identifies the intervals, so that we can scarcely fail to understand: "But two months dead, nay, not so much, not two," and thus we know the terminus a quo from which the action of the play springs. Then he tells us how long Gertrude waited after the death of her first husband before taking her second, and he conveys the intensity of his own outrage through his thunderous reiteration of the outrageous fact itself: "within a month," again "a little month," and once more "within a month." Even the most inattentive member of the audience would have gotten the point of disgraceful haste. The more acute would have sensed that the marriage followed the funeral amost at once, because it was impossible to bury a king or queen in Renaissance England in less than a month after the death, or at least it was never done more promptly.[17] What Claudius had spoken in sweeping generalities about "an auspicious and a dropping eye,/ With mirth in funeral and with dirge in marriage," Hamlet put directly when he observed that the shoes in which his mother followed his father's body at the funeral were scarcely broken in before her wedding, and that "the funeral baked meats/ Did coldly furnish forth the marriage tables" (1.2.11-12, 1.2.147-48, and 180-81). When Horatio admitted that the marriage "followed hard upon" the funeral, he was using the words in the Elizabethan sense of an almost immediate sequence (1.2.179). Hamlet views these developments not only as distasteful but as obnoxious and obscene. To understand whether or not that reaction was excessive, we need to consider it in the social context of Shakespeare's time. When so placed, Hamlet's social disgust at the haste will be as intelligible as his moral revulsion at the incest has already been shown to be. Even had it not involved a posting "to incestuous sheets," such precipitation from funeral to marriage would have impressed Shakespeare's original audiences as what Hamlet called "most wicked speed."

Death in the Renaissance was not quickly dismissed or easily forgotten, but involved social as well as liturgical rituals devised over the centuries to dignify the ultimate *rite de passage*. These social rituals would be observed not just for a few hours or a few days but for weeks and even months. For the death of a king, the whole kingdom should indeed be "contracted in one brow of woe." On the simplest level, this entailed not only mourning clothes but also mourning hangings and appointments for the royal household. After the death of Francis I of France on May 24, 1547, the Royal Great Hall was changed from the *Salle d'honneur* into the *Salle funèbre* or, as one contemporary described it, "changed from accoutrement of triumph and honor into that of mourning and lugubrious form" with "all the blue and gold draperies . . . replaced by black tapestries."[18] And all concerned were of course expected to wear appropriate garb for a long while after. A case in point is the death in 1586 of the English beau ideal Sir Philip Sidney: "so great was the lamentation for him," as one contemporary noted, "that for many months after, it was accounted indecent for any gentleman of quality, to appear at court or city, in any light or gaudy apparel."[19] Claudius, as brother of the deceased king, would have been expected to remain in black for several months at a minimum,[20] and for a widow or widower mourning was supposed to last considerably longer than for a brother or sister.[21] Sir Ralph Verney, for example, wore black for a year after his wife's death in 1650, and also required that his hairbrushes and other toilet articles be made of black.[22] Even the old King James I could not escape sardonic remarks at court when he shortened the mourning expected of a royal widower to three months after the death of Queen Anne. Thus the ironic court observer John Chamberlain wrote on June 5, 1619, that the king had shifted out of black into a "suit of watchet [i.e., pale blue] satin, laid with silver lace, with a blue and white feather, as also his horse was furnished with the like both before and behind; insomuch that all the company was glad to see him so gallant, and more like a wooer than a mourner. But what decorum it will be, when ambassadors come to condole (as here is one from the Duke of Lorraine with three or four and twenty followers, all in black), let them consider whom it more concerns."[23] Even for a king who had only a few more years of life expectancy, and who neither planned nor desired to remarry, three months of deep mourning was not considered sufficient. At the Danish court the shift was not only far more precipitate but more extreme than that of King James: not from mourner to appearing "like a wooer" but to actual honeymoon.

The change from funeral to marriage would create on the most obvious and visual level as massive a sartorial contrast as one could imagine. Gertrude, from having followed a corpse like Niobe, all tears and enveloped in black, is suddenly transformed into the blushing bride, full of smiles and joy. The electrifying contrast between the two roles, and the appalling rapidity with which his mother shifted from the one to the other, deeply scarred Hamlet's consciousness. He deplores her behavior, questions whether there is any honesty or sincerity in her being, even thinks of her as a prostitute who has been "whored" by Claudius (5.2.64). And when Gertrude, in the first line she speaks, appeals to Hamlet to forsake his mourning ("Good Hamlet, cast thy nighted color off"—1.2.68), she is urging him to endorse and join in the general indecency. But to Elizabethan eyes, Hamlet in his "customary" black would stand out against the gaudy dress of the rest of that court as the only decorous and seemly figure.[24]

When judged in sixteenth-century terms, Gertrude's behavior is utterly scandalous. Widows were held to even more rigorous and prolonged mourning than were widowers. In the Middle Ages, widowed queens were expected to stay for a year or more in darkened rooms hung with black, and although such harshness was somewhat remitted in the sixteenth century, strong feelings about mourning continued.[25] It was customary in England for widows to respect the so-called "dolefull month" during which they remained in apartments entirely hung in black,[26] and after that they "continued wearing black clothes for three or four years or even longer and often retained their heavy black veils for the rest of their lives."[27] In France, it was customary for royal widows to wear white mourning, as Mary Queen of Scots did for five years after the death of her first husband King Francis II until she launched upon the disastrous course of Scottish marriages and remarriages which notoriously contributed to her fall. Mary's granddaughter, and eldest daughter of Queen Anne and King James, Elizabeth the "Winter Queen" of Bohemia, was still in full mourning in 1642, ten years after the loss of her husband Frederick and continued in such mourning for many years thereafter.[28]

Whatever costume Gertrude wore on stage to befit her new status as a recent bride, it would have contrasted starkly with what Elizabethans felt was appropriate to a recent widow. In Hamlet's remembrance of his mother at the funeral about a month before, she would have been dressed in mourning quite similar to that worn by the Countess of Surrey at the funeral of Lady Lumley in 1578 (Fig. III.1). After the funeral, a less cumbersome but no less somber attire would have been put on, rather like that worn by an Italian widow in a portrait painted by Lodovico Carracci in about 1590 (Fig. III.2). For English mourning attire in the years between 1595 and 1600 we have direct evidence in the famous Unton panel, which shows Lady Dorothy Unton in mourning at the tomb effigy of her husband Sir Henry[29] (Fig. III.3).

Remarriages were frequent in Shakespeare's time, and indeed were rather expected, but there were legalities as well as proprieties to be observed. By English civil law, a widow was forbidden to remarry within a year of her late husband's death "unless there is a special dispensation from the prince," and Chief Justice Edward Coke cited an ancient custom that a widow who married in less than a year's time should forfeit her dower.[30] Although such legal provisions and judgments tell us nothing directly about the play (e.g., Claudius could have dispensed with the year's delay), they do serve to fill in for us the ambience of sordidness which Elizabethans would have intuited here as a matter of deeply ingrained social instinct.[31]

For acceptable remarriages, there were well-known proprieties, which most royal and noble families were careful to observe. A remarriage which violated

Within the image: *The Countesse of Surrey chiefe Mourner*

*John Selynger Knight / in sted of a Baron*

*Sir Thomas Browne Knight*

*Mrs Coote the Queenes / woman*

FIG. III.I. Countess of Surrey in Mourning at Funeral of Lady Lumley in 1578

decorum could, at least in sixteenth-century Scotland, contribute to armed conflict, as was twice the case with Margaret Tudor, left dowager queen in 1513 after the death of James IV at Flodden,[32] and as was also true of Mary Queen of Scots. In England the upper classes typically behaved with somewhat greater restraint, or at least discretion. Among titled Englishwomen, the redoubtable Bess of Hardwick was four times married and four times widowed, each time to her financial advantage, but it is worthy of note that she never married sooner than the second year after the death of her most recent husband. Henry VIII was the most-often married of English kings, outdoing even Chaucer's Wife of Bath, although of both it could be said that the official count was tallied "withouten oother compaignye." Of Henry's six queens, two were removed either by divorce or annulment (Catherine of Aragon and Anne of Cleves

86

FIG. III.2. Lodovico Carracci, *A Widow*, c. 1590

respectively), and two were executed under sentence for treasonous adultery (Anne Boleyn and Catherine Howard), and the last (Katherine Parr) survived him. Although there were scandals aplenty along the way of this virtuoso succession of marital adventures, none of these involved mourning as such. Indeed, only the third consort, Jane Seymour, died a natural death while sharing the throne, and she was therefore quite properly (according to custom) the only queen officially mourned by Henry and his court. That mourning was carried out with full propriety, and Henry did not remarry for over two years. That even Henry VIII so fully observed the proprieties on the sole occasion on which his loss of a queen was "mournful" indicates the powerful constraints exerted by such conventions and convictions.

That importance of observing a decent interval of something like one or two years between the loss of one spouse and the taking of another did not need to be recounted for the Globe audience: Shakespeare did all that was necessary by spelling out and repeating that Gertrude waited only "a little month." The audience could then be allowed to draw its own social conclusions.

What was stated in words by the dramatic characters was visually reinforced and underscored by the dressing of the actors on stage. Gertrude's costume when she first appears in scene two should be suitable for the marriage festivities which would still dominate the court and visually marked by the color and richness which accompanied royal weddings. Since Elizabethan stage furniture was minimal, and realistic scenery nonexistent, the major visual emphasis at the Globe would have been upon costuming. Numerous comments upon actors' dress were made during this period, and these demonstrate that spectacular costuming would have been expected and also that a company such as Shakespeare's could have mounted a convincing and sumptuous display of fashions to fit any mood.[33] A brief survey of English royal weddings between 1503 and 1613 will show the clothing felt to be appropriate and will give us some impression of the kind of dress which would presumably have been seen in the Globe's version. Always, however, we must bear in mind the stark visual and symbolic contrast between these styles and the isolated Prince in his suit and cloak of solemn black.

When Henry VII's daughter Margaret married King James IV of Scotland in 1503, the groom was attired in white damask worked with gold and lined with sarcenet, crimson satin, and black velvet, and scarlet hose, and the bride wore crimson velvet with a collar of gold. When Henry VII's younger daughter Mary married Louis XII of France in 1514, both were lavishly dressed in "goldsmith's work." In 1540 Anne of Cleves married King Henry VIII in a gown of cloth of gold, with attached flowers made of pearls (although unfortunately for Anne, Henry was not impressed), and the marriage of Queen Mary to Philip II of Spain showed both richly dressed in embroidered cloth of gold. When James I's daughter Elizabeth married Frederick the Elector Palatine in 1603 (a wedding to which we shall shortly return), the bride was dressed in rich goldsmith's work and adorned with jewels; her bridesmaids wore cloth of silver with several colored tissues and her ladies white satin.[34]

For direct visual evidence of a courtly wedding in Elizabethan England, we have little to go on, because if these events were actually painted, the paintings have not descended to us. We do, however, have a closely related

FIG. III.3. Lady Dorothy Unton in mourning for her
husband, anonymous *Unton Panel*, c. 1600

incident from 1600, in a painting associated with the marriage on June 16 of that year which united Lady Anne Russell with Henry Somerset, Lord Herbert, the son of Edward Somerset, fourth Earl of Worcester. The painting in question apparently does not represent the actual marriage procession, but it does contain principal members of both families, and of the Elizabethan court, along with the great queen herself, shown at the approximate time of the marriage celebration, and fully in its spirit. Long known incorrectly as *Queen Elizabeth Going in Procession to Blackfriars in 1600*, the painting is now more properly entitled *Eliza Triumphans*, or simply *The Procession Picture* (Fig. III.4). Here we find a visual record of the costumes and atmosphere surrounding a high courtly wedding in the very year in which Shakespeare's *Hamlet* most likely appeared. The richness, color, and variety of the clothing indicates what Elizabethans would have expected in a court circle at the time of a great wedding,[35] and something like what the costuming at the Globe would have sought to suggest.

It may be objected that these weddings do not exemplify that peculiar mixture of "mirth in funeral and dirge in marriage" to which Claudius alluded. Indeed they do not, because Elizabethans would not have thought such a combination conceivable where the wedding followed so "hard upon" the burial as Shakespeare indicates here. In the time span so carefully accounted in *Hamlet*, the "funeral baked meats" would indeed have been available to "coldly furnish forth the marriage tables," as the Prince says they did (1.2.180-81). Whether Hamlet's words are to be interpreted as a caustic figure of speech rather than as a caustic report of fact is immaterial: what matters is that such phrases as Claudius' "a defeated joy" or his "an auspicious and dropping eye" were not only rhetorical oxymorons, but also represent enacted social and moral oxymorons.

The closest we can come to an actual transition from royal funeral to royal wedding in Shakespeare's England is the uniting of King James' daughter Elizabeth to the Palsgrave Frederick, about a dozen years after the debut of *Hamlet*. This nuptial contract had been drawn up as part of a diplomatic alliance and Protestant league in Europe, but after the arrival of the Palatine prince in London in October of 1612 it developed into a love match as well. Unfortunately the wedding arrangements were disrupted by the unexpected and untimely death on November 6 of the bride's brother Henry, Prince of Wales. At first the wedding was indefinitely postponed, because as John Chamberlain

FIG. III.4. Attributed to Robert Peake the Elder, *Procession Picture* or *Eliza Triumphans*, c. 1600

wrote, "it would be thought absurd that foreign ambassadors coming to condole the prince's death should find us feasting and dancing."[36] The plan then was to delay it until May Day of the following year, but in view of Frederick's need to return more promptly to his principality in the Palatinate it was finally set for St. Valentine's Day.[37] The funeral of Prince Henry was hastened as much as possible and occurred on December 7, the solemn affiancing ceremony for Frederick and Elizabeth took place on December 27, and the wedding itself on February 14.[38] Throughout, the transition from dirge to mirth was managed with an exact sense of propriety, as we can see by noting the gradual change in royal costume during the period of over three months from the death of the brother to the marriage of the sister.

Dress worn at the affiancing on December 27 (three weeks after Henry's funeral) was chosen by the royal family so as to provide a seemly transition between the distinctive moods of the recently completed funeral and the coming wedding: the Princess herself wore a black velvet gown with silver thread and patterning and her surviving brother Prince Charles wore black velvet with gold lace.[39] At the wedding Queen Anne appeared "in white satin with much embroidery and diamonds," the white of course being appropriate both to the happy mother of the bride and to the bereaved mother of a dead prince. As for the King, he was dressed "in a most sumptuous black suit with a diamond in his hat." Bride and bridegroom both appeared in suits of "cloth of silver richly embroidered with silver."[40] The costumes worn by members of the court were less controlled, and often displayed flamboyant extravagance. Lord Montague spent fifteen hundred pounds upon the dresses for his two daughters, according to John Chamberlain who also referred more generally to "the curiosity and excess of bravery both of men and women, with the extreme daubing on of cost and riches." He singled out in particular the "extreme cost and riches" of the costume worn by the Earl of Dorset, which was fortunately memorialized in a portrait painted at the time[41] (Fig. III.5).

When the wedding occurred, even amid the sumptuous costumes of the court, careful transition had been negotiated by the royal family from the funeral atmosphere which followed upon the death of Prince Henry over three months before. For governmental and diplomatic necessities, the marriage had to be performed as soon as possible, but every effort was made to avoid any hint of social scandal. And in this marriage the dead prince had not been the king and husband of the bride, but only a brother.[42]

On the basis of such evidence of sixteenth- and seventeenth-century royal marriages, it is possible to establish a fairly compact spectrum of court dress appropriate to a great wedding, and since theatrical costumes were famous for their lavishness we may assume that Shakespeare's company would have sought to mount something of this kind. As for the early stage costuming of the court in *Hamlet*, there is only one piece of evidence, and it is not demonstrative. A shortened version of the play exists in a German text. This version was apparently taken to the Continent by a troup of traveling English actors under John Greene early in the seventeenth century, and somewhat later translated into German. It exists in a manuscript of 1710, preserving a considerably earlier text, which in turn seems to have been based upon the 1603 quarto.[43] In this German version of the play, the king explicitly describes the replacement of

FIG. III.5. Attributed to William Larkin, *Richard Sackville, Third Earl of Dorset*, 1613

93

"black mourning suits" with "crimson, purple, and scarlet, since my late departed brother's widow has become our dearest consort."[44] That description of stage costumes for the Hamlet story indicates much gaudier clothing than we find in historical accounts of actual courtly wedding festivities, and we have no assurance whether the Globe *Hamlet* would have come closer to those courtly models or to the derivative German variant of the play. However that may be, one thing is important for us to recognize: Shakespeare's staging of that opening court scene objectified in inescapable visual terms the stark moral and philosophical contrast between this prince and this court.

Hamlet is costumed in what his mother calls "thy nighted color" and what the Prince himself refers to as "my inky cloak [and] customary suits of solemn black" (1.2.68 and 77-78). The black suits are clear enough, and are suitable to mourning although not to mourning alone, because in this period such dress was customarily worn by those who wished to express a serious mind and spirit and a devotion either to scholarly concerns or to high administration of state affairs or perhaps to both. As Polonius said, and wisely was it said at least for once, "the apparel oft proclaims the man," so Hamlet's suits of black would associate him with such young Renaissance nobles and princes as so often appear painted by Moroni, Titian, Bronzino, Veronese, and others in elegant black costumes (Fig. III.6). As one case in point, Titian's portrait known as *The Young Englishman* (Fig. III.7) catches a Renaissance spirit similar to what Ophelia saw in Hamlet: "The courtier's, soldier's, scholar's eye, tongue, sword" (3.1.151). In similar paintings, a book placed in the hand would suggest the humanistic scholar, a sword would suggest the soldier, and the general cut and luxury would imply the courtier's rank. Such "customary suits of solemn black" were understood as expressing seriousness but not sickness of mind.[45]

But such a suit of solemn black would not have been what first caught the eye of the Globe audience. Indeed the suit itself would not even have been visible at first, for that "inky cloak" to which Hamlet refers would have enveloped him completely, leaving only his face and hands exposed. This is not the short cape to which we are usually treated in period costuming of *Hamlet*, but the voluminous outer mourning garment worn in the stately funerals of this period. Normally these cloaks were removed after the funeral or the funeral procession, because they were very bulky; the black suit was an equally appropriate mourning garment for wear after the burial and it was infinitely more comfortable. But Hamlet has continued to wear that cloak, covering him from

FIG. III.6. Veronese, *Portrait of a Man*

FIG. III.7. Titian, *Portrait of a Young Englishman*

head to foot, as though by it he could alone counterbalance the scandalous unseemliness and even irreverence displayed in the dress of all those about him. This identification of Hamlet's cloak was made over fifty years ago by Bertram S. Puckle in his *Funeral Customs: Their Origins and Development*, but so far as I can ascertain his identification has been ignored both in criticism and in the theater.[46] The point is important not only as providing the only instance in which we can be sure of what one of Shakespeare's tragic protagonists wears when he first appears on stage, but far more importantly because it shows how consistent and radical, even in visual terms, was Shakespeare's isolation of the Prince from the rest of the court.

Mourning cloaks are illustrated in numerous sixteenth-century prints and drawings, which show the costume to have been radically different from everything else in sixteenth-century dress, setting the wearer apart from ordinary

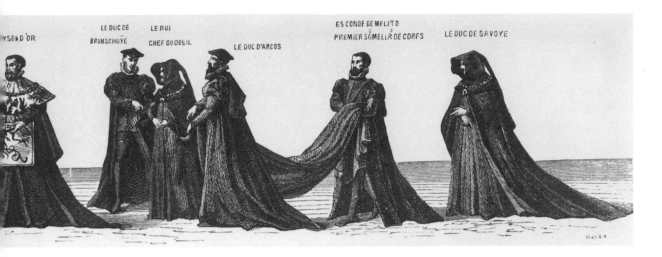

FIG. III.8. King Philip II as Chief Mourner in Funeral Procession of the Emperor Charles V, 1559

FIG. III.9. Robert Sidney as Chief Mourner and Funeral Procession of Sir Philip Sidney, detail from T. Lant, *Funeral Procession of Sir Philip Sidney*, 1587

clothing as though he were in a military uniform, or perhaps the effect might even more appropriately be compared to that of a monastic robe. Totally enveloping the body, the cloak was also provided with a hood, which could be drawn up over the head so that only the face was visible. In Shakespeare's age, the cut of these cloaks varied only slightly over the years and from one country to another. When the Emperor Charles V was buried in a sumptuous

FIG. III.10. Sir Walter Raleigh and Sir Robert Cecil as Mourners in Funeral Procession of Queen Elizabeth I, 1603, detail of William Camden's contemporary sketch, first printed in 1791

FIG. III.11. Edward Somerset, Fourth Earl of Worcester, as a Principal Mourner in the Funeral Procession of Queen Elizabeth I, 1603, detail of William Camden's contemporary sketch, first printed in 1791

funeral at Brussels in 1559, his son King Philip II of Spain walked in the procession as chief mourner, completely covered in black save for his hands and face[47] (Fig. III.8). The train worn by King Philip as chief mourner was longer than anything I have found in English mourning, but otherwise the gown is essentially the same.[48] For the funeral of Sir Philip Sidney, we find that the chief mourner was Sir Robert Sidney, the next brother in order of primogeniture and thus Sir Philip's heir[49] (Fig. III.9). Following Robert Sidney as chief mourner were the other principal mourners, of whom there were always several in every notable heraldic funeral—and all walk in mourning cloaks, hooded. Other important personages who were given a prominent place in the cortege, but who were neither chief mourner nor among the principal mourners, would wear the robe but with the hood pushed back upon the shoulders, and a hat on the head, as did Sir Walter Raleigh and Sir Robert Cecil in the funeral

98

FIG. III.12. Funeral Cortege of Henry, Prince of Wales, 1613, title page of George Wither, *Prince Henry's Obsequies*

procession of Queen Elizabeth in 1603 (Fig. III.10). Edward Somerset, fourth Earl of Worcester, whom we observed in lively and colorful court dress in the center foreground of *The Procession Picture* or *Eliza Triumphans* of 1600, was shown three years later (Fig. III.11) in the typical mourning cloak, as he leads the riderless horse of Queen Elizabeth in her funeral procession.[50] At the London funeral for Prince Henry in 1612, we see the principal mourners hooded and enveloped in jet black mourning cloaks as they walk beside the carriage conveying the coffin upon which lies the lifelike effigy of the Prince[51] (Fig. III.12).

At this juncture a bit of photographic realignment may be helpful. If we substitute the figure of Worcester in the darkened mourning robes he wore in Elizabeth's funeral procession for the figure of the same peer in the foreground of the chromatic procession picture, replete as that painting is with the ambience of a high courtly wedding, we see the stark contrast and theatrical impact of placing Hamlet in his inky cloak amidst the lively colored costumes and festive atmosphere of the Danish court (Fig. III.13). Shakespeare's masterly introduction of that first court scene made Hamlet look like a scholarly anchorite surrounded by a band of voluptuaries, in visual as well as verbal terms.

By enveloping the Prince from head to toe in a mourning cloak, Shakespeare insured that Hamlet would be the principal focus of the audience's attention from the first moment the court enters, even though the Prince does not speak until sixty-seven lines later. Hamlet is outweighed in power by Claudius, but it is equally true that Claudius is upstaged by Hamlet—which provides a finely calibrated introduction to the contest between these two mighty opposites. By visual emphases and contrasts, Hamlet dominates the stage long before the conversation turns to him, and he never loses that theatrical control during the five acts in which he struggles to establish a comparable political dominion in Denmark.

When Hamlet begins to speak or very soon thereafter, the hood must be pushed back from his face to lie on his shoulders, or his voice would be so muffled that a long speech could not be heard by the whole audience in the theater. Perhaps he thrusts back the hood when Claudius first addresses him, or when his mother asks him to "cast thy nighted color off," but it is also possible to assume that the hood is removed at the beginning of his first long speech when he says to his mother, "Seems, Madam? Nay, it is. I know not 'seems.'/ 'Tis not alone my inky cloak, good mother, . . ." (1.2.68 and 76-77). Once the cloak has served its primary function in this scene, it not only can but must be discarded, so that Hamlet will be free for his strenuous physical activities throughout the remainder of the play. Even after he has discarded the mourning cloak, Hamlet should continue to appear in his suits of solemn black—and always elegantly cut to suggest both his individual character and more generally what Milton later described as "staid wisdom's hue."[52]

The visual contrast Shakespeare staged between Hamlet and the court would have expanded the merely rhetorical oxymoron of Claudius' opening word play on "mirth in funeral and dirge in marriage," and would have objectified the moral, philosophical, and social polarities of the play. The patent misweighing of delight and dole, of the auspicious and the dropping eye, are far more important than the words "manners," "customs," and "ceremonies" usually suggest in our twentieth-century vocabularies.

FIG. III.13. Composite Picture to illustrate effect of introducing inky cloak of a
principal mourner into courtly wedding festivities

We have thus far traced the violation in Denmark of the incest taboo and
of the whole nexus of customs governing funeral and marriage, and have done
so in terms familiar to those first audiences for whom Shakespeare wrote the
play. With all that has been said of incest, and of the indecent rush into
remarriage, we have yet to consider the effect in 1600 of having a king murdered
and replaced by the assassin, both on the throne and in the royal bed. Would
Hamlet's reaction to those complications have appeared excessive or neurotic?
For our purposes, it is fortunate that by looking to the Scotland of 1567 we
can find an arresting historical analogy to those fictional events in *Hamlet*.
There a succession of brutal assassination of the king consort, and of widowhood and remarriage for the queen, precipitated Mary Queen of Scots from

her throne within four months of the murder of her former husband Henry Stewart and only one month after her marriage to his assassin, the Earl of Bothwell.

## IV. Burrio and Bridegroom: The Fall of Mary Queen of Scots

The parallels between those historical developments in Scotland and the fictional events in Shakespeare's Danish story are striking although not exact (parallels never are, except in geometry). Mary Queen of Scots had been wedded in 1565 in an ardent love marriage to her cousin Henry Stewart, formerly known as Lord Darnley but later addressed by official courtesy title as King Henry.[53] A little more than a year and a half after the Queen's romantic union, the king consort was assassinated, and three months thereafter Mary was married again—this time to the Earl of Bothwell who was universally recognized as murderer of her "precedent lord." Those events in Scotland are of interest to us not as a putative source or model for events underlying *Hamlet*, but because they will provide us with an objective criterion for appraising Hamlet's reaction in sixteenth-century terms. Those who hold that Hamlet's response to his mother's behavior is excessive, even diseased, should note that by the same standard the reaction of Scotland, England, and most of the Continent to the behavior of Mary Queen of Scots was equally excessive or even diseased. Prior to the assassination and remarriage, Mary's troubles as a Catholic sovereign with her Protestant subjects had been manageable and had been managed, and there was good reason to believe that Mary could have continued indefinitely as queen of Scotland despite her Catholicism. But now her behavior was perceived as so scandalous that she lost virtually all the support she had formerly had among Catholics as well as Protestants both at home and abroad, and she played directly into the hands of her enemies. Because that general European response against Mary establishes from yet another angle the normality of what Shakespeare's Prince thinks of Gertrude, the sequence of actions and reaction is worth noting in some detail. (See also Chapter Two, Part III.)

Early in 1565, Queen Mary fell madly in love with her cousin Henry Stewart, who like Mary herself was a great grandchild of the founder of the Tudor dynasty, King Henry VII, as well as a member of the Scottish royal family. They were married in July of that year, and on June 19 of the following year the future King James was born. Everyone at the Scottish court noted and many commented upon Mary's passionate attachment to Darnley; Antonia Fraser has described it as "violent infatuation" and (paraphrasing *Hamlet*) "the very first ecstasies of love." From contemporary reports it appears that Mary, like Gertrude with the elder Hamlet, "would hang on him/ As if increase of appetite had grown/ By what it fed on."[54] So things went at first between Mary and Henry, but as time passed, Mary's attitude toward her consort changed into suspicion, revulsion, and contempt. She considered getting a divorce from the husband upon whom she had so recently and so conspicuously doted, but divorce was found to be impossible. Her enemies later claimed that she had then attempted to poison him. "Certain black pimples . . . broke out all over his whole body" in what was officially diagnosed as smallpox, but after his murder at a later date these blotches were said to have been "certainly" the result of poison.[55] At best, relations between husband and wife were strained, and they lived apart.

But in early 1567 Mary made gestures of reconciliation. Henry, who was recuperating from an illness, was temporarily housed at Kirk o' Fields just outside Edinburgh, preparatory to rejoining the queen at Holyrood Palace in the capital. On the evening of February 9, Mary made a well-publicized visit to him there and showed every sign of having achieved a reconciliation. She returned to Edinburgh late that evening, and at about 2:00 A.M. on February 10, within a few hours after she had left the house, Kirk o' Fields was exploded with gunpowder and burned. King Henry's body was discovered after the explosion, unmarked by gunpowder but strangled, lying in the orchard or garden (*in horto reperiuntur prostrati* may be translated in either way). Everyone knew that the ruffianly Earl of Bothwell, widely reputed to be Mary's lover and soon to be her husband, was responsible for the murder, and many were fully convinced that Mary herself was his confederate in the plot. The English Ambassador to Paris was probably expressing the opinion of most and certainly of many when he declared that Mary had arranged the murder so that she could marry Bothwell.[56] The murdered King Henry was interred in shocking haste, without the customary royal ceremonies, at night by "pioners," in a flagrant disregard of public opinion at home and abroad. Queen Elizabeth instructed Lord Grey, her ambassador to Scotland, to make clear to Mary that "the contempt or at least neglect used in the burial" had "caused great indignation."[57] George Buchanan's words were more caustic: "she secretly in the night buried him without funeral pomp, or rather hid him like a thief" and thus did "plainly betray" her "inconstant counterfeiting of mourning."[58]

Mary did begin and very briefly continue to observe the customary mourning. On the very day after the assassination, however, she violated propriety by giving a conspicuous bridal feast to celebrate the wedding of one of her favorite attendants.[59] The Palace of Holyrood was nonetheless draped in black, and the period of mourning was properly initiated, but it was scandalously foreshortened in ways that played directly into the hands of Mary's enemies.[60] John Knox, the great Scottish reformer and steadfast adversary of Mary, wrote of the matter with the low-keyed restraint of a skilled rhetorician who knows when the facts should be simply recited and allowed to speak for themselves: "The Queen, according to the ancient custom, should have kept herself forty days within, and the doors and windows should have been closed in token of mourning; but the windows were opened, to let in light, the fourth day.[61] Before the twelfth day, she went out to Seton, Bothwell never parting from her side. There she went out to the fields to behold games and pastimes."[62] Because Mary was constantly observed in the doting company of her husband's assassin, the affair took on a deeply sinister complexion.

At about the time that Mary appeared in public on Bothwell's arm only a few days into her widowhood, placards began to appear in Edinburgh. Although we must presume that most of these were Protestant in origin, they never mention the divisive issue of religion, but instead concentrate upon the public scandal which shamed the entire nation. One of the most famous was a crude picture which spelled out in images an unmistakable message linking Mary with the assassin and the assassination (Fig. III.14). A mermaid (traditional symbol for prostitution and adultery) was shown crowned, and labeled with "M R" for Maria Regina. Below, a hare represented Bothwell's heraldic crest; it was labeled with the initials I. H. for his name, James Hepburn, and surrounded by a corona of daggers to signify assassination.[63] As the days passed, it became increasingly clear that the suspected adultery would soon be transformed into marriage. Robert Keith, the Scottish historian and bishop of the Anglican church in eighteenth-century Scotland, summarized the public impact of such a union between the widowed queen and the regicide: it was "an action for which her well-wishers were sorry and grieved at the heart, seeing by it she mightily increased the aversion already instilled into the people, and deprived

FIG. III.14. Edinburgh street placard,
"The Mermaid and the Hare," 1567

her friends of all just apology in her behalf; but an action which her enemies rejoiced to see accomplished, since by it she laid the foundation, as it were, of her own ruin, and advanced their wicked designs faster than they themselves could have looked for."[64] Honest men could and did disagree on the issue of Roman Catholicism, which Mary as queen kept powerful in Scotland, but it was virtually impossible to defend her for her attitude to the assassination of King Henry and her speedy marriage with the assassin. Froude has effectively summarized the effects of Mary's behavior: "Such a marriage under such circumstances . . . would be at once the consummation of an enormous crime, and a public defiant confession of it in the face of all men. . . . But to follow up the assassination of her husband by an open marriage with the man whom all the world knew by this time to have been the murderer, was entirely intolerable."[65]

One of the major differences between Mary's historical circumstances and Gertrude's fictional situation is that everyone was certain that King Henry had been brutally slain by Bothwell, whereas in the play the regicide is at first only suspected by the Prince, and later known only by him and by Horatio. But what is significant for us as readers of Shakespeare is that everyone (being as fully informed in fact as Hamlet was in fiction) reacted to the marriage of Mary and Bothwell with the same disgust and horror that Hamlet showed toward his mother's marriage with Claudius.

Between February and June, events in Scotland were followed with a mixture of fascination and abhorrence throughout Europe.[66] Mary's loyal ambassador Cardinal Beaton wrote to her from the Continent to say that she was the principal topic of conversation everywhere, much of it "mickle evil spoken" and "interpreted sinisterly," and advising that unless she behaved with more prudence, it would have been better for her to have "lost life and all."[67] On February 24, Queen Elizabeth wrote directly to Mary, expressing herself as "horrified at the abominable murder of her husband," equally shocked at Mary's relations with Bothwell, and urging her to behave herself so as to demonstrate to all that she is "a noble princess and loyal wife."[68] The French Chancellor Michel de l' Hôpital, who had earlier written a eulogy of Mary, now came to view the whole progress of events from the regicide through Mary's remarriage with horrified repugnance.[69] Mary's mother-in-law by her first marriage, the Queen Mother of France Marie de' Medici, wrote sternly to tell her that "if she performed not her promise to have the death of the King revenged to clear herself, they [in France] would not only think her dishonored, but would be her enemies."[70] The French king, who was Mary's brother-in-law and had been deeply devoted to her, instructed her ambassador to inform her that he would neither assist nor advise her because she "had behaved so ill and made herself so hateful to her subjects."[71] The Venetian ambassador to Paris feared that the cause of Catholicism in Scotland had been permanently confounded by her behavior, and of course he was very nearly correct.[72] At the same time George Buchanan widely publicized her shame.[73]

As her intent to marry Bothwell became increasingly apparent, protests arose from all sides. Mary's own Dominican confessor warned her against such an action, and sought to dissuade her from it. On the other side of the religious divide, John Craig, Presbyterian minister of St. Giles High Kirk in Edinburgh, at first refused to read the bans announcing the marriage; even when forced to do so by the Privy Council he made a public protest from the pulpit, declaring that Scripture, law, and reason united to call such a marriage "odious and scandalous to all that should hear of it."[74] Bishop John Leslie, Mary's strong champion, recorded the overwhelming opposition to the marriage among Scottish Catholics—"all the ecclesiastics and the greater part of the secular nobility"—because they knew it "was likely to bring great harm and shame upon her."[75] Despite all—"Scripture, law, and reason"—Mary and Bothwell were united in marriage on May 15, three months and one week after the assassination.

The pope, of all the leaders of Europe, had the strongest motives for defending Mary, because she represented virtually his last visible hope for restoring any or all of Great Britain to the Roman Church. But he too was alienated. After the marriage, he declared that he would have no further communication with her "unless in times to come he shall see some better sign of her life and religion than he has witnessed in the past."[76] Le Crock, the French ambassador to Edinburgh, was eager to preserve the Old Alliance between his country and Scotland, but he refused to attend the wedding feast, "thinking it did not sort with the dignity of his legation to approve the marriage by his presence which he heard was so universally hated."[77]

And the hatred of the marriage was indeed universal, being in no way restricted to the various lords spiritual and temporal. The Scottish populace—who had once loved the queen—were incensed.[78] Within less than a week of the murder, placards alluding to the joint guilt of Mary and Bothwell began to appear in Edinburgh, and the fury of these pasquinades was not assuaged by the passage of time. One, set up on April 13, "proclaimed that Bothwell had murdered the husband of the woman he intended to marry and had had her promise long before the murder."[79] The satirical versifiers minced no words.

> It is not enough the poor King is dead,
> But the miscreant murderer occupies his stead
> And double adultery has all this land shamed.[80]

Obviously, bringing shame upon the royal bed brought shame upon the nation itself. In another ballad, King Henry is portrayed as directly addressing the Scottish lords,

> For to revenge I leave in testament
> My saikless [innocent] blood, my murther and injury.

And the King's spirit continues:

> Hurt not your honors, the same to smuire [smother, conceal].
> First look to God, then to your liberty.[81]

Other ballads call Mary a Dalila, Jezebel, or Clytemnestra, associate her with other despicable women, and explicitly accuse her of murder as well as corrupting the royal bed.[82] The strongest revulsion concerns her having taken the regicide into her bed to replace the assassinated king;[83]

> Sair [hard] it was to see your Prince with murder pressed.
> Sairer, I say, him in his place possessed
> That did the deed; then Burrio, now Bridegroom.[84]

"Then Burrio, now Bridegroom"—first the Butcher and then the Bridegroom—sums up the reaction of the people, as

> The royal house, refuge to honest men,
> Was made a bordello and a thieves' den.[85]

The reference to Bothwell not only as a murderer but as a thief was not accidental, because it was quite clear that his ultimate goal was the crown of Scotland: first eliminate the king, then marry the queen, then ascend the throne.[86] The Scots regarded him as Hamlet regarded his uncle, as "a vice of king,/ A cutpurse of the empire and the rule,/ That from a shelf the precious diadem stole/ And put it in his pocket" (3.4.99-102). When Mary awarded Bothwell a ducal coronet (the only one in Scotland at the time) as well as possession of her bed, he was within reach of realizing the dream he shared with Claudius: his crown, his own ambition, and his queen (3.3.55).

But it had all gone too far and happened too fast. After the wedding on May 15, the Lords of the Congregation began to draw up their plans and to assemble their forces for a move against Mary and Bothwell. One month after the marriage the two opposing armies met at Carberry, but the queen's forces had no heart for a fight and steadily deserted. After some negotiation, Bothwell fled the field and eventually the country.[87] Then Mary was led back to Edinburgh, a prisoner to her own subjects. Antonia Fraser graphically conveys the scene and its significance:

> She, who all her life had been greeted publicly with adulation and enthusiasm, now heard the soldiers shout: "Burn her, burn the whore, she is not worthy to live," as they conveyed her along the road into Edinburgh. "Kill her, drown her!" they cried. . . . For the first time she began to realize what the effect had been on the ordinary

people of Scotland—the people who had once loved her—of her reckless action in marrying her husband's assassin, and of those weeks of propaganda by the enemies of Bothwell. To them she was now no longer their young and beautiful queen, but an adulteress—and an adulteress who had subsequently become the willing bride of a murderer.[88]

Mary's behavior during the three months between February and May, followed with scandalized fascination at home and abroad, were enough to turn the scales irrecoverably against her. On June 17, four months and seven days after the assassination and one month and two days after her marriage to Bothwell, the Scottish Lords imprisoned her at Lochleven and deposed her from the throne, to which she never returned.[89]

Significantly, the assaults upon Mary in the popular ballads and posters did not feature her religion. Religion was assuredly a factor, and a fundamental one, with most Catholics striving to maintain a credible loyalty to a Catholic queen and most Protestants desirous of having a more accommodating rule, but these considerations were often qualified on both sides. An interested English observer, John Jewel the Bishop of Salisbury, commented at the time that "many of the said queen's religion were against her, and many protestants were and are her friends."[90] Thus it was that the ballads and posters which both represented and sought to influence popular opinion were non-sectarian in approach, emphasizing instead the brutality of the regicide, the corruption of justice and loyalty, and that the court had become a bordello in which "filthy lust" was hypocritically cloaked by the "color of wedding." The principal modern student of the broadsides was able to find "no reference to her [Mary's] religious faith or to the underlying political issues in any of these numerous ballads; rather, the themes are those of lust, adultery, murder, abnormal sexual practices, promiscuity, and the like."[91] Mary's conduct played directly into the hands of her Protestant opponents, and made her own deposition inevitable on grounds other than religious, as her friends and Catholic supporters warned her again and again, but to no avail.

The differences between the actual Scotland of sixteenth-century history and the fictive Denmark of sixteenth-century drama are apparent, even inescapable, and would seriously hamper if not defeat any effort to argue that the Scottish history was a source for *Hamlet*, but that is not my argument here.[92]

My concern is to establish the patterns of reaction to killing a king and marrying with his widow, so that we may judge how people in 1600 would most probably have appraised Hamlet's reactions to Gertrude and Claudius. In the world of the play, Hamlet is virtually alone in knowing of the regicide, but his response to it and to the subsequent remarriage was essentially the same as that which everyone in Europe (from king and pope and lord to pamphleteer and peasant) had to Mary Queen of Scots. On the basis of the evidence, I suggest that no one in the sixteenth century would have argued as T. S. Eliot did in the twentieth, that Hamlet had no objective correlative to justify and explain the strength of his aversion.

Within the context of the audience and the time for which Shakespeare wrote, Hamlet's reaction to Gertrude's behavior simply would not have been regarded as either excessive or neurotic. The general attitude may be summarized in what Edmund Grindal, then Bishop of London and later Archbishop of Canterbury, wrote to Henry Bullinger in Switzerland, reporting the sequence of developments from Bothwell's assassination of King Henry to his marriage with Queen Mary: "it is impossible but that this infamous marriage must end in some dreadful tragedy."[93] In a more memorable phrase, Hamlet expressed a similar judgment of his mother's marriage with Claudius: "It is not nor it cannot come to good" (1.2.158). Any other response on the Prince's part would have struck Shakespeare's contemporaries as inadequate, irrational, unnatural, and perhaps even mad.

FOUR

# Choosing Sides

### 1. Thinkers and Non-Thinkers

THE FOUR Wittenberg students[1] who converge upon Elsinore differ radically in their attitudes toward life. Horatio epitomizes disinterested reason; he is not self-seeking, and does not try to promote a public career or advance his own profit. He is not unbiased or uncommitted—his loyalty to Hamlet is unfailing—but he is a scholar detached from concern for acquiring power at court or in the state. His commitment to reason and wisdom is thus unaffected by the ambiguities of practical politics and statecraft. Hamlet admires that unsullied rationality, that unblemished pursuit of wisdom, but however much his temperament may long for it, his place in society does not allow him that ultimate luxury.[2] He is not even permitted to return to Wittenberg, as he at first wished to do, and events quickly evolve in Elsinore which he and only he can resolve. The most rational of Shakespeare's heroes, he is forced to think and act in the highly irrational world of Denmark. Sharing Horatio's *recta ratio*, he cannot share his detachment.

Rosencrantz and Guildenstern, on the other hand, show neither detachment nor wisdom. They have accepted the King's emoluments and they know where their advantage lies: as they assure Claudius when they first appear on stage, "we both obey,/ And here give up ourselves in the full bent" (2.2.29-30). Later they go to meet their old friend Hamlet, who desperately needs their loyalty and support. Despite his eloquent appeals to "the beaten way of friendship," he soon finds that he cannot depend on them. They are actively in the service of Claudius and metaphorically in the service of Fortune—the two liveries being essentially the same in this play.

They are quite unindividualized: no one has yet succeeded in telling them apart by character or personality traits. They are ciphers, without discrete identities. Or worse still they are sponges: empty themselves, they exist only by absorbing what is around them. So Hamlet calls them, and when asked his

FIG. IV.I. Sycophants and Sponge from
Jeffrey Whitney, *Emblems*, 1586

meaning he explains that a sponge "soaks up the king's countenance, his rewards, his authorities. But such officers do the king best service in the end. He
keeps them, like an ape, in the corner of his jaw, first mouthed, to be last
swallowed. When he needs what you have gleaned, it is but squeezing you,
and you shall be dry again" (4.2.15-20). The image is utterly appropriate in
context of the play and of the time. The sponge, as we have seen, had a long
history as a symbol linking sycophants with tyrants, and Jeffrey Whitney's
*Emblems* (Fig. IV.1) contains a visual rendering of the same idea, but Hamlet
comes close enough to "drawing a picture" of the admonition for his erstwhile
friends, who nonetheless refuse to be enlightened or even alerted to what lies
in store for them.[3]

Rosencrantz and Guildenstern have cast their lot with the obvious, with
blatant power, and they show no sign of reflection or evaluation before or
after. Unsympathetic to Hamlet's appeals, threats, and warnings, they make
love to any employment which they think will bring them advancement. But
choose they do, as everyone must in this play, and like most of the characters
their choice is unexamined, as is the choice of Polonius, and of Fortinbras in
a different way, and of Gertrude until Hamlet confronts her in her chamber
and forces her to appraise herself. In a play in which the concept of conscience
is so pervasively important and in which the word "conscience" appears more
often than in any other Shakespearean tragedy, these characters show no in-

112

clination on their own to examine their consciences and to weigh the alternatives before them.[4] But choices are made, and the characters may be divided not only according to the sides they choose but also by the ways they make their choices. Hamlet of course is the most interesting of the choicemakers, but he is not the only one, and we should first look at the others, the characters who surround the Prince, who make up the community in which he lives. The living community of Elsinore is, after all, one of the greatest of Shakespeare's creative achievements in this play.[5]

One way of analyzing what Shakespeare gives us here is to approach the play in terms of the mythical antithesis between Wisdom and Fortune, and another is in ethical terms associated with cases or arguments and decisions of conscience. These surely do not exhaust the subject, but they do provide us entry into it in terms familiar in 1600. When Rosencrantz and Guildenstern first appear to Hamlet, they associate themselves with Fortune—neither the button of her cap nor the soles of her shoe, but about her waist in her secret parts, for as Hamlet observes, "she is a strumpet."[6] So she appears to him as a thinking and ethical man, and here we find one of the most striking iconographic antitheses of the play. Philosophically, poetically, and visually, a careful parallelism and systematic contrast is developed between the associated qualities of Reason, Prudence, and Wisdom on the one hand, and of Fortune and Vanity on the other. Reliance upon Fortune is the opposite of reliance upon Prudence or Wisdom. Both are frequently imagined as holding mirrors, but the mirror of Wisdom is symbolically associated with Truth, which endures, whereas that of Fortune concerns shifting and unstable appearances, which quickly emerge and as quickly vanish. One cannot choose both, and the wise man spurns the gifts of Fortune.

## II. Prudentia Bifrontis and Fortuna Bifrons

What Hamlet called the "discourse of reason" in his first soliloquy recurs in his last soliloquy as "such large discourse," which he then defines by metaphorical attributes assigned to Prudentia or Sapientia: "looking before and after." That conception, known in Renaissance art as *Prudentia bifrontis*, was splendidly visualized by Luca della Robbia in a terra cotta Prudence with two faces[7] (Fig. IV.2).

Such circumspection was necessary to the effective Christian prince, ac-

FIG. IV.2. Luca della Robbia, *Prudence*

FIG. IV.3. "Looking Before and After," from Jeffrey
Whitney, *Emblems*, 1586

cording to Erasmus, and it was also symbolized by the bifronted Janus in
Whitney's influential *Emblems* of 1586[8] (Fig. IV.3). Whitney's appended verses
note that his Janus-Prudence was

> call'd the God of war and peace, because
> In wars he warn'd of peace not to despair,
> And warn'd in peace to practice martial laws
> And furthermore, his looks did teach this sum,
> To bear in mind time past, and time to come.

Again, the ideal represented a cohesive and effective balance between thought
and action.[9]

Such images symbolize virtuous reason at work, but Prudence and Fortune
are consistently cast as opposites,[10] and are visualized in semantically inverted
pictures, so that similar presentations of Fortune are intended to suggest du-
plicity.[11] Just as Hamlet's reference to Reason "looking before and after" evokes
*Prudentia bifrontis*, so also his "Fortune's buffets and rewards" suggests what
was called *Fortuna bifrons*. That emblem may be defined in the words of
William Warner's *Pan his Syrinx* of 1584: "Fortune is painted with two faces,
frowning with the one, and smiling with the other."[12] So conceived, Fortune

115

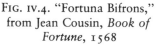

FIG. IV.4. "Fortuna Bifrons,"
from Jean Cousin, *Book of
Fortune*, 1568

FIG. IV.5. "Fortuna Bifrons,"
from Jean Cousin, *Book of
Fortune*, 1568

is morally understood as "two-faced," deceptive, unreliable. Jean Cousin's
illustrated manuscript *Book of Fortune*, dated 1568, shows Fortune seated like
a queen, and holding out gifts, in the one case a coronet and scepter to a
prosperous young gentleman, with a smiling countenance on that side of her
face, whereas the other or left side is shadowed as she hands a straw, reed, or
flagellum (it could be any one of these) to a hooded penitent[13] (Fig. IV.4).

Another drawing by Cousin in the same work represents *Fortuna bifrons*
with two separate faces. Again she passes out different gifts: with her right
hand she offers a royal scepter, a baton of command, and a bishop's crosier,
while with her left she presents a mace, a scourge, and a bundle of switches
or of straw[14] (Fig. IV.5). In the same vein, Aegedius Sadeler executed an engraving of Fortune precariously balanced on the ball which indicated her in-

FIG. IV.6. "Fortuna," from Theodor de Bry, *Emblemati Nobilitati et Vulgo*, 1592

stability, while she offers in one hand a cornucopia and in the other bolts of lightning.[15] In each of these works, Fortune's left hand offers her votaries equivalents of what Hamlet metaphorically calls "the slings and arrows of outrageous Fortune" (3.1.58).[16] Theodore de Bry varied the theme in 1592 by showing a seductively nude Fortune, her "sail" held up to the variable winds of chance, while to her right there is a scene of a peaceful and prosperous harbor, and to her left a radically different scene of a sinking ship and a city engulfed in flames[17] (Fig. IV.6). In every case we have visual counterparts to what Hamlet derisively calls "Fortune's buffets and rewards" (3.2.64).

Relevant here is Castiglione's praise of Duke Guidobaldi in *The Book of the Courtier*: that admirable prince suffered from disastrous health and much ill success in various enterprises, but "he always bore out with such stoutness

117

FIG. IV.7. "Prudence managing, Fortune leads
not," from G. B. Gelli, *I Capricci*, 1550

of courage that Virtue never yielded to Fortune, but with a bold stomach, despising her storms, lived with great dignity and estimation among all men: in sickness as one that was sound, and in adversity as one that was most fortunate." In the same spirit Hamlet praised Horatio as "one in suff'ring all that suffers nothing."[18] That conception was expressed in visual form in 1550 in *I Capricci* by G. B. Gelli (Fig. IV.7), the title page of which shows Prudence holding the mirror of truth and standing on firm ground, while a banderole carries the motto "Prudentia negoti . . . non fortuna ducat" (Prudence managing, Fortune leads not), while an emblem of 1593 (Fig. IV.8) by Theodor de Bry declares to the same effect "Expers Fortunae est Sapientia" (Wisdom is free from Fortune).[19] De Bry's engraving catches the spirit Hamlet associates with Horatio: Sapientia is seated at an altar-like desk, with an owl symbolizing wisdom and surrounded by the attributes of learning, ignoring the enticements of a city in the background and in the middle distance a nude Fortune sailing by with her meretricious gifts on display. As Shakespeare wrote elsewhere, "Wisdom and Fortune combatting together,/ If that the former dare but what

118

FIG. IV.8. "Wisdom is free from Fortune," by Theodor
de Bry, *Emblematum Liber*, 1593

it can,/ No chance may shake it," and again to the same effect that "Though Fortune's malice overthrow my state,/ My mind exceeds the compass of her wheel."[20]

The ideal of the wise man whose virtue keeps him safe from the vagaries of Fortune is further spelled out in Hamlet's praise of Horatio:

> blest are those
> Whose blood and judgment are so well commeddled
> That they are not a pipe for Fortune's finger
> To sound what stop she please. (3.2.65-68)

Those lines introduce the important musical attributes of Fortune, which were conveyed through the Italian proverb that "everyone dances for whom Fortune plays," and which were variously expressed in visual as well as verbal images. Della Bella engraved an illustration of the adage,[21] and Mitelli's *Proverbi Figurati* of 1678 (Fig. IV.9) shows a foppishly dressed young man dancing to the music of Fortune under the inscription "Assai ben balla, a cui Fortuna suona."

FIG. IV.9. "Dancing to Fortune's Tune," by Mitelli, *Proverbi Figurati*, 1678

FIG. IV.10. "Dancing to Fortune's Tune," from Guillaume de la Perrière, *Morosophie*, 1553

Those engravings show Fortune playing a stringed instrument whereas La Perrière's *Morosophie* of 1553, which provides many analogues to Shakespeare's verbal imagery, shows a nude blindfolded Fortune playing a pipe, while a modish young gentleman prances and dances to her tune[22] (Fig. IV.10). It is upon that conception that Shakespeare draws, but under his imaginative poetic adaptation the fool of Fortune is directly metamorphosed into "a pipe for Fortune's finger/ To sound what stop she please"—an image a visual artist could scarcely represent. Later in the same scene, Hamlet turns the image of Fortune's pipe against Rosencrantz and Guildenstern when, recorder in hand, he tells them, "call me what instrument you will, though you can fret me, you cannot play upon me" (3.2.356-57).[23]

When Hamlet refers in soliloquy to "the slings and arrows of outrageous Fortune," his imagination immediately extrapolates the related image of "a sea of troubles," an association which calls to mind the close connection between Fortune and stormy seas (3.1.58-59). Like the witches who served Hecate, the goddess Fortuna was a creator of tempests, and Seneca wrote that "a man who deserves to be mentioned with consideration . . . must . . . guide his bark through stormy waters; he must keep his course in spite of fortune."[24] That conception is visually conveyed by Hans Eworth's stunning mid-century Tudor allegory on the life of Sir John Luttrell (Fig. IV.11), where that worthy gentleman rises like Neptune out of a storm-tossed sea, and the inscribed label comments "the constant heart no danger dreads nor fears." Eworth's oil fully exploits the visual potential of "the sea of troubles," whereas Hamlet only alludes to it in passing as his thoughts race ahead.[25]

Just as a person who is slave to Fortune is an inferior human being, so a love which is similarly dependent is also inferior, whether it be love between man and wife, or between child and parent, or between friends. Such fortuitous loves abound in *Hamlet*, indeed outnumbering true and admirable loves. The love Gertrude bore the elder Hamlet was apparently led by Fortune, especially if it is judged by the standards which the Player King holds up for the Player Queen. In response to her protests of endless devotion, he warns her:

> This world is not for aye, nor 'tis not strange
> That even our loves should with our fortunes change,
> For 'tis a question left us yet to prove,
> Whether love lead fortune, or else fortune love.
> The great man down, you mark his favorite flies,
> The poor advanced makes friends of enemies;
> And hitherto doth love on fortune tend,
> For who not needs shall never lack a friend,
> And who in want a hollow friend doth try,
> Directly seasons him his enemy.          (3.2.191-201)

Whether that passage represents part of Hamlet's own insertion into the play of "some dozen or sixteen lines which I would set down," we do not know, but it does accord with his view of his mother's behavior (2.2.527-28).

It also recalls (without duplicating) the established iconography. If we return once again to Cousin's sketches of Fortune, we find one drawing in which Fortune has Cupid by the hand, leading him across a bare landscape under the caption "Fortuna et Amor." This emblem seems to answer the Player King's open question "Whether love lead fortune, or else fortune love," because here Fortune apparently leads; but then again the interpretation may be more complex, because Cousin shows both Fortune and Love blindfolded, in a fine visualization of the blind leading the blind[26] (Fig. IV.12). The visual landscape is as bleak as the human landscape which it symbolizes and which we see enacted in *Hamlet*. Otto Vaenius conveyed a similar conception in an emblem which shows a blind Fortune, complete with her billowing sail-cloth, putting a blindfold on Cupid, who stands precariously on her sphere, while her own foot also rests on the sphere as though she might at any moment kick it out from under him and send him sprawling (Fig. IV.13). The English translation, which appeared in 1608, carries this instructive commentary:

> Sometime blind Fortune can make love be also blind
> And with her on her globe to turn and wheel about,
> When cold prevails to put light love's fervor out,
> But fervent loyal love may no such fortune find.[27]

As with the Fortune-led love of wife for husband, so with the love of child for parent. Claudius raises this point with Laertes in the fourth act, in a speech reminiscent of that of the Player King:

> Not that I think you did not love your father,
> But that I know love is begun by time,
> And that I see, in passages of proof,
> Time qualifies the spark and fire of it.
> There lives within the very flame of love
> A kind of wick or snuff that will abate it,
> And nothing is at a like goodness still,
> For goodness, growing to a plurisy,
> Dies in his own too-much.          (4.7.109-17)

Again there is a pertinent emblem by Cousin: it shows Fortune seated on her rolling globe and holding out a clock, while Love plays aimlessly with the clock weights, over a banderole which links Fortune, Love, Time, and Place[28] (Fig. IV.14). The whole design conveys a sense of instability and of fleeting attachments, as do the words addressed by Claudius to Laertes. No love which is controlled by Time (or by Fortune) can long endure.[29]

The favors of the strumpet Fortune simply cannot be lasting or dependable. This conception was conveyed both by the rolling ball upon which Fortune stands or sits, and also by the image of Fortune's wheel. Sometimes Fortune

FIG. IV.11. *Sir John Luttrell*, 1550, by Hans Eworth

123

is shown astride that wheel, trying to ride it,[30] but more often the wheel appears rather like a Ferris wheel, which may be turned by a crank in Fortune's hand or may move without any external assistance. The purpose of all these representations of Fortune and her wheel was, as Fluellen told Pistol, "to signify to you, which is the moral of it, that she is turning and inconstant, and mutability, and variation," a risible but nonetheless accurate analysis (*HV.* 3.6.32-35). Awareness of these basic uses will help us to appreciate Shakespeare's obvious and not so obvious references to that wheel in *Hamlet.*[31]

Hans Burgkmair illustrated one version by showing a blindfolded Fortune turning the crank while three "asses" ride around the wheel like children in an amusement park[32] (Fig. IV.15). Here, however, the riders are not children, but mature adults grimly intent on self-aggrandizement. The first, who has just mounted the wheel from the viewer's left, has a human head and trunk, but his lower parts have already metamorphosed into the hind quarters of an ass. The figure at the top of the wheel has an ass's head, wears a crown and royal robes, and holds a scepter; he appears serenely self-assured, totally secure in the preeminence he had scrambled to achieve. The third figure, now divested of all the paraphernalia of royalty to be revealed as merely an ass, plunges off

FIG. IV.12. "Fortune and Love," from
Jean Cousin, *Book of Fortune,* 1568

FIG. IV.13. "Fortune and Love," from Otto Vaennius,
*Amorum Emblematum,* 1608

FIG. IV.14. "Fortune, Love, and Time,"
from Jean Cousin, *Book of Fortune,* 1568

125

FIG. IV.15. "Wheel of Fortune," from Hans
Burgkmair's illustrations for Petrarch's *Book of
Fortune*

the wheel as it steadily follows its rounds. We presume that another human
ass will soon grasp each place as it is vacated on the constantly turning wheel.

A variant version presents a self-propelled wheel, so that without the figure
of Fortune at the bottom it was possible to show a fourth phase of the wheel's
rotation[33] (Fig. IV.16). Thus another Hans Burgkmair print shows to the left
a richly dressed noble riding the wheel in its upward progress, his eyes intently
fixed upon a somewhat pretentious but imperial figure at the top. To the right,
another fool of Fortune heads downward on the wheel, still crowned, and
holding on for dear life, while at the bottom a fourth has just been thrown off
the wheel entirely, his regalia in disarray; he appears in danger of being crushed

GLORIOR ELATVS.

AD ALTA VEHOR.

DESCENDO MORTIFICATVS.

AXI ROTOR.

FIG. IV.16. "Wheel of Fortune," from Hans
Burgkmair's illustrations for Petrarch's *Book of
Fortune*

by the wheel on which he still maintains a slight but futile grip. Such, as
Shakespeare put it, was "the giddy round of Fortune's wheel."[34]

Two notable references to Fortune's wheel occur in *Hamlet*, both evoking
the standard image and both going beyond it in interesting ways. The first
comes when the First Player declaims Aeneas' speech on the destruction of the
royal house of Priam at Troy:

Out, out, thou strumpet Fortune! All you gods
In general synod take away her power,
Break all the spokes and fellies from her wheel,

127

And bowl the round nave down the hill of heaven,
As low as to the fiends.                                    (2.2.481-85)

Most of that is conventional enough, perhaps even hackneyed, but it does introduce a hill for Fortune's wheel to roll down to destruction. In Shakespeare, that hill is first mentioned here in *Hamlet*, and it recurs in a strikingly original variation a bit later in a passage to which we shall shortly turn, and also in *King Lear* and *Timon of Athens*. In the latter play, the Poet says, "I have upon a high and pleasant hill/ Feigned Fortune to be throned." Below are people of all states, and many a one among them bows "his head against the steepy mount/ To climb his happiness," only to find after reaching the summit and enjoying a period of adulation that "Fortune in her shift and change of mood/ Spurns down her late beloved." When that happens, all the sycophants and parasites of the once fortunate man desert him, and "let him slip down,/ No one accompanying his declining foot" (*Timon*, 1.1.63-89). A mutation of this image occurs in *Lear* when the Fool says:

> Let go thy hold when a great wheel runs down a hill, lest it break thy
> neck with following. But the great one that goes upward, let him draw
> thee after. When a wise man gives thee better counsel, give me mine
> again. I would have none but knaves follow it since a fool gives it
> (*Lear*, 2.4.69-73).

Chew finds Shakespeare's hill of Fortune remarkable for its rarity in visual iconography, and he asks whether the introduction of the hill may "express Shakespeare's own distaste for the image, staled by innumerable repetitions, of Lady Fortune and her gyrating wheel? . . . Was it because he was tired of representations of this piece of hoisting machinery that he makes his Poet in *Timon* imagine a hill of Fortune? The concept is almost unique, paralleled only once or twice in all the lore of Fortune."[35] Chew does cite a similar but not identical literary use in Ariosto's *Satires in Seven Famous Discourses*, as published in Robert Tofte's translation in 1608, but he has apparently found no instances in visual iconography.[36]

There was a visual parallel in an emblem (now lost) embroidered by Mary Queen of Scots during her long imprisonment, when the exiled monarch used her needle for diversion. The emblem showed a "wheel rolled from the mountain in[to] the sea," with a motto suggesting a fall without hope, *senza speranza*.

It all fits with Mary's situation, and also with Shakespeare's general allusion, and I suspect that other visual examples will come to light from time to time, but for the moment this is all I have found of the hill as such, with a wheel of ill fortune plunging down it. An engraving by an unnamed sixteenth-century monogrammatist illustrates a related conception (Fig. IV.17). Instead of a hill, this print gives Fortune a tower or castle, at the top of which she stands, enticing her devotees to hazard the ascent. And hazard it they do, using siege ladders, ropes, and bare hands. As each seeks "to climb his happiness," many tumble down head-over-heels to destruction or despair on the plain below. And among the aspiring climbers, no one shows the slightest concern for the fallen.[37] All such images focus our attention upon segments of humanity entirely and madly given over to the pursuit of Fortune's meretricious favors, and thus entirely devoid of wisdom and of grace.

This serendipitous analysis brings us back to the second and more significant, as well as original, reference in *Hamlet* to the wheel plunging down a steep incline. It comes in a sycophantic speech which Rosencrantz addresses to Claudius. The Mousetrap play has just been broken off, and the conversation is now focused on that play's scarcely veiled threats to Claudius' life and throne. Rosencrantz's lines are permeated with unintended irony which would not have been lost on Elizabethan theatergoers familiar with the wheel of Fortune to which the ambitious cling as they aspire to the crown, obtain it, and are at last thrown down in disaster:

> The cess of majesty
> Dies not alone, but like a gulf doth draw
> What's near it with it; or 'tis a massy wheel
> Fixed on the summit of the highest mount,
> To whose huge spokes ten thousand lesser things
> Are mortised and adjoined, which when it falls,
> Each small annexment, petty consequence,
> Attends the boist'rous ruin.

There is a double irony in this flattery of Claudius: in the first place, his own murder of his brother has already brought the realm close to "boist'rous ruin," and in the second place there is the unmistakable association of the wheel of Claudius' majesty with the wheel of Fortune. Whatever the mediocre Rosencrantz may have intended to convey in this pompous compliment, the shrewd

FIG. IV.17. "Fortune," anonymous sixteenth century

Claudius may be expected to have caught the allusion to a wheel of Fortune on which ambitious majesty revolves, to its own ultimate loss. Like the jettisoned king who drew his sword against the wheel from which he fell in Burgkmair's engraving, Claudius responds decisively with "we will put fetters upon this fear" (3.3.15-26).[38]

## III. The Conscience of the King

When Claudius vows to put fetters on this fear he means quite simply that he will arrange for Hamlet to be assassinated at the end of a speedy voyage to England. A single murder was not sufficient, and he knows that what he has gained from the assassination of the former king may be lost unless he now also destroys the heir apparent. In this and in other ways he is much like Macbeth; indeed I suspect that the creation of Claudius gave Shakespeare the germ of the idea for casting a murderous usurper and tyrant with a guilty conscience as the protagonist of a tragedy. Both men attain the throne in the same way, both hold it by recognizing that "Things bad begun make strong themselves by ill," and both suffer the agonies of the damned even in this life (*Macb.* 3.2.55).

Claudius is the first character in this play to refer to his own conscience. As he and Polonius are about to set an eavesdropping trap for Hamlet, using a praying Ophelia as bait, Polonius comments that

> We are oft to blame in this,
> 'Tis too much proved, that with devotion's visage
> And pious action we do sugar o'er
> The devil himself.

Those words trigger an immediate reaction from Claudius in an aside:

> O, 'tis too true.
> How smart a lash that speech doth give my conscience!
> The harlot's cheek, beautied with plast'ring art,
> Is not more ugly to the thing that helps it
> Than is my deed to my most painted word.
> O heavy burthen!                                    (3.1.46-54)

That provides our first hint from Claudius that he is guilty, a hint which whets our curiosity and sharpens suspense as we approach the Mousetrap playlet. But he tells us nothing specific about the nature of his guilt, which could be solely caused by his having posted with such dexterity to incestuous sheets and have no relevance to the Ghost's charge of an even heavier guilt.

But just as Claudius is the first character to refer to his own conscience, so also the first reference to conscience in the play concerns him, as Hamlet in soliloquy deliberates on his own dilemmas and the King's secret. Recognizing the ambiguities of the Ghost, and the uncertainty surrounding its charges, Hamlet seeks "grounds more relative"—more relevant, that is—to solving the enigmas with which he has been challenged. He thus concludes: "The play's the thing/ Wherein I'll catch the conscience of the king" (2.2.589-91). Hamlet's assumption here is straightforward, and follows one meaning of conscience which can be traced back continuously at least as far as the reference in Xenophon's *Apology* to the false witnesses responsible for the death of Socrates that they "must feel in their hearts a guilty consciousness of great impiety and wickedness."[39] That embodies the classical Greek meaning of conscience, or *syneidesis*, a meaning which did not go appreciably beyond a recognition of the painful weight of one's own guilt, or what Claudius calls his "heavy burthen."

Hamlet designs "The Murder of Gonzago" in direct reference to the King's conscience. The play-within-the-play is no endeavor of art for art's sake, but is devoted to an utterly empirical end—forcing Claudius to a clear manifestation of his guilt. Hamlet plans to inspire at least a tell-tale flinching from his uncle— "if 'a do blench,/ I know my course"—and because that flinching is precisely what he gets, we have paid too little attention to two of his speeches which indicate that he also hopes for a great deal more, even for goading his uncle into an immediate public confession that he has attained the throne by murdering the former king:

> I have heard that guilty creatures sitting at a play
> Have by the very cunning of the scene
> Been struck so to the soul that presently
> They have proclaimed their malefactions.                    (2.2.575-84)

Although "presently" in modern parlance has an indefinite time reference, it more often meant "at the present moment" in Shakespearean and Elizabethan usage. The verb "proclaim" is even more important, and its significance in

132

Shakespeare is consistent. If it does not mean "to make known to the public by criers or advertisements," which it cannot mean here because the King is expected to speak for himself, then it means "to declare or announce openly, either by words or in another way; . . . to make one's declaration openly and publicly."[40] What Hamlet plans to achieve by catching the conscience of the King is an unequivocal public confession of his crimes. Such a "proclaiming" by the King before the court would vastly simplify Hamlet's task of setting right what is out of joint in Denmark.

The possibility of an immediate public confession is broached once again just before the play begins, when Hamlet expresses to Horatio the hope that his uncle's "occulted guilt" will "itself unkennel in one speech" (3.2.77-78). These words have often been read as meaning that Claudius will react to that "speech of some dozen or sixteen lines" written by Hamlet for insertion in the play (2.2.525-27), but the syntax does not support that interpretation. If that is what Hamlet meant, he should have predicted that Claudius' guilt would unkennel itself *at* one speech, or in response *to* it. To say that guilt reveals itself "in one speech" means that the guilty person will himself confess his guilt "in one speech,"—just as in Hamlet's earlier reference to "guilty creatures sitting at a play" who "have proclaimed their malefactions." Hamlet expects a very great deal indeed from the theater, even more than many Shakespeareans have recognized.[41]

To achieve such conclusive results depends, however, upon "the very cunning of the scene." It must be entirely convincing—not a melodramatic tearing of passion to tatters or "o'erdoing Termagent." To "split the ears of the groundlings" may induce applause in a public theater, but on this occasion Hamlet would focus everything upon exposing his uncle, or more precisely upon leading him to expose himself. Like Herod, Claudius had broken the ban against incest by marrying his brother's wife and the commandment against murder by assassination within his own family, but according to Hamlet's dramatic principles a person who has repeated Herod's sins would not recognize himself in an actor on stage who "out-herods Herod" as though a town crier spoke the lines. The play must inspire conviction in its own terms before it can reach beyond itself to "catch the conscience of the king," or of anyone else. Conviction on one level, in other words, must precede conviction on the other, which accounts for Hamlet's careful tutelage of the players.

The players do not live up to his instructions, and their performance of the Gonzago murder falls short of the utter credibility by which Hamlet hoped to impel Claudius to proclaim his guilt before the whole court. First comes the dumb show, in direct contradiction of Hamlet's direction, and as the play itself reaches its crisis, Hamlet has to break in to curb the out-heroding of Herod: "Begin, murtherer. Leave thy damnable faces and begin" (3.2.243-44). This acting scarcely displays the discretion and the modesty of nature which Hamlet required, and so the public admission of guilt is not elicited. Even so, the King is moved—not to a full and open revelation of his guilt but quite sufficiently to convince Hamlet.

But Hamlet is not the only one to learn from the Mousetrap. Until now he and Claudius have each been probing the mystery of the other, and trying to devise effective strategies of response. If the Prince now knows the King to be an actual regicide, the King in turn now sees in the Prince a regicide in the making. Morally the advantage is more than ever in Hamlet's favor, but strategically the score is even.

How the actor of Claudius in Shakespeare's original production responded to the Mousetrap we do not know, but Claudius is typically a cool operator and it is possible that he saw the dumb show miming his crime and that he was still able to contain himself—thereby increasing the suspense as to whether he was guiltless of regicide. But the re-enactment of the same scene in the playlet itself, accompanied by Hamlet's running commentary, broke down his reserve. "Frighted with false fire," he starts to his feet, cries "Give me some light! Away!" and rushes from the stage, as Polonius calls for "Lights, lights, lights" (3.2.244-60). The incident has great theatrical power: at first Claudius responds in a way which seems to falsify the Ghost's allegation, but he cannot twice maintain such steely control, and his response tells Hamlet and Horatio what they need to know. But it is a response which would not necessarily seem excessive to the court on stage, because he merely behaved as a monarch would be expected to do when offended by a play. Thus on one occasion when Queen Elizabeth was infuriated by a performance before her, she rushed from the room taking all the lights with her as a sign of passionate disapproval, and leaving the indoor stage in darkness.[42] In her case, the disapproval was of religious irreverence, whereas the Danish court would have assumed Claudius to be offended by the obvious lese majesty of the players and the Prince.

Claudius has regained his customary *sang-froid* when we next see him. With ruthless aplomb, he arranges the details for dispatching Hamlet to England

and to his death. Rosencrantz and Guildenstern are the appointed agents of this plot, but the printed text of the play does not make clear whether or not they are fully aware of what is involved. The Prince thinks that they are, and I am inclined to follow his judgment, but without demonstrable assurance. That issue would have been clarified by the kinetic action of the Globe performance—another interesting detail on which we would like information we cannot now obtain. We do know that Claudius arranges for the elimination of his nephew with dispassionate efficiency, and that he then coolly prepares to pray for the forgiveness of his earlier murder. And so the audience learns the truth of the regicide, and the King himself learns that he cannot repent.

He certainly ponders repentance, and deeply. The agonizing of his conscience in this scene elicits a sympathy for Claudius which he has not previously enjoyed, and when Hamlet stands above him with drawn sword to speak the most bloodthirsty soliloquy in the play, an Elizabethan audience might well have wondered whether Shakespeare were about to reverse the roles between his two mighty opposites, casting Hamlet as a vicious murderer and Claudius as a sympathetic penitent (3.3.36-98). Had Claudius' "make assay" succeeded when he bows his "stubborn knees"—and during Hamlet's bitter soliloquy we do not know for certain whether this prayer may become genuine—the play would indeed have taken a new direction, but of course it does not. The reasons for the failure of Claudius' silent prayer are made clear in his own reflections both before and after.[43]

In his magnificent prelude to prayer, he freely and frankly acknowledges his guilt (or rather a part of it), he affirms the need for repentance and the availability of mercy, and yet he declares "Pray can I not." There are two reasons for this inability. The first—which he does not mention—is that he is plotting another murder even as he seeks forgiveness for the first. Latimer's words define this first impediment: "As long as he is in purpose of sin, he cannot pray"—and the King here is certainly "in purpose of sin."[44] A. C. Bradley has brilliantly described his situation: "it is one of the grimmest things in Shakespeare, but he puts such things so quietly that we are apt to miss them—when the King is praying for pardon for this first murder he has just made his final arrangements for a second, the murder of Hamlet."[45] Modern readers may miss the irony here, and missing it has allowed some to conceive an unwarranted admiration for Claudius. A literary parallel may be found in *A Mirror for Magistrates* where the personified Remorse is described as "tossed and tormented with the tedious thought/ Of those detested crimes" she has committed, but has not genuinely repented.[46] The crucial distinction between true and false repentance is made by Henry Bullinger: "false or counterfeit repentance proceedeth of a feigned heart: and though at a blush it seem to have the circumstances of true repentance, yet for because it wanteth a turning to God and a sound confidence in him, it is unsincere and utterly false."[47] Under the circumstance of the play at this point we should and do feel sympathy for Claudius, but not admiration.

Beyond the impediment of his plot to commit a second assassination, Claudius' attempt to pray is also blocked by his unwillingness to restore what he has already gained from crime, as he admits:

> But, O, what form of prayer
> Can serve my turn? "Forgive me my foul murther?"
> That cannot be, since I am still possessed
> Of those effects for which I did the murther,
> My crown, mine own ambition, and my queen.
> May one be pardoned and retain th' offense?          (3.3.51-56)

What he really wishes, but knows he cannot have, is suggested in that last line, to enjoy both the fruits of his crimes and forgiveness for them. Protestants and Catholics alike recognized that a wrongdoer must not merely admit his guilt but also "recompense his trespass with the principal thereof," according to the still applicable Mosaic requirement of Numbers 5:7, "and give it unto him against whom he hath trespassed." If the injured party be dead, then the restitution should go to his nearest kinsman, in this case Prince Hamlet. What St. Augustine wrote on this subject is directly pertinent: "if men be able to make actual restitution, and do it not, their repentance is no repentance and their sin shall not be pardoned until actual restitution is made."[48] That essential point was made in virtually every sermon, treatise, or even simple reference devoted to repentance throughout the sixteenth century, and long thereafter.[49] Claudius is fully aware of all this, as his soliloquy demonstrates, but he is ultimately unwilling to pay the price of a true and effective repentance. He is in a state which might be called attrition rather than contrition, or anguish rather than penitence.[50] As he expects, then, his attempt at prayer is doomed from the start, even as he tries to assume the proper physical and spiritual stance: "Make assay,/ Bow, stubborn knees, and heart with strings of steel,/ Be soft as sinews of the new-born babe./ All may be well" (3.3.69-72).

On the basis of Claudius' own description of his prayer, it is apposite to recall the words Tyndale used to define "a false kind of praying, wherein the tongue and lips labor, and all the body is pained, but the heart talketh not with God, nor feelleth any sweetness at all, nor hath any confidence in the promises of God."[51] Claudius eventually finds no more relief than he had expected. A handbook on prayer by John Norden, published in 1596, commented of such a petitioner that "when he hath spent many words and much time in speaking in the air, his prayer returneth unto himself in vain," because without the full commitment of faith and life a prayer such as that of Claudius is "but as wind passing by and from our lips, and by reverberation of the air makes a sound, but to no profit."[52] As Claudius put it, "my words fly up, my thoughts remain below./ Words without thoughts never to heaven go" (3.3.97f.).

Claudius is thus left with the continuing burden of a guilty conscience. For him conscience is pervasively retrospective, concerned only with distress over past conduct, whereas for Hamlet conscience is prospective, linking past, present, and future, a guide (at least potentially) for what he yet may do. Claudius' use of conscience is essentially pre-Pauline and pre-Stoic whereas Hamlet's is essentially post-Pauline and post-Stoic, as we shall see. The classical Greek sense of *syneidesis*—unmellowed by later developments—may be cited as all that Claudius can muster, although he knows more to be available if he were willing to sacrifice "the wicked prize." He suffers as did those responsible for the death of Socrates, whose guilt left them "conscience-stricken about much impiety and wickedness." A passage from Plutarch is also pertinent. Citing Euripides' play in which Menelaus asks Orestes what troubles him, Plutarch integrates Orestes' reply into his own sentence so as to conflate Euripides' comment with his own: " 'My conscience, since I know I've done a dreadful deed,' like an ulcer in the flesh, leaves behind it in the soul regret which ever continues to wound and prick it."[53] So it is with Claudius. Temporarily he can profit from the fact that "In the corrupted currents of this world/ Offense's gilded hand may shove by justice," but he knows that ultimately "There is no shuffling." Seneca had long since observed that "where there is an evil conscience something may bring safety, but nothing can bring ease."[54] Unwilling to sacrifice as he must for repentance and a clear life ensuing,

Claudius must live out his life, in his own phrase, as a "limèd soul, that struggling to be free/ Art more engaged."

Unable to deceive himself, Claudius is nonetheless skilled at deceiving others. From the beginning there is the court, and Gertrude and Polonius, but for the latter part of the play his adept manipulation of that fiery wildcat of a young man, Laertes, is even more important. It was first necessary for Claudius to calm the fury with which Laertes stormed the royal presence, and to quiet if not quite tranquilize his passion; that he does brilliantly. Next he must rearouse that fury and redirect it against Prince Hamlet. Much insight into Claudius' own character may be gained from two related incidents in this entrapment and corruption of Laertes.

Claudius begins by asking whether Laertes really loved his father. It is an unnecessary question from any rational point of view, because the intensity of Laertes' devotion could not be more patent, but the question does serve to arouse emotion:

> Laertes, was your father dear to you?
> Or are you like the painting of a sorrow,
> A face without a heart? (4.7.106-08)

We can understand this "painting of a sorrow" as a flat, visual personification of grief, and if so we will catch well enough the taunting antithesis between actual emotion and painted abstraction. But Claudius' point is sharper still: he is here referring to those crude and unconvincing figures of widows and children in stereotyped postures of mourning which adorned tombs in Tudor and early Stuart England.[55] Beneath the stiff recumbent figure of the dead parent were ranged the equally stiff heirs as "weepers" or "sorrows." Examples from the 1590's may be seen on the tomb at Bottesford for John, fourth Earl of Rutland who died in 1591, and on that for the second Earl of Southampton who died in 1592 (Fig. IV.18). On the latter, at St. Peter's Church in Titchfield, we may see Shakespeare's onetime patron the third Earl kneeling opposite his widowed mother (Fig. IV.19) in rigid poses as unmoving emotionally as they are immobile physically. Usually the carvings were painted, and although the paint has generally been lost, we occasionally find examples where it has been preserved or faithfully restored, as in the tomb dated 1616 at Wichenford for a family of country gentry named Washbourne (Fig. IV.20). Here we have exactly the kind of thing Claudius called "the painting of a sorrow,/ A face without a heart."

Such funerary displays were coded signposts announcing grief, but rarely if ever in sixteenth-century England did they *show* grief in believable faces or physical postures.[56] The evocation of individual personality was clearly beyond the ability and may not even have been the intent of English sculptors at this time.[57] Some British oil paintings may have been a bit more sophisticated, though not much, and in the *Darnley Memorial* (Fig. IV.21) we see in the kneeling figures of Darnley's son, brother, and parents the familiar, standardized pose of painted "sorrows." Such representations were merely conventional announcements of grief, mechanical in execution and conventional in meaning, and Claudius can effectively allude to them as the purely stereotyped or even hypocritical feigning of grief. Asking Laertes whether he is like one of those "sons" is a goading, taunting question, calculated to arouse this passionate young man to passionate avowals—as indeed it does when he swears that he would even cut Hamlet's throat in church. Thereupon Claudius proposes the treacherous fencing match, which Laertes gladly accepts, adding the provision of the poisoned rapier, which Claudius in his own turn accepts, then adding the poisoned chalice to cap off the plot.

That exchange establishes Claudius' conception of funerary art as showing artificial grief, unfelt posing, and even outright hypocrisy. In the next scene, Claudius himself assumes exactly the same posture on stage, as he kneels beside the grave of Ophelia and declares to the court, "This grave shall have a living monument" (5.1.284). We thus see the King acting out in pantomime, as it were, "the painting of a sorrow," which he has already defined as the role of "a face without a heart." It is a role in which he has always demonstrated great skill.[58]

## IV. Laertes Dares Damnation

Laertes is three times directly associated with the word "conscience": he uses it twice himself, and Claudius once cites it in an appeal to him. That appeal comes when the King concludes his argument for his own innocence in Polonius' death by saying, "Now must your conscience my acquittance seal,/ And you must put me in your heart for friend" (4.7.1-2). Conscience here is subject to two possible interpretations: it could suggest a meaning which has by our time been largely lost, but which was still current in 1600, namely a sense of general consciousness or knowledge. On this basis, the King would

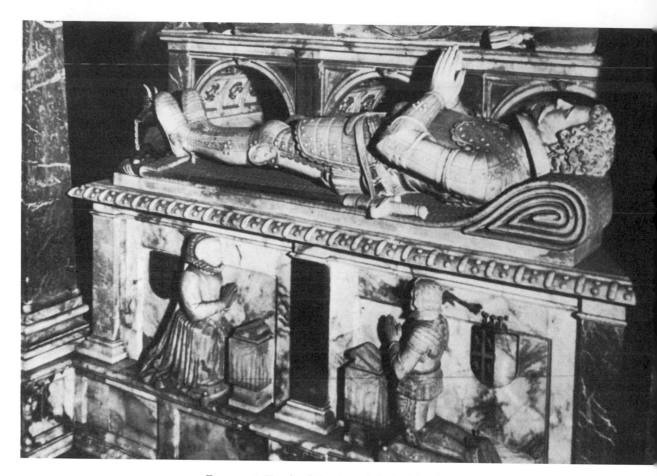

FIG. IV.18. Tomb of the Second Earl of Southampton, 1591

be saying in effect that Laertes must excuse, not accuse, him in the death of Polonius now that he has full consciousness of the knowledge just shared with him. The other possible meaning is the more usual one of an inner conviction of right and wrong: in other words, your conscience will make you excuse me, for to do otherwise would be wrong. Either meaning is possible, and the issue is not weighty enough to justify long consideration.

When Laertes himself uses the word, on the other hand, he refers to that particular sense of right and wrong which incorporates late Stoic and early Christian developments of *syneidesis* or *conscientia*. Whereas Claudius' use of conscience is purely retrospective, the guilt-ridden evaluation of evils already done, Laertes uses conscience prospectively—to apply a sense of right and wrong to present choices and future actions. In doing this, Laertes is neither sophisticated nor subtle, his mind seeming always to operate on a simple plane.

FIG. IV.19. Detail of the Second Earl of Southampton's Tomb, showing
Shakespeare's onetime patron and his mother as "sorrows"

FIG. IV.20. Son as "sorrow" on 1616 Washbourne
tomb in Wichenford Church

141

Even on that superficial plane, he does not debate issues, deliberate over them, or evaluate them. In this of course he is radically different from Hamlet. Also, Laertes does not come to an ethically correct decision, even though the two cases of conscience to which he refers are as elementary as one could desire. Thus, during his fencing match with Hamlet, he assures Claudius that he will now kill the Prince with the poisoned rapier, but he adds in an aside, "And yet it is almost against my conscience" (5.2.285). That is after he has accepted Hamlet's offer of reconciliation, and has already assured the Prince that "I do receive your offered love like love,/ And will not wrong it" (5.2.240f.). Yet he goes on to play the treacherous game with murder as its goal, justifying himself only by saying that it is almost against his conscience. That line evidences what is at best a palsied conscience, but it is somewhat better than what we find in Laertes' first reference to the subject.

Bursting into the royal presence at the head of a riotous band, Laertes demands satisfaction for his father's death. Acknowledging conscience along with divine grace and human vows of allegiance, he nonetheless excludes them from his consideration, because they would stand between him and the unlimited vengeance he seeks:

> How came he dead? I'll not be juggled with.
> To hell allegiance, vows to the blackest devil,
> Conscience and grace to the profoundest pit!
> I dare damnation. To this point I stand,
> That both the worlds [i.e., this life and the next] I give to negligence.
> Let come what comes, only I'll be revenged
> Most throughly for my father.                    (4.5.129-36)

Everything here sets Laertes in contrast to Hamlet. The Prince acknowledges that he is "prompted to my revenge by Heaven and Hell," and that the Ghost may be a devil that "abuses me to damn me," but he struggles, both morally and intellectually, over the challenges confronting him as Laertes never does (2.2.570 and 589). A quintessential Renaissance gentleman, Hamlet expects himself to combine thought with action and to neglect neither in favor of the other—a conception we shall investigate further in the next chapter. In seeking to maintain his balance, he at one point overemphasizes "the pale cast of thought" and at another the bitterness of passion, but he continues the struggle within himself until he has attained a resolution (3.1.85 and 3.3.73-

FIG. IV.21. Livinus de Vogelaare, *Darnley Memorial*, detail of Fig. II.2

96, for example). He is even willing to run the risk that conscience may make a coward of him, whereas Laertes with an adolescent assertiveness banishes conscience, even swears it away, to avoid any such possibility. Hamlet's overall struggle with his challenges and the resolution he eventually achieves (although not everything he does along the way) would have seemed almost equally impressive to a pagan Roman philosopher and to a Christian theologian, whereas Laertes might have aroused the sympathy of both but would have had the approval of neither.

Yet Laertes must be contrasted to Claudius as well as to Hamlet, and Shakespeare has managed the story in such a way that the Globe audiences would not have lumped Laertes together with Claudius as the villains of the piece. He probably would have appeared to be a moral simpleton to those

Elizabethan theatergoers who thought about the issue, yet we all know that moral simpletons can be attractive people, and there is indeed a good deal to be said in defense of this one. His anger over his father's death requires no explanation, but it is important to note that he is just as much concerned with the manner of his burial as with the matter of his death. He lists his specific grievances as follows:

> His means of death, his obscure funeral—
> No trophy, sword, nor hatchment o'er his bones,
> No noble rite nor formal ostentation—
> Cry to be heard, as 'twere from heaven to earth,
> That I must call 't in question.          (4.5.211-15)

His allegations are contained in the first three lines, running to a total of twenty-one words, and of these only the first four refer to the killing itself, the remaining seventeen being concentrated upon particular details of the hugger-mugger interment.[59]

We may assume this concentration upon expected social form to be but another example of Laertes' superficiality. Beyond his early concern for his sister, ethical issues typically elude him: his immediate acceptance of Claudius' treacherous plot for the fencing-murder and his own addition of the poison to the unbated tip of the rapier would have put him in no more favorable light with the Globe audience than with us today. But the issues as Shakespeare presents them are complex, and Laertes' distress over the violation of expected ceremony in his father's funeral was not in itself calculated to make him look unappealing in the eyes of the audience for which Shakespeare was writing. Indeed, his righteous indignation (the phrase is appropriate) over that disgraceful funeral would probably have been one of the most sympathetic things about him. The observance of order and ceremony was too basic to life in the sixteenth century to be taken lightly, for in many ways form spoke louder than words, and the disposition of Polonius' burial brought disgrace not only on the old man but through him upon his son.

We will be in a better position to understand Laertes' reaction to his father's obscure funeral if we consider a representative funeral of a prominent Elizabethan nobleman, ceremoniously closing the official life of the father while affirming and consecrating the succession of the son. The fullest account preserved for such an occasion describes the solemn exequies in 1572 for Edward

144

Stanley, and the symbolically important transference of his title and power as Earl of Derby to his son. Stanley had been a Privy Councillor to Elizabeth, as well as a Knight of the Garter, and the arrangements for a sufficiently elaborate funeral to do justice to his interment required about six weeks' time.[60] The funeral procession itself consisted of some nine hundred participants, with all three heraldic kings-of-arms participating and assisting in the direction. The chief mourner was the young Earl of Derby, now succeeding his father in the title. In the church, the officiating clergyman stood beside the son while the other principal mourners brought forward the trophies and hatchments of the dead man. These "honorable hatchments" of the father were presented to the clergyman who then presented them to the son—an impressive ceremonial which indicated in unmistakable fashion that "the hatchments now symbolized the heir's inheritance, blessed by the church." Finally the standard and banner were offered up, and when they were offered the esquires who brought them forward pushed back the hoods which had shrouded their heads, indicating that the formal ritual commemorating the dead father was coming to a close, and that the young earl was now the successor. The chief household officers broke their staffs of office by the side of the grave, and shortly after again received new staffs from "the new Earl their lord and master."[61]

At least three important things were accomplished in such ceremonies. In the first place, the hatchments recognized the achievements of the deceased (it is pertinent to note that "hatchment" is merely a shortened form of "achievement").[62] In the second place, the natural succession of son and heir was confirmed, as the young earl succeeded to the role of his father. In the third place, both of the former elements were given the blessing of God by the rituals of the church. Seen in this historical light, Laertes' objections to his father's interment were in no sense trivial. The "trophy, sword, and hatchment" to which Laertes referred were not only fitting summaries of one man's life, now closed, but they were also regarded as symbols of an honorable tradition passed on to his heir to continue. In them Laertes saw the tangible evidence of what he knew to be his parental heritage, but also the ritual expression of what he expected would be his own future. Because of the official downgrading of his father's burial, Laertes had every reason to feel that his past had been blighted and his future clouded.

The Derby funeral in 1572 is the most fully explained[63] of such heraldic and ecclesiastical ceremonies, so that from it we can best understand the significance of the events. In pictorial terms, the most fully preserved and publicized records were for the funeral of Sir Philip Sidney in 1587. Thomas Lant, the Windsor Herald, made a long, narrow drawing of the procession later engraved by De Bry and published in the same year under the title *The Famous Funeral Procession of Sir Philip Sidney*. Of the several thousand mourners involved, Lant's sketches illustrate only about two hundred participants; the scroll-like shape of his picture make it impractical to reproduce.[64]

Fortunately for us, the heraldic scroll-drawing of the funeral procession of Queen Elizabeth I was later redesigned and presented in a more manageable, rectangular format. Although based upon William Camden's original sketches of the procession, Badoureau's nineteenth-century engraving is not entirely accurate, but it is sufficiently so to provide a useful general impression of such a ceremony (Fig. IV.22). Only the funerals of royalty would have contained the effigy of the deceased carried upon the coffin, but in other regards this particular engraving gives a clear impression of the formality of such occasions, although so simplified here as to fall short of what was commonplace for noble funerals at the time. Even the funeral for the relatively unknown Sir John Savage, who was buried at Macclesfield in 1597, involved a longer procession than is shown here, and it was headed by a trumpeter "sounding a dreadful note" for the occasion.[65] The Badoureau engraving thus illustrates the least that should have been done in an important heraldic funeral, and what Polonius did not get.

On the basis of the evidence preserved for us, virtually all ranks of Elizabethan society regarded marked and formal distinction in ceremony as part of the natural order of things, and viewed the disruption of that order with intense suspicion. Richard Hooker, that master spokesman for the Elizabethan settlement, maintained that funerals should render the deceased "that honor generally due unto all men," but beyond this he asserted that "some man's estate may require a great deal more."[66] Queen Elizabeth herself insisted that this "great deal more" should be carefully observed in funeral ceremonies, and on at least two occasions in the later fifteen nineties she intervened personally to insure proper heraldic funerals for her noblemen. Despite her well-known parsimony, she involved herself in the funeral of the third Earl of Huntingdon in 1595 even to the point of bearing part of the cost so as to be certain that decorum was observed, and she paid over one thousand pounds toward the

FIG. IV.22. Funeral Procession of Queen Elizabeth, by Badoureau after William Camden's original roll of sketches

burial solemnities in 1596 of her kinsman Lord Hunsdon, who as Lord Chamberlain was the patron of Shakespeare's dramatic company.[67]

Whether under Queen Elizabeth or King James, Shakespeare's contemporaries were accustomed to regarding ceremonial form as an outward expression of social fact. Within this context, an obscure funeral for a high official or great noble would have suggested that the deceased was guilty of a capital crime or major disgrace, or was a threat to the national well-being. An axiom of Charles the Fair is pertinent: "those who die in the King's Prison are deservedly deprived of funeral pomp, lest they should be thought to have been thrown into prison wrongfully." That axiom was cited as justifying the obscure and non-heraldic burial of Arabella Stuart in 1615. Because of her royal descent and close connection by blood to King James, this unfortunate lady was always treated with suspicion by the court, and when she died as a prisoner in the Tower, "she was interred at Westminster, without funeral pomp, in the night."[68] The case is not isomorphic with Polonius', but it can provide helpful insights. When the funeral of a prominent person was obscured, with "no noble rite nor formal ostentation," the effect was not only to deprive him of additional honor, but actually to dishonor him—to de-fame and also to defame.

Polonius' death had repercussions beyond anything that we see that verbose councilor achieve during his lifetime. The most obvious and immediate effect, of course, was to send Hamlet packing abroad, an exile from Denmark, doomed to execution in England. But Claudius himself was not unaffected by the assassination of his chief minister, which posed very great problems for him. He solved those problems, after a fashion, but in a way which was only temporary and which was certain to invite even greater problems at a later date.

Claudius never shows the slightest sign of grief for the death of Polonius as a valued friend and advisor. Instead, his thoughts turn instantly to the possible repercussions upon himself: his concern is not so much for the "bloody deed," as for the expectation that it will be "laid to us" (4.1.16-27). He concentrates upon how to strike the most cautious political balance, as "this vile deed/ We must with all our majesty and skill/ Both countenance and excuse" (4.1.30-32). And so he proposes to call up his "wisest friends," while calculating the odds of damage. He intends to achieve safety for himself, with no apparent consideration or regard for Polonius or his children. He appraises the problem under the image of artillery (which he so much favors), and he schemes to maneuver so that "the cannon . . . may miss our name/ And hit the woundless air" (with an easily overlooked punning reference to striking down the heir, who of course is Hamlet), but he later acknowledges that his disposition of Polonius' body has backfired and "like to a murd'ring piece, in many places/ Gives me superfluous death" (4.1.42-44 and 4.5.95-96). Under these circumstances, the people became understandably confused and suspicious about "good Polonius' death," and Claudius admits to Gertrude that "we have done but greenly/ In hugger-mugger to inter him" (4.5.83-84).

A hugger-mugger burial of a great figure was bound to create suspicion. In North's *Plutarch*, Mark Antony was able to persuade the conspirators to allow him to conduct Caesar's funeral by arguing that Caesar "should be honorably buried, and not in hugger-mugger, lest the people might thereby take occasion to be worse offended."[69] Hugger-mugger funerals inevitably brought suspicion either upon the person buried or upon the person responsible for the burial. In another context we have already noted a most famous example in Edinburgh in February of 1567, when King Henry, the consort of Mary Queen of Scots, was brutally assassinated, and the Queen arranged for an obscure funeral, which haunted her thereafter. George Buchanan made the most of this scandalous behavior, describing how "she secretly in the night buried him without funeral pomp, or rather hid him like a thief," while John Knox described the procedure with more restraint but equal effect: "The Queen caused his corpse to be carried by some pioners in the night without solemnity, and to be laid beside the sepulchre of David Riccio."[70] That interment (especially beside the grave of the detested Italian scribe Riccio) was seen as prima facie evidence of Mary's villainy by her enemies, and aroused suspicion among her friends as well. Mary's denial to her murdered spouse of solemn burial with trophy, hatchment, and noble ostentation was but one of the ways in which she scandalized immemorial custom and expectation, as we have already seen.

In somewhat the same way, Claudius' choice of a hugger-mugger interment for Polonius was an invitation to misunderstanding and perhaps even to insurrection because it virtually forced Laertes onto a collision course with the crown. That disposition of Polonius' body shows Claudius to be an imprudent as well as an unjust ruler. On the other hand, the cunning he displays in dealing with the consequences reveals him at his Machiavellian best, as he uses his well-practiced skills of persuasion to extricate himself. When Laertes and his riotous band overbear Claudius' Swiss guards, the King is temporarily reduced to complete impotency. With only his wit and courage to protect him, he negotiates so adeptly that he is soon able to reestablish himself in a position of absolute control.

When both pluses and minuses are assessed, and the favorable as well as the discreditable elements are balanced, the overall effect of Claudius' relations with Polonius and his children once again puts him in an unfavorable moral light with the Globe audience. The King's attitude toward his dead councilor would, in sixteenth-century terms indicate the response of a tyrant rather than of a just monarch. Tyrants, as Erasmus wrote, "look out for their people only insofar as it redounds to their personal advantage, hold their subjects in the same status as the average man considers his horse or ass. For these men take care of their animals, but all the care they give them is judged from the advantage to themselves, not to the animals."[71] So Claudius had regarded Polonius in life, and so he had disposed of him in death.

Ophelia's funeral was just as disgraceful as her father's. That her suicide was due to mental derangement could not be made more clear in the play. For a thousand years, church law and church practice had affirmed the right of such *non compos mentis* suicides to burial by the full rites of the church. In England, furthermore, the decision of a coroner's inquest on this matter could not be legally overruled, and we are told that the "crowner's quest" decided for Christian burial in Ophelia's case. The establishment of these points of doctrine and practice is fully laid out in an appendix, but here it should be said that Laertes appears to be fully correct in the demands he makes upon the "churlish priest" who officiates at the "maimèd rites" of his sister.[72] I have found no way to justify those "maimèd rites" in terms of the Elizabethan expectations and reactions as we can now reconstruct them, and the fact that both Laertes and the audience in the Globe would have been shocked by this degraded funeral service tends to increase the explosive impact it has on the play.

Once again, Laertes' plight would have elicited the sympathy of the Globe audience, if not entirely its approval: the corruption of Claudius' Denmark is such that even his friends cannot be assured of a decent burial.[73] Yet the King's unscrupulous cleverness is such that he can turn almost everything to his own advantage (even the results of the corruption endemic under his own reign). He is thus able to use the intensely passionate but largely sympathetic resentment of Laertes to convert Laertes into an instrument for his own plots. Hamlet's blunder in thrusting through the arras at the wrong man has even more importantly played into Claudius' hands, but the maimed funeral of Ophelia also contributes: it increases Laertes' fury, pushes Hamlet beyond restraint, and in the fifth act sets these two young men at each other's throats in a struggle which will end only in their mutual destruction. To that matter we shall return in Chapter Six.

## v. Gertrude's Mirror of Confession

Claudius and Laertes are each aware of conscience, although only partly and in different ways, but Gertrude seems oblivious to it. She does not suffer from its retrospective guilt as does Claudius, nor does she feel the need to foreswear its prospective control as does Laertes. And she certainly does not scrutinize it, dissect it, and weigh it as does Hamlet. She never so much as mentions the word "conscience." Even to say that she ignores conscience may imply a larger awareness than she shows, because she simply does not seem sufficiently conscious of its existence to feel the need to ignore it. She is in a sense amoral, if such a condition exists: she wishes to please and to be pleased, and it never occurs to her that in doing so she may offend.

The speed with which she rushed from the grave of one husband to the bed of another was shameful, even disgraceful in terms of the contemporary social mores, but it was not on the plane of her two other faults, actual and potential. She is patently guilty of incest, and Hamlet fears that she may also be involved in murder. It is to these faults, one certain and the other suspected, that Hamlet draws his mother's attention during their interview in her chamber. That scene is critical to the development of her character, just as the preceding prayer scene was for Claudius, and it is upon it that we shall concentrate.

The play-within-the-play had elicited from Claudius the evidence Hamlet needs to confirm the Ghost's report, but its effect upon Gertrude is at best superficial. The play has irritated her because it offended her current husband, but the dramatization of the original murder touches her not at all. Indeed, she does not even perceive the connection, and when Hamlet levels the explicit charges of regicide—"almost as bad, good mother,/ As kill a king, and marry with his brother" (3.4.29-30)—her astonishment at "kill a king" is so patently innocent that Hamlet never again suspects her of complicity in that crime, and never mentions it again.

But there remains the sin of incest, the union of brother- and sister-in-law, and as we have already seen it was regarded as a major sin indeed, for which Elizabethan penalties expressed social disgust and revulsion.[74] It is upon this sin that Hamlet focuses his attention, and in his interview with Gertrude he is intent upon making her recognize her own guilt, repent of it, and reject it.[75] To that end, his speeches are direct, forceful, and even crude. He forces her, unwilling though she is, to confront the full implication of her evil—apparent hypocrisy, clear lust, and depraved judgment. The more distanced mirror up to nature the playlet affords having failed to move her, Hamlet now confronts her with a highly personalized mirror of her own soul and he calls her to repentance. Within the pertinent Elizabethan frames of reference, Hamlet's reproaches of his mother are skillfully designed to express the ultimate kindness, even through a seeming cruelty, or as he puts it, "I must be cruel only to be kind" (3.4.179).

Yet Hamlet's confrontation with his mother in her chamber has seemed puzzling or outright distasteful, in one degree or another, to a number of twentieth-century observers. Many would even agree with G. B. Shaw: "This scene is an unnatural one: the son's reproaches to his mother, even the fact of his being able to discuss the subject with her, is more repulsive than her relations with her deceased husband's brother."[76] Such opinions can provide lively stimulus and provoke reactions, but these are not to be confused with the stimulus and reaction which passed between Shakespeare and the Elizabethan public for whom he wrote.

Neither Hamlet's reproaches to his mother, nor the scene as a whole, would have appeared "unnatural" or "repulsive" in 1600. Gertrude was guilty of violating one of the most ancient and widespread human laws, and Elizabethans would have regarded her incestuous marriage with her brother-in-law as reprehensible in all the ways Hamlet points out, as we have already seen. Under these circumstances, her bland self-assurance (ignoring her guilt as though there were none) would have seemed especially shocking. Elizabethan audiences would have been fascinated to see how Hamlet might proceed with his mother when he faces her alone in her chamber. He begins, significantly, with a looking glass in which she is to see her inmost parts. The implications of that mirror of self-knowledge provided Elizabethans with initial understandings which Shakespeare proceeded to develop throughout the scene, and to render immensely theatrical. (See Della Robbia's *Prudence*, Fig. IV.2 above.)

A stage tableau is promptly set when Hamlet seizes a mirror and forces his mother to study her own face and even more importantly her soul:

Come, come, and sit you down. You shall not budge.
You go not till I set you up a glass
Where you may see the inmost part of you.                    (3.4.19-21)

That glass which Hamlet holds up to Gertrude is fundamentally metaphorical, and stage productions today usually show no actual mirror, but the visual tradition of a woman studying herself in the mirror of self-knowledge was so widespread and so popular that the early Globe audiences would surely have recognized the visual allusion which Shakespeare here enacted. It is a fine example of Hamlet's theatrical dictum of suiting the word to the action and the action to the word: the staging would have been easy, and would have required no elaborate properties. Elizabethan ladies frequently had mirrors about them, either suspended from the girdle or carried by hand in a fan-mirror as in an engraving executed by Jost Amman in 1582 (Fig. IV.23). On the Globe stage, Hamlet need only have seized Gertrude's glass and held it up to her face,

FIG. IV.23. Lady with fan-mirror, detail from
"Lady and Fowler" by Jost Amman

153

or have forced her to hold it there. (For the development and meaning of mirror symbolism generally, see Appendix A.) When so staged, the observed action of the two characters would have reinforced the verbal arguments the Prince uses througout the scene, as he forces her to recognize herself as she is and to repent.

The image of a woman gazing at herself in a mirror could convey a number of implications in addition to self-knowledge. As an attribute of pride, the mirror could indicate smug self-approval and a concentration upon the self in disregard of virtue or of the claims of other individuals. Venus gazing into a mirror suggests lust, as focusing upon the attractive surface of the flesh which characterizes venery. A mirror held by Fortune implies the transience and fragility of her gifts, because images reflected in a mirror are seen only temporarily, and the glass itself is proverbially frangible. In various ways, each of these suggestions might be appropriate to Gertrude,[77] but in all the arts we must observe the context if we are to understand the primary significance of a particular mirror. When Hamlet confronts Gertrude in her closet, Shakespeare carefully develops the context of self-knowledge, converting a static image into an intensely dramatic scene.

From at least as early as Giotto's painting of Prudence for the Arena Chapel in Padua, Europeans had been familiarized with the allegorical figure of a woman appraising herself by studying her reflection in a glass. Within this established iconography, Prudence was not restricted to the merely common-sensical or cautious virtue which we think of today, but was far closer to what we mean by wisdom. *Prudentia* was given eminence among the cardinal virtues because it was the ability to discriminate between good and evil (or gradations within the two) and to choose according to that discrimination. Thus the *Speculum Virginum* taught that "Maidens look into mirrors to see whether there is an increase or decrease of their beauty, but Scripture is a mirror from which they can learn how they can please the eternal Spouse. In this mirror they can find themselves and understand what they ought to perform."[78] Much the same was said of the Virgin Mary as a *speculum sine macula*, but the reference also went beyond the Bible or the Virgin to apply quite generally to a knowledge of the self in the light of human virtue very broadly conceived.[79] In the sixteenth century, Guillaume de la Perrière's emblem book, *Le Théâtre des Bon Engins*, shows a woman looking at her face in a stand mirror, while the appended French verses advise that (Fig. IV.24)

154

Beaulté de corps tourne à desconfiture
S'elle se plonge en plaisirs reprouvez.
Ici noter peult toute creature,
Que les miroirs à ces fins sont trouvez.[80]

When this charming work was published in an English translation in 1614,[81]
the accompanying verses elaborated La Perrière's original point. The motto
reads, "Herein the chiefest cause is taught,/ For which the glasses first were
wrought," which is true enough for the symbolic mirror, if not for the artifact.
The English verses spell out the moral meaning:

A woman should, and may well without pride
Look in a looking glass, and if she find

That she is fair, then must she so provide
To suit that beauty with so fair a mind.
If she be black, then that default to hide
With inward beauty of another kind.

George Wither continued the tradition in his *Emblems* of 1635, showing a
maiden or a wife (his commentary allows for either) looking into a hand-mirror
(Fig. IV.25). The introductory couplet advises "In all thine actions have a care./
That no unseemliness appear," while the expansive commentary refers to the
woman who uses her glass to be sure that her attire will "please her lover's or
her husband's eyes," which Wither interprets as

A documental sign remembering us
What care of all our actions must be had.
For he that in God's presence would appear
An acceptable soul, or gracious grow
With men that of approv'd conditions are,
Must by some faithful glass be trimmed so . . .

so trimmed, that is, as to win approval, whether divine or human.[82]

Hamlet's arguments to Gertrude in her closet focus upon divine considerations, rather than social.[83] He does not directly mention the reactions within
a corrupt society to her lustful union (Claudius has already said that the court
has "freely gone/ With this affair along"), and Hamlet declares that "in the
fatness of these pursy times/ Virtue itself of vice must pardon beg,/ Yea, curb
and woo for leave to do him good" (1.2.15-16 and 3.4.154-57). His appeals
are specifically "for love of grace," with the hope that she may become "desirous
to be blest" (3.4.145, 172). Holding up the glass of self-knowledge for her,
Hamlet acts the part which George Wither recommended of "a wise companion
and a loving friend" who "stands nearer" and "serveth well to such an useful
end":

For he may be thy glass and fountain too.
His good example shows thee what is fit;
His admonition checks what is awry,
He by his good advice reformeth it;
And by his love thou mend'st it pleasedly.

FIG. IV.25. Lady and hand-mirror, from
George Wither, *Emblems*, 1635

But if thou do desire the perfect'st glass.
Join to the moral law the law of grace.

Gertrude is like La Perrière's fallen woman—"elle se plonge en plaisirs reprouvez"—and Hamlet tells her that "rank corruption, mining all within,/
Infects unseen" (3.4.149-50). Like Wither who urges his woman with the mirror
to "Join to the moral law the law of grace," Hamlet pleads "confess yourself
to heaven,/ Repent what's past, avoid what is to come" (3.4.150-51).

An allegorical print executed half a dozen years before Shakespeare's *Hamlet* is especially pertinent to the Prince's persuasion of his mother. The Dutch artist Stradanus (Jan van Straten) executed in 1594 an instructive picture called "The Frailty of Human Life, or the Presenting of the Mirror of Life" (Fig. IV.26). Set in a chamber replete with luxury, the print shows a seated lady of indeterminate age, with withered flowers in her lap. She is addressed by a robed counselor, completely hooded, who holds up to her the two tablets of the Mosaic law, and below these a double mirror. The larger glass reflects the lady's face, while a smaller panel extended out to the right reveals a death's head. On the wall to the right is a picture of Adam and Eve being expelled from the Garden—probably the most universal of all visual incentives to penitence—and above the picture yet another mirror. Symbolically we have here an extensive visual counterpart to Hamlet's mission in his mother's chamber.[84] Like the robed counselor in Stradanus' engraving, Hamlet holds up a mirror in which Gertrude sees her inmost part.

One final example should be cited, from an English pictorial commonplace book dated 1608 (Fig. IV.27). In it, Thomas Trevelyon has drawn and colored the traditional figure of Prudence, who grasps the serpent symbolizing wisdom in her right hand and the mirror of self-knowledge in her left. Beneath the picture are several relevant verses of Scripture, including Proverbs 19:25, "Smite a scorner (recall Hamlet's purpose to show 'scorn her own image') and the foolish will beware: and (if) the prudent be reproved, he will understand knowledge." What Trevelyon quotes in the abstract, Hamlet applies concretely: like Wisdom crying aloud (also cited by Trevelyon from Proverbs 1:20), the Prince "roars . . . loud and thunders" accusations against his mother (3.4.53) smiting her hardened conscience as he seeks to convert her from the image of scorn to that of virtue.[85]

The stage tableau of Gertrude with her mirror takes on greater richness when seen in the context of such visual traditions, and it effectively sets the stage for the strategy Hamlet employs with her throughout the scene. For a full understanding of his words and of her response, however, we must consider certain influential and representative Elizabethan treatments of guilt and repentance. Two Biblical passages are basic to these. James 5:16 admonishes "confess your faults one to another, and pray one for another, that ye may be healed," and in Ezekiel 3:18 God declares that the righteous must warn the wicked and specifies that if "thou givest him not warning, nor speakest to warn

FIG. IV.26. "The Frailty of Human Life, or Presenting the Mirror of Life," 1594, by Stradanus

the wicked from his wicked way, to save his life; the same wicked man shall die in his iniquity, but his blood will I require at thine hand."

In the Church of England in Shakespeare's lifetime, there was no sacrament of penance, but repentance was nonetheless an absolute necessity for everyone. Ultimately, confession must be to God, for which a clergyman was not regarded as essential. In sixteenth-century Roman Catholic teaching, on the other hand, penance was a sacrament which "cannot be ministered but by a priest," as Father Thomas Harding wrote in an attack upon the Church of England practice, yet the Catholic tradition also recognized the possibility of valid confession to a layman in case of necessity. Thus Peter Lombard wrote that in the absence of a priest "thou must make thy confession unto thy neighbor or unto thy fellow," and the Decretals of Pope Gregory IX declared that "in the case of

159

necessity a layman may both hear confessions and absolve."[86] In a prayer of St. Thomas Aquinas translated into English and included in the Anglican prayer books of Edward VI and of Queen Elizabeth, there is the entreaty that the petitioner may "tell my neighbor his faults charitably without dissimulation."[87] In both Catholic and Protestant doctrine, Christians were urged to assist in bringing sinners to repentance.[88] Although Catholicism did not exonerate laymen from that responsibility, Protestantism placed a greater emphasis upon the laity. Because Shakespeare tells us four times that Hamlet was a Wittenberg student (and that he was eager to return to Wittenberg), we can scarcely avoid recognizing that the Prince was schooled in Martin Luther's own university, the birthplace of the Protestant Reformation; it is therefore appropriate to consider his "shriving" of his mother primarily in terms of the Protestant understanding familiar to Shakespeare's original audiences at the Globe Theatre.

Bishop John Jewel defended the exclusion of penance from among the Protestant sacraments by declaring that James 5:16, already quoted,

> speaketh not of priest or minister, but of every one of the faithful. Every Christian may do this help unto another, to take knowledge of the secret and inner grief of the heart, to look upon the wound which sin and wickedness hath made, and, by godly advice and earnest prayer for him, to recover his brother. This is a private exhortation, and as it were a catechizing or instructing in the faith, and a means to lead us by familiar and special conference to examine our conscience, and to espy wherein we have offended God.[89]

At this point, the often misunderstood Protestant conception of the priesthood of all believers was quite clear-cut.[90] Thus Archbishop Cranmer wrote that even when a priest is available, the layman is not bound to confess to him, but only to God,[91] and William Fulke, in his defense of Anglicanism against Rome, summarized that doctrine when he wrote that "the layman must shrive the priest, as well as the priest shrive the layman."[92]

As such "shriving" was never a Protestant sacrament, it had no single name: in addition to Fulke's use of the traditional word "shrive," he and Cranmer also referred to it as confessing, Jewel called it a familiar or special conference, Thomas Becon treated it as "consideration," Henry Bullinger saw it as "consultation," Latimer as reproof, and Tyndale as smiting.[93] The name

FIG. IV.27. "Prudence," from *Picture Commonplace Book of Thomas Trevelyon*

161

was immaterial, "so long as ye understand what is meant thereby," Tyndale said, and "if thou study not to amend thy neighbor, when he sinneth, so art thou partaker of his sins," and worthy of punishment for it, "but if thou do thy best . . . to keep thy land [i.e., nation] or neighbors from sinning against God; then (though it help not) thou shalt bear no sin for their sakes when they be punished."[94] Whether or not the offender requests such assistance is immaterial, because even if a sinner "demandeth not [consultations], and thou dost see thy brother to be in danger, charity again commandeth thee to admonish him that is so in danger, and to handle him as a brother,"[95] to quote a passage from Bullinger which is typical of Protestant conviction on this matter. Thus, if Hamlet had not admonished Gertrude, he would have been partaker both of her guilt and also of his own for ignoring the imperative of charity. His response combines love of her with love of himself as mandated in the commandment that we should love our neighbor as ourself.[96]

It is thus a work of charity which Hamlet performs in his mother's chamber. First he levels the charge of regicide, and he finds that her guiltlessness on that score is so obvious that he never mentions it again. But the sin of incest is another matter, and Gertrude's extreme peril on this count is evidenced by her shocking lack of moral or spiritual awareness before Hamlet shows her the parlous state of her soul. Had he not spoken, she would presumably have continued in the grip of the rebellious hell and cozening devil to which he refers (3.4.77-83). Even after he has begun his reproof, she still professes ignorance of any sin worthy of such notice—asking first "what have I done that thou dar'st wag thy tongue/ In noise so rude against me?" and again "what act/ That roars so loud and thunders in the index?" (3.4.40f. and 52f.). However she may wring her hands, there is no sign that she has ever wrung her heart, so Hamlet must bring her to it:

> Peace, sit you down
> And let me wring your heart, for so I shall
> If it be made of penetrable stuff,
> If damnèd custom have not brazed it so
> That it is proof and bulwark against sense. (3.4.35-39)

Hamlet accuses her of being "stewed in corruption" (3.4.94), much as Bishop Pilkington had described hardened sinners as "wallowing in sin" until "they feel no remorse of conscience, are desperate and almost past all recovery."[97]

Hamlet is aware that it may be too late for his mother, that her heart may already be too hardened to repent. The Epistle to the Hebrews 3:13 commands Christians to exhort one another while there is time, "lest any of you be hardened through the deceitfulness of sin." It is to break down that hardening of the heart that Hamlet labors, wringing and pounding his mother's heart into malleability, forcing her to see herself, restating all the evil of her incest in terms so graphic and repugnant that if there be yet any conscience alive it may awaken and bring her to virtue again. Romans 2:5 describes the state into which he fears that she may have fallen, which the Bishop's Bible translated as "stubborness and heart that cannot repent" and Geneva as "hardness and heart that cannot repent."[98]

Under these circumstances, he cannot in conscience come to her with a subtle and tactful suggestion that she might do well to consider repentance, and he certainly cannot leave her alone, as G. B. Shaw might have preferred— she is far too deeply involved for such a simple solution. Bishop Hooper treated such deep sin under the traditional metaphor of desperate illness (which Hamlet also uses), describing how one who is gravely imperilled "with a dangerous disease, and yet feeleth not the grief thereof, shall never find remedy, neither have the ill removed," and adding that "the next way unto health is the knowledge of the disease."[99] Hamlet first brings his mother to a recognition of her sin, using words as knives to dissect and reveal the moral disease which like "rank corruption, mining all within,/ Infects unseen" (3.4.149-50).

He has made significant progress when the Ghost appears, and this episode provides Gertrude with a diversion and a possible excuse for dismissing Hamlet's argument as mere madness. As Bishop Ridley said, a sinner "is ready to find and invent some color to cloke his conscience, to do that thing that his heart desireth," and Hamlet acts swiftly to prevent her from using any such rationalization:[100] "Lay not that flattering unction to your soul/ That not your trespass but my madness speaks" (3.4.146ff.).

Throughout most of the interview Hamlet is "smiting" Gertrude, to employ the verb Tyndale applied to correction. And yet this smiting should be done in love, as Tyndale insists: "May a man be angry with love? Yea, mothers can be so with their children. It is a loving anger, that hateth only the vice, and studieth to mend the person"; and again he wrote, "a mother can smite and love."[101] It is in this spirit that faults are to be recognized, communicated, and corrected, "and so may the son do to his father, and a servant to his master, and every man to his neighbor."[102] That is the spirit in which Hamlet attempts to confront and correct his mother. Even in his overwrought soliloquy just before he stumbled upon Claudius at prayer, the Prince had declared of Gertrude that "I will speak daggers to her, but use none" (3.2.381), which roughly approximates the advice which Luther gave to Protestant "confessors": "you should so inflict the wound that you can both mitigate and heal it; you should be so severe as not to forget to be kind,"[103] a conception very close to Hamlet's "I must be cruel only to be kind" (3.4.179). The Prince "smites" his mother in the ways that might be expected of one who was educated at Wittenberg.

Gertrude's reaction shows that Hamlet has indeed succeeded in holding the mirror up to her inmost part in the confessional sense. The standard vocabulary employed in religious writings again and again refers to revealing the "spots" left by sin. As Bradford put it, "let us consider the heart, and so shall we see the foul spots we are stained withal at least inwardly, whereby we the rather may be moved to hearty sorrow and sighing."[104] Alexander Nowell's *Catechism*, required for study in every Elizabethan grammar school, advised all people to behold "as it were in a glass, the spots and uncleanness of their souls"; Latimer referred to the moral law as "a glass which showeth us the spots in our faces, that is, the sin in our hearts"; and Calvin recommended it as revealing our weakness and wretchedness "even as a glass representeth to us the spots of our face."[105] The frontispiece of Sir Walter Ralegh's 1614 *History of the World* shows the personification of Ill Fame covered with spots. The conception was everywhere. John Donne need not, and indeed was not, thinking of Hamlet's tactics with Gertrude and her glass when he wrote of turning "the looking-glasses of women to a religious use, to show them . . . the spots of dirt, which they had taken . . . that they might wash themselves clean."[106]

When we recognize that sixteenth-century vocabulary, the confessional implication of Gertrude's response becomes as clear to us as it was to Shakespeare's contemporaries:

> O Hamlet, speak no more!
> Thou turn'st mine eyes into my very soul,
> And there I see such black and grainèd spots
> As will not leave their tinct.                    (3.4.89-93)

Hamlet has successfully brought Gertrude to the path of virtue. The process to this point may be usefully summarized in the words of Thomas Becon:

Ye know that a man's face shall be long defiled, spotted, and deformed, before he shall perceive it, except it be either told him of other, or else that he himself seeth it evidently in some mirror or glass. Semblably, the soul of a Christian man shall be spotted with sin a great space, before he perceiveth it, and be truly contrite and sorry for it, except it be either told him of other by declaring the law of God to him, or else he himself looketh in the glass of truth, which is the law of God, and by that means perceiveth his own deformity, misery, and wretchedness.[107]

Even after Gertrude has acknowledged those inward spots, more remains to be done. The recognition and acknowledgment of guilt is only the first step in repentance—necessary, to be sure, but merely provisional—as we have seen in the case of Claudius. Gertrude has taken no more than that first step when she sees and admits the "black and grainèd spots" which mar her soul. Hamlet is gratified but unwilling to leave his mother on this preliminary way-station to grace, as it were. True or full repentance goes far beyond regret or remorse; it involves a restored right relationship with heaven and a turning away from evil on earth. To the "passion or grief of conscience" Gertrude has demonstrated—to use Becon's terms—she must next add an acknowledgment of sin to God and finally "an amendment of [her] former evil life . . . to take away and banish the evil, to bring in and establish the good" with a "full, determined purpose to amend."[108] Hamlet lays out the basic program. Calling explicitly upon the "love of grace," he urges the full progression upon her: "Confess yourself to heaven,/ Repent what's past, avoid what is to come" (3.4.145-51). When she replies, "O Hamlet, thou has cleft my heart in twain," he at once answers with a reinforcing admonition: "O, throw away the worser part of it,/ And live the purer with the other half" (3.4.157-59).[109] And his advice moves beyond the general principle of amendment to spell out the precise implications for Gertrude: "go not to my uncle's bed/ . . . Refrain tonight," and then again, and again, each abstinence making the next easier as she establishes a new life which, in Bradford's words, lets "your sorrowing for your evils demonstrate itself by departing from the evils you have used."[110] Such amendment of life will show that she is "desirous to be blest," and when she has shown that, Hamlet adds, "I'll blessing ask of you" (3.4.172f.).[111]

Hamlet's final comments upon his mother come late in the play's last scene. After the fencing match, his first action is to turn to his mother, who has now drunk the cup, and to ask, "How does the queen?" The answer to that question is quick and distressing. Later, as she lies dead and as he is dying, Hamlet addresses her for the last time: "Wretched queen, adieu" (5.2.297 and 322). The "wretched" here is subject to various interpretations, and it has sometimes been read as a sign of Hamlet's continuing reprobation of his mother. There is no absolutely certain way to establish the nuance here, but the best we can do is to consider Shakespeare's usage elsewhere. In that light, "wretched queen" more likely conveys pity and sadness than moral condemnation. In his study of Shakespeare's words, Alexander Schmidt finds that Shakespeare only twice used the word "wretched" in the sense of hateful, abominable, or evil, and occasionally as contemptible or paltry. In the overwhelming majority of cases, Shakespeare used it to mean miserable or very unhappy[112]—providing a far more charitable assessment.

In view of Shakespeare's practice elsewhere and of the context here, I assume that Hamlet's "wretched queen, adieu" expresses a sense of tragic waste, instead of moral condemnation. Whereas Hamlet had been obsessed with his mother's depravity through the first three acts, after their interview he never again censures or criticizes her, nor does he even speak of her with sarcasm. It would appear therefore that he thinks he has succeeded in bringing her to repentance and an amendment of life.[113] The flowers Ophelia gives her in the fourth act suggest the same conclusion, for "herb of grace o' Sundays" was a recognized symbol for repentance (4.5.180). The individualized mirror of the closet scene apparently served its purpose.

That point about Gertrude is not entirely demonstrable, of course, but it is less important than Hamlet's own situation, because he has cleared his own conscience by acting responsibly toward his mother. We have already cited Ezekiel's prophetic admonition that if we make no effort "to warn the wicked man from his wicked ways to save his life, the same wicked man shall die in his iniquity, but his blood will I require at thine hand." In the very next verse, however, Ezekiel offers this assurance from the Lord: "Yet if thou warn the wicked, and he turn not from his wickedness, nor from his wicked way, he shall die in his iniquity; but thou hast delivered thy soul" (Ezek. 3:18-19). Regardless of whether Hamlet was or was not successful in appealing to his mother, he has quite clearly discharged his own moral obligation in her case.[114]

# FIVE

# The Deliberate Prince

### 1. The Prince and His Problems

THE PRINCE in *Hamlet* is so beset with problems that his characterization is not only colored but even shaped by the nature of the challenges he confronts. To understand the Prince and his play, we must recognize that Shakespeare has introduced energizing problems which would have elicited no consistent or consensus response from his Globe audiences. A simple comparison with the other major tragedies may be helpful here, for in them a consensus response was elicited at least on the basic launching actions of each: in *Lear*, it is clear that the old King should not have divided his kingdom and exiled his only faithful daughter; in *Othello* it is clear that the Moor should not have trusted Iago rather than Desdemona and Cassio; and in *Macbeth* it is clear that the title character should not have killed Duncan and usurped the throne. Each of those three plays contain important ambiguities, but Globe audiences would not have been seriously divided on those initial issues.

In *The Tragedy of Hamlet*, on the contrary, Shakespeare has so developed plot and characterization that his intended audiences would have been denied that kind of initial assurance. Hamlet's first problem is posed by the Ghost—whether it be "a spirit of health or goblin damned" (1.4.40). But the Ghost, as Shakespeare presents him, is not finally identified in the familiar terms of Elizabethan pneumatology. That mystery is given no consistent resolution either by the comments of the Prince or by the words of the play as a whole. Yet whatever may be its nature, the Ghost issues challenges Hamlet cannot ignore: as crown prince, he must rid the royal bed of "luxury and damned incest" and he must deal with an alleged murder which appears to have been the perfect crime, leaving no clue behind. Even after the mystery of that murder has been solved to the satisfaction of the protagonist and the audience, Hamlet must still resolve what he can and should do next. What is the proper response to a tyrant? And that question again was subject to radically different answers which keep the play in an atmosphere of uncertainty and suspense until the final act.[1]

As a dramatic form, the Elizabethan revenge tragedy itself exploited suspense, but generically this was suspense of an obvious and melodramatic kind. The principal interest in the revenge hero concerned the fascinating horrors he would devise in return for the horrors which had been inflicted on him, and also the Machiavellian intrigues and counter-intrigues employed along the way. That was the theatrical tradition Shakespeare inherited, and he gave his audience full measure of suspense in this kind. Had he done no more, however, his *Hamlet* would be no more noteworthy than the other blood and horror shows of this genre. But Shakespeare has given us suspense of three kinds: the suspense inherent in the tradition of the revenge play itself, plus the suspense of variations upon that form so that the audience was often kept wondering whether the Prince ever would achieve revenge at all, and (of far more lasting interest) the suspense of probing the ultimate mysteries of human nature and destiny. All of this is done with a poetic power and philosophical depth which goes beyond merely topical and time-bound concerns. But we understand it all better for ourselves even today if we can see it in the context of the concerns of the time and audiences for which it was created.[2]

Early Tudor doctrine forbade all resistance to established authority in England, even if such authority were to become tyrannical and abusive, and advocated instead a passive acceptance of the inherited status quo. Yet that apparently uncomplicated attitude still produced such contradictory responses to the same royal succession as we have seen in Cranmer and Hooker (see above, Chapter II). On the other hand, Elizabethan doctrine publicly recognized and approved quite different initiatives among foreign princes from those countenanced in England. At the opposite extreme from the passive resistance advocated for England by Anglicanism was the course followed by Scottish Calvinism. George Buchanan called for all-out opposition to a tyrant, and urged people of all ranks in society to initiate action and apply any degree of force necessary to overthrow and remove what was perceived to be unjust authority. In addition to these two positions was the course advocated and followed by the Huguenot magnates: a prince of the blood was obligated to act against a tyrant, but only he could initiate such action and only when certain of his ground and of his conscience. This summary somewhat simplifies the alternatives which late sixteenth-century audiences would have sensed as available to someone in Hamlet's situation, but should remind us of what has already been covered in greater detail. The Prince's choices were, in short, intensely disturbing and problematic.

In comparison, the options before the other characters in the play are relatively simple binary choices. Polonius has already decided when the play opens that his loyalty will go to the new king, not to the old one or to his son. Rosencrantz and Guildenstern upon their return to Denmark promptly elect to align themselves with Claudius, rather than with their old schoolfellow Hamlet. Ophelia chooses to trust her father and the King rather than the man she loves. Even Claudius, who is the most complex and interesting of these characters, debates what is essentially a straightforward either/or choice: to repent or not to repent. And Laertes forthrightly rejects his conscience in order to murder Hamlet with the poisoned rapier. In each of these cases, the chosen course is wrong, but also in each the choice is either utterly or comparatively uncomplicated.

The landscape for most of these binary choices is as clear and simple as that sketched by Ophelia early in the play. Laertes has just given her some worldly-wise advice about preserving virtue, and she replies:

> but, good my brother,
> Do not as some ungracious pastors do,
> Show me the steep and thorny way to heaven,
> Whiles like a puffed and reckless libertine
> Himself the primrose path of dalliance treads
> And recks not his own rede.           (1.3.46-51)

The advice is good, it is pointed, and it is as unoriginal as most good advice usually is. It is cast in the familiar imagery of the paysage moralisé. Scores of paintings and prints represented moral choice as the selection between two pathways, one moral but therefore difficult and challenging, and the other wicked but easy and apparently delightful. In a tradition going back to classical Greek myth-making, the "chooser" in these little dramas is often Hercules, but actually the person or persons addressed by the picture or story are expected to think of themselves as the choosers.[3]

A woodcut in Alexander Barclay's often-reprinted English version of *The Ship of Fools* (Fig. V.1) illustrates the choice as a dream vision presented to Hercules, shown asleep in the center of the print: on the left, "the primrose

FIG. V.I. "The Choice of Hercules," woodcut
from Alexander Barclay, *The Ship of Fools*,
c. 1570

path of dalliance" leads to a naked *Voluptas* who literally displays primroses, while on the right "the steep and thorny way" of virtue is symbolized by thorns and the figure of *Virtus* personified. Other pertinent visual treatments of the choice might be cited, for there were many, but for our purposes it is enough to recognize that Ophelia has verbalized one major and widely recognizable tradition of the paysage moralisé.[4] In the innocent and unsophisticated image she sketches, one must simply choose between Good and Evil as clear-cut options, unmistakably labeled.

Hamlet's choice is far more complex and difficult. Although strong and unequivocal moral judgments underlie both action and character in *Hamlet*—Denmark is an unweeded garden, the King is a murderer as well as a mildewed ear, the Queen is deeply stained by lust and incest, and the Prince is born to set it right—yet precisely what to do about all this is far from self-evident. Few in Shakespeare's theater would have been so naive as to know exactly what Hamlet should do, or how he should do it, but they would have been engrossed by his developing response to the challenge. The Prince was involved in what would in 1600 have seemed an extraordinarily dramatic and fascinating "case of conscience."

## II. The Ideal: Mars and Mercury

Hamlet's response is to deliberate, in the full sense of weighing and evaluating the alternatives before him, which in turn involves him in delay, and about that he repeatedly expresses guilt feelings which cannot be ignored.[5] Both the concern for delay and the guilt it engenders are important elements of his characterization, but as Maurice Charney warns us, we should not adopt a romantic notion that "hesitation about murdering your uncle is the product of a deliciously morbid introspection, so that Laertes is an altogether healthier and more natural young man than Hamlet," or some other similarly distorting interpretation.[6] Hamlet's inaction irritates him and may derivatively irritate us, but delay in a prince is not necessarily a bad thing. Giovanni Botero, an eminent sixteenth-century authority on practical statesmanship, advised that a ruler should avoid extremes but should be "deliberate and judicious, inclining rather to slowness than to haste because slowness has some affinity with prudence and haste with rashness."[7] Delay in a prince could nonetheless be exasperating. Thus Pope Gregory XIII complained of the "everlasting delays" of King Philip II, but it was the only fault he found in him. Here as elsewhere, the context is important and balance of view imperative.[8]

As a liberally educated Christian humanist, Hamlet approaches his problems by thinking about them, by attempting to reason them out, before taking action. The ideal of the nobleman or prince in Shakespeare's culture was a man of action who was also a man of thought, and Hamlet is to be understood primarily within that frame of reference. It is thus that Ophelia thinks of him, even after the traumatic encounter in which he angrily ordered her to a nunnery, when she is convinced that he is wildly insane, with his once "noble and most sovereign reason/ Like sweet bells, jangled, out of tune and harsh." Burdened with the pathos of contrasting past and present, she recalls the noble Prince she had formerly known in words which define the ideal Renaissance gentleman:

> The courtier's, soldier's, scholar's, eye, tongue, sword,
> Th' expectancy and rose of the fair state,
> The glass of fashion and the mould of form,
> Th' observed of all observers. . . .         (3.1.150-61)

Within the world of the play, the Prince appeared to be such an ideal figure not only to Ophelia, but also to those whom she calls "all observers," presumably including the common people whose devotion to him twice elicits comments from Claudius (4.3.4 and 4.7.18).[9]

Hamlet points to the same Renaissance ideal in his father's combination of the qualities of Mars and Mercury, representing the god of war and the messenger of the gods who symbolized the graces of reason and understanding. According to the son, the elder Hamlet displayed

> An eye like Mars, to threaten and command,
> A station like the herald Mercury
> New lighted on a heaven-kissing hill—
> A combination and a form indeed
> Where every god did seem to set his seal
> To give the world assurance of a man.         (3.4.58-63)

That uniting of Mars with Mercury is made visible in an English emblem published in *The Mirror of Majesty* two years after Shakespeare's death, where the appended verses define the meaning (Fig. V.2). The figure is divided neatly down the middle: one half is fully armed and holds spear and shield like Mars, representing victorious action, while the other half is clothed like Mercury, the patron of the arts. The engraving with its appended verses serves to illustrate the qualities which Hamlet saw combined in his father:

> What coward Stoic, nor blunt captain will
> Dislike this union, or will not labor still
> To reconcile the Arts and Victory?

The ideal was to unite the philosopher (here characterized by the emblematist as "coward") with the captain (characterized as "blunt") so as to achieve rational and proportioned action. The emblematic verses continue:

> Since in themselves Arts have this quality,
> To vanquish error's train: What other then

FIG. V.2. Mars-Mercury, from *The Mirror of Majesty*, 1618

Should love the Arts, if not a valiant man?
Or, how can he resolve to execute,
That hath not first learned to be resolute?

The "cowardice" of the philosopher and the "bluntness" of the soldier should so qualify and temper each other, so associate thought with action, as to achieve princely virtue. The same book which conjoins Mars and Mercury presents another pertinent emblematic figure, designed to similar effect (Fig. V.3). The appended verses make clear the significance of the picture, in which a whole man is composed of two equal halves, one half being a black-gowned scholar holding a book and the other a fully armored knight grasping shield and spear: "Forces united germinate their force," we are told, and "the noblest parts of wisdom" are defined as "clear wit, high courage" which move forward together at "a passant pace/ Till Wisdom seat you in your wished place."[10] Both emblems

Fɪɢ. ᴠ.3. Soldier-Scholar, from *The Mirror of Majesty*, 1618

visually objectify the Renaissance ideal to which Ophelia refers Hamlet, and to which Hamlet refers his father.

It is interesting that the Mars-Mercury emblem was dedicated to Shakespeare's sometime patron the Earl of Southampton, and the Scholar-Soldier emblem to Lord Carey of the family of the Lord Chamberlain who gave his title and patronage to Shakespeare's theatrical company, but I doubt that the emblematist was directly inspired by the words of Hamlet. It seems more probable that the artist and the dramatist were alike drawing upon the broad Renaissance tradition of mythological symbols. Some quarter of a century or more before Shakespeare wrote *Hamlet*, the soldier-poet George Gascoigne had chosen the motto *Tam Marti, quam Mercurio* to recall his combination of notable military service in the Dutch wars with an influential literary career.[11] A greater soldier and poet, Sir Philip Sidney, was posthumously described in 1596 as "England's Mars and Muse."[12] And again some forty years later George

Wither presented an emblem to the same effect, although without direct reference to Mars and Mercury: here we see the figure of a king, not divided into Mars and Mercury, but holding a sword in his right hand and an open book in his left, with an appended couplet explaining that "a prince's most ennobling parts/ Are skill in arms and love to arts."[13]

Both implicitly and explicitly, Hamlet's soliloquies record his efforts to achieve a similar resolution. In the play no one else is shown with that concern for synthesis, but among the dramatis personae two characters respectively embody the scholar and the captain, or the devotee of Mercury and the devotee of Mars—Horatio and Fortinbras. Neither of these seeks to broaden himself to include the "force" of the other, and both serve as foils to the Prince in his struggles to achieve thought without cowardice, and decisiveness without recklessness. Because he must combine the attributes of Mars with those of Mercury, Hamlet cannot model himself solely on Horatio or on Fortinbras, but must combine the best qualities of both.[14] His struggles to attain such a combination are fraught with much agony and some error. Most notably, the unalloyed rashness of the captain betrays him when he stabs through the arras in his mother's chamber to kill the wrong man, and thus sets in motion a train of events which will lead to his own destruction.

But more often he feels that he has to struggle against the timidity of the scholar, and he repeatedly indicates his fear of being dominated by fear, of allowing the rational reflection of the scholar to paralyze the resolution of the captain. At the conclusion of act two, he is acutely anxious lest his careful deliberation may be merely a mask for fear, and he cries out "Am I a coward?" (2.2.556). The specter of cowardice in Hamlet's thought is closely related to his ideal of combining the qualities of Mars and Mercury, but cowardice also figures prominently in the important sixteenth-century conception of cases of conscience, to which we shall shortly turn. What Hamlet says about cowardice in his soliloquies elicits all these resonances. In his great "to be or not to be" soliloquy he goes so far as to assert that

> Thus conscience does make cowards of us all,
> And thus the native hue of resolution
> Is sicklied o'er with the pale cast of thought,
> And enterprises of great pitch and moment
> With this regard their currents turn awry
> And lose the name of action.                    (3.1.83-88)

In the fourth act, as he reflects on the army of "such mass and charge" led by Fortinbras, he returns to the same necessary self-scrutiny:

> Now, whether it be
> Bestial oblivion, or some craven scruple
> Of thinking too precisely on th' event—
> A thought which, quartered, hath but one part wisdom
> And ever three parts coward—I do not know
> Why yet I live to say, "This thing's to do,"
> Sith I have cause, and will, and strength, and means
> To do 't.                                    (4.4.39-46)

His thoughts have still not opened the way to action, for he has not yet fully parsed the grammar of doubt and of decision.[15] It is only later, when he returns to Denmark in the final act, that his uncertainties have been resolved, and the conscience he has so painfully consulted is now fully committed to a single just and decisive action. That resolution is not clear to us until the last scene, and until the very end we follow the action with suspense and excitement.

Combining the "courtier's, soldier's, scholar's, eye, tongue, sword" requires a union of disparate and even conflicting qualities, easier to achieve in Ophelia's blank verse or in the emblematic engravings than in the harsh realities of life, particularly in the rotten state of Denmark. Reason is central here—what Horatio calls "the sovereignty of reason" and what Ophelia calls "that noble and most sovereign reason" (1.4.73 and 3.1.157). It involves avoidance of such forms of haste as characterize "a beast that wants discourse of reason" (1.2.150). And it requires balance, as opposed to what Hamlet describes as "the o'er growth of some complexion" or some habit "that too much o'er-leavens/ The form of plausive manners," and it opposes anything that tends toward "breaking down the pales and forts of reason" (1.4.27-30). The Prince recurs again and again to reason. Not only does reason distinguish man from the beasts, but it reflects the divine image:[16]

> What a piece of work is man, how noble in reason, how infinite in faculties, in form and moving how express and admirable, in action how like an angel, in apprehension how like a god: the beauty of the world, the paragon of animals! (2.2.300-4)

Even though he adds that "this quintessence of dust" delights him not, the

Prince maintains the highest regard for reason. It can be perverted, of course, as when "reason panders will" for the satisfaction of lust (3.4.89), but that is the abuse of reason, and in his last soliloquy he again affirms the primacy of this divine gift:

> Sure he that made us with such large discourse,
> Looking before and after, gave us not
> That capability and godlike reason
> To fust in us unused.                                   (4.4.36-39)

His own task, as he sees it, is to deploy the "excitements of my reason and my blood" (4.4.58) so that Mercury and Mars, the deliberation of the thinker and the rashness of the captain, may be united in virtuous and wise action. Whether he really wants to achieve such a union may be in doubt at points in the play, and whether he will be able to achieve it at other points—all of which contributes to Shakespeare's masterly development of suspense, both for character and for plot.

## III. Hamlet and Conscience

Hamlet brings to these problems a superb intellect, evidencing the finest mind of any literary character in our tradition. But he is pervasively aware of human sin and shortcomings, particularly in himself. This should not be surprising, because he was created in the same cultural milieu which produced the great words of the General Confession repeated at morning prayer in parish churches throughout Shakespeare's England: "We have left undone those things which we ought to have done; and we have done those things which we ought not to have done; and there is no health in us."[17] The Prince's repeated criticism of himself is also appropriate for one who was educated at Wittenberg, a university whose most influential professor, Martin Luther, had taught that "if the sins of which I am conscious in my heart were evident to the world, I should deserve to be hanged."[18] Hamlet brings that general understanding of human nature directly to bear upon himself when he says to Ophelia that

> I am myself indifferent honest, but yet I could accuse me of such
> things that it were better my mother had not borne me: I am very
> proud, revengeful, ambitious, with more offenses at my beck than I

have thoughts to put them in, imagination to give them shape, or time to act them in. What should such fellows as I do crawling between earth and heaven? We are arrant knaves all; believe none of us (3.1.122-29).

On an earlier occasion, Hamlet had said also to Polonius that "to be honest, as this world goes, is to be one man picked out of ten thousand" (2.2.178f.). As Martin Luther had declared, "if all those were hanged that are thieves and yet would not be called so, the world would soon be desolate, and there would not be either hangmen or gallows enough."[19] Such views are pervasive in Hamlet, who always recognizes not only the immensity and complexity of the challenge before him but also that all human responses (not excluding his own) are flawed, even when they represent the best that can be done. Thus when Polonius promises to use the players "according to their desert," Hamlet quickly retorts, "God's bodkin, man, much better! Use every man after his desert, and who shall scape whipping?" (2.2.515-17). That conception was ancient and widespread in Christianity, far antedating both Luther and the General Confession of the *Book of Common Prayer*, as we find in the assertion of St. Augustine that "if you shall be paid what you deserve, you must be punished."[20] Here we see a fundamental difference between the Stoic Brutus and Hamlet, as Camille Wells Slights puts it: "Like Brutus, he is challenged to accept responsibility for destroying a source of evil, but, unlike Brutus, he does not rely on the purity of his intentions to obliterate moral doubt."[21]

But however imperfect and flawed Hamlet feels himself to be, and however massive the problems confronting him, he never doubts that he was "born to set it right." Laertes had made a comment upon him early in the play which was addressed to a different problem, but it applies here as well.

> His greatness weighed, his will is not his own,
> For he himself is subject to his birth.
> He may not, as unvalued persons do,
> Carve for himself, for on his choice depends
> The safety and health of this whole state. . . . (1.3.17-21)

Viewed in the adjacent contexts of Shakespeare's play and of the world in which it was written, Hamlet's birth carried with it not only privilege but even more pertinently obligations he could not evade. To this he agrees in the fictive world of the play, and to this Shakespeare's theater audiences would also have agreed. There was no such agreement as to which precise and specific acts would discharge that obligation, but there was general agreement that the answers should be sought through the examination of conscience.

Conscience unites reason, moral obligation, and fear in ways which would have seemed self-evident to an audience in 1600. As a word, "conscience" is used more often in this play than in any of the other tragedies, and as a concept it is even more important. It is specifically employed on eight different occasions, twice each by Claudius and Laertes and four times by Hamlet. Hamlet's first use of the word refers to Claudius—"The play's the thing/ Wherein I'll catch the conscience of the king" (3.2.589-91)—where the reference is to the most primitive sense of conscience as an accuser and revealer of former misdeeds.

Hamlet's typical use of the word conscience is broader and more significant than that, and may be read as a conflation of Hellenistic and Roman with Christian influences extending from the Apostle Paul into Shakespeare's own time. Going well beyond a guilty feeling or revelation of guilt, it points forward as well as backward in time, and provides guidance to action. It is this conception we have inherited under the Latinate form "conscience." As St. Paul and later Christian writers held, conscience accused or excused acts (both past and future) as judged by rational thoughts (*ton logismon* in Paul's Greek), under God. It operated in the light of the natural law available to all men and even more fully in light of the special revelation of Scripture.[22] On this basis, all people, whether pagans or believers, are capable of appraising their thoughts and their actions in a moral as well as practical way.

In its broader sense, the word conscience is capable of extraordinarily complex use. The Latin etymology gives some clue both to its meanings and to its ambiguities: *Conscientia* means a "knowledge with." From the junction of *con* with *scientia* arises the potential of "conscience" both for rich expression and loose communication: knowledge (*scientia*) with respect to (*con*) whom or what? So understood, the word can refer to consciousness, without any specifically ethical reference, but as its usage developed the ethical sense predominated and the word applied to a means (or faculty, or standard, or judgment, or dictate) of ethical conduct. But still, ethical knowledge with what basis? Is it ethical knowledge with respect to God, or the Word of God, or the Natural Law, or the positive law and accepted morality of a culture, or is it the act and process of inner reflection by an individual who takes several or all of these criteria into consideration? All these possibilities exist in *Hamlet*, as in the usage of Shakespeare's time, but one other meaning must be excluded, even though popularly associated with conscience in later centuries: it was only in more recent times that people began to assume that the dictates of their consciences would automatically bubble up in their minds, that these were inevitably correct for them, and were to be followed without question and without fear. Few if any thinkers in the sixteenth century regarded conscience that simply.

Here it may be instructive to consider the appeals to conscience by the Catholic Thomas More and the Protestant Martin Luther. Risking their lives to uphold opposing religious convictions, both men appealed to conscience and took stands on the basis of conscience. When More refused to accept the religious supremacy asserted over the church in England by Henry VIII, his beloved daughter Margaret Roper sought to persuade him to reconsider, and in response he chided her for trying "to make him swear against his conscience, and so send him to the devil."[23] But we simply cannot take More to mean that in following his conscience he was acting upon a radical individualism (such as developed during and after the Romantic movement) and on the sole basis of his inner light. Such an interpretation would run counter to his whole insistence upon the Catholic tradition and its validity as a bulwark against individual whims and errors.

As for Martin Luther, when he took his stands on conscience at Augsburg and Worms, he was also jeopardizing his life, and he was surely not doing so on the basis of any glib assurance of his own automatic "inner" infallibility of perception. Luther refused to accord infallibility to any human authorities, all of which he regarded as fallible, from purely individual insights up to and including papal pronouncements—somewhat as More had refused to accept the elevation of an English king to comparable authority, as he saw it. More held to the authority of church tradition and Luther to the authority of scripture, but neither was a subjectivist in religion, and neither would raise conscience to the status of independent and unexamined authority. Luther in fact declared that his conscience was open to change and correction on the basis of evidence drawn from scripture. He was impelled to hold to his convictions so long as he was convinced, but "he saw no necessary connection between the truth of his theological position, and whatever subjective experience of certainty it might engender."[24] Thus Luther "based his refusal to recant on the principle that to act against conscience is wrong, that even the erroneous conscience is, until enlightened, a binding authority in the sense that it is not to be violated."[25] But he also held that it was to be scrupulously examined and evaluated. Operating on the same assumptions about conscience, More and Luther risked their lives (on opposite sides) for what they recognized might be wrong but what they were convinced was right.

For Catholic and Protestant alike, conscience was not autonomous, being subject to the judgment and will of God, whether conveyed through church tradition or scripture or both.[26] But when one had conscientiously reached a firm judgment, one should hold to it, even if it were wrong, so long as one was convinced. Suppose that conscience directed a person to commit an evil act, then as one Catholic scholar summarizes the choices, "a man is placed in the peculiar situation of sinning whether he obeys or disobeys; he sins by obeying his conscience, since he acts contrary to God's law; and he sins by disobeying the same conscience, for though the act he does contrary to conscience is a good act, he believes the act to be evil, and thus acts with a wrong intention."[27] Protestantism offered no less awesome prospects. Writing at about the same time that Shakespeare was engaged in producing *Hamlet*, William Perkins summed up the problem in three propositions: "(1) Whatsoever is done with a doubting conscience, is a sin. . . . (2) Whatsoever thing is done in or with an erroneous conscience, it is a sin. . . . (3) What is against conscience though it err and be deceived, it is a sin in the doer."[28] In view of such conceptions of conscience, we should not be surprised by Hamlet's conclusion that "conscience does make cowards of us all" (3.1.83).[29]

In that phrase, Hamlet's second explicit mention of the word, conscience goes beyond a focus upon ethics alone, although that is included, to embrace reasoned judgment and deliberation or weighing of alternative courses of action. William Perkins expressed the general tradition when he placed conscience among rational powers, and restricted it to reasonable creatures (beasts lack "true reason," or "discourse of reason").[30] As such, conscience was a power, faculty, or created quality "from [which] knowledge and judgment proceed as effects," either in evaluating actions already committed or in appraising actions which might be committed in the future.[31] Perkins saw a just conscience as founded in the will of God, whether expressed in the revelation of scripture or in the natural law of general creation, but the conclusions of conscience are not automatic, instinctual, or self-evident. Instead, conscience gives judgment "in or by a kind of reasoning or disputing." This he calls the operation of "practical syllogism," citing Romans 2:15 where St. Paul refers to "their reasoning accusing or excusing each other." All this Perkins calls "a kind of argumentation" which involves accusing and condemning, or excusing and absolving, or a mixture of all these.[32]

Perkins does not describe this "kind of reasoning or disputing" as pleasant, although it can produce great rewards. But in process of accusing and condemning actions, a person's conscience will especially "stir up" five different "passions and motions in the heart." One of these is shame, which Hamlet specifically cites when he reflects upon the activist Fortinbras and his unthinking army that "to my shame I see/ The imminent death of twenty thousand men," while in more general terms at another point he calls himself a rogue, a peasant slave, and a very drab (4.4.59f. and 2.2.534-73). Next is sadness or melancholy and Hamlet repeatedly refers to such effects in himself, whether as the recent loss of "all my mirth" or as "my weakness and my melancholy," or in other expressions (2.2.293 and 587).[33] The third attendant disorder is fear, and, as we have seen, Hamlet repeatedly accuses himself of being inactive because of fear. There is also "perturbation or disquietness of the whole man," which is close to "Hamlet's transformation—so call it,/ Sith nor th' exterior nor the inward man/ Resembles that it was" (2.2.5-7 and also 290-99). And there is desperation, the fifth concomitant of this conscience which, as Perkins wrote, "made Saul, Achitophel, and Judas to hang themselves . . . [and] makes many in these days to do the like," a temptation to suicide which Hamlet more than once considers.[34] All examiners of their consciences do not suffer from all these "motions of the heart," as Hamlet does, but Perkins regards them as effects especially stirred up by the conscience.

Now this is not to imply that Shakespeare's *Hamlet* is directly founded upon or indebted to William Perkins' theological treatment of cases of conscience, any more than it was said to be so related to the historical instances we have already traced of cases of conscience in practical statesmanship,[35] but these backgrounds should all help us to approach the play in terms familiar to Shakespeare and the original audiences for which he wrote. Again and again, Hamlet's soliloquies weigh the cases for or against action, and do so by a combination of references to right and justice, the operations of ethical awareness, and the deliberations of reason—which was exactly what St. Paul cited in Romans 2:14-15 as constituting the law within the heart of Gentiles as well as Jews and Christians.[36]

Paul's reference to classical culture serves to remind us of the depth and breadth of the tradition Shakespeare develops in *Hamlet*. For Horace, conscience could not only correct past faults but direct us away from future wrong: "Be this our wall of bronze, to have no guilt at heart, no wrongdoing to turn us pale."[37] Thus Seneca advised his inept pupil Nero to direct his conscience so as to avoid guilt and to preserve the pleasure of subjecting "a good conscience to a round of inspection."[38] To arrive at such a clear conscience by disciplined "rounds of inspection" was not easy. Quoting Epicurus' judgment that a knowledge of our guilt is the beginning of health, Seneca advises: "You must discover yourself in the wrong before you can reform yourself. . . . Therefore, as far as possible, prove yourself guilty, hunt up charges against yourself; play the part, first of accuser, then of judge, last of intercessor."[39]

Again and again we see Hamlet casting himself in just the role Seneca here advises for the good man—accusing himself of guilt, testing himself, hunting up charges against himself. "O what a rogue and peasant slave am I," he cries, going on to call himself "a dull and muddy-mettled rascal" (2.2.534-52), and again he declares "how all occasions do inform against me," as indeed he makes them do (2.2.534 and 552; and 4.4.32). Like Seneca, Martin Luther advised that a person should judge himself, but for Luther this was also associated with the Christian obligation to judge himself before judging others, as he said in his typically colorful and extravagant way: "Hans, take hold of your own nose, and reach into your own bosom. If you are looking for a villain on whom to pass judgment, you will find there the biggest villain on earth."[40]

The purpose of all this self-scrutiny was not negation but affirmation. If this process were properly followed, pagan and Christian ethicists agreed, it should lead one beyond self-accusation and condemnation "to excuse and absolve" oneself. The purpose was not to revel in the perpetual examination of one's conscience, but was to avoid occasions for an evil conscience and to establish oneself so as to act with a good conscience. In this way one might eventually claim Horace's promise of that "wall of bronze, to have no guilt at heart," or the promise of Perkins that "the excellency, goodness, and dignity of conscience, stands not in accusing, but in excusing."[41]

## iv. Early Deliberations

In the meanwhile Hamlet goes through the *agon* of the tragedy, that accusing and condemning of himself and that painful weighing of alternatives recommended by Seneca, Luther, and Perkins. In his first soliloquy he pours forth the disgust, even revulsion, he feels for the corruption of the Danish court, and especially his mother (1.2.129-59). This speech, following upon the initial court scene, serves to establish Hamlet in the eyes of the audience: it is the spiritual counterpart to the long mourning cloak in which he alone was enveloped amongst that gaudy and popinjay retinue, and it establishes the essential congruity between "that within which passeth show" and "the trappings and the suits of woe" he wears (1.2.85f.). It is as great as an expository or protatic soliloquy can be. As yet he has not heard the Ghost's denunciation of his uncle for regicide and he concentrates upon pouring out his nauseated aversion to the incest and the disgracing haste of the marriage. His reactions here would have seemed quite normal and responsible to the Globe audience. But he feels himself immobilized: "It is not nor it cannot come to good./ But break, my heart, for I must hold my tongue."

When Horatio and the guards bring him word of the Ghost he is eager for the encounter, but he must wait—the first of the waiting scenes Hamlet must endure until he can find his way—and so he can only say, "Would the night were come!/ Till then, sit still my soul. Foul deeds will rise,/ Though all the earth o'erwhelm them, to men's eyes" (1.2.256-58). The stroke of midnight signals the Ghost's arrival, and Hamlet shows no hesitation in following his lead offstage for he knows not what kind of encounter. Horatio and Marcellus as wise friends attempt to prevent him from going, because the Ghost may be luring him to death or damnation or both, but the Prince will not be restrained: "Unhand me, gentleman./ By heaven, I'll make a ghost of him that lets me" (1.4.84f.). Here the audience gains its first insight into Hamlet's faith and fortitude—the faith because he is confident at this point that the devil cannot harm his soul, and fortitude because he demonstrates in action as well as words that "I do not set my life at a pin's fee" (1.4.64-67). The evaluation of his life remains constant, but he will come to recognize that the Ghost is indeed able to place his soul in jeopardy.

The Ghost's overtures to Hamlet contain no such melodrama as tempting him "to the dreadful summit of the cliff," to topple headlong down. On the contrary, the Ghost speaks largely of ethical concerns, of crime in high places, of violence unpunished, and of sexual corruption. He calls upon Hamlet to seek revenge of the kind which launches other revenge tragedies, but he surrounds that call with high moral outrage. In effect, he delegates Hamlet to reform the state. If this be a temptation of the devil, it is the most subtle of such temptations, the seduction to fall through a wrong devotion to virtue— the kind of strategy the devil reserves for idealistic spirits. When Hamlet stands with sword drawn over the praying Claudius in act three, he displays exactly the kind of self-righteousness which such a demonic strategy might be designed to achieve. And if the Ghost is not a devil, its moral challenges still burden Hamlet with Herculean tasks. The issues are so imperative that Hamlet determines to "wipe away all trivial fond records" to be replaced by "thy commandment all alone." This determination is expressed in the soliloquy delivered directly after the departure of the Ghost. The Prince here makes a commitment similar to that which the parents of King Henry Stewart, assassinated consort of Mary Queen of Scots, sought from their grandson, the future King James I: "that he shut not out of his memory the recent atrocious murder of the king his father, until God should avenge it through him."[42] To a comparable "parental" mandate, Hamlet responds that he will exclude all but the Ghost's story "from the table of my memory" (1.5.92-112).

When he is rejoined by Horatio and Marcellus, he continues in a high state of nervous agitation. With "wild and whirling words" he describes the apparition as "an honest ghost," but he also addresses it as "old mole." With the time out of joint, Hamlet commits himself to "set it right." Although he does not yet perceive how massive his task will be, he provides some protective coloring for himself by planning "to put an antic disposition on." On the basis of that announcement and of the words he speaks to his mother two acts later, the audience is told that "how strange or odd some'er I bear myself," nonetheless "I essentially am not in madness,/ But mad in craft" (1.5.170-72 and 3.4.188f.). So understood, Hamlet's "antic disposition" implies not only the fantastic and bizarre behavior we see the Prince assume, but also the sense of "disguised" which Robert Cawdrey associated with the word "antic" in the section devoted to hard and unusual English words in his 1604 *Table Alphabetical of English Words*.[43]

Such feigning of madness to achieve some desired effect was so ancient and widespread that in literary criticism there is even a special word—morology—to cover it.[44] The Roman Emperor Claudius assumed the pose of foolishness as a protection before his accession to the purple, thus following the first Brutus who played the fool to safeguard himself from the Tarquins before he overthrew their dynasty and established the Roman Republic. In the Old Testament, after King Saul had driven David into exile, this future king had to take refuge among his enemies the Philistines where he acted the madman to escape from their vindictive hatred.[45] And in the development of the Hamlet legend prior to Shakespeare, the Prince is repeatedly said to have assumed the disguise of madness as a protection. In earlier times than our own, madness was invested with an almost religious aura, deserving the special protection of gods and men. It thus serves Hamlet as a valuable camouflage. How convinced the King and Danish court are of his madness may be uncertain—like so much else in the play—but they are sufficiently confused to give Hamlet valuable time to maneuver. At points the King and Polonius will refer to Hamlet as though they were certain of his madness (2.2.92-95 and 3.1.4), while at other times they make comments such as Polonius' "though this be madness, yet there is method in 't," and the King's "what he spake, though it lack'd form a little,/ Was not like madness" (2.2.203f., and 3.1.163f.). Even Guildenstern can qualify by calling it "a crafty madness" (3.1.8). Ophelia's description of his deranged and unkempt appearance when he came to visit her represents this antic disposition in its most extreme form, far more blatant than any which Hamlet ever assumes on stage.

Melancholy was another matter. Hamlet's "customary suits of solemn black" would have given visible expression to this temperament through the contemporary code of dress, as we have already seen.[46] As a seriousness of temperament it was often characteristic of noble minds not only among scholars and artists, but among soldiers and statesmen as well. It was easy to overplay and thefore easy to parody, as we may recall from Shakespeare's amusing treatment of the melancholy Jaques in *As You Like It*. At the University of Wittenberg in the latter half of the sixteenth century, a student skit was enacted in Latin which satirized the fashionable pose of learned melancholy, along with other forms of "cony-hood," all translated into English and published in London in 1595:

That cony-hood which proceeds of melancholy is, when in feastings appointed for merriment, this kind of cony-man sits like *Mopsus* or *Corydon*, blockish, never laughing, never speaking, but so bearishly as if he would devour all the company, which he doth to this end, that the guests might mutter how this his deep melancholy argueth great learning in him and an intendment to most weighty affairs and heavenly speculations.[47]

That parodic tone would be far more appropriate to the melancholy Jaques than to the melancholy Dane. There were and still are many perils to acting on stage the part of Prince Hamlet, but we can be confident that when Burbage introduced the role, he incorporated appropriate humor in it without exposing it to parodic laughter.[48]

The first two acts of the play have provided Hamlet with enough challenges to keep his serious mind seriously occupied, and in the soliloquy which closes act two, we see the nature of his reflections (2.2.533-91). As the dialogue later suggests, we are at this point two months removed from the Ghost's first visit.[49] This two months' hiatus in the action is the only substantial amount of time available to Hamlet to act against the King, but he does not act. Now he lacerates himself for being sluggish, inert, even supine. Here for the first time the issue of cowardice is introduced, and he declares that "I am pigeon-livered and lack gall." On the one hand he says that he is "prompted to my revenge by heaven and hell" and so he feels that he should be able to respond, but on the other hand his problem arises from that very double prompting: the spirit "may be a devil . . . [who] Abuses me to damn me." He thus projects the play-within-the-play to test the King's guilt.

That soliloquy generates high tension and suspense. Hamlet begins by castigating himself for inaction, leveling charge after charge at himself for some forty lines. He is caught between the obligation to act and the concomitant obligation to avoid precipitous action. It was axiomatic in 1600 that whereas "prudence is a virtue . . . overscrupulousness [is] a vice."[50] On the basis of those underlying and pervasive assumptions, Hamlet then concludes the soliloquy by explaining why he should not, indeed cannot, act until he has tested the story of a potentially demonic ghost. Although he was suspicious of his uncle's guilt even from the beginning, having had in his "prophetic soul" a sense of foreboding even before he first encounters the Ghost, he also knows that he cannot act until he is certain of the fact of regicide. Thus this soliloquy not only concludes the first two acts which launched and developed the plot, but also projects us forward to the climactic third act. As elsewhere in Shakespeare, this central act contains not only the turning-point or -points but a turning radius or turning area where various actions combine to effect the future development of the play.[51]

## v. To Be or Not To Be

When Hamlet returns to the stage early in the third act, he at once launches into a soliloquy which is almost certainly the most famous and perhaps the most discussed passage in Shakespeare (3.1.56-88). He begins by posing the most basic of all antitheses: "To be or not to be." That is the question indeed, and it is a broader question than might at first appear, because it epitomizes a logical approach to discussing any issue. Thus Abraham Fraunce, in his popular manual *The Lawyer's Logic* of 1588, wrote of "a disposition of one argument with another, whereby we judge a thing to be or not to be."[52] In 1596, William Perkins made a functional definition of intelligence that it "simply conceives a thing to be or not to be."[53] Hamlet's question "to be or not to be" was assigned under a Latin version to students at the University of Edinburgh in 1607, 1612 and 1615, and presumably in other years as well.[54] What Hamlet poses thus appears to have been a fairly standard formula for appraising alternate possibilities, at least among the better-educated of the time.[55] Beginning with a posing of existence against non-existence, he immediately shifts to a weighing of action against inaction. He later recurs to the desirability of death, which he still later repudiates because of "the dread of something after death" as a punishment for willful suicide. But throughout he shifts back and forth between considerations of whether existence or non-existence is to be preferred, and whether action or inaction is better. In terms of Hamlet's analysis, the two issues are closely related, perhaps indissolubly so.[56]

His first extensive analysis in this soliloquy weighs action against inaction: "whether 'tis nobler in the mind to suffer/ The slings and arrows of outrageous fortune/ Or to take arms against a sea of troubles/ And by opposing end them." That question could not have been raised in 1600 as though in some hermetically sealed philosophical isolation, because it was fundamental and divisive throughout western Europe in the latter third of the sixteenth century. As we have already seen, prominent Jesuits recommended violent action when necessary to achieve virtuous ends, and prominent Calvinists in France, Holland, and Scotland not only advocated but actually did "take arms against a sea of troubles," and by opposing did in some sense end them, overturning regimes and replacing monarchs by their own combination of activism and faith. On the other hand there was the opposite position, represented by the Elizabethan *Homilies* and by many Anglican spokesmen, that it was "nobler in mind to suffer" than to "take arms." The official Tudor view had held, at least until the appearance of Bishop Bilson's *True Difference* in 1585, that any taking arms to change "the law's delay,/ The insolence of office" and all the other abuses, real or imagined, would merely lead to other and far worse ills, both in this world and in the hereafter. The deliberation or weighing of these alternative views had to be handled with some tact on the London stage in 1600, but Shakespeare has managed it in a generalized context which the authorities would not find seditious, but which intelligent theatergoers would find exciting. Hamlet unequivocally poses the question, equivocally appraises the major responses, and reaches no conclusion. We have here what is surely the greatest aporia (in the sense of a debate about an issue and weighing of its sides) in Shakespeare. The terms of its proposal would have intrigued Elizabethan audiences, and its inconclusiveness increases the suspense of the play.

After first debating the issue of passivity and action, Hamlet's mind returns to the underlying issue of life and death. Suicide would release one from having to decide upon whether and how to act, because death would end all possibility of action and of suffering through action—but not the eventual possibility of passive suffering. Because the Everlasting has "fixed/ His canon 'gainst self-slaughter," as Hamlet recognized in his first soliloquy, there is still the fear of bad dreams, so that suicide offers no sure and attractive release. Recognizing that retribution may be expected by those who commit murder upon themselves, Hamlet deduces that "conscience does make cowards of us all." Immediately thereafter, however, the Prince's focus shifts from the life/death alternative back to the active/passive alternative, or perhaps the two merge into a single question again. At all events, the conscience which forestalls the particular action of suicide broadens out to forestall unspecified "enterprises of great pitch and moment" and so *all* "lose the name of action."

The immense popularity of this soliloquy lies in the brilliance of its poetic arguments and counterarguments, but theatrically its ambiguity is equally significant. Here the Latin meanings of certain root words are pertinent: *ambigo* means not only to be uncertain, but also to argue or debate about something, to consider arguments for and against; *ambiguitas* means a double sense or equivocalness; *ambiguus* means not only uncertain and doubtful but a "going about," showing equal predilections to all sides.[57] All these senses are applicable to the "to be or not to be" soliloquy. But its ultimate importance to the tragedy arises just as much from the exciting clash of ideas stunningly expressed as from the increase of an audience's suspense and uncertainty. Act two had closed with signals pointing forward to the play-within-a-play as a catalyst for resolving uncertainty about the alleged murder of Hamlet's father. In this first soliloquy of act three, the audience sees that the Prince is undecided about even more basic matters than his uncle's guilt.

Shakespeare has made him analyze his indecisions in much the same way that John Donne was doing at about the same time in his anguished quest for assurance. Recognizing that truth and falsehood often appear to be "near twins," Donne affirmed the need to "doubt wisely."

> On a huge hill,
> Cragged and steep, Truth stands, and he that will
> Reach her, about must and about must go,
> And what the hill's suddenness resists, win so.
> Yet strive so that before age, death's twilight,
> Thy soul rest. . . .

As yet Hamlet's soul is nowhere near to rest, for he still must go about it and about. In his perplexity he doubts even the value of doubting, but he continues the debate within himself in a similar spirit to that which Donne showed:

> in strange way
> To stand inquiring right is not to stray;
> To sleep, or run wrong, is.[58]

That Hamlet was undecided in this way would not have inclined the Globe audience to dismiss him either as constitutionally weak or chronically indecisive. It was too early in the drama to reveal Hamlet's final resolution: to do so would destroy suspense as well as credibility. What counts here is to show the protagonist involved in great issues and attempting to solve them in terms of great patterns. We have already dealt considerably with the theory and practice of violent action among the Huguenot magnates and it will now be appropriate to examine a Huguenot tract written about the inner uncertainties of a Biblical heroine as to whether or not she should kill a tyrant. In 1579, Seigneur du Bartas wrote a poem intended to furnish a Biblical model for the inner debates of French Protestant nobles and princes. In pedestrian verses, the Israelite heroine Judith soliloquizes an aporia as to whether she should or should not assassinate Holofernes, the tyrannical oppressor of her people:

Then said she, "Judith, now is time, go to it,
And save thy people": "Nay, I will not do it."
"I will," "will not". . . .

. . . .

"Alas, are they not murderers slays their prince?"
"This tyrant is no prince of my province."

Poetically, this is the poorest kind of stuff, but it makes its point. Judith, universally interpreted as a virtuous tyrannicide, is shown struggling, woodenly but impressively, between action and inaction, until she resolves to act in reliance upon the providence of God:

"Alas, my heart is weak for such a deed";
"Th'are strong enough whom God doth strength at need."[59]

Hamlet's soliloquy at this point shows him at a considerable remove from that resolution, but it also shows him in the throes of such an examination of his own conscience.

There is another case of conscience from the late years of the sixteenth century which should be cited in connection with Hamlet's melancholy debates over his own action and inaction in the face of Claudius' continuing threat to him and to his kingdom. This is the case of Queen Elizabeth I, as she sat in gloomy isolation and wavered back and forth over what to do about Mary Stuart. The deposed Scottish queen, although a captive in England, proved a continuing threat to Elizabeth's reign and to the peace and even the independence of England. Mary was the heir presumptive to Elizabeth's throne, and many international leaders of Catholicism (including Philip II of Spain) maintained that her title was in fact better than Elizabeth's.[60] She was thus a magnet attracting every would-be conspiracy, a center of allegiance for all those who wished to assassinate or depose the English queen. And there can be little or no doubt that Mary actively encouraged many such plots against her cousin and rival, keeping England in a continuing state of anxiety and crisis for some twenty years.

Elizabeth's closest advisers urged her to destroy this enemy, before she herself should be destroyed, and there was surely provocation enough. But Elizabeth temporized year after year, recognizing the strength of the arguments and utterly distrustful of Mary, but also fearful of the consequences of striking at another crowned (even though deposed) monarch. To kill Mary would dispose of certain ills, but would invite (to apply the words of Hamlet) "others that we know not of," unknown ills which could apply both in this world and in the world to come.[61] For Elizabeth, as for Hamlet, such a problem indeed "puzzles the will," and it may be said of her too that "the native hue of resolution" was "sicklied o'er with the pale cast of thought."

Then came the final provocation of the Babington Plot in 1586. Sir Anthony Babington and other recusant conspirators projected a Catholic uprising to be assisted by a foreign invasion, culminating in the murder of Queen Elizabeth, and the placing of Mary on the throne. Mary wrote an explicit approval of the plot, including the assassination of Elizabeth, and that letter was intercepted by Walsingham, the chief of Elizabeth's intelligence service. The evidence, now documentary and as incontrovertible as that later discovered by Hamlet in Claudius' letter, was used by Walsingham and others to urge upon Elizabeth the imperative necessity of executing Mary. The Parliament "with one voice" affirmed that "the Queen's safety could not be secured as long as the Queen of Scots lived." Again Elizabeth declared her reluctance to kill Mary, asserting that she was "in greater conflict with myself than ever in all my life" and desired that "some other means" might be found out to preserve her own safety and the security of the nation. Seeing both sides of the issue, she requested Parliament to "excuse my doubtfulness, and take in good part my answer answerless."[62]

William Camden, the principal Elizabethan historian of her reign, described the Queen's mind as "wavering and perplexed," and declared that "being naturally slow in her resolutions, [she] began to weigh in her mind whether it were better to put [Mary] to death or to spare her."[63] She would resolve to kill Mary, and "the next day, while fear dreaded even her own designs, her mind changed." Rather like Hamlet, she agonized over every contending doubt, arguing pro and con. As Hamlet admitted that he had of late "lost all my mirth, foregone all custom of exercises" (2.2.293f.), so it was said of Elizabeth that the liveliness and enjoyment of company she had typically displayed were no longer evident, but were replaced by melancholy and disquiet. Camden's description is pertinent:

> Amongst these pensive and perplexed thoughts, which troubled and staggered the Queen in such sort that she gave herself over to solitariness, sat many times melancholy and silent, and often sighing muttered to herself, *Aut fer, aut feri*, that is either bear strokes or strike, and out of I know not what emblem, *Ne feriare, feri*, that is, Strike lest thou be smitten.[64]

The point is not that Shakespeare modeled his fictive Prince upon his historical queen, which I do not for one moment believe he did, but is rather that the decision laid upon Hamlet was no more perplexing to him than a similar decision was to the ablest ruler in the Europe of Shakespeare's time. It might be necessary and one's moral duty to strike down a crowned sovereign, but it was not morally easy, even when one already wore a crown oneself. A question such as Elizabeth's "*aut fer, aut feri*" or Hamlet's "To be or not to be" inevitably "puzzles the will."

## VI. To Drink Hot Blood

The Mousetrap play in the scene following this soliloquy resolves the question of Claudius' guilt, but leaves unsettled the even more basic questions which Hamlet debates as to what he can and should do if the King is in fact a regicide. The playlet thus introduces one new certainty without altering the other uncertainty, and that combination of certainty and uncertainty brings us just within the turning radius of the tragedy. Aristotle had approved such a change or peripety in the central episodes of a drama, and we see it operating here. One suspense (the mystery of the old king's death) is superseded, and another suspense (for which we have already been prepared by Hamlet's inner debates) now occupies the foreground of our attention; the continuing question of what if anything the Prince will do takes on a new urgency. The soliloquy (3.2.373-84) delivered between the Mousetrap play and the discovery of Claudius at prayer suggests that Hamlet may now have abandoned the difficult task of balancing Mars and Mercury, and have accepted wholeheartedly the singleminded, stereotyped response of the bloody avenger. To put it differently, the Prince's words and actions now open the possibility that for the remainder of the play we may be following a character cut to fit the flat mold of a simple revenge protagonist, who pursues blood without limit and without qualm.

But until the end of the play every presumption is qualified by another, and here the qualification comes in Hamlet's attitude toward his mother. Before he goes to meet her, he excludes "the soul of Nero" from his own "firm bosom," and declares "Let me be cruel, not unnatural;/ I will speak daggers to her, but use none." The restriction is important, but even so it introduces the subject of lethal daggers and of a mad Nero killing his own mother, so that it evokes visions of the very behavior which it apparently rejects, thus leaving the audience in a double suspense. The rest of the soliloquy is enough to curdle the blood:

> 'Tis now the very witching time of night,
> When churchyards yawn, and hell itself breathes out
> Contagion to this world.

The focus narrows here when compared to Hamlet's first encounter with the Ghost and first question as to whether he brings with him "airs from heaven or blasts from hell," whether his intents are "wicked or charitable" (1.4.41f.). Now the Prince refers only to the dark contagions of hell and witchcraft. We could find no apter motto for the one-sided avenger than Hamlet's "Now could I drink hot blood." Those six short words provoke a chilling *frisson*.

The next scene shows Claudius kneeling in prayer, when the Prince unexpectedly enters, draws his sword and stands above him, poised and ready to strike. That tableau suggests a personified Vengeance prepared to kill an evil-doer in retribution for his crime.[65] When William Perkins envisioned a wicked man like Claudius at the very height of glory and power, controlling kingdoms and riches, he added: "but withal suppose one standing by, with a naked sword to cut his throat, or a wild beast ready ever and anon to pull him in pieces: now, what can we say of this man's estate, but that all his happiness is nothing but woe and misery?"[66] Hamlet here stands like a tableau figure, cast to represent such an inhuman nemesis, awaiting the moment to strike.[67]

A stereotyped revenger—and Hamlet's most recent soliloquy makes him sound like just that—might have killed Claudius here without compunction. Shakespeare tantalizes his audience with the possibility that Hamlet will implacably slice Claudius into bits, just as the "baked and impasted" Pyrrhus had done with helpless old Priam in the play for which Hamlet had earlier expressed such great admiration (2.2.440-506). But although Pyrrhus, after a moment of frozen indecision, again and again slashes away at his victim, Hamlet does not. If Hamlet had been allowed to re-enact Pyrrhus here, Shakespeare would thereby have killed not only his villain but also his hero and his play: the fascinating complexity of Hamlet's characterization would have been negated, and the Prince reduced to a simple thug. And the play would have ended halfway through.[68]

But if Shakespeare cannot allow Hamlet to become a simple-minded as-sassin here, neither can he allow him to sheath his sword and simply walk away—which would be a dreadful, even ludicrous, anticlimax. In terms both of plot development and of characterization, Hamlet must respond powerfully, and so we have the "more horrid hent" of the soliloquy delivered over the praying Claudius (3.3.73-96). And horrid enough it surely is, yet with the intellectual sophistication we would expect not from a thug but only from a Prince Hamlet or a Prince Lucifer. Like that first among angels who sought to assume the prerogatives of God and so became the fiendish (but clever) Satan, he here rejoices in the prospect of entrapping his victim to the endless tortures of hell. The tone of the soliloquy is appropriate to one who, only a short while before, had rejoiced that "hell itself breathes out/ Contagion to this world" (3.2.374f.). He envisions a revenge even more revolting than the drinking of hot blood. Nothing, Hamlet declares, can now satisfy him short of the ultimate perdition of Claudius—"that his heels may kick at heaven,/ And that his soul may be as damned and black/ As hell, whereto it goes." In the ultimate so-phistication of horror, Hamlet here at once usurps and blasphemes both the judgment of God and the hope of man.[69]

To do the right deed for the wrong reason is the greatest treason, as T. S. Eliot has reminded our time.[70] In this soliloquy Hamlet combines a right af-firmation (he will act against Claudius) with the worst of reasons. The depravity of the Prince at this point would have seemed evident from every point of view in 1600. Thus Thomas Aquinas had written that "in the matter of vengeance, we must consider the mind of the avenger. For if his intention is directed chiefly to the evil of the person on whom he takes vengeance and rests there, then his vengeance is altogether unlawful." And Thomas adds: "nor is it an excuse that he intends the evil of [i.e., to] one who has unjustly inflicted evil on him, . . .

for a man may not sin against another just because the latter has already sinned against him since this is to be overcome by evil."[71]

On that point Thomas Aquinas expresses the basic Christian understanding, operative in the Protestant as in the Catholic conscience, and presumably binding upon the unbeliever as well. John Calvin writes of the magistrate's obligation to act against evil, but he speaks with equal force of any who "broil with unappeasable rigor" (as Hamlet does here) against those they punish, and he quotes Augustine to the same effect: "But all magistrates ought here to take great heed that . . . if they must punish let them not be borne away with a headlong angriness, let them not be violently carried with hatred, let them not broil with unappeasable rigor, yea let them (as Augustine saith) pity common nature in him in whom they punish his private fault."[72] In the seventeenth century, Sir Thomas Browne would warn similarly against going beyond the *lex talionis*, "requiring too often a Head for a Tooth."[73] William Tyndale had earlier treated just retribution with his usual directness: For him who is "a ruler thereto appointed," there was a duty to act against evil doers; "them smite, and upon them draw thy sword, and put it not up until thou hast done thine office; yet without hate to the person," and "not of malice."[74] Shakespeare's contemporary William Perkins summed up these teachings in the memorable distinction between the sinner and the sin: "We must put a difference between the *person* and the *offense* or sin of that person. The sin of the person is the proper object of anger, and not the person. . . ."—a vital distinction which Hamlet at this point totally ignores.[75]

It is quite possible for the avenger (even the avenger of a great crime) to act in such a way that he becomes worse than the criminal upon whom he brings retribution, as all acknowledged in 1600. Erasmus warned those who execute justice upon a wicked man to "beware, lest in avenging his lewdness we become lewder ourselves."[76] At this point in the play, Shakespeare renders Hamlet less sympathetic than Claudius. While Claudius struggles on his knees to release himself from his admittedly great guilt, Hamlet towers arrogantly above him in his freshly chosen role as judgmental gatekeeper of hell. We wonder for a time whether Shakespeare may be creating a great reversal in which hero and villain will exchange roles in the play.[77] Stunning in its theatricality, this reversal is itself later reversed, but it provides suspense by the very fact of interjecting a false or temporary peripety in the characterization of the Prince. Ophelia's earlier judgment now comes closest to being true, although not in the sense of her limited vision, that "a noble mind is here o'erthrown" (3.1.150).

The venomous fury Hamlet vented over the kneeling Claudius has prepared the audience for sudden violence at the next opportunity. That moment comes early in the following scene when an enraged Hamlet thrusts through the arras to kill one whom he imagines to be the King, only to find that it is that old busybody Polonius. In this action there is no sign of deliberate control by a judicious mind: Mars has usurped, even apparently obliterated, Mercury. An intensely passionate man, the Prince usually keeps his passion under some measure of control and he genuinely admires the man who "is not passion's slave," but here he unreservedly allows himself to become the slave of passion (3.2.69). In a popular work published in the year of *Hamlet*'s appearance, John Downame wrote that anger "perverteth judgment, overthroweth counsel, and puteth out the eyes of reason, making it the slave of passion, fit to execute those works of darkness in which rage employeth it."[78] Downame's words are apposite: at this juncture the eye of reason—"looking before and after"—has been put out in the Prince, and he is left with responsibility for the murder of a man whom he had ridiculed but not intended to kill, and whose most blatant offenses are insensitivity, officiousness, and a meddlesome stupidity—scarcely capital crimes.

From having been the agent of nemesis, seeking to bring deserved retribution to another, Hamlet now suddenly becomes himself the prey of nemesis, upon whom just retribution is also due. He not only regrets his rash action, but he goes beyond regret to make an explicit repentance: "For this same lord,/ I do repent"—which contrasts sharply with his uncle's admission that he "cannot repent" (3.4.173f. and 3.3.66). Hamlet declares that he "will answer well/ The death I gave him," and he is prepared to suffer the consequences (3.4.177f.). That blindly passionate rapier thrust into an unseen body behind the arras determines much of the remainder of the play: Hamlet's dispatch to England (and presumably to instant execution) becomes irreversible; Ophelia goes mad; Laertes returns and allies himself with the King against the Prince. Although Hamlet cannot tell exactly what lies ahead, he knows full well that "Thus bad begins, and worse remains behind" (3.4.180).[79]

In the second half of the third act we thus have a series of related peripeties which together constitute the turning radius upon which the play pivots. The play-within-the-play provides the evidence Hamlet requires to settle any lin-

gering doubts that his uncle is a regicide, and Claudius' soliloquy at prayer
further convinces the audience of his guilt. After the playlet Shakespeare introduces two soliloquies by the Prince which suggest that he has now adopted
the role of the total and stereotyped avenger. His thirst for hot blood carries
him beyond any humane concern for proper justice and into the usurpation of
divine prerogative so that like Lucifer he seeks the everlasting torture of Claudius in hell. Then follows the "rash and bloody deed" of killing Polonius, with
which counterforces of nemesis are triggered upon Hamlet himself. Thus unexpected lines of action are extrapolated, and old suspense is reinforced with
new, as we move into the fourth act.

The counteraction against Hamlet is launched at the very beginning of the
fourth act when the King learns that Hamlet has killed Polonius, and draws
the obvious inference: "It had been so with us, had we been there" (4.1.13).
Fully aware that he cannot be safe so long as Hamlet is at large, he gives orders
to secure Hamlet's immediate arrest. Rosencrantz and Guildenstern are put in
charge of a search party or posse to find and secure the Prince: "Friends both,
go join you with some further aid . . . [and] seek him out" (4.1.33-36). The
following stage directions (4.2.3 and 4.3.11) show their reappearance with
"others" and with "all the rest," presumably referring in each of these instances
to Claudius' mercenary guard of Switzers. When Hamlet is brought before the
King, he is no longer a free man, but as Rosencrantz is careful to tell the King,
he is "guarded" (4.3.14), thus making explicit the neutralization of the Prince.
Surrounded as Hamlet is by those armed Swiss guards, the King is safe at least
for the time being.[80] All that the Prince can do at this point is to taunt his
adversary with the verbal banter at which he is unmatched, but this does not
imply that he is capable of nothing more than verbal assault. Claudius patently
was under no such delusion when he declared that "we will fetters put upon
this fear," a plan which Rosencrantz, Guildenstern and the Switzers have put
into effect for him: the Prince cannot now strike down the King (3.3.25).

Throughout the play, Hamlet's opportunities to kill the King have been
severely limited by Shakespeare's presentation of the action. Until he can find
convincing confirmation of the murder, Hamlet cannot take action, for reasons
he himself made clear in the soliloquy spoken at the end of act two; furthermore,
the plan to use a play to reveal the King's guilt could not take shape until the
arrival of the players. After their arrival, Hamlet schedules the performance at
the earliest possible time—"tomorrow night" (2.2.521 and 525). Within some

ten minutes of stage time after that performance has provided the needed evidence, Hamlet first refuses to kill the King at prayer, and then almost immediately thereafter strikes through the arras of his mother's chamber to give him the fatal blow. His conviction that he has killed the King is made explicit in the words he speaks over the dead Polonius, "I took thee for thy better" (3.4.33). Guarded by the Switzers until his speedy dispatch to England, his next opportunity does not appear until the fifth act, when he returns on the morning of Ophelia's funeral. He dispatches Claudius that afternoon.[81]

Of course we do not know (because Shakespeare does not choose to show us) what Hamlet would do in his encounter with the King just before he is shipped to England if he were not surrounded by that platoon of armed guards—and that uncertainty contributes to the suspense of what he will do if he is ever again free to act, but whether he ever will be so is another element of suspense. And we must surely be unsure whether Hamlet himself yet knows. The Luciferian stance he adopted after the Mousetrap play does not suit him for long, nor does the prospect of drinking hot blood hold a lasting appeal for him. The peripety which showed him moving in the direction of such a stereotype was not permanent. Shakespeare makes this clear just before the Prince boards ship for England, as he analyzes and appraises the pomp-and-circumstance display of that "rash captain" and demi-Mars, Fortinbras. In this soliloquy, his last, Hamlet is still the deliberative prince, still weighing the available alternatives.

## VII. The Last Soliloquy: Fortitude and Vanity

If we were able to find among our acquaintances today a living incarnation of Shakespeare's Hamlet, I suspect that he would prefer a university professorship at Wittenberg to the throne of Denmark,[82] but then even Shakespeare might not have been able to write the world's most exciting tragedy on the life of an academic don, and at all events that choice is not made available to the Prince in this play. Nor would it have been available to any actual prince known to the Globe audience in 1600, for a prince was born to act and to lead: as Laertes said, "on his choice depends/ The safety and health of this whole state" (1.3.20f.). The extent to which Hamlet succeeds in fulfilling his role has been much debated by critics, but in the judgment of Fortinbras he was a soldier who deserved the rites of war and who "was likely, had he been put on,/ To have proved most royal" (5.2.386f.).

Hamlet's attitude toward Fortinbras, on the other hand, is more complex. He is one of the two living characters in the play who provide Hamlet with possible models upon which he most extensively comments. The Prince's lengthy commendation of Horatio in act three suggests his own predisposition, but his reflections on Fortinbras are equally extensive, although not so uniformly flattering (3.2.51-71, 4.4.25-66). With his dying voice, he explicitly supports Fortinbras as successor to the vacant Danish throne, and he clearly admires the Norwegian for his decisiveness and courage.[83] Yet in the soliloquy delivered before his departure for England, he shows himself almost equally drawn to, and put off by, his Norwegian counterpart. We sense in Hamlet here an underlying concern that Fortinbras may have chosen the more admirable as well as the simpler approach to life—that of a Viking adventurer, a Mars unalloyed by Mercury: in him there is surely no sign of any "craven scruple/ Of thinking too precisely on th' event." But as Hamlet works out his response to this example, he is willing to accept only part of what it offers him.

That army of "twenty thousand men/ [who] for a fantasy and trick of fame/ Go to their graves like beds" serves Hamlet as a catalyst for action, in somewhat the same way that an ancient Athenian cockfight served the Greek hero Themistocles in a famous instance recounted by Aelian:

> At what time Themistocles was captain to an army of citizens . . . against the barbarous and foreign people, he saw two cocks fighting fiercely together. . . . Of which game or sight he did not show himself an idle gazer, but gathering his whole army round about him, made this short oration unto them.
>
> "These two cocks endanger themselves, as we see to the death, not for their country's cause, not for the household gods, not for the privileges of their honorable ancestors, not for renown, not for liberty, not for wife or children: but that th' one might not overcrow or beat the other, or that the one should give ground or game to the other, as the worse to the better, the weaker to the stronger"; which words being beautified with the flowers of policy, ministered marvelous encouragement to the hearts of the Athenians, which stoutness and audacity he wished and also willed to be put in practice, that thereby they might purchase perpetual remembrance.[84]

As Themistocles used the cockfight to encourage his Athenian army, so Hamlet uses Fortinbras to encourage himself with that "stoutness and audacity he wished and also willed to be put in practice." Combining recognition with irony, Hamlet deduces that "Rightly to be great/ Is not to stir without great argument,/ But greatly to find quarrel in a straw/ When honor's at the stake." When compared to the cause which energizes Fortinbras, Hamlet's cause is massively significant, involving values fundamental to the civilized life of individuals and societies.

Yet beyond his obvious qualities of fortitude and decisiveness, Fortinbras does not satisfy Hamlet as a model for himself. There is something more than ridiculous about fighting "for a plot/ Whereon the numbers cannot try the cause,/ Which is not tomb enough and continent/ To hide the slain." But no such consideration ever clouds the simple directness of Fortinbras' brain: one must act, and if one cannot find a great cause it is no matter, because a trivial cause will serve just as well. He is, literally, a flat character, utterly predictable almost to the point of personifying action for action's sake, risking everything even for eggshells and straw.[85]

The introduction of straw is quite significant and perhaps even definitive. References to Fortinbras' debating "the question of this straw" and to finding "quarrel in a straw" do not represent the idiolect of one man, but invoke a well-established and widespread proverbial motif rich in connotations of triviality which would not have escaped sixteenth-century audiences. We have already seen Jean Cousin's drawing of Dame Fortune presenting a bundle of straw or switches,[86] but the symbolism was both more explicit and more widespread than one example can testify.

For a century before and after Shakespeare, the recognition of Vanitas as straw or hay was standard in the proverbial wisdom of England and of the Continent. A proverb in Flemish refers to the struggles for vain possessions and vain eminence as *al hoy*, or all hay, and in Holland the expression "to drive the haywagon" indicated cheating and misrepresentation.[87] In the folklore of the Low Countries, hay and straw were repeatedly equated with Vanitas. Much the same meaning is found in English proverbs, as Tilley's research has demonstrated.[88] Such proverbial use of hay and straw was naturally carried over to the Elizabethan stage. Thus Dekker wrote of one who, "drawing out one handful of gold and another of silver, cried . . . 'I have made my hay whilst my sun shined,' " and in *3 Henry VI* the rising King Edward IV refers with unwitting irony to his conquest of the kingdom as "our hoped-for hay."[89] Such expressions are based partly in the common observation of the cheapness of hay, and of the ease with which it dries into worthless straw, but they also have roots in lingua franca of Biblical imagery. Thus the Book of Common Prayer in its Order for the Burial of the Dead requires the saying or singing of verses from the thirty-ninth and ninetieth Psalms, including the reference to grass that "in the morning it is green, and groweth up but in the evening it is cut down, dried up, and withered."[90] In 1635, we find among Wither's *Emblems* one displaying hay with the descriptive couplet, "All flesh is like the wither'd hay,/ And so it springs and fades away."[91]

In the visual arts, the best-known development of this motif of hay and straw comes in *The Haywain* by Hieronymus Bosch where Bosch has painted a disorderly march about a huge wagon loaded with hay. The wain is drawn by devils and followed by the high and mighty of the earth, while ordinary humanity (impelled by greed, ambition, and deceit) fight and scramble and claw at the hay to grasp a futile handful.[92] Bosch varied this vision in a later painting, now lost, which became the basis for the Haywain tapestry at the Royal Palace in Madrid.[93] The hay-cart continued as a lively and popular visual image during another century and a half. In 1559 it appeared in a print attributed to Bartholomeus de Mompere. In 1563, a festival procession through the streets of Antwerp featured an allegorical hay-cart "ridden by a devil named Deceitful, and followed by all sorts of men plucking the hay, so as to show that worldly possessions are *al hoy*." A popular song as early as 1470 made the same point, and was echoed by another in the second half of the sixteenth century which declared that "In the end it is *al hoy*."[94] An anonymous *Allegory on Conditions in the Low Countries* repeats the theme, Jacques Horenbault used it in an engraving in 1608, and the subject was still popular enough later in the seventeenth century to justify Jan Siberechts' painting of his *Haywain*.[95]

In addition to the verbal proverbs about hay and straw and to the visual parables of haywains, we fine these symbols closely associated with Dame World, a cater-cousin to Dame Fortune in the allegorical family of Vanitas figures. In about 1585, J. Vrints engraved a copy of Abraham Bosse's "The Dance around Dame World" (Fig. V.4) which shows at her feet a crown resting on a bundle of straw conveniently labeled *Vanitas*. Everything in this work suggests vanity: Dame World is crowned with a globe to identify her (but the cross on the globe above her head indicates that true sovereignty is not hers).

FIG. v.4. J. Vrints after Abraham Bosse, "The Dance around Dame World"

Richly dressed, she holds a jeweled chain in her right hand, and in her left a bubble to suggest the true value of her favors. The tables of the Mosaic law have been cast to the ground in the left foreground, and two drinking vessels rest on them, one overturned and spilled as another reminder of emptiness. A fool peeps out of the front of her robe, holding a mask as the symbol of deceit, and a peacock's tail appears from beneath her train.[96] The peacock-feather motif recurs in the hat of the musician as a reiteration of pride and presumption, and the dancers represent humanity acting just as foolishly as those who, in Hamlet's words, become a pipe for Fortune's finger to play what tune she will.

Hamlet's sardonic observation that Fortinbras has been able "greatly to find quarrel in a straw" evokes this popular background of words and images,

epitomizing in a single phrase a rich variety of traditional expression. Fortinbras' noble army of twenty thousand men is willing to die for "a fantasy and
trick of fame," as Hamlet observes:

> This is th' impostume of much wealth and peace,
> That inward breaks, and shows no cause without
> Why the man dies. (4.4.27-29)

This passage on "th' impostume of much wealth and peace" has sometimes
been interpreted as though Fortinbras had spoken it, rather than Hamlet, and
is thus understood to affirm that the invasion of Poland for "a little patch of
ground" is healthy for society. In my view, on the contrary, Hamlet interprets
that war as a mark of disease, a trivial but bloody pursuit of Vanitas. So
understood, his final soliloquy combines affirmation with scepticism into the
splendid irony of viewing the example of Fortinbras in both positive and negative terms: made admirable by his fortitude, and trivial by his pursuit of straw.
As for himself, Hamlet has struggled to keep "the excitements of my reason
and my blood" in balance, but he feels that "all occasions do inform against
me" for allowing "that capability and godlike reason/ To fust . . . unused."
Thought must be embodied in action, as action must be tempered by thought.
The ideal of combining Mercury with Mars remains intact.

For Hamlet, "bestial oblivion" may consist both in acting wrongly and in
the failure to act at all. Fortinbras' army is Shakespeare's counterpart to Bosch's
*Haywain*. It is a catalyst for reflection, appraisal, and decision, but Hamlet's
sardonic comments indicate that he has not accepted it as his ideal model for
action. Fortinbras has here chosen an action which requires only blood, but
Hamlet's ideal requires thought as well. His final soliloquy does not reach a
logical synthesis of the two, but it does conclude with a rhetorical synthesis:
"O, from this time forth,/ My thoughts be bloody, or be nothing worth."
Whether and how that synthesis may be expressed in action, we have yet to
discover.

# SIX

# The Prince amid the Tombs

## 1. Drawing to an End

THE FINAL ACT of *Hamlet* opens in a graveyard, continues with the reflections of the Prince among the tombs, moves through the blood and thunder of duel and retribution, and closes with four captains taking up the body of the protagonist on a bier to the accompaniment of soldiers' music and the rites of war. That dénouement of the plot is paralleled and coordinated with the development in the characterization. The Prince whom we watch in the two scenes of this fifth act grows into a maturity beyond anything which we have seen in the first four acts of the tragedy. The earlier "wild and whirling" demeanor breaks out for the last time in the struggle over Ophelia's corpse, but before and after that incident he displays a new and impressive serenity. This serenity, however, is not superimposed and does not cancel out the underlying passion of the nature Shakespeare has thus far portrayed. We have here the same character, developed into what Elizabethans would have regarded as a fuller (although by no means complete) wisdom and vision. The basic problems which preoccupied him before recur here, but within a greater breadth and depth of understanding. Shakespeare's careful and systematic construction of words and actions early in this act prepares the audience to accept the composure, balance, and self-assurance Hamlet displays in the play's last scene— qualities which may be summarized as a kind of tranquility.

Coming to terms with his own mortality is central here. The Renaissance was schooled in the contemplation of death. The importance of such contemplation was emphasized by Latin Stoicism, by the Christian past, and by the great spokesmen of their own times. Seneca wrote that "the mind will never rise to virtue if it believes that death is an evil; but it will so rise if it holds that death is a matter of indifference." Hamlet's reflections over Yorick's skull would have been approved by Seneca, who wrote that man's mind "is never more divine than when it reflects upon its mortality, and understands that man was born for the purpose of fulfilling his life, and that the body is not a permanent dwelling, but a sort of inn (with a brief sojourn at that)."[1]

The differences between the teachings of Christ and of Seneca were great, but both emphasized the acceptance of the end, and preparation for it. Thus we read in Matthew 24:36 and 44: "That day and hour no man knoweth. . . . Therefore be ye also ready." And in Elizabethan times, Sir Philip Sidney's characterization of Euarchus praised this ideal ruler because he showed "no more affected pomps than as a man that knew, howsoever he was exalted, the beginning and end of his body was earth."[2] Hamlet's reflection on death invests him with what the Renaissance regarded as a particularly admirable maturity and tranquility.

This tranquility (if that be the proper word for it) is obviously neither complete nor unshakable—Hamlet is not a Stoic, nor was meant to be—and we find his equanimity not only strained but shattered at its most vulnerable point when he watches Ophelia's pathetically shrouded body lowered into her grave. His control of himself and of his situation may be almost complete, but this incident demonstrates that the passionate substratum is still present, ready to burst out, as it does when he comes forward to assist in the interment of the woman he loves, and is caught up in a violent struggle with her brother. That incident establishes continuity with the vehemence and impetuosity we have seen before, but the previous reflections on grave-making, on Yorick's skull, and on the famous and powerful dead, would have indicated to the Globe audiences that the Prince has also attained a new balance, maturity, and wisdom.

## II. Introducing Skeletons and Skulls

The tableau of Hamlet contemplating the skull of Yorick in the graveyard of Elsinore is one of the most famous in the Shakespearean canon. For actors and playgoers alike, it is a lasting favorite, and perhaps more than any other action in the play it has been engraved on the popular mind as providing the most memorable single image of the melancholy prince. Shakespeare's presentation of that scene was, as far as we can now tell, a striking innovation on the London stage where he introduced it in or about the year 1600.[3]

In his innovation upon the stage, however, Shakespeare was not creating *de novo*. There was a well established and very popular tradition of showing

206

a young man with a skull, or commenting upon it, and numerous examples of this visual *topos* exist in various art forms. The greatest of these is Frans Hals' oil of *A Young Man with a Skull* (Fig. VI.1) which was executed about 1641 and which in the nineteenth and early twentieth centuries was confidently identified as a painting of Shakespeare's Hamlet, but that is unlikely and in any case it is scarcely the point.[4] What matters to us is that both Shakespeare and Hals were working in a broad and encompassing tradition. If we contemplate Hals' painting, we will see that it conveys something quite different from what we in the twentieth century might expect in the portrait of a youth holding a skull. Where we might anticipate a mood of anxiety, Hals shows that the face and indeed the whole posture reflect security, ease, even serenity. In the age of Shakespeare and Hals, that was the result expected from a serious contemplation upon death.

That tradition was well known to Shakespeare and to the audiences for whom he wrote, being readily accessible in England as on the Continent through prints and engravings, paintings, and mortuary sculpture. In tracing this visual iconography,[5] which Shakespeare evokes by a stage tableau and through the visual imagery of his words, I shall cover a broad spectrum of art works, where feasible in chronological order, but basically according to the motifs employed.

Strangely enough, the skull has not always been used as the standard visual symbol of death. Its popular use in Christian Europe began a little more than a century before Shakespeare's birth,[6] as it was introduced within the space of a single decade in Northern and in Italian art. About the year 1450, Rogier van der Weyden executed a triptych for Jean de Braque, and on the verso he painted a picture of a skull; in 1458 an Italian medal by Giovanni Boldú showed on its reverse side a bas relief of a skull.[7] From these modest beginnings, the usage spread widely and continued in vogue for several centuries, appearing on tombs throughout Europe, including Shakespeare's wall monument in Stratford-upon-Avon. The allegorical carvings above the poet's figure show a putto with a spade representing labor on the left, and on the right another putto with an inverted torch of life representing rest, whose hand rests on a skull, while the whole monument is crowned by a skull.[8]

One of the most frequent uses of the skull in the visual arts was as an attribute of saints, and although our concern here is with Hamlet (who is never reported to have been beatified) and not with hagiography, we should give this important part of the developing tradition a brief and summary treatment.

FIG. VI.I. Frans Hals, *Young Man with a Skull*

Dürer first employed a skull in the iconography of St. Jerome in his celebrated engraving of 1514, in which the scholarly saint is deeply yet tranquilly working at his reading desk in a light-filled study. The lion, his identifying attribute, sleeps peacefully adjacent to a pet dog in the foreground. There is a comfortable window seat, with scattered pillows and books; below are the saint's slippers and above, placed with almost equal casualness, a skull rests on the window sill "pleasantly transfigured by the sunshine," as Panofsky put it.[9] In this representation, the skull is not being contemplated by the saint, who is absorbed in his scholarship at the far end of the room. The whole scene is redolent of contentment, even serenity.

A later consideration of Jerome with the skull comes in Dürer's pen drawing now in Berlin. Here the saint is no longer shown as a full-bodied figure in voluminous robes, but as a half-naked ascetic. Further, instead of concentrating upon his research, he is concentrating pensively upon the skull before him on the small table, its jaw gaping as though it were speaking to the saint whose eyes are fixed upon it in a melancholy stare. The next stage of the development comes in Dürer's oil of St. Jerome which was completed, after at least five preparatory sketches, in March, 1521. Here Jerome stares directly at the viewer, his brow furrowed in melancholy and puzzled thought, his index finger pointing to the skull, while the skull itself seems to fix us with an eyeless and bony stare.[10] This visual conception of Jerome with the skull was soon adopted by Lucas van Leyden, Marinus van Reymerswalle, and Jan van Hemessen; Joos van Cleve's studio proliferated reproductions and variations upon Dürer's basic conception of the saint. Such replicas were often labeled "Homo bulla" ("Man the bubble") to spell out the meaning. The long career of the saint contemplating a skull was firmly launched, and soon spread to representations of St. Mary Magdalene, St. Francis of Assisi, and others.

Our concern here is not for the association of the memento mori with saints, but with secular figures, and, as we shall see, that association was both widespread and varied. We find one Italian example dating about 1530 in a portrait by Lorenzo Lotto at the Borghese in Rome. Here a romantic-looking gentleman gazes out at us in what the Renaissance admired as a thoughtful and melancholy mood, while the placing of his right hand calls our attention to a little pile of fallen rose petals, themselves symbolic of the beauty and the transiency of life. And among those petals we can identify a small but exquisitely carved skull.

Small ivory skulls were very popular among sixteenth-century gentlemen and ladies. Several are preserved in the British Museum, and of these two examples should be described as representative of this subgenre. Whereas in Lotto's painted version the skull is presented without embellishment beyond its miniature representation, others emphasized the comparison between the living and the dead. One shows a woman's living head on one side, and on the other the skull and shoulders of a skeleton—with a motto to the effect that "it is not possible to escape," where the sense is close to Hamlet's "to this favor she must come," the message he contemplates sending to "my lady's chamber" along with Yorick's skull. Another ivory, without identifying the sex, emphasizes decay even more drastically—showing a clean skull on one side, but a shriveled and decaying head on the other, where the remaining flesh is being consumed by worms and beetles. These particular figures are French, and are paralleled by a more restrained Danish memorial medal for Queen Dorothea dated 1560, which shows her head on one side and a skull with crossed bones on the other.[11] All these works were small, suitable for placing in a cabinet, on a dressing table or desk, or for hanging on a wall. All were designed as appropriate for intimate use, mementoes for private chambers, whether "my lady's" or "my lord's," and they appeared in both. Even mirrors had skulls and bones etched onto the glass: "In Northern France and the South of the Low Countries mirrors were made, till the early eighteenth century, for lady's dressing tables in the glass of which were engraved a skull and crossing bones: beauty and finery could only be contemplated through the image of decay."[12] Hamlet's thought of sending the skull to his lady fits with these fashions, which at the time were regarded as neither crude nor unsympathetic.

There was even a vogue for skull-shaped watches in the sixteenth century: Mary Queen of Scots and King Henry III of France are said to have used such watches, and others surely did. The one I show (Fig. VI.2) has traditionally been associated with Mary, and although that particular association is dubious, the watch dates from Shakespeare's age and it does represent the kind of death's-head timepiece which was popular among his contemporaries. The Fall of Adam and Eve is engraved along the side of the silver-gilt skull. On the forehead a skeletal figure of Death holds a scythe, and pushes with one foot against the door of a palace and with the other foot against the door of a poor cottage, a patent appeal to humility. One could not open the face of such a watch to tell

FIG. VI.2. Skull-shaped watch, supposedly
belonging to Mary Queen of Scots

the time without being reminded that each passing hour brought one closer to death.

> And so from hour to hour, we ripe, and ripe,
> And then, from hour to hour, we rot, and rot.[13]

Such *memento mori* were worn on chains about the person, and must frequently have been taken in hand—rarely, I should think, without inspiring reflections similar to those of Hamlet holding Yorick's skull.[14]

As with such death's-head timepieces, so other visual fashions reached England from the Continent, for even though the country was not creatively involved in the most exciting currents in the visual arts of Europe, it was not entirely isolated. Englishmen traveled abroad and came home with new ideas; foreign art works were imported into England, especially prints and engravings, which were the primary means for spreading artistic knowledge throughout Europe. Finally, foreign artists moved to England, most notably of course Hans Holbein who worked in the court of Henry VIII, and a later succession of lesser artists from the Low Countries and elsewhere.

For secular portraits, Holbein was apparently responsible for introducing into portraiture in England both the skeleton and the death's-head—with significantly different implications for each. In a portrait of Sir Brian Tuke, now in Munich, Holbein presented this early Tudor patron of learning in a seated pose, with an hourglass about to run out, while he points to the Latin of Job

10:20 ("Will not the number of thy days be soon ended?"). Behind him is the leering figure of Death, prepared to cut Sir Brian down with his scythe.[15] A similar and derivative treatment of this motif appears in a painting by Marc Gheeraerts the Elder, now in the collection of Lord Methuen at Corsham Court: executed at about the same time that Shakespeare was completing *Hamlet*, the painting shows the aged Queen Elizabeth with her prayerbook, flanked on the left by the weary figure of Time, and on the right by a menacing skeleton holding an hourglass with one hand and a coffin with the other.

The skeleton in these portraits obviously portends approaching death, usually of an elderly person, whereas the skull need not carry any such imminent threat of death. Taken by itself, the skull was a *memento mori* symbol in a more general sense—warning that death was inevitable, no matter how long postponed—and thus putting life in the meanwhile into proper Christian perspective. As such, the skull was equally appropriate when associated with young, middle-aged, and elderly people. Sometimes we find an art work which brings together a skull with a dead body to present a message with blatant clarity. A powerful example may be found in an English painting dated 1560, known as *The Judd Memorial* (Fig. VI.3). This oil was among the earliest bequests to Dulwich College, established by the great Elizabethan actor Edward Alleyn, who was Burbage's principal rival as a tragedian. It may have come as part of the 1626 gift from Alleyn's private collection, which had hung in his own home, or it may have been donated as part of the Cartwright bequest of 1686. In either case, the sixteenth-century artist has graphically exploited one of the favorite themes of Shakespeare's England. As Roy Strong has written, the "*memento mori* emerges as one of the few subjects congenial to Elizabethan collectors," and he cites examples in the collections of Lord Lumley, the Earl of Leicester, and Archbishop Parker, although these and many others like them have been lost.[16]

Shakespeare's contemporaries obviously found appealing the very thing some moderns may find appalling here—the combination of the portrait with *memento mori*. Beneath the seated husband and wife is a shrouded and rotting corpse, to which the husband points, while both have placed their hands on a skull beneath such standard symbols of transitoriness as flowers and a candle. The man is identified as forty-seven years of age, and the woman twenty-eight. Above the skull are the words, "Behowlde ower ende," while beneath the cadaver we read "lyve to dye and dye to lyve etarnally"—which is a precise if

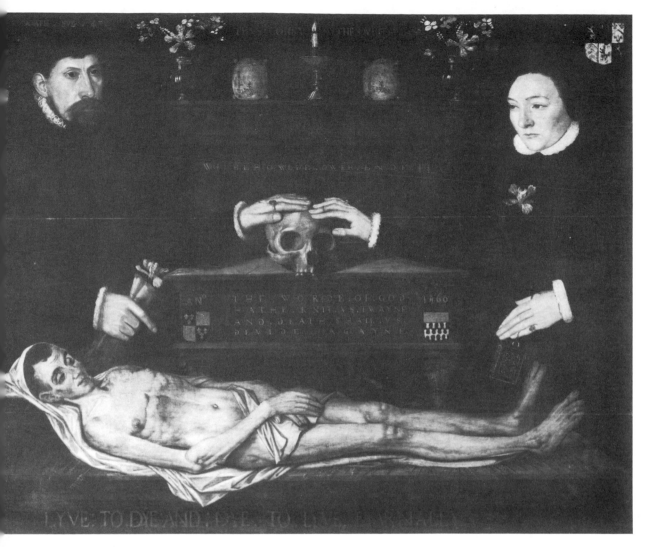

FIG. VI.3. Anonymous, *The Judd Memorial*

somewhat flat-footed summary of the *memento mori* tradition. Typical examples of that tradition are not always so naively explicit, but the meaning is there nonetheless.

### III. Young Men with Skulls

But the contemplation of a skull was not restricted to saints nor to older persons nor those on the verge of death: it was at least equally common to picture a young gentleman with a skull, and it is with such pictures that we are principally concerned. Indeed, the first published version of a man actually

213

holding and pointing to a skull involved the secular figure of a young man about Hamlet's age. In about 1519 Lucas van Leyden executed an engraving of a richly dressed young man attired as a nobleman or courtier (Fig. VI.4), who holds a skull within the folds of his cloak, and points to it, while gazing thoughtfully into the distance.[17] Here we have the earliest known example of the basic visual *topos* that Shakespeare gives us when Hamlet takes Yorick's skull from the Gravedigger, and says to Horatio, "I knew him, Horatio," going on to comment on the lack of lips, the "chapfall'n" bones, and so forth (5.1.173ff.). I do not suggest that Shakespeare knew this engraving, but rather that it introduced into the visual arts the tableau he introduced on the stage some eighty years later. The original Lucas van Leyden conception soon became popular, and many later examples can be cited prior to Shakespeare's adaptation. About 1530, Jacob Binck engraved a self-portrait which is a sentimentalized version of Lucas' more forceful and thoughtful rendition (Fig. VI.5).

The first example in England of a portrait which associated young men with a skull is Holbein's *The Ambassadors* now in the National Gallery, London. It represents two French nobles, Jean de Dinteville and Georges de Selve, standing on a distinctive mosaic pavement of Westminster Abbey during their visit to England in 1533. Although the background symbolism of the painting is complex almost to the point of allegory, the principal figures and shelved objects are represented in a straightforward way—except for a strangely spectral shape which seems to float menacingly between their feet. That shape is actually a skull, painted in a manner which we now technically refer to as anamorphic, and which was called "a perspective" in Shakespeare's time, when its presence made this painting a famous attraction, widely commented upon in London. When viewed in the usual way, it appears amorphous and confusing, but from a particular angle or viewpoint it takes on the unmistakable form of a skull. Shakespeare described such effects in *Richard II*: "when rightly gazed upon [they]/ Show nothing but confusion; eyed awry, [they]/ Distinguish form."[18] When the visual game was properly played out, a viewing device attached to the frame allowed spectators to see the skull on the floor. That skull in turn echoes a small skull brooch on Dinteville's cap.[19] This double association of the skull with the young nobleman (Dinteville was twenty-nine, Selve twenty-five, as the painting indicates) places them and all their earthly concerns in the perspective of mortality. This is the first example of the introduction of the skull into portraits in England.

FIG. VI.4. Lucas van Leyden, *Young Man with a Skull*     FIG. VI.5. Jacob Binck, *Self-Portrait with Skull*

Eleven years after *The Ambassadors*, we find an interesting but anonymous portrait of Sir Thomas Gresham (Fig. VI.6), standing upon the threshold of a brilliant financial career which would include the founding of the Royal Exchange. Although the painting was apparently executed about 1565, Gresham is pictured at the age of twenty-six or thereabouts, for the painting was apparently commemorative of his marriage in 1544 to Anne Ferneley. In the upper right we see two pairs of initials, her "AG" and his "TG" with loveknots, connected by the words "Love, Serve, and Obey," based upon the marriage vows. Gresham has the alert, penetrating, and prudent gaze of one who looks confidently to the future as he had every reason to do, both because of his native abilities and because of his strong faith in providence. The frame is lettered with four repetitions of "Dominus mihi audiutor," the familiar verse of Hebrews 13:6, "The Lord is my helper and I will not fear what men shall

215

FIG. VI.6. Anonymous, *Sir Thomas Gresham*

FIG. VI.7. Anonymous, *William Clowes*

do unto me." Next to Gresham's right foot is a conspicuous human skull, a reminder of the fragility of even the strongest men, and of their ultimate dependence upon God, "Dominus mihi audiutor."[20] In Holbein's *The Ambassadors* and in the portrait of Sir Thomas Gresham, the skull is on the floor, but nonetheless casts its aura over the whole scene, suggesting that each of these handsome and healthy young gentlemen is actually standing in the shadow of death.

After Holbein's painting came *The Judd Memorial* of 1560, and a few years later a portrait of William Clowes which shows this successful young Englishman with his hand on a skull. As Gresham was the most outstanding financier of his time, so was Clowes one of the most notable physicians and surgeons.[21] Born in 1544 (Fig. VI.7), Clowes became a distinguished surgeon in Elizabethan naval, military, and civil life, and wrote several authoritative books during his many years of medical practice in London. The anonymous and undated portrait shows him as a young man richly dressed in a furred

FIG. VI.8. Remigius Hogenberg, *English Gentleman*

gown with a golden chain, a ring on his hand, and a jewel in his cap. Like Gresham, he is scarcely an ascetic repudiating the world,[22] but rather an active young man, successfully challenging the possibilities of life and the responsibilities of his profession. His hand rests upon the skull on the table as a tangible reminder of the inevitability of death, and of the need to conduct life *sub specie aeternitatis*. Such was the whole purpose of the skull as *memento mori*.

In 1579, about the same time as the Clowes portrait or perhaps a few years later, an engraved portrait of an unknown Englishman was executed by Remigius Hogenberg: it represents a thirty-four-year-old gentleman with his left hand on a skull (Fig. VI.8). The motto "Never to Forget" appears behind the subject's head, while verses on the panel spell out the significance of the young man with a skull:

Death, why should I fear thee
Since thou canst not hurt me
But rid me from misery
Unto everlasting glory.[23]

Theodor de Bry was, like Hogenberg, a Protestant emigré who worked in England, but he was at once more famous as an artist and far more distinguished—indeed, he was one of the major graphic artists of the sixteenth century. With his self-portrait dated 1597 (Fig. VI.9), we are within about three

218

FIG. VI.9. Theodor de Bry, *Self-Portrait*

years of the appearance of *Hamlet* as we now know it. The self-portrait carries the label "Nul sans Soucy," and on the balustrade the Latin inscription which may be translated as "Lord, teach me to pass the remainder of the days of my life so that I live and die in true piety."[24]

The various examples we have now rehearsed should clearly establish for us the social and intellectual milieu in which Shakespeare's contemporaries were accustomed to seeing and understanding a meditation upon a skull. Hamlet's reflections upon Yorick's skull fit within that general context, but of course expand and elevate it. It is important for us to recognize this fact, if we are to avoid a flaccid twentieth-century assumption that Shakespeare's prince was uniquely morbid in the comments he makes in the graveyard at Elsinore. Shakespeare's contemporary audience in the Globe Theater can be presumed to have seen Hamlet here as being at once most realistic and most rational. Within this context, Hamlet's reflections on Yorick's skull prepared the original audience for accepting and understanding the serenity of mind and conscience Hamlet displays in the following scene which concludes the play.

Here as elsewhere, Shakespeare's use of tradition was that of the master who transmutes what has gone before him into powerful and original visions. Each generation interprets these according to its own lights, but we miss much of the force of Shakespeare's conception if we do not seek by every means at our disposal to understand what he wrote within the context of meaning in which his dramatic scene would have been judged by the contemporaries for whom he wrote. If we view the graveyard scene in Elsinore only or even primarily in terms of those typically twentieth-century attitudes which seek to ignore or euphemize death, we may regard Hamlet at this point as morbid in soul and sick in mind. But if we reestablish the sixteenth-century context and recall representative examples of the raw materials upon which Shakespeare's imagination worked, we see a Hamlet here thinking through the ultimate realities of death to arrive at what becomes, for him as it had for others, a new sanity and even serenity.

## IV. Encounters Among the Tombs

The contemplation of a skull became so popular a theme in European art that even the great anatomist Vesalius could not resist it (Fig. VI.10). In his revolutionary study of the human body which appeared in 1543, and in many successive editions, there is a superb engraving of a skeleton in a graveyard leaning upon a tomb and contemplating a skull. In purely visual terms, this engraving exploits the ironies implicit in the motto which frequently accompanied skeletons and skulls in the visual tradition ("as you are now, so once I was; and as I am now, so you will be") by presenting the viewer as no less osseous than the skull he contemplates. We sense a similar irony in the graveyard at Elsinore as Hamlet, who is so soon to die, contemplates death.

The Vesalius engraving not only exploits the contemplation of a skull, but illustrates a visual tradition which sets that contemplation alongside a tomb. The tradition of an encounter between prosperous young men and death-figures alongside graves or open coffins was spread throughout Europe in the middle ages by the popular story of "The Three Living and the Three Dead," in which noble or royal huntsmen in the excitement of the chase come suddenly upon

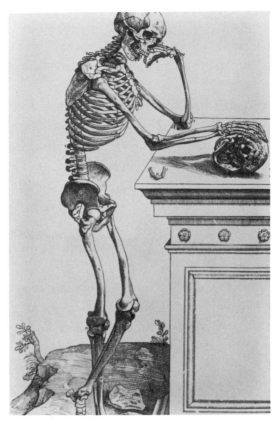

Fig. vi.10. Vesalius, Skeleton Contemplating a
Skull, *De Corporis humani*

three cadavers who rise from open coffins to address them, and to shock them
into recognizing their transience. The tale was given its early literary form in
thirteenth-century France, with later developments in other European lan-
guages. The theme, as would be expected, also became immensely popular in
art. Perhaps the finest version is found in the frescoes of the Camposanto in
Pisa, executed in the mid-fourteenth century by Traini or Orcagna. These murals
illustrate the terror which struck throughout Europe after the initial and horrifying onslaught of the bubonic plague. The same story is known to have been
represented by at least thirty paintings in England, of which twelve are now
extant, although none is on the artistic level of this Italian work.[25] In it, the
surprise encounter with the remains of the dead gave rise not only to nausea
(one rider holds his hand over his mouth, as though to control a gagging
reaction, such as Hamlet mentions in "my gorge rises at it"—5.1.176) and

later, according to contemporary expectations, would lead to constructive thought on the relativity of human life on earth as compared to the purposed destination of the soul.

Another point along the way of this developing tradition comes in a late fifteenth-century French Book of Hours.[26] Only one figure is involved, for a counterpart to Prince Hamlet has not yet been introduced into the confrontation, and it is only we as viewers who are confronted by the spectral figure of Le Roi Mort. A dark, cadaverous Death with a crown and dart emerges from an open tomb to fix us with a vacant yet ominous stare. In his left hand he displays a skull, but he does not present it to anyone within the picture frame; indeed, there is no one there to whom he can present it. Instead, he appears to present the skull to the viewer.

Numerous variants developed out of this basic graveyard confrontation. When precisely it first appeared in England I cannot say, but it became associated with the Dance of Death and was featured in mural paintings. One example was executed in the latter half of the fifteenth century on the wall of the Hungerford Chapel in Salisbury Cathedral (Fig. VI.11). Here a modishly dressed young man is confronted by a cadaverous figure in a shroud, with an open coffin by his feet on a ground sown with thorns and thistles.[27] The appended verses convey the standard moral and religious doctrine. About a century later, in 1568, Stephen Bateman illustrated his didactic poem *The Travayled Pylgrime* with a picture of the Pilgrim escorted by Memory into a cemetery with numerous funerary monuments. A skeleton lies at his feet, while he and Memory behold and comment upon "the ancient show and funerals of mighty conquerors past," after somewhat the same fashion as Hamlet's reflections on Alexander and Caesar.[28] The picture has a certain quaint charm, but it surely is not high art in any sense. Its significance for us is its visual staging of an encounter with bones and the memory of the great dead within a graveyard, but it lacks key features of Shakespeare's play.

Some twenty-five years later, and only eight years before the generally accepted date of *Hamlet*, Theodor de Bry engraved (Fig. VI.12) a striking vision of a young man in a graveyard.[29] The youth is attired in the height of late sixteenth-century fashion—he might in this regard at least be taken as "the glass of fashion and the mould of form"—and he holds a rose, symbolic at once of the beauty and fragility of life. A skull and logget bones are at his feet, and a brooding skeleton contemplates him from a sarcophagus, upon which

222

FIG. VI.11. Fashionable Youth and Death by open coffin, Hungerford Chapel, Salisbury Cathedral

223

FIG. VI.12. Theodor de Bry, *Young Gentleman in Graveyard*

FIG. VI.13. *Contrasto del Vivo e
del Morto*, Florence, 1572

is carved a conventional *memento mori* warning: "Fui, non sum es, nõ eris"—
"I am not as I was, you will not be as you are." Almost forty years after the
appearance of *Hamlet*, Rembrandt etched a scene in which a well-dressed couple
(she holding a flower) are accosted by a skeleton who emerges from an open
grave to confront them with an hourglass.[30]

In none of these instances does the figure of Death hold out a skull to the
young man, although the French Mors does present the skull to us, the viewers.
It is in Italy that we find the closest approximation to the scene Shakespeare
dramatized, although the Italian artist cast a skeleton in the role of Shakespeare's Gravedigger. A sixteenth-century Florentine woodcut (Fig. VI.13) shows
a fashionably dressed young gentleman in a cemetery, who is accosted by a
skeleton with horrid cadaverous hair, as the skeleton rises from an open grave
to hold out a skull to the astonished passer-by. Formally, there is much here
which we find in *Hamlet*—bones scattered about as though someone played
"at loggets with 'em"—but there is no human gravedigger, only the osseous
figure who performs his function in the open grave and presents the skull for
contemplation. The woodcut appeared in a religious tract called *Contrasto del
Vivo e del Morto* published in Florence in 1572, but the style of the young
gentleman's costume suggests a much earlier date, and this design apparently
had a long history of publication.[31]

These visual counterparts to Hamlet contemplating Yorick's skull are useful to us as readers of Shakespeare because they clearly establish the cultural
and intellectual context Shakespeare invoked. As for the gravedigger with whom
Hamlet shared that scene (and it is typical of Shakespeare that instead of an
allegorical figure of Death he would employ a flesh-and-blood sexton), there
was no visual convention so well known and so frequently represented as to
establish equally strong iconographic resonances. The First Gravedigger with
whom Hamlet banters is therefore not much enhanced by visual analogies, but
there is one analogy so curious that I cannot resist introducing it. It is the only
sixteenth- or seventeenth-century portrait of an actual sexton I have been able
to discover, and it represents Robert Scarlett, the sexton of Peterborough Cathedral, as memorialized in that cathedral (Fig. VI.14). Scarlett was born in
1498 and died in 1594, six years before the entrance of Shakespeare's
Gravedigger at the Globe Theater. Most of his ninety-six years were spent
interring all kinds and conditions of humanity at Peterborough, in the course
of which he buried two queens, Catherine of Aragon in 1536 and Mary Queen

FIG. VI.14. Robert Scarlett, Gravedigger, Peterborough
Cathedral, engraving from J. Caulfield, *Portraits of
Remarkable Persons*, 1813

of Scots in 1587. His clientele was thus at least as good as that of his confrere
in Elsinore, but regrettably for his posthumous fame he never had the opportunity to present Yorick's skull to Hamlet. His portrait does show, however,
that he had a skull ready to hand (or rather to foot, for it is behind his feet,
resting on his pickaxe), while he holds his spade to his right. The coat of arms
suggests that he made some pretensions to gentility, not unlike his counterpart
in Elsinore who claimed that grave-makers are "ancient gentlemen" who "hold
up Adam's profession" (5.1.27-30). Executed at about the time of Scarlett's
demise in 1594, the painting has suffered from various "restorations," and I

226

reproduce it here from the earliest version I have been able to discover, an engraving published in 1813.[32] To the painting were appended explanatory verses in a typical sixteenth-century exhortation:

> He had interred two queens within this place
> And this town's householders in his life's space
> Twice over: but at length his own turn came:
> What he for others did, for him the same
> Was done: no doubt his soul doth live for aye
> In Heaven, though here his body clad in clay.

## v. Decay, My Lady Worm, and the *Transi*

One of the first things Hamlet notices about the fictional counterpart of Robert Scarlett is that "this fellow [hath] no feeling of his business, that 'a sings at grave-making" (5.1.62f.). He accepts Horatio's reply about the customary "property of easiness" and his natural curiosity becomes engaged by the lore of a trade which built habitations to "last till doomsday" (5.1.56). Against that background which extends till worldly time is no more, he asks the Gravedigger a pointed question: "How long will a man lie i' th' earth ere he rot?" The reply is disconcerting: "Faith, if 'a be not rotten before 'a die (as we have many pocky corses now-a-days that will scarce hold the laying in), 'a will last you some eight year or nine year" (5.1.153-56).

This reference to the rottenness of the living is primarily a moral metaphor, as is so much of the *memento mori* material we are discussing, but two important visual prototypes did show living figures who were rotten: there were the sculptured representations of Frau Welt and of the World Tempter or Prince of this World. The first of these we have already encountered as Dame World with her Netherlandish attribute of a bundle of straw in the engraving which helped to illustrate the Vanitas element in Hamlet's appraisal of Fortinbras (see above, Fig. V.5). Along with the Prince of this World, she was an important allegorical personification. Both were frequently carved in the late thirteenth and early fourteenth centuries in Germany and France, as at the Sebalduskirche in Nürnberg and at the cathedrals in Basel, Freiburg, Regensburg, Worms, and Strasbourg. Both the male and female personifications represented the deceptions of the world, and appear highly attractive when viewed from the front, but are revealed as naked and rotten behind, with their bodies riddled by snakes or worms and devoured by toads, as illustrated in the Prince of this World at Strasbourg[33] (Fig. VI.15). I have found no sculpture in England which provided so literalistic a parallel to the Gravedigger's remark, but the Strasbourg Prince of this World does provide a fine visual metaphor for the rottenness which Hamlet finds so pervasive and so revolting in Denmark and its king. With the two views, front and back, juxtaposed, we find a visual equivalent to the contrast between appearance and reality, between what seems and what is, which is thematically so important in *Hamlet*, and which is at least subliminally evoked in the Gravedigger's reference to the "many pocky corses now-a-days," rotten even before they die.

To the mixture of concern for moral as well as physical decay in such allusions must be added that concentration upon physical rot and the ravages of "my Lady Worm" which powerfully deflate human pride and pretension (5.1.82). Hamlet has already evidenced that approach in the fourth act. During his conference with the King, he describes the most tactile details of worms devouring Polonius, fattening themselves upon his decaying corpse, and then suddenly he turns the focus directly upon the King himself, as he narrates the passage of a dead king's body into a banquet for worms, followed by a fish eating that worm, and a beggar eating that fish, until finally what remains of the monarch goes "a progress through the guts of a beggar."[34] Death is the great leveler, by whom all social and economic distinctions are destroyed, so that "your fat king and your lean beggar is but variable service—two dishes, but to one table"[35] (4.3.19-31). Like all forms of the *memento mori*, this concentration upon worms was traditionally understood as an incentive to charity, humility, and faith; but Hamlet obviously has no hope of changing Claudius, and is merely goading him rather than evangelizing him.

Hamlet's references in the graveyard to Alexander and Caesar are not directly associated with Claudius, whom Hamlet regards as merely "a king of shreds and patches" (3.4.103), but they do continue and in some sense conclude the Prince's earlier reflections on that Norwegian conquering hero, Fortinbras, who "with divine ambition puffed . . . [exposed] what is mortal and unsure/ To all that fortune, death, and danger dare." And for what was all this done? Psychologically it was because "honor's at the stake," and objectively it was "for a plot/ Whereon the numbers cannot try the cause,/ Which is not tomb enough and continent/ To hide the slain" (4.4.47-66). These themes Hamlet

FIG. VI.15. Prince of this World, or "Le Tentateur," front and rear views
of sculpture from Strasbourg Cathedral

broached in this fourth act soliloquy recur and are expanded in his graveyard reflections.

First Hamlet reflects on the burial of a lawyer who in his time was "a great buyer of land" but who is in the end reduced to a little patch of earth which measures no more "than the length and breadth of a pair of indentures." Indeed, "The very conveyances of his lands will scarce lie in this box, and must th' inheritor himself have no more, ha?" (5.1.91-104). As with Fortinbras' army, the lawyer's efforts have brought him at his final rest scarcely enough land to bury the dead. This theme was a commonplace in Shakespeare's works and in his culture. At the end of the minor tetralogy, the dying Warwick declared that there "is nothing left me but my body's length," and Calvin had written that "we must have no more ground than our own length, wherein to rot and consume away to nothing."[36]

The end was no different for the great world-conquerors. Thus Hamlet's imagination traces "the noble dust of Alexander till 'a find it stopping a bung-hole," following "him thither with modesty enough, and likelihood to lead it; as thus: Alexander died, Alexander was buried, Alexander returneth to dust; the dust is earth; of earth we make loam; and why of that loam whereto he was converted might they not stop a beer barrel?" The attention then shifts to Caesar:

> Imperious Caesar, dead and turned to clay,
> Might stop a hole to keep the wind away.
> O, that that earth which kept the world in awe
> Should patch a wall t' expel the winter's flaw!     (5.1.190-204)[37]

Beginning in the fourth act and culminating in the graveyard, Hamlet's various comments upon human death, decay, and dissolution provide the finest literary expression of a tradition which was centuries old in 1600. A few years after *Hamlet*, Shakespeare's *Measure for Measure* gave words on the same subject to Claudio as he awaits execution: "To lie in cold obstruction and to rot,/ This sensible warm motion to become/ A kneaded clod" (*Meas.* 3.1.119-21). Both Hamlet and Claudio point to the same morbid decomposition, and both do so with great realism, but there are major differences between their attitudes. Hamlet's reflections in the graveyard make no mention of divinity, heaven, or providence; but even without any such direct assertions of faith here, one familiar with the *memento mori* traditions would suspect or expect from the Prince's words a yet-to-be-stated completion of the standard argument, a conclusion which in fact he shortly states in three separate affirmations of faith in the following scene. With Claudio's speech, on the contrary, the major thrust is in a different direction. Claudio's words lack the heroic tone of Hamlet's, not only because he is terrified where the Prince is undaunted, but also because he expresses no concern beyond himself, as though he were *sui generis*, whereas Hamlet considers the tragic lot of all humanity through representative types. Between these analyses of death, the greatest similarity lies in their utter sensuousness. In these passages, death is no pale abstraction, but a tangible reality which claws us in its clutch: we can feel it, sense it, touch it, smell it until we empathize with the very processes of dissolution. The effect is powerfully synaesthetic.

The same effects were sought by *memento mori* and mortuary art. Tomb effigies until the middle of the fourteenth century had typically showed the deceased peacefully stretched out in the panoply of the appropriate rank or profession, calmly awaiting the general resurrection. Such figures are known as *gisants*. But under the terrible scourge of the bubonic plague in the mid-fourteenth century and the devastations of the Hundred Years War which continued after it, Europeans began to add tomb carvings of fleshless skeletons, or cadavers in the process of decay.[38]

The stately *gisant* continued to appear on the top of the tombs, but below it there now appears another and more alarming figure, the *transi*. The *transi* includes several subtypes of figures, which trace the effects of death on the human body. First in the normal progression was the *caro vilis*, the merely lifeless corpse, usually unclothed and perhaps showing the embalmer's incision (conspicuous, for example, on the *transi* of King Louis XII of France in St. Denis); next came the *vermis*, with the flesh now rotting away and worms crawling in and out, along with beetles, toads, and perhaps snakes; finally, there was the *pulvis*, either a shrunken, mummified cadaver or a skeleton.[39] In mortuary sculpture, it is rare to find more than one of these later phases represented in addition to the stately *gisant*, but the juxtaposition of two stages cannot fail to bring a powerful shock of recognition and awareness.

An influential example may be found in the early fifteenth-century tomb of Cardinal Lagrange (d. 1402) in Avignon, where the upper figure illustrates the cardinal as a mighty prince of the church, while the lower shows a shockingly shrunken cadaver. Professor Kathleen Cohen writes that this monument "served as the prototype" for the group of tombs which used "the corpse as a symbol of the nemesis of worldly glory," and cites the carved inscription, "Miserable one, what reason have you to be proud?"[40] The effect is similar to that which Hamlet achieves as he proposes to trace "the noble dust of Alexander till 'a find it stopping a bunghole" (5.1.192-93).

Within a few decades, such tombs began to appear in England. A famous tomb in Canterbury Cathedral shows Archbishop Chichele (d. 1443) (Fig. VI.16) in full episcopal regalia above, and as a shrunken cadaver below, partly covered by his shroud. This was the first *transi* monument in England, and was carved in 1424, almost twenty years *before* Chichele's death and under his personal supervision. Chichele is an unnamed but important character in Shakespeare's *Henry V*, where as Archbishop of Canterbury he urged Henry to undertake the conquest of France, and contributed heavily to financing the French Wars. Like many men of the cloth in his time, he was at least as much a prince of the state as of the church, and he wielded immense power in England, especially when Henry was abroad in France. His tomb, however, represents an exposé of the shallowness of worldly glory. Thus Chichele's inscription declares, "Now I am cut down and ready to be food for worms. Behold my grave: Whoever you may be who passes by, I ask you to remember you will be like me when you die, all horrible, dust, worms, vile flesh." In addition, there are various appeals for his soul and for harmony with God.[41] Such sentiments were not only for the benefit of later observers, but served as attestation of the spiritual health and religious sanity of the person who ordered them placed on his tomb.[42] Before he died, Archbishop Chichele had generously provided for the foundation of All Souls College, Oxford, but neither this great act of beneficence nor any of his major achievements in the state and the church are recorded on his tomb: there, as in the rotting cadaver below the effigy, the emphasis is on the decay of a glory now reduced to food for worms, and on the hope for salvation.[43]

That emphasis upon a stark and unrelieved contrast was applied to the tombs of women as well as men. A valuable example is a tomb in the church at Ewelme, Oxfordshire, which commemorates Chaucer's granddaughter Alice, who died in 1475 as Duchess of Suffolk. The duchess is represented on two biers, one above the other. On the upper bier, she is shown in what M. D. Anderson has described as "idealised beauty and splendid array," for an effect

FIG. VI.16. Archbishop Chichele Tomb

which is both touching and beautiful, while the lower bier presents her as a ghastly cadaver.[44]

These contrasts between feminine beauty and decay reached England shortly after the two-bier tomb was introduced by Chichele. An English manuscript *Disputacioun betwyx the Body and Worme*, dating from 1435-40 (Fig. VI.17), features a crudely drawn, but nonetheless revealing, illumination based upon such two-stage tombs. Above we see a lady who is both beautiful and beautifully dressed; below is her corpse infiltrated by worms and gnawed by beetles and other dark, creeping things. Here "my lady" is literally devoured by "my lady worm" (5.1.82).

233

FIG. VI.17. Manuscript illustration, *Disputacioun betwyx the Body and Worme*, 1435-40

Such treatments were even more popular on the Continent. One of the most emotionally powerful of these tombs was executed only about a dozen and a half years before Shakespeare wrote *Hamlet*, and it shows in two stages the figure of Valentine Balbiani. Valentine was the wife of René de Birague, Chancellor of France in the fifteen seventies, who after the death of his spouse entered holy orders and was made a cardinal. Before his death in 1583, he commissioned this monument from Germain Pilon. Above, Pilon showed the elegant figure of Valentine, half reclining as she pensively turns the pages of a book. Her face is both lovely and serene. The vision provided by the bas relief on the sarcophagus below is utterly different. The once gentle face is now a cadaverous mask, the figure is emaciated, and bones begin to protrude through the flesh, as a heightened naturalism has been used to stimulate emotional response. What the widower and sculptor agreed to achieve here in visual terms was essentially the effect Shakespeare sought through Hamlet's words[45]—although Hamlet does not carry his imagination to this extreme when he declares of the lady, "to this favor she must come."

Such contrasts, whether skilfully or crudely executed, were to be seen almost everywhere. A fine tomb at Arundel shows John, Earl of Arundel (d. 1435), above "in armor covered by an heraldic tabard: beneath . . . is a cadaver—a gruesome reminder of mortality."[46] Similar treatments are found in the tomb of Sir Marmaduke Constable (d. 1520) at Flamborough in Yorkshire, John Wakeman (d. 1530s) at Tewkesbury, Henry Lord Windsor at Tarbic in Warwickshire (1605), Sir John Golafre at Fyfield, Berkshire, and a Mr. Blount at Mamble, Worcestershire (1563). And, among similar brasses, there is that for Ralph Hamsterly (d. 1518) at Oddington.[47] The coming of the Renaissance and of the Reformation created no break in the steady production of such mortuary monuments.

Approximately a century separates the tomb of Archbishop Chichele from that of the humanist reformer and Dean of St. Paul's, John Colet, who died in 1519, and whose tomb dated from about 1522. Although the tomb was destroyed in the fire of 1622, it is known through an engraving preserved in William Dugdale's *History of St. Paul's Cathedral*.[48] On the wall above the tomb was a bust of Dean Colet within the scallop shell, as a symbol for pilgrimage and immortality. There was no reference to an endowment of masses, and no appeal for prayers from the living. The epitaph did refer to the skeleton on the sarcophagus below in admonitory fashion as a guide to the living—"the glory of the body returns to this"—and it immediately went on to make an appeal: "Die to the world that you might live for God." The tone of inscription and of monument is the willing sacrifice of life, and a faithful confidence that beyond the vile flesh there will be new life, in the providence of God.[49] This double emphasis, entailing a devaluation of earthly and fleshly glory and a confident expectation that flights of angels would convey the soul to its rest,[50] was implied by the very structure of the double-decker monument.

One of the more notable examples in England was erected only a dozen or so years after *Hamlet* appeared. When Robert Cecil, First Earl of Salisbury and principal minister to King James, died in 1612, he was buried in a tomb for which he had already contracted, which Lord David Cecil has beautifully described: "He was buried at Hatfield; by his own wish privately and quietly. 'I desire,' he had said, 'to go without noise or vanity out of this vale of misery, as a man that has long been satiated with terrestrial glory.' He had, three years earlier, approved a design for a tomb which was erected after his death in Hatfield church. It is in the allegorical manner of the high Renaissance, and is a visible image of his moral situation as it presented itself to him in his last years. On a slab of black marble supported at each corner by white figures representing the cardinal virtues of Justice, Prudence, Temperance, and Fortitude, lies the figure of the dead man clad in his Lord Treasurer's robes and with his actual Treasurer's staff in his hand. Beneath the slab a rough pallet props up his skeleton, macabre witness to the condition to which all mortal greatness must in the end come; and awaiting the verdict to be delivered on him by his Creator on the final Day of Judgment."[51] The purpose and the effect had changed relatively little in the course of some two hundred years, except that under the Stuarts England began to attract or develop more sophisticated artists and Cecil both could and did afford the best. The skilled hand of Maximilian Colt has dramatized the contrast between the magisterial peer above, still holding his staff of office, and the grinning skeleton beneath.

Although English tombs did not feature the extremes of decay that are found on the Continent, their displays of shrivelled and dried cadavers may appear quite shocking enough. The pertinence of all this to our understanding of Shakespeare is the recognition that for Shakespeare and his contemporaries, Hamlet's references to death would not have seemed abnormal or out of the ordinary for a thoughtful person. And when Hamlet's vision of death is considered along with many *memento mori* art works on the Continent, the Prince will appear by comparison to have been remarkably healthy, even to the thanatophobic eye of the twentieth century.

A few examples will make the point. In 1604, Jacopo Ligozzi painted a matched pair of portraits of a young man and young woman, presumably an engaged or married couple, and each portrait contained a *memento mori* painting on the reverse side of the panel (Fig. VI.18). In the next section of this chapter we shall consider the treatment of the woman, but here we will concentrate upon the man. The front of this panel shows a fashionably but soberly dressed young man holding a pikestaff—a patently thoughtful young man not far from the age of Hamlet—and on the reverse side Ligozzi has represented the frightfully shrunken flesh of a cadaverous head, the mouth drawn back into an impotent grimace.[52] Among the acknowledged masters in this vein of painting was the devout seventeenth-century Spanish Catholic Valdez Leal (1622-90), and his *End of the Glory of the World* at the Hospital de la Caridad in Seville is so overwhelming in its total impact that we almost feel we can smell the decomposing but richly arrayed "vile flesh" laid out to rot in the splendid robes of a bishop. Like Hamlet overwhelmed by the stench of death in the graveyard, we feel, with a shudder of revulsion, "how abhorred in my imagination it is! My gorge rises at it. . . . Pah!" (5.1.175-88).

## VI. Hamlet's Imaginary Dance of Death

Hamlet's graphic words imaginatively recreate many different aspects of the *memento mori* traditions—indeed this whole ambience has never been more finely invoked in literature. As the Prince holds the skull in his hands and converses with the Gravedigger among the tombs, Shakespeare establishes a visual tableau on stage which was already visually familiar to his audiences. Furthermore, Hamlet's reflections themselves provide to the mind's eye a vivid procession of the Dance of Death pictures which were standard fare of the time.

The *danse macabre*[53] was first conceived in France no later than the first part of the fifteenth century, and spread over Europe from there, producing innumerable mural cycles in England as on the Continent, including a cycle in the cloister of old St. Paul's, and a famous sixteenth-century example painted in Whitehall by Hans Holbein.[54] Unfortunately, these like so many others are now lost, but between 1523 and 1526 Holbein made a series of drawings of

FIG. VI.18. Jacopo Ligozzi, *Memento Mori Portrait of a Young Man*, front and back

the *danse*, which were converted into woodcuts by Hans Lützelburger, who then sold the lot to Treschel, the Lyons printer, who added other prints and published the first edition in 1538. The work proved so popular that eleven editions were published in Lyons alone within the next twenty-four years; the remaining years of the sixteenth century saw as many as a hundred copies and imitations issued elsewhere. These immensely popular prints may have had the incidental effect of "somewhat domesticating the dreadful fatality," but the primary purpose was to supply an incentive "to maintain a state of readiness—readiness to die gracefully (in both the theological and social senses), to face the judgment of God, to be snatched away from all one has ever known."[55]

Hamlet's poetic *danse macabre* begins with "Cain's jawbone, that did the first murder" (a reference which brings to mind Claudius' explicit association of himself with Cain as a fratricide), and it ends with "Here comes the King" (5.1.72-204 and 3.3.36-38). But although the Prince begins and ends with allusions to Claudius, he manages to touch on many of the memorable figures in the *danse*. When he takes Yorick's skull in his hands, his thoughts are of the jester, whom he recalls with great affection. Then his mind turns to woman, and he imagines dispatching the skull as a bony exemplar of the futility of cosmetics to "my lady"—but to which lady we do not know, whether his mother or Ophelia. His reference to cosmetic painting does cohere with his earlier verbal assault upon Ophelia: "I have heard of your paintings too, well enough. God hath given you one face, and you make yourselves another" (3.1.142-44), but either woman could have been suggested, or perhaps both. At all events, the picture he paints is unforgettable: "Now get you to my lady's chamber, and tell her, let her paint an inch thick, to this favor she must come. Make her laugh at that" (5.1.180-82). Holbein has three relevant woodcuts. The first represents a queen visited by an antic figure of Death wearing a fool's costume with cap and bells over his osseous body (Fig. VI.19). Here we have the union of two common motifs Hamlet also evokes: the visit of Death to a lady, and the appearance of the macbre emissary as a jester (Hamlet of course varies the *moros-mors* topos by imagining the dispatch of a jester's skull as a messenger). Other woodcuts show Mors visiting the lady in her chamber, as Hamlet directs: in one, he calls upon a duchess in her bed and in the other he actually assists a countess at her *toilette*, adjusting her necklace (Fig. VI.20). The visit paid by Death to a young and beautiful woman was so standard in this period that a book has recently appeared on the subject.[56]

*Le portrait macabre*, as Réau calls it,[57] even became a popular sub-genre to portraiture, of which we have already noted one example in Ligozzi's 1604 portrait of a young man (Fig. VI.18 above). As a tandem to that piece, Ligozzi also painted a living woman on one side of a panel (Fig. VI.21), and a dead image on the other. In this way, the most horrific effects were possible: first we see the young woman in the full flower of her beauty, and on the other side her cadaverous head, reflected in a mirror to compound the macabre effect, while scattered about are the jewels she wore and the *toilette* she used in life. Here, surely, we have the *reductio ad horrificum* of Hamlet's "tell her, let her paint an inch thick, to this favor she must come." There were, of course, some poignantly lovely *memento mori* paintings, as for example the *Vanity of Earthly Love* by Luca Cambiaso (1527-85), in the New Orleans Museum of Art, which shows a beautiful nude woman who has just been deprived of Love (i.e., Cupid), by the winged figure of Time, while she gazes intently at a skull. Within either

FIG. VI.19. Death and the Queen, Holbein, *The Dance of Death*

the horrific or the gentle context, Hamlet's intent to send the skull to "my lady" would have strong iconographical support, inducing a concern for the lasting within which merely transient beauty should be understood.[58]

Also popular in Shakespeare's time was the anamorphic *portrait macabre* which showed two different pictures when viewed from different angles. One such was a portrait of Mary Queen of Scots, now in the National Gallery of Scotland (Fig. VI.22). Painted on a corrugated surface, the queen appears in one perspective in all her much-praised human beauty (or at least in as much of it as this stiff painter could convey), whereas from another angle what appears

240

FIG. VI.20. Death and the Countess, Holbein, *The Dance of Death*

is a death's-head. The great Elizabethan miniaturist Nicholas Hilliard did at least one similar painting, showing a woman and Death, and there were many others.[59] The culture which encouraged such works—and we should also recall the skull-watches and the miniature ivory death's-heads we considered earlier in this chapter—would not have misinterpreted Hamlet's thought of sending a jester's skull to his lady's chamber.

Under the stimulus of the Elsinore cemetery, with its disinterred skull and bones, Hamlet's mind does not concentrate only upon Yorick and his lady, but races through a wide succession of social types, all of whom have been

241

FIG. VI.21. Jacopo Ligozzi, *Memento Mori Portrait of a Young Woman*, front and back

struck down by the grisly dancing skeleton representing Death: first a politician and courtier, then a lawyer and rich man, then a lady, and finally the two emperors Alexander and Caesar—social types all found in the visual cycles of the *danse*. At the end of the list he breaks off his reflections to declare, "Here comes the King." The implications would have been clear to alert members of a sixteenth-century audience, both as to Hamlet's state of mind and as to Claudius' future. Just as Claudius comes on stage directly after the mention of Caesar in Hamlet's list, so in Holbein the death of the emperor is followed by the death of the king, who is served his cup of "Rhenish" by the osseous figure of Death. The appended biblical motto is from Ecclesiasticus 10:10—"And he that is today a king, tomorrow shall die"—and the emblematic verses comment that

> He who today is yet a king,
> Tomorrow shall entombèd be,

Nor carry with him anything
Of all his transient royalty.

There is no reason to assume that Shakespeare knew precisely this version, but the broad general tradition was widely diffused, and in the next scene Hamlet affirms with Horatio that the time "will be short," and purposefully adds, "the interim is mine" (5.2.73). Shakespeare's management of Hamlet's contemplation of death has not only deepened his characterization, but has advanced the plot toward its ultimate dénouement.

## VII. Laying Ophelia to Rest

But although Hamlet is personally prepared for his own death, and equally prepared to execute the King, his ruminations on the transience of human life have not prepared him for the shock of encountering the funeral of the woman he loves.[60] He can contemplate sending her a death's-head with a *memento mori* message, but his equanimity is shattered when he discovers that she has already been visited in deadly earnest by the dancing Mors. At first he watches unseen, in a kind of stunned silence, but when he sees her shrouded corpse being lowered into the earth he steps forward to participate in that final rite. The impact of his sudden appearance unleashes the pent-up fury of Laertes, and the ensuing struggle becomes in itself an enacted, theatrical dance of death, presaging the end of the tragedy.

The body of Ophelia is brought on stage as a "corse," according to the directions of the basic quarto text.[61] Reconstructing the stage action in the light of contemporary Elizabethan practice, we can envision the pallbearers bringing forward a bier on which lay Ophelia's body, closely wrapped in a shroud, tied immediately above the head and below the feet, with no more than perhaps a slight parting around the face to make the features visible.[62] The poor were customarily buried in such a way, with the shrouded body placed in the earth unprotected by any coffin. The body could be brought to the graveside on an open, stretcher-like bier, or a coffin (sometimes called a "shell") could be borrowed or rented from the local church wardens, so that the body might be carried into the cemetery in some style, but once there the body would be lifted from the bier or the coffin and placed in the grave with no protection other than the winding sheet. All of this, as the First Gravedigger sang, "for such a

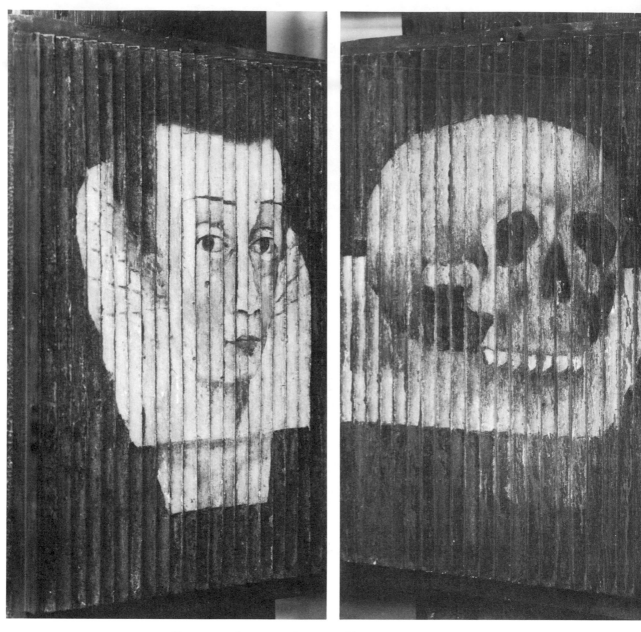

FIG. VI.22. Anonymous anamorphic portrait, Mary Queen of Scots

guest is meet," and it represents what would have happened in the vast majority of burials in Elizabethan England (5.1.90).[63]

One of the most obvious distortions of the "maimèd rites" was the unprotected display of a shrouded body in such a distinguished funeral procession.[64] Those who were "of some estate," whether nobility or merely prosperous citizens, were almost invariably buried in coffins (often in double coffins) and were given their final resting-place within the church, not in an outdoor churchyard[65]—unless of course they were convicted of some major and disgraceful crime. I shall not repeat here the evidence presented elsewhere in this volume that Ophelia's "maimèd rites" were a violation of immemorial and contemporary burial practice for an insane suicide, but merely refer to those treatments (see Chapter Four, Part IV, and Appendix C). Again we see the distortion of expectation and of ceremony in Claudius' Denmark, but that is not the principal effect of introducing the shrouded body of Ophelia exposed on a bier. Here Shakespeare develops an intensely theatrical scene, in a way which would have made considerably more sense in 1600 than it does today. When Laertes takes Ophelia's body in his arms,[66] he is quite literally and quite simply burying his dead.

For those who could afford burial in a coffin, its placing in an open grave in 1600 was not radically different from what we know today: the pallbearers would simply see to lowering the casket by means of ropes or straps. The burial of the vast bulk and coffined splendor of Henry VIII is described in a manuscript of the herald's office: "fifteen strong yeomen of the guard took the coffin, and with five strong linen towels . . . let it into the vault."[67] But most burials involved removing the corpse from a bier or at best from a rented coffin and then placing it in the grave in a far more personal way. This is a very different procedure from anything with which we are familiar today: someone had to take the corpse into his or her arms and put it gently in place. Contemporary descriptions of the burial of the poor are scanty, in comparison with wealthy funerals, but this necessary placing of the body seems to have been performed either by the sexton or by members of the family of the deceased.

We can best reconstruct these scenes by a combination of pictorial and written records. The interment of a woman's body and the valedictory embrace at the grave is graphically portrayed in a sixteenth-century German engraving by Hans Burgkmair, which traces its subject, "Marriage," from wedding cer-

FIG. VI.23. Hans Burgkmair, "Marriage," detail of burial

emony to funeral with apparent reference to the theological conception of "till death do us part"[68] (Fig. VI.23). Interments of this kind had changed very little over the years, and we observe essentially the same action pictured in a French manuscript dating from about 1470 (Fig. VI.24). Such scenes would have been intimately familiar to Elizabethans in 1600, when life expectancy was short and death was a more frequent occurrence among one's family, friends, and neighbors. In the seventeenth century, when the keeping of journals and diaries became increasingly common, we begin to get more circumstantial accounts of the actual laying in the grave of the shrouded corpse. Thus Nicholas Assheton of Downham records the birth and death within half an hour of his child on February 16, 1617/18, and then the burial of the baby: "My mother with me laid the child in the grave."[69] In May of 1650, a country parson and prosperous farmer at Earls Colne named Ralph Josselin recounts how his daughter Mary

246

Placebo.

FIG. VI.24. Burial illumination, Eugene B. Power *Book of Hours*, c. 1470, by follower of Maître François

247

"fell asleep": "she was eight years and forty-five days old when she died." As with the Assheton burial, more than one person was involved in the placing of the corpse in the grave: four pallbearers having brought the girl's body to the churchyard, "Mrs. Margaret Harlakenden and Mrs. Mabel Elliston laid her in the grave," but the diarist also describes himself as a participant in the actual "laying up." As he writes, "I kissed her lips last, and carefully laid up that body; the soul being with Jesus, it rests there till the Resurrection."[70] That final kiss, reminiscent of Laertes' farewell embrace, appears to have been an ancient practice, and is mentioned in an account of funeral customs in Christian communities as early as the year 500.[71]

Such scenes must have been highly emotional, indeed can only have been so, as the dead body was taken in arms and placed in the open earth by one or more of the closer relatives and friends. Under ordinary circumstances, the act of interring a young woman like Ophelia might and I expect would have been performed jointly by her brother, as her closest relative, and by her prospective husband, but of course the circumstances in Elsinore are by no means normal. Even so, an understanding of the normal background of expectation will prepare us to understand the climactic incidents in the burial of Ophelia, and the struggle between Laertes and Hamlet. The Prince wishes to participate in the final act of interment and of farewell, and Laertes repels his efforts to do so. Although neither of these young men understands the point of view of the other, the Globe audience would have understood and in good measure sympathized with both.

The ensuing quarrel is scandalous enough for the most melodramatic tastes, but it was not entirely beyond the realm of credibility in the sixteenth century, when disputes over precedence and procedure in funerals were not confined to the stage.[72] In France, royal funeral processions were so subject to disruption and violence that King Henry II found it necessary to take strong action "to avoid those differences, combustions and debates which before have so often occurred in such affairs and assemblies."[73] Even at the funeral of King Henry IV in 1610, members of the funeral cortege produced a notable wrangle in the effort to achieve greater prominence, so that there was much "jostling and shoving."[74] In England, "disputes over precedence could cause serious delays" in funerals, as in the notable delay of Queen Anne's burial occasioned by the rivalry of noble ladies over which should achieve the place of chief mourner, and a similar problem occurred a few years later over another "question of precedence when the French ambassador made his displeasure known with the place assigned to him in the procession for the funeral of King James I."[75] On a different social level, another kind of dispute completely disrupted a funeral in 1598 at Wrabness when one Thomas Bett "did go into the grave made for the body of Edward Godfrie and did there arrest the body [for unpaid debts] with very unseemly, unrelevant, intemperate speech, whereby our minister would not bury him or read the burial service for him."[76] When judged against such sixteenth-century backgrounds, the struggle between Laertes and Hamlet in the graveyard is no less scandalous, but it is not unique. At the same time, we should recognize that Laertes' precipitating action in taking Ophelia in his arms was neither scandalous nor unique.

When Laertes took the body of his sister into his arms, he was neither "arresting" her nor the funeral service, but was completing the service by the familiar Elizabethan practice of taking into his own hands the final act in the burial of his dead. Distraught not only because of his loss, but also because of the degrading of the insane Ophelia's right to a full and proper ceremony, he breaks out in an emotional "speech of fire," as though he would himself compensate for the meager and demeaning words thus far bestowed upon her in the maimèd rites:

> Hold off the earth awhile,
> Till I have caught her once more in mine arms.

Then, holding the shrouded body in his arms as he stands in the grave, he continues:

> Now pile your dust upon the quick and the dead
> Till of this flat a mountain you have made
> T' o'ertop old Pelion or the skyish head
> Of blue Olympus. (5.1.237-41)

At this point Hamlet's emotions also become strained beyond endurance, and he steps forward from his concealment. He too has a claim upon Ophelia, as Gertrude had just reminded the audience when she scattered flowers over the bier,

> I hoped thou shouldest have been my Hamlet's wife.
> I thought thy bride-bed to have decked, sweet maid,
> And not have strewed thy grave.       (5.1.231-33)

With greater cause of grief, and deeply moved beyond restraint, the Prince later justifies his own intervention into the final act of laying the dead body in the earth:

> I loved Ophelia. Forty thousand brothers
> Could not with all their quantity of love
> Make up my sum.       (5.1.256-58)

He says this to Laertes after their fight, when explanation is already too late, but we should not overlook that fact that the Prince had first come forward to the graveside with relatively restrained words:

> What is he whose grief
> Bears such an emphasis? whose phrase of sorrow
> Conjures the wand'ring stars, and makes them stand
> Like wonder-wounded hearters? This is I,
> Hamlet the Dane.       (5.1.241-45)

Although these words are highly emotional, they are not necessarily offensive in themselves, unless the actor chooses to deliver them in an offensive manner. It is true that modern actors and critics alike usually read them as though Hamlet has begun by rebuking Laertes in a gratuitously caustic way, thus inviting the quarrel which ensues. But I would suggest that this is to "read in" here the undoubtedly angry tone of the later speeches, delivered after Laertes has attempted to strangle him. A more likely (although not demonstrable) sequence seems to me to run as follows: Hamlet steps forward to join in the mourning and to participate in the actual placing of the body in the grave, as would seem appropriate for one who had hoped to marry Ophelia. Instead of intending to start a quarrel with Laertes, he intends to take part with him in that final and familial act of interment. But what might in other and more ordinary circumstances have been a joining in common grief over the laying to rest of a dead sister and an intended bride quickly flares into a bitter and potentially deadly struggle.

Hamlet, utterly unprepared for the shock of stumbling upon the burial of the beloved Ophelia, is so obsessed with his own overwhelming emotions that he gives no thought to the sensitivity of Laertes. Laertes, on his own part, not only knows that Hamlet has killed his father but also regards him as directly and callously responsible for the madness and suicide of his sister, and so he is in no mood to accept any overture of common grief. Both points of view are understandable. Thus as Hamlet advances toward the grave to take part in the mournful laying to rest, Laertes responds with the bitter oath, "the devil take thy soul," and lunges for his jugular. To this physical assault, Hamlet's initial response is moderate, in words if not in action:

Thou pray'st not well.
I prithee take thy fingers from my throat,
For, though I am not splenitive and rash,
Yet have I in me something dangerous,
Which let thy wisdom fear. Hold off thy hand.           (5.1.245-50)

Exactly what happens thereafter is not spelled out either by the dialogue or by the stage directions, but the overall development is clear. Once aroused, that "something dangerous" in himself to which Hamlet refers is given full vent in his counterattack upon Laertes. Perhaps he responds in kind to Laertes' attempt to choke him, and in his fury almost throttles him before others intervene to tear him away. In whatever way, he gives him a thorough thrashing, so that Laertes is unable to speak again in this scene, even though he is directly addressed at least once by the Queen, twice by the King, and again and again by Hamlet. Hamlet obviously gets the better of the fray, both physically and verbally. His fury is unbridled, so that the Queen must plead with him and Horatio calls, "good my lord, be quiet." Even the King commands "Pluck them asunder"—which he certainly would not do if he thought Laertes might succeed now in killing or at least humiliating Hamlet. What the Prince says[77] and does after he has torn Laertes' hands from his throat indicates not only that he is violently enraged by the curse and assault upon him, but also that he had expected no such response and is puzzled by it. What the King had earlier described in Hamlet as a nature "most generous" has naively expected acceptance rather than antipathy (4.7.133f.), but Laertes' response disabuses him of that over-simple assumption, and the Prince shortly indicates that he will be prepared for whatever may follow. In his last speech in the scene, he asks Laertes,

> Hear you sir,
> What is the reason that you use me thus?
> I loved you ever.

Laertes does not answer that overture, and Hamlet now seems to sense that there can be no diverting of the forces which rush toward a catastrophe:

> But it is no matter
> Let Hercules himself do what he may,
> The cat will mew, the dog will have his day.[78]           (5.1.275-79)

Hamlet's reactions at Ophelia's funeral demonstrate an essential continuity in his passionate nature. His earlier reflections on death show that he is resigned to the common mortality of man, but his is no stoic resignation. In another play, Shakespeare has given us an example of one distinctively stoic response to the death of a beloved woman when Brutus reflects dispassionately upon his wife's death by suicide: "Why, farewell, Portia. We must die, Messala./ With meditating that she must die once,/ I have the patience to endure it now."[79] Whether we like it or not, that is stoicism, but it is not Hamlet. He has, however, arrived at an attitude toward death in general, and toward his own death in particular which is admirable in a stoic as well as in a Christian perspective, although primarily developed in Christian terms.

At this point we can return to our starting place, to Hamlet holding the skull and meditating upon the mysteries of life and death, and to Hals' portrait of another young man in essentially the same posture (Fig. VI.1). Although there is presumably no direct connection between the two works, they do represent the highest achievements in painting and in poetry of a very widespread tradition. Considered in the terms of their own time, neither would have been understood to convey emotional sickness or morbidity, but rather a sane grasp of the realities of human life and destiny.[80] The visual *memento mori* we have examined in connection with the *memento mori* dramatization in *Hamlet* did not trap a person in the spiritual cul-de-sac of a sterile preoccupation with death. On the contrary, they were directed toward life, and toward the effective living of life which, however long or short, should be lived in confident reliance upon the providence of God. Thus Sir Thomas Gresham's *memento mori* portrait is framed with the fourfold reiteration, "Dominus mihi adiutor," and thus Hamlet declares that "There is a divinity that shapes our ends,/ Rough-hew them how we will." Indeed, it is Hamlet who gives the whole tradition its finest summation: "There is a special providence in the fall of a sparrow. If it be now, 'tis not to come; if it be not to come, it will be now; if it be not now, yet it will come: the readiness is all" (5.2.10-11, 208-11). Hamlet's reflections in the graveyard provide the transition between his earlier uncertainties and that settled assurance which he displays in the final scene of the play.

# SEVEN

# Finale

## 1. Providence, Death, and Readiness

Hamlet's reflections upon life and death in the graveyard provided for Shakespeare's Globe audiences a credible transition between his indecision and agony in the earlier acts and the serenity and assurance which he displays in the final scene of the play. Conversely, those *memento mori* reflections are completed and put into context by his affirmations of faith in providence early in the last scene. The continuity is there, and Elizabethans would have recognized a unity in the dramatic construction which has sometimes escaped modern readers. Each dramatic element leads to the next with what may be called a narrative logic in the unfolding of plot and of character.

As part of the dénouement of tragedy, Aristotle called for the protagonist to experience anagnorisis—the discovery or recognition of his own true situation—which Hamlet shows in the fifth act. In the first scene of this act, he explores and defines, in the face of death, the vanity of human pretensions—not, be it noted, of all human effort, but rather of pride and self-sufficiency, which he exemplifies in his procession of dance-of-death figures. In the modern age, anagnorisis often leads to a sense of despair and nihilism, or to a concentration only upon the individual existence: we are familiar with such reactions in our time, and it is easy to read them back into this Renaissance play. But as we have already seen, the implications of Hamlet's reflections among the tombs would have been differently understood in 1600. And early in the last scene of the play those implications are explicitly drawn and defined in Hamlet's insistence upon divine providence.

The first reference comes early, as he explains to Horatio how he came to discover the King's perfidious order for his execution in England:

> Rashly,
> And praised be rashness for it—let us know,
> Our indiscretion sometime serves us well

When our deep plots do pall, and that should learn us
There's a divinity that shapes our ends,
Rough-hew them how we will—                                    (5.2.6-11)

Thus Hamlet ascribes his experience on shipboard, and his later deliverance, to the active surveillance of divinity. This conception of the divine oversight of individual lives was widely held in Shakespeare's time, and we find a roughly comparable treatment in Calvin:

> If a man light among thieves or wild beasts, if by wind suddenly rising he suffer shipwreck on the sea . . . , if having been tossed with the waves, he attain to the haven, if miraculously he escape but a finger breadth from death, all these chances as well of prosperity as of adversity the reason of the flesh doth ascribe to fortune. But whosoever is taught by the mouth of Christ, that all the hairs of his head are numbered, will seek for a cause further off, and will firmly believe that all chances are governed by the secret counsel of God.[1]

By a kind of cultural coincidence (and I do not suspect direct influence), Calvin illustrated the workings of providence by experiences similar to those Shakespeare later attributed to Hamlet. Hamlet is one who was "tossed with the waves," who did "light among thieves," who did "escape but a finger breadth from death," and who came to believe firmly that all these "chances are governed by the secret counsel of God." In the same vein, Richard Hooker saw "every particular nature, every mere natural agent, only as an instrument created at the beginning, and ever since the beginning . . . to work his [God's] own will and pleasure withal."[2] And Bishop Lancelot Andrewes preached that "if a sparrow fall not to the ground without the providence of God . . . much less does any man or woman which are more worth than many sparrows. And if any one man comes not to his end (as we may call it) by casualty, but it is God that delivers him so to die."[3]

Hamlet's first affirmation of faith in providence refers directly to his experience of deliverance from the death to which Claudius had sent him. That reference to his narrow escape reminds us of his extensive analyses of death in the graveyard. His coming to terms with death in the earlier scene is integrally related to his faith in the "divinity that shapes our ends," and prepares the audience to recognize it as dramatically credible. In a 1567 Elizabethan *Book of Common Prayer,* the prayer for trust in God opens thus: "The beginning of the fall of man was trust in himself. The beginning of the restoring of man was distrust in himself and trust in God."[4] Although no one would have regarded that sequence as logically inevitable it was so common a part of Christian experience and teaching that it would have struck audiences in 1600 as psychologically convincing. When judged in this context, Hamlet's comments on Yorick's skull demonstrate distrust in mortality, whereas his comments on his deliverance demonstrate the concomitant trust in divinity.

Hamlet next recounts to Horatio how Rosencrantz and Guildenstern "go to 't" (5.2.56) because he was able to substitute one warrant of execution for another. Under the circumstances, his only hope of avoiding execution himself was to make certain that they would be so speedily executed that they would have no chance, however brief, to explain that Claudius actually intended the sudden death of Hamlet. The presence of the royal seal in his purse thus makes possible Hamlet's escape from execution, and the execution instead of his former friends and present enemies, which again raises in his mind the issue of providence, and he declares, "Why, even in that was heaven ordinant" (5.2.48).

There follows a brief but decisive comment on conscience (to which we shall shortly turn), and then the arrangements for the fencing match. As Hamlet awaits the arrival of the court and the staging of the contest, he expresses his misgivings to Horatio—"thou wouldst not think how ill all's here about my heart. But it is no matter." Horatio, concerned by his friend's premonition, offers to forestall the match, but Hamlet refuses to allow him to do so. Regarding himself as completely in the hands of divinity, he is prepared for whatever may come:

> we defy augury. There is a special providence in the fall of a
> sparrow. If it be now, 'tis not to come; if it be not to come, it will
> be now; if it be not now, yet it will come. The readiness is all. Since
> no man of aught he leaves knows, what is't to leave betimes? Let be
> (5.2.201-12).

The only dependable knowledge is not human, but is the knowledge with which divinity acts, and that is what Hamlet is now prepared to "let be." Three years before the appearance of Shakespeare's play, a devotional book called *Brad-*

*ford's Beads* was published, containing a reflection instructively similar to Hamlet's thought here:

> This ought to bee unto us most certain that nothing is done without thy providence, O Lord; that is, that nothing is done be it good or bad, sweet or sour, but by thy knowledge, that is, by thy will, wisdom, and ordinance (for all these knowledge doth comprehend in it), as by thy holy word we are taught in many places that even the life of a sparrow is not without thy will.[5]

A similar reliance upon divine knowledge is apparent in Hamlet's comments. Furthermore, the Christianity which has been implicit in each of his comments upon providence up to this point now becomes explicit with the evocation of the fall of a sparrow, one of the most familiar sayings of Jesus.[6] As Matthew 10:29 puts it, "are not two sparrows sold for a farthing? And one of them shall not fall on the ground without your Father."[7]

Readiness, too, is repeatedly emphasized in the New Testament. In Matthew 24:42 and 44, Jesus commanded, "Watch therefore, for ye know not what hour your Lord will come," and again, "Therefore be ye also ready; for in such an hour as ye think not the Son of Man cometh," and similarly in Luke 12:40. In Revelation 3:2, the angel advises, "Be watchful and strengthen the things which remain, that are ready to die," and Saint Paul wrote in II Timothy 4:6 of the coming end of his own life as a sacrifice offered to God: "For I am now ready to be offered, and the time of my departing is at hand."[8] Based upon such biblical emphases, exhortations to readiness appear from all quarters. St. Francis de Sales wrote: "Happy are they who, being always on their guard against death, are always ready to go."[9] Similarly Martin Luther said Christians "should behave as those who are at every moment ready for death," and Calvin advised that we should always be ready and that "we ought to live as if we were every moment about to depart this life."[10]

Richard Hooker, the great spokesman for Elizabethan Anglicanism, wrote that we should "provide always beforehand that those evils overtake us not which death unexpected doth use to bring upon careless men, and that although it be sudden in itself, nevertheless in regard of our prepared minds it may not be sudden."[11] Coverdale taught that each person should prepare "to the intent that at all hours he may be found ready" and Latimer also admonished that

God wishes us to be "ready at all times."[12] Archbishops Grindal and Sandys similarly pointed to the certainty of death but the uncertainty of its timing as incentives "that we always be in readiness."[13]

That is the frame of reference to which Hamlet's "the readiness is all" refers, and his expiring words pick up the same theme. First he provides for the orderly succession of Fortinbras to the Danish throne (a subject to which we shall return) and sends his chosen successor a message, but his strength fails him and he breaks off in mid-sentence, unable to continue, and says simply that "the rest is silence" (5.2.347). That reference to "silence" has been read by some intelligent twentieth-century critics as suggesting non-existence, but it did not carry that implication in 1600.[14] The meaning is twofold, that Hamlet cannot complete his message and that he cannot continue his life. In the second sense, the reference to death as silence occurs frequently in the Bible, and would have been familiar to Shakespeare's Elizabethan audiences, summarizing as it did the end of all human effort and of an individual's capacity to express himself in the world.[15] In the same sense, the official Elizabethan *Homilies* refer to death as "quietness, rest, and everlasting joy."[16]

Interpretations of the biblical metaphor of death as silence or quietness were generally agreed upon in Shakespeare's time. The central view, which could be documented across the range of major Christian groups, may be conveniently illustrated in Calvin's commentaries. On the treatment of the dead as voiceless in Isaiah 38:18, Calvin wrote that the prophet, like others speaking of the silence of death, "did not consider what kind of condition awaited them after death," but referred instead to the loss of the power to speak and do God's will in this world.[17] He treated Psalms 94:17 in the context of bodily impotence in the tomb, before the general resurrection: the Psalmist here "speaks of 'his life dwelling in silence,' for the dead lie in the grave without feeling or strength." And he interpreted Psalms 30:9 as meaning "but my death . . . reduces me to eternal silence" as a reference to the fear of dying without children to continue the family line.[18] Any and all of these suggestions may be pertinent to Hamlet's final words, but the main point is simple and direct: the expression of Hamlet's mind and will in this world has come to that ending for which he had declared that the readiness is all. Now, that "fell sergeant, Death,/ Is strict in his arrest" (5.2.325).

## 11. Perfect Conscience

Hamlet's references to conscience in the final scene occur within the context of providence, death, and readiness.[19] The cases of conscience which had preoccupied, troubled, and perplexed him are now resolved. Here there is no more fear that conscience will make him a coward, and no more of that vexing uncertainty which had so disturbed him during his soliloquies. Both retrospectively and prospectively, his conscience is at peace. He has already repented for the death of Polonius; as for his towering passion with Laertes, he expresses his sorrow for that privately to Horatio and he later provides a handsome and gracious public apology to Laertes.[20]

For the execution of Rosencrantz and Guildenstern, on the other hand, he has no regrets. When they had arrived in Denmark in the second act, he had eloquently appealed to them for their loyalty, but they had chosen instead to soak up "the king's countenance, his rewards, his authorities," as he put it when he tauntingly addressed them as sponges before he and they departed for England (4.2.15-20). To his mother he had said of these two that "they bear the mandate," and had predicted that as his arresting marshals they would conduct him to whatever knavery the King had planned. He referred to them in two metaphors, both revealing. First he says, "I will trust [them] as I will adders fanged," which identifies them with the only poisonous (and indeed deadly poisonous) reptile known in England. I suggest that we are to read this not as hyperbole, but as a straight, factual appraisal: to Hamlet, they are lethally venomous serpents, and given the opportunity, he is sure that they will strike him dead. The other metaphor is equally telling, drawn from warfare: they are military engineers who, in besieging a city, tunnel under its walls, plant explosives, and then blow these up so as to destroy the defenses and capture the prize. Hamlet's response is that of the defending soldier who counters the enemy stratagem by digging a deeper tunnel under that of his attackers, and then destroying them by setting off their own explosive. The military analogy fairly blazes as Hamlet asserts to Gertrude his confidence that he can outmaneuver his enemies:

> Let it work.
> For 'tis the sport to have the enginer
> Hoist with his own petar, and 't shall go hard

But I will delve one yard below their mines
And blow them at the moon. O, tis most sweet
When in one line two crafts directly meet.                    (3.4.203-11)

Hamlet regards himself and his two schoolfellows as soldiers actively maneu-
vering to destroy each other in the life-and-death struggles of a war.

The Prince's eventual defeat of these adversaries comes very close to the
projection he made to his mother. When he opens their packet aboard ship,
he finds that they bear a mandate to the tributary king of England "That on
the supervise, no leisure bated,/ No, not to stay the grinding of the axe,/ My
head should be struck off" (5.2.23-25), and he reverses that mandate so that
it will apply to them, thus precisely hoisting them with their own petar (3.4.207).
There is a rational symmetry here which obviously appeals to Hamlet, as the
offenders are destroyed by their own offensive, the attackers by their own
attack. He believes that they have knowingly consented to be the King's agents
in killing him, and he has no qualms about turning their plots against them.
But if Hamlet's stratagem is to succeed, the utmost speed is essential: Rosencrantz and Guildenstern must be executed as soon as he and they arrive in
England. When Hamlet substituted the warrant of execution, he was still aboard
ship: he had no notion of the impending encounter with the pirates, and he
still expected to arrive in England with Rosencrantz and Guildenstern—indeed,
in some sense under their guard. They must have no opportunity to expostulate,
lest they reveal Claudius' actual intent, and achieve Hamlet's execution. So his
rewritten mandate orders their immediate execution, "without debatement further, more or less" (5.2.45).

There follows another provision which occasionally raises problems for
readers. Hamlet provides that England "should the bearers put to sudden death,/
Not shriving time allowed" (5.2.47). According to one interpretation, Hamlet
is here willfully and purposely assuring the damnation as well as the death of
Rosencrantz and Guildenstern, by denying the Roman Catholic rites of penance
and of extreme unction before death.[21] Now if Hamlet were characterized in
the play as a Roman Catholic, that appraisal would be a possible analysis of
his intentions and frame of mind, although even then it would be questionable.
Here we should remember that when the young Dominican Jacques Clément
struck down the French King Henry III in 1589, he himself was promptly
stabbed to death by the king's attendants, so that shriving time was not allowed

either for the king or for his assailant. In the controversy over this act of regicide or tyrannicide (depending upon the point of view), I have been able to discover no argument that Clément's actions willfully assured the king's damnation, even among those who thought the king to be damnable, nor that Clément's unshriven death assured his damnation. As for the assassin, he was honored as a martyr by the Catholic League and by the preachers of his order, and the Pope regarded his success as a sign of providence. In short, Clément "was proclaimed from the pulpits of Paris as 'the holy martyr of Jesus Christ' who had delivered France from 'that dog of a Henry of Valois.' "[22] I suggest, therefore, that even from the Catholic point of view it is dubious to argue that Hamlet would have been accused of willfully insuring the damnation of Rosencrantz and Guildenstern.

But that point aside, one of the clearest things about this play is that Shakespeare has carefully and consistently cast Hamlet as a Protestant. In the first scene in which he appears, Hamlet is four times explicitly identified as a student at Wittenberg, and as one who wishes to return there as soon as possible. In 1600, it would have been inconceivable for a Catholic prince to attend Wittenberg, the very birthplace of the Reformation and a university devoted to the Protestantism Martin Luther had launched there. Believing that "the readiness is all" and that extreme unction was "a flattering unction" (3.4.146), Hamlet could not have believed that his denial of it to his former schoolfellows would have doomed their souls. When Hamlet wished to send an adversary to hell, he could make it plain (as he did in his horrifying speech over the praying Claudius), but here he did not.

Aside from that point, Hamlet's disposition of Rosencrantz and Guildenstern still seems callous to some critics of the play. What Horatio thinks of all this may be debated. How did Shakespeare's original actor read Horatio's laconic line, "so Rosencrantz and Guildenstern go to 't"? It could be read so as to suggest the justness of their punishment, or the sudden turning of Fortune's wheel, or it could have registered wonder at Hamlet's resourcefulness, or perhaps some measure of shock at his indifference to the life and death of former friends. The manner of delivery would be the key, and there is no way to determine or demonstrate that now, but Hamlet's own attitude could not be more clear:

Why, man, they did make love to this employment.

They are not near my conscience; their defeat
Does by their own insinuation grow.
'Tis dangerous when the baser nature comes
Between the pass and fell incensèd points
Of mighty opposites.                              (5.2.57-62)

I can sympathize with sensitive modern readers who regard this as insensitive, but I cannot believe that many Elizabethans would have been much disturbed by it.[23] Rosencrantz and Guildenstern had elected to play a deadly game against their prince, whereupon he took their own play, turned it against them, and won.

Several sixteenth-century reactions can be postulated here. We can see Hamlet either as the rightful king who executes justice upon two would-be assassins; or we can take Hamlet's own analogy of a war in process, and assume that Hamlet as a combatant has the rights of war, allowing him to kill his enemies before they can kill him; or we can apply an argument which was used from the Middle Ages into the seventeenth century to brand tyrannical agents like Rosencrantz and Guildenstern as traitors: thus John of Salisbury held of "the overthrow of the laws by the tyrant. . . . [that] any citizen who fails to avenge it when he can is thereby proved false to himself and to the commonwealth," and Johannes Althusius in Shakespeare's time declared of those who will not assist the true prince but support the tyrant instead that "those who refuse to help the resisting ephor with their strength, money, and counsel are considered enemies and deserters."[24] There is no way to deny that Rosencrantz and Guildenstern were in fact "enemies and deserters" who "refuse to help the resisting ephor," and I am confident that most of the Globe audience in 1600 would have accepted some such arguments as justifying Hamlet's attitude, and that few if any would have felt that his conscience should be disturbed by the execution of Rosencrantz and Guildenstern, who were merely cat's-paws for the assassin Claudius.

Claudius clearly exhibited the most conspicuous characteristics of a tyrant, as we have already seen in some detail, and to those public evils are added the depravities of private life the play reveals. The challenge of acting against him rests in this play upon Hamlet and upon Hamlet alone, as prince of the blood. Under the circumstances Shakespeare dramatizes, there would at first have been differences of judgment within the audience as to whether Hamlet should strike him down, and as we have seen the Prince debates these with himself in his agonizing case of conscience. During four acts, he examines his conscience through the whole range of possible doubts. Then in the final scene of the play he has come to that degree of assurance which casuists from the Stoics through Catholics and Protestants alike had predicted as the proper conclusion of a full analysis of conscience, a degree of assurance which would undergird action.²⁵ He expresses his conviction through rhetorical questions which indicate the affirmative answers and actions that most members of the Globe audience would by now have been prepared to applaud in him:

> Dost it not, think thee, stand me now upon—
> He that hath killed my King, and whored my mother,
> Popped in between th' election and my hopes,
> Thrown out his angle for my proper life,
> And with such coz'nage—is't not perfect conscience
> To quit him with this arm? And is't not to be damned
> To let this canker of our nature come
> In further evil? (5.2.63-70)

Basically, that statement stands as the conclusion to Hamlet's forensic soliloquies. The Globe audience would have recognized the perplexing issues Hamlet had debated as he debated them, and his considerations were so inclusive that he would, I think, have elicited the sympathy of most people in the theater. This is not to say that all or even most would have adopted his final view as their own—which is not after all the purpose of the theater—but the sympathy he generated would have been sufficient to secure their acceptance of him as morally heroic within the confines of the theater.

The social climate in 1600 afforded the keyboard, with various notes, harmonies, and instruments, from which Shakespeare produced his tragic symphony, and he constructed his play so as to exploit and develop the precedents for treating a virtuous tyrannicide as heroic. The Greeks and Romans notably admired and honored those who would kill a tyrant. In England, the hereditary principle was so strong that most Englishmen would have assumed Claudius to be a usurper until they were told in the last scene that the Danish monarchy was elective. Thus for most of the play, and for the whole time of Hamlet's inner debates, many would have assumed as had Bishop Hooper that the mere process of coronation "maketh not a king, but the laws of God and of the land, that giveth by succession the right of the kingdom to the old king's first heir male in England and other realms," so that Claudius would have seemed "a traitor [who] may receive the crown, and yet [be a] true king nothing the rather."[26] That judgment would not in itself have solved Hamlet's problem, nor the audience's perplexity as to what he should do. The Protestant monarchomachs went far beyond such arguments to establish inclusive justifications for overthrowing a tyrant. Even though he might not be a usurper, a ruler who "violates the bonds and shatters the restraints by which human society has been maintained," as Althusius put it, would in this view leave magnates and princes of the blood no other recourse than to take up arms. In striking down a tyrant, according to Buchanan, they would be engaged in "the most just of wars."[27] Not only did princes and magistrates have the right to destroy a tyrant, but they had the duty to do so, according to teachings shared by Calvinists and Jesuits. As the Huguenot du Plessis-Mornay put it, they are not only permitted "to use force against a tyrant . . . but obliged as part of the duty of their office, and they have no excuse if they should fail to act."[28] In a somewhat more general context, Calvin wrote of inactive magistrates that if they "put up their sword and hold their hands pure from blood while in the meantime desperate men do reign with murders and slaughters, then they shall make themselves guilty of most great wickedness."[29] Those phrases remind us of the sixteenth-century point of view which Hamlet finally accepts when he declares not only that it is "perfect conscience/ To quit him with this arm" but also that it would be "to be damned/ To let this canker of our nature come/ In further evil." And at least for the purposes of the theater, Shakespeare's original audience would by and large have agreed, by the end of the play.

## III. Election, Succession, and the Dying Voice

In addition to announcing Hamlet's hard-won assurance, the "perfect conscience" speech supplies one other new piece of information, and it is very important: here for the first time in the play, the Globe audience is informed of something few could be expected to have known when they entered the theater, namely that the Danish monarchy was elective. That information is reiterated at the end of the play when Hamlet casts his "dying voice" for the election of Fortinbras to the now vacant throne (5.2.65 and 344f.).

The introduction of that factor into the play at this very late point, just as Hamlet is about to kill the King, requires explanation.[30] Shakespeare's practice in other tragedies offers no earlier precedent nor later parallel for interjecting equally crucial information this close to the end of a play, so we must presume that what he does here is uniquely appropriate to this particular story. Furthermore, in no other play does he present the killer of "a Christian king" in so favorable a way as Hamlet, and I suggest that these two factors are connected.

The final Elizabethan doctrine concerning the use of force against a tyrant was, as we have seen, contained in *The True Difference between Christian Subjection and Unchristian Rebellion*, which was issued three times between 1585 and 1595. In that work, commissioned and rewarded by Queen Elizabeth, Bishop Thomas Bilson justified Protestant princes and nobles who led wars against kings and emperors in order to "defend themselves from injustice and violence" as well as "to save the state from open tyranny." Although his arguments are not altogether consistent, they are quite instructive for our purposes. An hereditary monarch who becomes a tyrant may be opposed and restrained by force of arms, but he "may not be deposed." That restriction, however, does not apply to elected kings. If a ruler owes his crown to election, princes and nobles "may lawfully resist him . . . or else repel him as a tyrant, and set another in his place by the right and freedom of their country."[31] Thus, an elected tyrant such as Claudius is fair game.[32]

In this light, Shakespeare's late announcement that Denmark is an elective monarchy becomes considerably more intelligible: by classifying Claudius as an elected king just before and just after he is killed by the Prince, Shakespeare has presented Hamlet in a more favorable way while protecting himself and his company from the danger of dramatizing a scene in which a sympathetic and attractive hero kills a crowned king. Should the authorities object, the Lord Chamberlain's Men could point to the official Elizabethan doctrine as presented by Bishop Bilson. These precautions are particularly appropriate when we consider them in connection with contemporary events in London.

Although we are not certain of the specific date when Shakespeare's *Hamlet* first appeared on stage, we do know that our primary text of that play was first published several years after the crisis of the Earl of Essex's uprising against Elizabeth early in 1601. Investigations and trails following this conspiracy revealed that followers of Essex had paid the Chamberlain's Company to stage

Shakespeare's *Richard II*, complete with the deposition and eventual assassination of Richard, on the day before their attempted coup. Essex and his followers took to the streets of London on Sunday, February 8, 1601, attempting to gather popular support for their insurrection, but it was abortive, and within a few hours the principal rebels were all captured. Trials of the conspirators followed almost at once, and Essex himself was beheaded on February 25.

The part of Shakespeare's company in this sequence of events was carefully investigated, and they were so fully exonerated of willful complicity that they were invited to present another play before the Queen and her court on the night before Essex's execution. Nonetheless, attention was publicly focused upon the potentially incendiary influence of the theater, and for some time the acting companies were subject to more than ordinary suspicion and surveillance. In the prosecution of Essex's steward, Attorney General Coke cited the fact that he had arranged for the performance of a play which "set forth the killing of a king upon a stage."[33] And in that offending play, as students of Shakespeare well know, Bolingbroke, who deposed a lawful and hereditary English king, was by no means so attractive a figure as Hamlet the Dane, nor did Bolingbroke himself take a hand directly in killing the reigning monarch. To present the killer of a king as a sympathetic character could entail misunderstanding on the part of the authorities and also of the audience. Precautions were thus advisable so as to avoid giving offense either to the English throne or to loyal English citizens in the theater. Thus Shakespeare introduced the fact that Denmark was an elective monarchy just before the Prince actually kills the King, and he reminds the audience of that fact once again shortly after the King's death.[34] Without compromise either to his story or to his protagonist, Shakespeare has thus managed to dramatize a broadly topical subject and has gotten away with the murder of a tyrannous king, to the applause of his Elizabethan audiences. Within the rules of the game, Claudius deserves no better than he gets, and as prince of the blood Hamlet gives it to him fairly and squarely.

Finally, Hamlet acts to avoid the onset of anarchy as a consequence of the tyrannicide and of his own death. It will be recalled from our earlier reconstruction of attitudes toward rebellion that there was a persistent fear lest the violent replacement of a tyrant might lead to a social chaos worse even than the tyranny. Thus Thomas Aquinas had allowed that overthrowal of tyranny "is not strictly sedition except perhaps in the case that it is accompanied by such disorder that the community suffers greater harm from the subsequent disturbances than it would from the continuance of the former rule." It was on this basis that the official *Homilies* could argue that rebellion is inevitably "worse than the worst government of the worst prince that hitherto hath been." Although the continental reformer Henry Bullinger would not go that far, and although he like others maintained that wise and just resistance was possible, he nonetheless warned that a tyrannicide may be "so far from doing good in killing the tyrant, that it is to be feared lest he do make the evil double so much as it was before."[35]

Hamlet's support of Fortinbras for election to the throne has understandably troubled many readers: it is a less than ideal choice, but Shakespeare is holding a mirror up to nature, and human societies usually find themselves forced to make less than ideal choices. Hamlet's own attitude toward Fortinbras, as expressed in his soliloquy in act four, was ambivalent. He admired his decisiveness and fortitude (qualities which will be sorely needed in the new Danish king),[36] but depreciated his pursuit of straw and eggshells in Poland. At the same time, we must recognize the sixteenth-century view that although tyranny was unacceptable, perfection in a ruler was unattainable. Thus du Plessis-Mornay, one of the greatest of the monarchomach theorists, had written that "we should not look for perfect princes, but consider ourselves fortunate if we have men of middling virtue as our rulers."[37] On that count, Fortinbras qualifies. Furthermore, he is the only other prince available in the play and he has familial connections and hereditary claims upon the throne. As for the other remaining characters, none has those royal credentials. Even if someone wished to argue that a Globe audience would have credited the election of a commoner to the throne (which I doubt), the options open to Hamlet are severely limited. He could scarcely have cast his voice for Horatio with any plausible expectation of decisive royal leadership from that admirable but self-effacing scholar; Osric would be utterly inconceivable, and Laertes is dead. So of the choices available to him, Hamlet takes the only one creditable to his judgment. It may be said that Shakespeare could have introduced and developed another character more acceptable to modern readers than Fortinbras, but that would have required him to have extended the length of the play considerably beyond its present length of four and a half hours of stage time—which scarcely seems feasible for a play already the longest in the canon.

All things considered, Shakespeare has done everything necessary to satisfy his own contemporaries, who constituted the audience which concerned him. Elizabethans would have accepted the end of the play as insuring the restoration of order. In those terms—which are decisive—Hamlet wisely supports Fortinbras as successor to the crown. Horatio as Hamlet's delegated spokesman announces the Prince's choice and places it in the context of assuring an orderly succession: "let this same be presently performed,/ Even while men's minds are wild, lest more mischance/ On plots and errors happen" (5.2.382-84).

The establishment of order in Denmark is but one part of Shakespeare's careful guidance of the audience's response to Hamlet at the end of the play. The Prince has resolved his own conscience, and he now shows no sign of that satanic rage to see Claudius suffer in hell which he had earlier expressed. Once he is prepared in mind to act, he waits calmly for providence to provide his cue and the propitious moment. This comes when Gertrude cries out to him that she has been poisoned by the drink Claudius prepared and when, immediately thereafter, Laertes reveals that the rapier was also poisoned, so that "in thee there is not half an hour's life" (5.2.298-309). Hamlet's instant response is to drive that rapier into the King. Suffering from that deadly thrust, Claudius gasps for air, and as he does so Hamlet forces the dregs of the poisoned cup down his throat. The words Hamlet addresses to Claudius here are deeply, passionately felt, but they also have about them something of the quality of those Elizabethan summaries of crimes committed by a criminal which were read at public executions:

Here, thou incestuous, murd'rous, damnèd Dane,
Drink off this potion. Is thy union here?
Follow my mother. (5.2.313-15)

That verdict culminates the Prince's weighing of possibilities through five acts of the play, and epitomizes the retributive justice that Claudius, who has lived by poison and sword, should now die by the very instruments of his own treacherous devising. That poisoned chalice which Claudius prepared and from which he must now drink may most appropriately be glossed by words Shakespeare wrote a few years after *Hamlet*, words spoken by Macbeth on retribution: "This even handed justice/ Commends th' ingredience of our poisoned chalice/ To our own lips" (*Macb.* 1.7.10-12).[38]

## IV. Final Judgments within the Play

But Shakespeare does not leave that conclusion merely implicit in the nature of the event, although it is surely there. In addition, he spells out in some detail three different appraisals of the Prince and his actions. These appraisals come successively from Laertes, Horatio, and Fortinbras. Laertes affirms the essential justice, the rightness, of the nemesis which has come upon him and the King, and he speaks from the vantage point of one who has himself been destroyed; Horatio speaks from his own uniquely intimate knowledge of Hamlet's mind and character, and assesses him as a human soul *sub specie aeternitatis*; finally, Fortinbras speaks with the objectivity of one who has not been involved in the play's central issues, and who judges Hamlet as a man of action, a prince and a potential king.

Laertes' first response comes after Hamlet has wrested the unbaited rapier from him, and wounded him with it. Calling himself "a woodcock to mine own springe," he underscores the fact that he has been caught in the very trap he had treacherously laid for the destruction of Hamlet: "I am justly killed with mine own treachery." He quickly explains to Hamlet what has happened, and again underscores the justice of such retribution:

> The foul practice
> Hath turned itself on me. Lo, here I lie,
> Never to rise again. Thy mother's poisoned.
> I can no more. The king, the king's to blame.      (5.2.295-309)

There is no sentimentality here, no evasion, no search for excuses, but instead only the clear-eyed perception of honest death. Laertes has received his just deserts, and he admits it; he knows the King is to blame, and he says that too. When Hamlet has poured the drink down Claudius' throat, Laertes comments that

> He is justly served.
> It is a poison tempered by himself.      (5.2.316f.)

That judgment is all the more significant coming from one who had himself been subverted by the sophistries of the King. Laertes is of course not alone in succumbing to Claudius' appeal: a number of modern critics have also been taken in. But Laertes is not permanently deceived, and repudiates his own gullibility. His dying affirmation of the essential justice of Hamlet's actions must be allowed to clear the air of cant. As one who classed himself among Hamlet's enemies, he affirms the rightness of the Prince's final action. Whereas this affirmation comes from one who opposed Hamlet, the next is from his intimate confidant and unfailing supporter.

Horatio responds to Hamlet's dying words with one of the most beautiful benedictions in our literature:

> Now cracks a noble heart. Goodnight, sweet prince,
> And flights of angels sing thee to thy rest.[39]　　　　　(5.2.348f.)

The image Horatio invokes is traditional, and rich with associations both ancient and modern. From the New Testament onward, "rest" was taken as a shortened equivalent for heavenly rest (recall the familiar "Rest in Peace" carved on many tombstones), and many Old Testament passages which mention rest were interpreted as referring to the serenity of souls in the company of God in Paradise. This was a standard interpretation among Catholics and Protestants alike of Christ's promise to those who believed that "I will give you rest" and "ye shall find rest unto your souls" (Matt. 11:28-29). The fourth chapter of the Epistle to the Hebrews interpreted the Old Testament promise to believers that they would enjoy the Promised Land as a promise of rest, and emphasized the fact that the name Jesus was only a Greek equivalent to the Hebrew Joshua, who led the original chosen people into the land of promise. What the Old Testament Joshua opened up as an historical and geographical reality had since been elevated into a new and everlasting life in an eschatological reality by the second "Joshua" who promised the "rest" of heaven. The author of Hebrews thus appeals to readers: "Let us labor therefore to enter into that rest" (Heb. 4:11). It is this heavenly rest which Horatio envisions for Hamlet. Ultimately, the conception was traceable to the rest of God on the seventh day, after the works of Creation (Gen. 2:2).

As for the "flights of angels," the ultimate source would of course be Luke 16:22, where Jesus described how the poor beggar Lazarus died, "and was carried by angels into Abraham's bosom." Scenes of Abraham holding the souls of the faithful in his bosom were frequent in paleo-Christian and Byzantine art, and developed into later art in ways we shall shortly trace, but the imagery was equally popular in verbal expressions. An antiphon in the Roman Catholic service for the dead runs, "*In paradisum deducant te angeli*," or "May the angels lead thee into Paradise," and those Latin words continued to be familiar to most Englishmen until the Reformers introduced a different service in the English *Book of Common Prayer*.[40]

Reformation theologians maintained the popularity of this conception. "At death," Luther declared, "I know not whither I go, but my guides, the holy angels, know it well," while Calvin spoke of "a soul, unspeakably precious, which is carried by angels to a blessed life," and Henry Bullinger wrote that the redeemed are conveyed to heaven "by angels carrying up our souls with a most swift flight or moving."[41] The usage can be traced through the early church back to Judaism,[42] and continued in England after the Reformation. Robert Hill urged believers to remember at death that "the angels stand at your bed's head to carry your soul into Abraham's bosom, where you will see God the Father." Matthew Griffith taught that after death "our souls are immediately carried (as the Lazar's was) by elect angels into Abraham's bosom," and Richard Brathwait imagined heavenly "angels coming forth to meet thee, the whole host of heaven to conduct thee to the palace of eternity."[43]

Biographical references between 1600 and 1603 to particular individuals who would, it was believed, be conducted to heaven attest to the currency of Horatio's conception. In 1600 Phillip Stubbes recounts how his good wife on her deathbed saw angels gathering about her to be her guides to heaven as they were with "the good prophet Elizeus [Elisha]." In February, 1601, the Earl of Essex, awaiting the end, twice prayed publicly to God to "send thy blessed angels to be near me, which may convey [my soul] to the joy of heaven."[44] In one of the memorial elegies for Queen Elizabeth in 1603, we read that she is now "Glorious in heaven, thither by angels borne,/ To live with them in bliss eternally," while another elegist named John Lane applies to the poor dead queen a ludicrous vulgarizing of Shakespeare's words: "Farewell (sweet Prince) wherever thou do bide/ Whether in earth, or by some angel's side"—ineptly suggesting that Lane was less sure of Elizabeth's future company than Horatio was of Hamlet's.[45] One can imagine Elizabeth's response to Lane's doggerel had she been in a position to respond, but fortunately for him she was not.

A knowledge of exactly how angels conveyed the blessed to heaven is not one of the major imperatives of scholarship, the crucial points about Horatio's valediction being its accepted meaning and its wide provenance. But that provenance was as much visual as verbal, and it might be interesting to trace briefly.[46] As early as the twelfth century in France, artists represented angels as holding

Fig. vii.1. Tomb of Eleanor, Lady Percy, at Beverly
Minster. Late fifteenth-century sculpture, showing
angels conveying soul in a sheet to God

a sheet in which souls were conveyed to heaven.⁴⁷ This conception was brought
to England rather early, and was popular in various art forms. An altar cloth
used at St. Gregory's Church in Norwich when mass was celebrated for the
dead objectified the "in paradisum deducant te angeli" antiphon: it showed
"many angels holding sheets" with a small naked figure of a man or woman
in each "to represent that by their [i.e., the angels'] ministration the souls of
the righteous are conducted to heaven."⁴⁸ Above the tomb of Chaucer's granddaughter, the Duchess of Suffolk (who died in 1475), there is a choir of angels
singing her soul to rest,⁴⁹ and in other English examples the angels symbolically

272

uphold the head of the recumbent tomb effigy.[50] At Beverly Minster, the tomb niche of Eleanor, Lady Percy, who died in 1488, shows one of the most common representations used alike for men and women. A carved figure of the deity is shown seated, his right hand raised in benediction, and his left gently supporting the praying hands of a nude figure of the deceased who has been conveyed to God in a sheet held by angels on either side of the throne (Fig. VII.1).[51] Many stone monuments in these forms were erected in English churches, as Gough's massive study testifies, but their popularity began to wane at the end of the Middle Ages.

In the Renaissance, a different visualization gained popularity, and was spread largely through woodcuts and engravings. This new approach may be illustrated from the "Bruder Clause" series of woodcuts executed by Dürer in 1488 (Fig. VII.2). Reiter's *Mortilogus*, published at Augsburg in 1508, illustrates the actual death, as the soul in the form of a small human figure emerges from the mouth of a dying man to be caught up by an angel.[52] Day's *Book of Christian Prayers*, a popular English devotional book published in 1578 and often reprinted thereafter, has many charming illustrations of angels taking the saved, and devils the damned, to their final destinations (Fig. VII.3).[53] This popular motif continues in book illustrations through Francis Barlow's engraving for Edward Benlowes' *Theophila* of 1652, where the allegorical print shows Theophila (personifying the love of God) fighting the temptations of the World, the Flesh and the Devil, while in the upper right her triumphant soul is conveyed to heaven by angels (Figs. VII.4 and 5).[54] The last example I know shows the apotheosis of the great eighteenth-century Shakespearean actor David Garrick.[55]

At least two major artists—El Greco and Rubens—did oil paintings of the subject. During Shakespeare's lifetime the greatest representation was probably by El Greco in *The Burial of Count Orgaz*. This great painting—El Greco called it "my sublime work"—is so full of action that as we look at the whole we are likely to miss the detail of the angel in the upper center. When we move our focus ever more tightly, we recognize that this angel is in fact conveying an amorphous and tiny form, representing the soul of the dead Count, to his heavenly rest. Now I cannot conceive of Shakespeare's ever having visited the Church of San Tomé in Toledo, for which El Greco executed this superb painting in 1586, but it is interesting as the finest contemporary analogue in oils to Shakespeare's verbal painting. In the sixteen-thirties, Rubens executed

FIG. VII.2. Soul Transported to Heaven by Angels,
from Bruder Claus woodcuts, 1488 by Dürer

a painting of the reception into heaven of King James I, conveyed of course by angels, which may still be seen on the ceiling of the Banqueting House in Whitehall. Some years earlier, Rubens had painted a somewhat sentimental but still rather moving picture of a dead child being carried to heaven by little winged cherubs (Fig. VII.6). Because the human soul was often portrayed as a child, this Rubens painting can be read as broadly symbolic of the destiny of all faithful souls. On the other hand, Ellis Waterhouse has very tentatively suggested that this may also have been a private document, commemorating the death of one of Rubens' own children.[56] On either count, the role of the transporting angels is clear.

The painting perhaps most directly relevant to Horatio's comment about

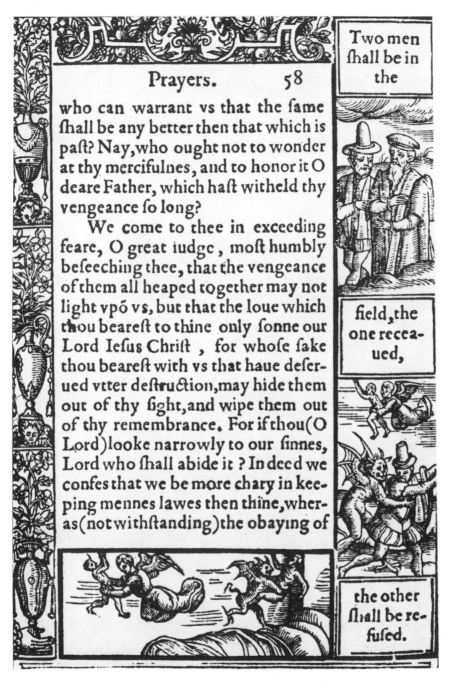

who can warrant vs that the same ſhall be any better then that which is paſt? Nay, who ought not to wonder at thy mercifulnes, and to honor it O deare Father, which haſt witheld thy vengeance ſo long?

We come to thee in exceeding feare, O great iudge, moſt humbly beſeeching thee, that the vengeance of them all heaped together may not light vpō vs, but that the loue which thou beareſt to thine only ſonne our Lord Ieſus Chriſt, for whoſe ſake thou beareſt with vs that haue deſerued vtter deſtruction, may hide them out of thy ſight, and wipe them out of thy remembrance. For if thou (O Lord) looke narrowly to our ſinnes, Lord who ſhall abide it? In deed we confes that we be more chary in keeping mennes lawes then thine, wheras (notwithſtanding) the obaying of

Two men ſhall be in the

field, the one receaued,

the other ſhall be refuſed.

FIG. VII.3. Souls Transported to Heaven by Angels, and to Hell by Devils, from R. Day, *Book of Christian Prayers*, 1578

FIG. VII.4. Theophila's Warfare, and her Soul
Transported to Heaven by Angels, by Francis Barlow,
from Edward Benlowes' *Theophila*, 1652

FIG. VII.5. Detail of Fig. VII.4 above,
showing Soul Transported to Heaven by
Angels

Hamlet is an anonymous English oil dating from about 1570, entitled *Allegory of Man*, and now in the collection of Derek Sherborn, Esquire, of Fawns Manor (Fig. VII.7). It recounts the final story of a human soul which has won the last of its earthly battles and trials. Through clouds where cherubim unite in songs of praise and thanksgiving to God, the soul is lifted by another angel into heaven.[57] Horatio's benediction "Flights of Angels sing thee to thy rest" was far from a frozen metaphor or a refurbished reference to past conceptions when it was spoken on the Globe stage in 1600. Instead, it would have evoked a strongly emotional imagery, which was still full of vitality and meaning.

The third commentary upon Hamlet comes after Horatio's and is as different from it as one could imagine. It is not that the two disagree nor that they contradict, but they represent unmistakably different emphases and points of perspective. Whereas Horatio has emphasized Hamlet's spiritual state, Fortinbras concentrates entirely upon him as a secular figure, a soldier and prince (5.2.384-92).[58] There is no movement of angel wings, no sound of angelic song, but instead "the soldiers' music and the rites of war/ Speak loudly for him." Fortinbras is a practical ruler and leader of men, commenting on Hamlet as one of his own class, a prince whom he can and does respect. Hamlet had understood all of Fortinbras, but Fortinbras can recognize and understand only that part of Hamlet he can find also in himself. We, as Shakespeare's audience, know more of Hamlet of course, or we should, although we probably can never assimilate all of the rich diversity and depth Shakespeare has given us.

FIG. VII.6. Rubens, *Dead Child Carried to Heaven by Angels*

But we should try to encompass that whole, and an important part of that whole is what Fortinbras sees and says at the very end, as he has Hamlet borne

> like a soldier to the stage,
> For he was likely, had he been put on,
> To have proved most royal.

These three climactic appraisals of the Prince come after he has already affirmed in the most explicit terms his own confidence in the justice of his cause and the clearness of his conscience, and they thus give external validation to his own judgment. Nowhere else does Shakespeare provide so well-orchestrated a dramatic endorsement for a tragic protagonist, but then he did not elsewhere

FIG. VII.7. Anonymous English Painting, *Allegory of Man*, c. 1570

face a protagonist with the same bewildering challenges. The speeches of Laertes, Horatio, and Fortinbras amount to separate endorsements of Hamlet from the three different points of view of a fiery adversary, an intimate confidant, and an unbiased rival. Each of these picks up certain major themes and lines of development over which the Prince and the audience have agonized in the course of the play.

The issue of retribution is one of these, and it is in effect addressed by Laertes when he affirms that Hamlet's dispatch of the King was just and deserved. The responsibility of retribution was not all that perplexed Hamlet, however: he was equally concerned lest he might obey that command in a way which would "damn me." Horatio's words are broadly applicable, of course, but perhaps their primary force is to affirm the state of Hamlet's soul through his own assurance that angels will convey the Prince to his rest. Then there are the Prince's persistent doubts of his own adequacy as a man of action, and these are met by Fortinbras' expression of confidence in him as a soldier and ruler.

In none of his other great tragedies does Shakespeare give us anything comparable to this crescendo of affirmation for the tragic hero at the end of his life. Just as the challenges and problems Hamlet must meet exceed in complexity those of Shakespeare's other protagonists, so does his end receive unmatched approval from all the other major characters who can speak of him after the tragic catastrophe. In this, as in many other ways, *The Tragedy of Hamlet* is unique. When all things are considered, Prince Hamlet, with all his faults, stands not only as Shakespeare's most interesting but also as his most admirable protagonist.

# Appendices

## The Mirror up to Nature: Artifact,
## Metaphor, and Guide

*This appendix provides background for the treatments of mirrors in the body of this book: Chapter I discussed the general significance of Hamlet's advice to the players as a beginning point for our approach to the tragedy as a whole, and Chapter IV treated the play-within-the-play as a moral and dramatic stratagem addressed to Claudius, and the mirror of confession addressed to Gertrude. Because the material treated in this appendix is pertinent to each of these three analyses, but obviously could not be given at all of those points, it is brought together here as a general background for understanding.*

Hamlet's advice to the players is easily the most famous piece of literary or dramatic criticism in English (3.2.1-42). It begins very near the midpoint of the play,[1] and it pivots exactly upon the image of drama as a mirror held up to nature:

> the purpose of playing, whose end, both at the first and now, was and is to hold, as 'twere, the mirror up to nature, to show virtue her own feature, scorn her own image, and the very age and body of the time his form and pressure (3.2.19-23).

In only forty-two lines, Hamlet's advice in these speeches says everything which is absolutely basic to narrative and dramatic literature (including *Hamlet*) as well as to acting and stage production. Beyond that, he also epitomizes representational aesthetics in all the arts.[2] It is indeed as close as we can find to a definitive statement—definitive, that is, if we are willing, as the Renaissance was, to go beyond a conception of art as self-fulfilling design, or the creation of a fictive world independent of ordinary life, or a self-expression of the artist's individual vision, or an end in itself, or pure entertainment and diversion, although those conceptions may be subordinated in a qualified way to Hamlet's more inclusive vision of drama. Here we also have the Renaissance affirmation that art should teach as well as delight, and that it should do so through a recognizable imitation or picture of life.

The "mirror up to nature" which is cited by Hamlet seems crystal clear, but it can lead to considerable misunderstanding, and some readers have found in it a prescription for the univocal fidelity of art to nature, a virtual reproduction rather than an imitation. Thus Virgil K. Whitaker has rightly protested that Hamlet's definition too often "has been taken to imply a doctrine of verisimilitude, or even something approaching the 'slice of life' sought by some modern writers."[3] To correct such misunderstandings as those to which Whitaker and others have objected, we shall first examine the actual mirrors and then the metaphoric references to mirrors familiar in Shakespeare's time. The movement, then, will be from a consideration of the vehicle of the metaphor to a consideration of its tenor or tenors.

The glass mirrors Shakespeare and his Globe audiences knew were small instruments: few if any Elizabethans can be expected to have seen a plane or flat mirror measuring more than a foot or so in size, and most would have measured no more than a few inches across. Many and perhaps most of the glass mirrors available in England at the time (and these were the mirrors Shakespeare knew) were not plane at all, but convex instruments whose spherical shape yielded inevitable distortions, no matter how skillfully made. The point is inescapable if we consult the famous *Self-Portrait in a Convex Mirror* by the sixteenth-century painter Parmigianino, who makes no attempt to compensate for the distortions of the image (Fig. Ap. 1). Although the head was placed in the center of the mirror's sphere, so that the curvature would apply equally in all directions, the reflection is far from realistic. Not only is the extended hand grotesquely enlarged, but, as Sir John Pope-Hennessy notes, the mouth diminishes in a "disconcerting fashion on the right" and the eyes "appear to rest on two quite different planes." What such mirrors yielded was at best a mere approximation.[4] In addition to such glass mirrors, reflectors were made from polished metal. Although these were flat, they also presented less than accurate reflections, due to irregularities in the casting, to polish lines and scratches on the surface, and of course to misrepresentation of color.

On the most basic technical issues of the size and fidelity of reflections, then, there were differences between what Shakespeare's Elizabethan and his twentieth-century audiences could expect mirrors to show. Modern technology can supply huge sheets of silvered glass which reflect sweeping panoramas of

*[handwritten margin note: Mirrors of this time were very distorted]*

FIG. AP.I. Parmigianino, *Self-Portrait
in a Convex Mirror*

nature, with all details accurately represented. As early as the eighteenth century, "landscape mirrors" were made for placing over mantels in English country houses, which would accurately reproduce broad vistas of the gardens and landscaped grounds outside the windows. In the later seventeenth century, the extremely wealthy might have many smaller panels of mirrors joined together so that whole walls, or even entire rooms, were converted into reflecting surfaces—the Hall of Mirrors at Versailles being the most famous example. Nothing of the kind, and nothing approaching it, was available anywhere in Europe in Shakespeare's time, and such developments did not even begin until several generations after his death. In the late seventeenth and eighteenth centuries, glass manufacture had advanced beyond anything known to the Elizabethans, and landscape mirrors or even whole walls of mirrors in rich houses "replaced the heavy woven tapestry of the past and competed successfully with the painted vistas of landscapes and cities."[5]

The mirrors with which Shakespeare and his English contemporaries were familiar were very different indeed. The center of glass-making in Europe was still in Venice, and the Venetian state so profited from the industry that it imposed the most stringent measures to preserve the secrets of the processes.[6] Sixteenth-century developments there in the making of plane mirrors were notable, and greater accuracy of reflection was achieved, but the size of the mirrors remained relatively small and the costs were high. Even at the Venetian center of the industry, the size of mirrors did not exceed that of an ordinary twentieth-century bathroom mirror fixed over a washbasin. A relatively large sixteenth-century mirror may be seen in Titian's sumptuous *Toilet of Venus* in Washington, and it cannot be estimated to measure more than about twelve by thirty inches, at the very most. Venetian technology made possible the production of these flat or plane mirrors which reflected accurately, but still gave only a limited view.

No looking glasses were manufactured in England prior to Shakespeare's death in 1616,[7] so that all had to be imported at very considerable expense. Only the wealthiest Elizabethans could have afforded a fine Venetian mirror of the size Titian shows,[8] because costs of manufacture and the added hazards of shipping such fragile articles from Italy would have imposed a price beyond the means of all except the most affluent Londoners. Most of the mirrors were of a size that a woman might hang from her girdle or carry about with her, as in Jost Amman's 1582 woodcut of a fashionably dressed lady receiving birds from a fowler, while she holds a small mirror surrounded with feathers. Even smaller mirrors were sold at fairs by peddlers such as Shakespeare's Autolycus in *The Winter's Tale*, and these were probably about the size (but not the quality) of a modern purse or compact mirror.[9] From this size they might range up toward the six-to ten-inch diameter of the stand mirror which could be placed on a table or cabinet[10] (for illustrations, see above, Figs. IV.22 and 23). Elizabethans would not have been tempted to confuse what such mirrors showed with anything approaching a "slice of life" in the modern sense. Their only practical use was for observing the face, and from that use developed their most persistent metaphorical significance, which originated in the classical world.

"Know Thyself," the famous motto on the ancient Temple of Apollo at

Delphi, contributed one of the most basic and consistent elements of Platonic and neo-Platonic philosophy. As we read in Plato's *The Charminides*, "self-knowledge would certainly be maintained by me to be the very essence of knowledge, and in this I agree with him who dedicated the inscription, 'Know Thyself!' at Delphi. That word, if I am not mistaken, is put there as a sort of salutation which the god addresses to those who enter the Temple."[11]

It may seem surprising to us that neither Plato nor Socrates themselves connected that dictum with the mirror as a means or symbol for self-study, but this was presumably because reflections in the polished metal mirrors available in those times usually gave dark and shadowy rather than clear representations. Even in the first century A.D., the Apostle Paul referred to the obscurities in the mirrors he knew, when he wrote in I Corinthians 13:12 of seeing "through a glass darkly" (Geneva version) or "in a dark sort" (Rheims-Douay version), where "glass" is a mistranslation of the Greek word for a metallic mirror. Such metal mirrors were also common in Elizabethan England (recall George Gascoigne's *The Steel Glass* of 1576), and apparently offered no clearer reflection than their counterparts in the Roman world. Returning to Plato, we find him comparing art to a mirror in *Republic* X, 596, but he uses this comparison so as to discredit both art and artists. For Socrates, the images to be found in the mirror of art were just as deceptive as the famous shadows cast on the walls of his cave of ignorance.[12]

Six centuries or so after Socrates' death, neo-Platonists attributed to him a different attitude toward mirrors. By the early third century A.D., Diogenes Laertius' *Lives of the Philosophers* (II, 33) could record a tradition that Socrates had "advised his young disciples to look frequently at themselves in mirrors in order to make themselves worthy of their beauty, or if they were ugly to compensate and cover their imperfection through education."[13] However dubious that story may be for an historical knowledge of Socrates, it influenced the way Europeans came to think of themselves: self-scrutiny, symbolized by the mirror, was pursued for the twin objectives of identifying and eliminating vice, and of identifying and reinforcing virtue. And the mirror came to symbolize that process.[14]

The tradition recorded by Diogenes Laertius presumably reached St. Augustine, either directly or indirectly, and it is to him that we are indebted for the popularizing of the looking-glass metaphor in the post-classical West. In Christian teaching after his time, the mirror became a standard symbol for self-knowledge, and derivatively for all kinds of knowledge. The Apocryphal book known as the Wisdom of Solomon (7:24-26) had provided an early and nearly canonical precedent in its eulogy of the personification of Wisdom as a spotless mirror and receptor of the majestic will of God—or as the Vulgate has it, *speculum sine macula Dei maiestatis.* For St. Augustine in the patristic age, and later for the Protestant Reformers of the sixteenth century, that "mirror without spot" was to be found in the Holy Scriptures, and to a derivative extent also in Christian teachings generally. If we seek self-knowledge through that mirror, Augustine wrote, it will show us the virtues we should display and also the spots or deformities in ourselves which we should confess and reform.[15] That twofold mirroring was repeated in varied but consistent forms right down until Hamlet appeals first to the mirror of drama "to show virtue her own feature, scorn her own image" and later to the mirror of repentance to show his mother her sin and to warn her from it.

Hamlet is not, however, invoking a conception which was only theological or only neo-Platonic in his choice of the mirror as a symbol for drama. Literature in the most general sense had also long been taken as effectively mirroring wisdom in the human and natural realms.[16] Thus Plutarch had commented that "I began writing the *Lives* for the sake of other people, but now I take delight in continuing them for my own sake. Using history as a mirror, I try in one way or another to order my own life and to fashion it in accordance with the virtues of those lives."[17] What Plutarch found in the mirror of history and biography, others found also in the fictive mirrors of creative literature. Drama was explicitly cited as such a didactic mirror by Aelius Donatus, the fourth-century rhetorician whose works were standard texts in European schools for centuries. Donatus, citing Cicero, defined comedy as an imitation of life, mirror of manners, and image of truth, a conception which runs through the dramatic theory of the Renaissance, in England and on the Continent.[18] Explicit references to drama as an instructive mirror occur also in plays by Skelton, Wager, Fulwell, Jonson, and Randolph, among others, and was incorporated into the title of the play by Thomas Lodge and Robert Greene, *A Looking Glass for London and England* (1594).[19]

In referring to drama as a mirror, Hamlet gave that critical topos its finest expression, as well as its most profound, but he was building upon a popular understanding. Several decades later, we find it all given graphic form on the illustrated title page of a Leiden edition of six plays by Terence, where Prudence

FIG. AP.2. Frontispiece, *Publii Terentii Commediae Sex*

holds up an hexagonal mirror in which are reflected the haloed figure of Truth along with the costumed figure of Simulatio with a theatrical mask to represent acting or, as Hamlet calls it, "playing"[20] (Fig. Ap. 2). In a well-ordered human life, it was the function of Prudence or Wisdom to acquire self-knowledge (and other forms of knowledge as well) by holding up a mirror to Truth, whether reflected through the medium or drama, or of history, or of philosophy, or of divine revelation. The mirror had become an almost universal symbol for instruction, knowledge, and understanding.

In the sixteenth and seventeenth centuries, hundreds of books, pamphlets, and broadsides were published in England which proffered mirrors, glasses, looking glasses, and *specula* upon one important subject or another.[21] A comprehensive list of these titles has been painstakingly assembled by Herbert Grabes, and the list runs to sixty-five pages.[22] Throughout this vast literature run the twin themes of achieving the good and rejecting the evil—in a medical treatise the choice being between health and sickness, in an agricultural treatise between harvest and dearth, in a treatise on navigation between a successful voyage and shipwreck, and in a treatise on war between victory and defeat. Throughout, the "Socratic" and Augustinian emphasis continues, with the mirror as an instrument or symbol for informed choice. As for the subjects presented in the mirror books which proliferated during the Middle Ages and the Renaissance, the most useful system of classification remains that which was invoked by Alanus de Insulis (1114-1203) when he referred to three mirrors: of Scripture (divine revelation and theology); of human nature (humanities and social studies in our terms); and of creatures or creation (the sciences and technology).[23]

In the visual arts, the mirror was important in similar ways as symbol and metaphor, but it also took on an instrumental function as a useful tool. During the Renaissance and for generations thereafter, artists would often study the reflections of their paintings in a mirror, so as to get a fresh point of view on their works and polish them to a higher perfection. Alberti was not the first to recommend this procedure, but he made clear what it contributed, when he advised painters that "a mirror will be an excellent guide," going on to say "I do not know how it is that paintings that are without fault look beautiful in a mirror; and it is remarkable how every defect in a picture appears more unsightly in a mirror. So the things that are taken from nature should be emended with the advice of a mirror."[24] Although Alberti is here concerned with the technique of art rather than with human wisdom or the conduct of life, his practical concern for emphasizing strong points and eliminating weak points in an art work parallels the Augustinian concern for improving virtue and eliminating vice in life.

As artists under the influence of the Renaissance increasingly sought to create convincing pictures of physical reality, along with conceptions of its meaning, the mirror served as both a tool and a metaphor. We must recognize of course that the spiritualizing vision characteristic of Byzantine and medieval art was not abandoned, but it was modified and united with a more accurate

mirror of Human nature.

delineation of physical nature in its larger and smaller details. Thus Leonardo da Vinci asserted that "a successful painting will always give the impression that it is a piece of nature seen in a large mirror."[25] This does not mean that Leonardo demanded photographic accuracy, and he was in fact quite capable of creating contradictory arrangements of light and space within single paintings (as in the *Mona Lisa*), but he was concerned that paintings should "give the impression" of reality. It was in this sense that he advised artists, "you should take the mirror for your guide."[26] These associations of art with a mirror, originating on the Continent, spread to England as well, where paintings were frequently referred to as mirrors.[27]

A famous painting from the Northern Renaissance affords an opportunity for us to bring together many of these aesthetic approaches and themes. When Jan van Eyck in 1434 painted his influential *Giovanni Arnolfini and his Bride* (Fig. Ap. 3), he introduced in the background a mirror which was important both technically and iconographically. As Panofsky demonstrated in a pivotal essay in 1934, the mirror up to nature we find in this painting has relevance to understanding all the visual arts of the Renaissance and succeeding centuries.[28] Giovanni Arnolfini and his bride Jeanne de Cenani were Italians transplanted to Bruges, where Arnolfini was an important official of the Burgundian court. They stand here with hands joined in *fides manualis*, the essential feature in plighting their troth, and the artist's signature line, inscribed just above the mirror, reads "Johannes de Eyk fuit hic. 1434"—meaning that he was himself a witness to the sponsal, which the painting renders as an "artistic marriage certificate."[29] The single lit candle in the chandelier (quite unnecessary from a practical point of view in a room flooded with daylight) represented both the all-seeing wisdom of God and the traditional marriage candle which was lit in the home of the newly married couple. The marriage bed appears to the right, and the armchair against the back wall is surmounted by a small carved figure of St. Margaret, who was invoked in expectation of childbirth. The pert-looking terrier between the feet of the couple was a familiar symbol of fidelity, and the shoes in the left foreground suggested the sacred aspects of marriage: "Loose thy shoe from off thy foot, for the place whereon thou standest is holy." Not only does the mirror reflect the whole scene from a different direction, but its ten projecting panels each contains an exquisitely detailed episode from the life and ministry of Christ—so that the mirror of art and the mirror of nature

FIG. AP.3. Jan van Eyck, *Giovanni Arnolfini and his Bride*

are placed within the context of the mirror of God.[30] And the mirror's reflection of the painter himself suggests that the artist is also a faithful reflector of reality.[31]

Panofsky revolutionized the study of Renaissance art by showing that the lovingly wrought material details in this painting were not mere ends in themselves, as had previously been supposed, but were "significant attributes . . . disguised, so to speak, as ordinary pieces of furniture." We have, then, what Panofsky called "a transfigured reality," which he described as follows:

> Jan van Eyck's landscapes and interiors are built up in such a way that what is possibly meant to be a mere realistic motive can at the same time be conceived as a symbol, or, to put it another way, his attributes and symbols are chosen and placed in such a way that what is possibly meant to express an allegorical meaning at the same time perfectly "fits" into a landscape or an interior apparently taken from life.[32]

In the half-century since Panofsky wrote those words, continuing research has confirmed his hypothesis not only for Van Eyck but for a large number of art works of all kinds produced between the Renaissance and the eighteenth century.

The mirror of art was created to provide a believable imitation of nature, not a literal transcription of it, but even more importantly it was to convey a significant understanding in aesthetically satisfying forms. That is the critical context in which Hamlet's words would have been understood in Shakespeare's time. Drawing upon general and broadly applicable principles, Hamlet deduces the consequences for theatrical art in general and for the production of particular plays, including both "The Mousetrap" play-within-a-play and the *Tragedy of Hamlet* itself.

Word and action are to be suitably coordinated—"suit the word to the action, and the action to the word," as he tells the actors—so that what Claudius sees in the performance will be understandable in its purposed meaning, at the furthest remove from "inexplicable dumb shows and noise." Movements, actions, and tableaux in the theater (as in painting) are to be significant, not inexplicable, and with these the verse is to be harmonized into a unitary effect. This combination of event, word, style, and meaning should "acquire and beget a temperance that may give it smoothness." Leonardo's dictum that "a successful painting will always give the impression that it is a piece of nature seen in a large mirror" corresponds to Hamlet's requirement that a stage performance be credible and convincing. For that reason, he repudiates "o'er doing Termagant" and theatrical characterizations that

> neither having th' accent of Christians, nor the gait of Christian, pagan, nor man, have so strutted and bellowed that I have thought some of Nature's journeymen had made men, and not made them well, they imitated humanity so abominably (3.2.29-33).

If the impression revealed in the mirror of art is not a convincing imitation of nature, no one will give it credit and "the purpose of playing" will be defeated. The requirement to "o'erstep not the modesty of nature" is to preserve the ultimate end, the *telos*, of art.

All this background should help us to understand Hamlet's "mirror up to nature" not only within the context of his entire speech, but within the context of the time and environing culture for which both speech and play were written. It is not that members of the Globe audience would have made mental correlations between Hamlet's words and this background: that would not have been necessary, and the speed of stage action and speech would have precluded the possibility even for the best-informed people in the theater. But their responses would have been shaped by these traditions. Hamlet's words not only evoke the kinds of mirrors which were familiar in Elizabethan England, but also evoke for his purposes an ancient and still vital ambience of meaning.

In this milieu, Hamlet's directives for dramatic art are remarkably inclusive: art begins with and refers back to reality, but without a slavish copying; art increases our moral awareness, but without preachiness; and art is subject to temperance and decorum. Between the polarities of verisimilitude and fantasy, it presents a transfigured reality.

## Claudius on Stage and in Hamlet's Mind

Hamlet is not unbiased in his view of his uncle, and the Globe audience would not have expected him to be so. Neither, indeed, would that audience have been. As we have observed in Chapter Two, Claudius displayed major characteristics of the tyrant, as tyranny had been defined in Europe for some two thousand years from the time of Aristotle to that of Shakespeare. In addition to his own words and actions, the fact that Claudius was accompanied on stage by "my Switzers" (4.5.97)—the most famous mercenaries of the sixteenth century—would have conveyed a kinesic message which could not be ignored. All of this fits well with his inescapable, and admitted, guilt for fratricide and regicide.

There are, furthermore, the conditions of his marriage, as treated above in Chapter Three. In his first appearance, Claudius makes clear that he is guilty of incest by marrying his brother's widow, and we have seen the emotional revulsion which Elizabethans typically felt for such a union. On a less heinous plane, but nonetheless socially distasteful and even shocking, were the implications of this "o'er hasty marriage," even apart from any consideration of incest. All this places Claudius under the condemnation of the audience. His eavesdropping, general spying, and exploitation of others as pawns in his own game disincline us from developing a warm regard for him: we may (and I think should) accord him a measure of sympathy, but he never becomes a lovable villain. The text of the play clearly and palpably justifies Hamlet's description of him as "A murderer and a villain, . . . a vice of kings,/ A cutpurse of the empire and the rule" (3.4.97-102). That summarizing judgment is factual, readily documented, and almost legal in its specificity.

But on secondary matters we may still question how accurately the Prince's verbal abuse of the King expresses what the Globe audience would have observed of the King as his part unfolded on stage, or whether it distorts that enactment while principally expressing only the Prince's personal frustration and fury. Certainly the latter is important: hyperbole should be expected from a character in Hamlet's circumstances, and he is eloquently good at it. To describe Claudius to Gertrude as "A slave that is not twentieth part the tithe/ Of your precedent lord" and as a "king of shreds and patches" (3.4.98-103) is rhetorically superb. But it is also a judgment reinforced by the play's presentation of Claudius as unfit for the throne. Even on the plane of effective statesmanship, Claudius' decision to permit that fiery young adventurist Fortinbras to march through Denmark with a battle-ready army of twenty thousand soldiers shows remarkably impractical judgment for a monarch. For this and other reasons, very few of us would wish to live in a nation ruled by Claudius.

Personal appearance is another matter, and it is impossible to establish firmly after the lapse of almost four hundred years from the original stage production. Physical ridicule is a part of Hamlet's arsenal for disparaging his uncle, whom he views as a satyr (a proverbially ugly as well as lascivious creature) and as a mildewed ear (1.2.140 and 3.4.65). These verbal assaults are morally and psychologically significant, but whether and how they correspond with the King's appearance on Shakespeare's stage we simply cannot demonstrate.

Drinking and drunkenness are also repeatedly associated with Claudius, and it would be helpful to know the stage presentation so that we could evaluate Hamlet's charges on this score, but we do not have conclusive evidence. The Prince repeatedly refers to his uncle's bad habits in this regard, but we do not know whether he is exaggerating what the Globe audience would see on the stage. Thus, while Hamlet is looking forward to his revenge, he anticipates striking the King "when he is drunk asleep" (3.3.89), which implies repeated drunkenness, but he never explicitly says that he is what we would call an alcoholic, and although he regrets that other nations call the Danes drunkards, he does not quite call Claudius that (1.4.19). When Guildenstern tells Hamlet that the King "is in his retirement marvellous distempered," the Prince wittily retorts, "with drink, sir?" (3.2.289f.). No one else accuses Claudius of overindulgence, but this negative fact should not lead us to assume that he is temperate, because no one else accuses him of incest, either, and he is certainly and patently guilty on that score. The Danish court, as characterized throughout this play, is neither observant nor outspoken, whereas Hamlet is both. It is difficult to see why Hamlet would complain about the court's custom of "heavy-headed revel" if the Globe audience did not see much of it on stage. And there are repeated references. Claudius makes much of his own drinking, accompanying it with the machismo sounds of drums, trumpets, and artillery salvoes:

No jocund health that Denmark drinks to-day

But the great cannon to the clouds shall tell,
And the King's rouse the heaven shall bruit again,
Respeaking earthly thunder.                                    (1.2.125-28)

When Horatio asks Hamlet to explain the flourish of trumpets accompanied by cannon fire, he responds:

The King doth wake tonight and takes his rouse,
Keeps wassail, and the swaggering upspring reels,
And he drains his draughts of Rhenish down
The kettledrum and trumpet thus bray out
The triumph of his pledge.                                     (1.4.8-12)

Whatever else one may make of that drinking style, it is in pompously bad taste.[1] And it would also become tedious, this living in a court where music moves only in the direction of *The 1812 Overture*, without quite achieving even its disputable subtlety.[2] The whole thing is typically and dreadfully overdone. In the final scene of the play, Claudius declares "The king shall drink to Hamlet's better health," and then orders the whole adolescent rodomontade repeated once again:

    Give me the cups,
And let the kettle to the trumpet speak,
The trumpet to the canoneer without,
The cannons to the heavens, the heaven to earth,
"Now the King drinks to Hamlet."                       (5.2.260 and 263-67)

Shortly after that, he cries out once more, "Stay, give me drink" (271). Even as he tries to poison Hamlet, Claudius repeatedly indulges his own strong taste for strong drink. It is not that we today can demonstrate that he was ever drunk, although we often enough see him drinking. In comparison with his other faults, it is a small one, but it does tie in with the "king of shreds and patches" allusion. "The King drinks" was, after all, one of the major themes of the Twelfth-Night revels in which an elected parodic monarch "reigned" and drank. Paintings by Jan Steen at Buckingham Palace and at the Museum of Fine Arts in Boston and by David Teniers the Younger at the National Gallery in Washington give us visual evidence of what those peasant revels were like. We do not need to imagine that the Danish court on the Globe stage would have been modeled after such a revel, but Hamlet views it morally and socially in some such terms.

Where we are dealing with Elizabethan attitudes we can recover, as we are doing in the body of this book, we can cite demonstrative evidence that an English audience in 1600 can be expected for the most part to have agreed with Hamlet's judgments of his uncle. Fortunately, those issues are the most substantive in the play. On other matters such as personal appearance and fondness for drink, we lack the same large measure of assurance, but here again the evidence which the text supplies, even if not determinative, suggests that the Prince's view of his uncle is not far from the mark of what the Globe audience would have observed on stage.

# Ophelia's Funeral

*Ophelia's funeral has been discussed in Chapter Four, Part IV, and more fully in Chapter Six, Part VII, and in both places I have claimed that Laertes' protests against the "maimèd rites" would have seemed justified in Elizabethan terms. This appendix provides the evidence for that claim, by a detailed sorting out of historical materials which can more appropriately be presented here than in the body of the book.*

## I. Contradictory Views

Ophelia's funeral as dramatized in the fifth act of *Hamlet*, is strikingly different from the normal burial customs with which the Globe audience would be familiar, and that difference is not only staged but signalized by the play's dialogue. Two conflicting views are presented by the officiating clergyman and Laertes: the priest declares that the funeral should have been far more fully degraded; Laertes maintains that the degradation we see is unwarranted and unjust. Their contention should be read in full:

LAERTES. What ceremony else?
DOCTOR. Her obsequies have been as far enlarged
  As we have warranty. Her death was doubtful,
  And, but that great command o'ersways the order,
  She should in ground unsanctified have lodged
  Till the last trumpet. For charitable prayers,
  Shards, flints, and pebbles should be thrown on her,
  Yet here she is allowed her virgin crants,
  Her maiden strewments, and the bringing home
  Of bell and burial.
LAERTES. Must there be no more done?
DOCTOR.            No more be done.
  We should profane the service of the dead
  To sing a requiem and such rest to her
  As to peace-parted souls.
LAERTES.           Lay her i' th' earth,
  And from her fair and unpolluted flesh
  May violets spring! I tell thee, churlish priest,

A minist'ring angel shall my sister be
When thou liest howling.
(5.1.210-29)

The contradiction could not be more absolute. In this radical discord, where should our sympathies lie? Shakespeare has provided no chorus to direct our response, as a Greek dramatist might have done, but he has written into the play everything that was necessary to allow his original audience to choose between these opposing views without explicit coaching. From what we can reconstruct of Elizabethan attitudes, I am confident that the Globe audience would for the most part have endorsed Laertes' view both emotionally and ethically. The reasons for this are at once interesting and significant, and a full analysis will throw considerable light on the play. Modern readers who accept the arguments of the churlish priest (and many do) miss the full pathos of the scene and overlook one further instance of the depravity which besets this kingdom under Claudius.

## II. Suicide and Madness

Ophelia's suicide is clear in the one sense that was crucial in Shakespeare's time: her death was directly related to her madness. In 1600, that direct relationship carried with it many implications—ethical, theological, legal. At this late date, we can fully recover these implications only by historical research, but the audience for which Shakespeare wrote would have grasped them almost instantaneously, and without conscious effort.

Basic to any clear understanding is a recognition of the power of Ophelia's great mad scene, one of the most affecting scenes of madness in any literature (4.5.1-198). Moving on and off stage, Ophelia indelibly impresses the pathos of her madness upon the other characters in the play and upon the audience. In every sense that counts for the drama, she is "a document in madness" (4.5.177). This kind of dramatic document differs from legal or medical documents because it does not require the forensic arguments of legal demonstration nor the techniques of medical analysis, but is sufficient if it strongly convinces those on stage and in the theater. No one knew better than Shakespeare how to create such dramatic conviction, and nowhere does he do it better than here. Other characters comment upon her "madness," describe her as "indeed distract," as "incapable of her own distress," as "Divided from herself and her fair judgment/ Without the which we are pictures or mere beasts," and see her as proof that "a young maid's wits [are] as mortal as an old man's life" (4.5.156, and 2; 4.7.177; 4.5.85f. and 159f.). Even moderately competent acting can mesmerize an audience with Ophelia's madness. As for her drowning, we know that she came to it "as one incapable of her own distress,/ Or like a creature native and indued/ Unto that element" (4.7.177-79). Whether these lines mean that in her madness Ophelia felt herself to be in no danger from the water, because she was a "creature native" to it, or that she was, also due to her madness, otherwise "incapable" of recognizing the danger in which she found herself, is largely immaterial, but one thing is and remains inescapable: Ophelia's death was not willful. No Elizabethan audience, seeing this play, would have found her guilty of intentional suicide, and it would have seemed only natural that the coroner's jury sitting on the case "finds it Christian burial" (5.1.4).

Over the centuries prior to 1600, both church practice and doctrine consistently held that a person so patently mad as Ophelia should receive the full rites of Christian burial. Her death, however apparently suicide, was not "by her fault" in the sense of rational and responsible choice, but was brought on by her madness, either directly or by the loss of a sense of consequences. Contemporary attitudes in 1600, buttressed by over a thousand years of church history, attest to the rightness of Laertes' claims for his sister.

As early as 563 A.D., the Council of Braga or Bracara had excluded from the full rites of Christian burial only those suicides who inflict death on themselves "by any fault," a qualification which was consistently interpreted as protecting the rights of those who commit suicide "when they are so far deprived of reason as not to be responsible in the sense of doing it by 'any fault,' willfully and consciously." The Canon of Braga appeared in English church law as early as the excerpts of Egbert in 740 A.D., and recurred among the Penetential Canons of 963 A.D.[1] The *Decretals* of Gratian, composed in the mid-twelfth century and influential for several hundred years thereafter, emphasize the same point in declaring that only those who *voluntarily* commit suicide, shall not be given the rites of the church at burial.[2] In the thirteenth century, the influential English legalist Henry de Bracton wrote of insane suicides "that a madman is not liable"; in his consideration of suicide by "the deranged, the delirious, and the mentally retarded," including any who "laboring under a high fever drowns himself," he concluded that "since they are without sense and reason and can no more commit an *injuria* or a felony than a brute animal, since they are not far removed from brutes."³ Ophelia's deprivation of reason had, as Claudius commented, rendered her "divided from herself and her fair judgment./ Without the which we are pictures or mere beasts" (4.5.85-86). At this point in the play, we may wish to recall Hamlet's comment in the immediately preceding scene that the Creator had given us that large discourse of reason, "looking before and after," without which a man becomes "a beast, no more" (4.4.35-39). Deprived of "her fair judgment," Ophelia is no more morally responsible for her actions than a beast would be, to use the terms just quoted from Bracton's analysis. In the fifteenth century William Lyndwood declared to the same effect in his *Constitutiones Legatinae* that the canon law prohibiting burial to willful suicides "extendeth not to idiots, lunatics, or persons otherwise of insane mind."⁴

That ancient conception was maintained in the Church of England throughout the century of the Reformation, and long thereafter. When traditional and continuing church practice was codified in the Anglican *Constitutions* of 1603, canon 68 declared that the right to full Christian burial was not to be denied to those who committed suicide while insane. Specifically, this canon directed that the minister could not degrade the funeral of a suicide whose death was attributed to madness or accident by verdict of a coroner's inquest, as was the case with Ophelia (5.1.1-5).⁵ In 1621 Robert Burton summarized the whole tradition in *The Anatomy of Melancholy* when he wrote of a man who commits suicide in insanity that "in regard he doth this not so much out of his will, as from violence of his malady, we must make the best construction of it."⁶ The "best construction" was indeed put on self-inflicted death by coroner's juries. Typically, these decisions showed what had been aptly called a "stretched humanity," the coroner's courts being "unwilling to suppose it [suicide] could be the act of reason,"⁷ but seizing upon even the remotest possibility of insanity to justify Christian burial for a suicide. That understanding had governed Christian thought and practice for over a thousand years when the enacted funeral cortege brought the "corse" of Ophelia onto the Globe stage.

Both the coroner's verdict of "Christian burial" and the audience's direct observation of Ophelia's madness (is there anywhere a more blatant example of *non compos mentis* behavior on stage?) would have led theatergoers at the Globe to expect something very different from what now appears. Instead of the mandated normal rites of Christian burial, Ophelia's funeral is degraded through "maimèd rites" until it approaches, although it does not reach, the rituals of abhorrence inflicted upon sane and willful suicides.

### III. The Burial of Suicides in Shakespeare's England

A sane person who chose suicide, on the other hand, was regarded as willfully guilty of murder, and of murder in a most obscene and reprehensible degree. A person had no more right to kill himself or herself than to kill another, and the crime of murder was rendered all the more damaging by the fact that suicide, if immediately successful, left no opportunity for repentance. Thus Elizabethan and Jacobean Englishmen regarded suicide with particular revulsion, and referred to it degradingly as "self-slaughter." Thomas Rogers Forbes summarizes the reactions: "The Elizabethans abhorred a *felo de se*, one who had committed the felony of self-murder, a sin and a crime. An exception was made if the victim was mentally deranged. But if the act was considered to have been done 'voluntarily and maliciously,' there was no compassion."[8] A conscious reverence for life was involved here: self-slaughter was regarded as the ultimate rejection of the greatest conceivable gift, the gift of being, and it was therefore made subject to the most abhorrent rituals which could be devised.

Suicide was sufficiently evident in Shakespeare's England, as well as sufficiently notable and scandalous, that his audience would have been quite cognizant of it, and of the specific ecclesiastical and social means of dealing with it. For one thing, there was a shocking increase in recorded instances of *felo de se* in the sixteenth century.[9] Prior to the year 1500, suicide rarely figures in the official records, with perhaps no more than two or three cases a year. In the decades of the fifteen thirties through the fifteen fifties, there was a tremendous increase, as indicated by the researches of Terence R. Murphy. The increase in numbers during those decades was not reversed even temporarily at any point, and in the fifteen eighties reached a stabilized rate of at least five times the annual incidents recorded as late as the early fifteen thirties. Shakespeare's Warwickshire, in the three decades between about 1560 and 1590, recorded an average of three suicides certified at the assizes for each of those thirty years, with five each for 1564 and 1574, and seven for 1587. At Stratford-upon-Avon, suicides occurred in 1567, 1573, 1577, and 1585, with two in 1589. John Shackspere of Balsall in Warwickshire who hanged himself on July

23, 1579, may have been a kinsman of the dramatist.[10] For London and Middlesex during the fifteen nineties and early sixteen hundreds, the fragmentary record indicates that a minimum of between ten and twenty suicides occurred each year during Shakespeare's residence there.

Professor Murphy's studies have meticulously analyzed legal records from the Tudor and Stuart dynasties, from 1500 to 1700. Because the primary evidence has been preserved in fragmentary and uneven ways, Murphy has been unable to determine accurately the total number of actual cases, but during those years he has documented the minimum as roughly 20,000 instances. Of these perhaps 14,000 contain some biographical data as to class or occupation, circumstances of death, and the like. In terms of social history, final judgments on the rapid and striking increase in the incidence of suicide in the sixteenth century records will have to await the completion and publication of Murphy's research.[11] Fortunately for our literary purposes, however, other publications already provide sufficient evidence of how suicides (both sane and insane) were buried in Shakespeare's England so that we can appraise the funeral of Ophelia against that background of familiar practice.

The burial of sane and willful suicides typically involved interment at night under a mere scattering of shards or pebbles, outside the sanctified ground of the churchyard, usually at a crossroad, with a stake driven through the breast.[12] The most famous suicide in England prior to Shakespeare's lifetime involved the eminent jurist Sir James Hales, who drowned himself in a shallow river in August of 1554. As the inheritance of property was involved, Sir James being a well-to-do man, every effort was made to prevent the court from adjudging him *non compos mentis* because if he were adjudged a willful suicide his property would therefore be forfeit.[13] The intense religious conflicts of the times were also involved in this case, because Hales was a famous Protestant layman, and as such was a target of attacks from the Roman Catholicism Queen Mary had recently reestablished in England: branding him a willful and premeditated suicide would serve to discredit him and also the Protestant movement with which he was prominently associated.[14] After unusually prolonged debate, Hales was adjudged sane, and "a verdict of *felo de se* was returned. Under this finding his body was to be buried in cross-road, with a stake thrust through it, and all his goods were forfeited to the crown."[15] That standard treatment of the willful suicide was applied to the body of Amy Stokes in September, 1590, and also to Elizabeth Wickham, who was buried in November, 1595, in the same alley where she hanged herself, also with a stake driven through her body.[16] In a similar but less detailed record we are merely told that Agnes Miller "who killed herself with a knife was put into the ground" on 27 August, 1573, where the stark reference to "putting in the ground" signifies that the burial was in "ground unsanctified" and not in a churchyard. Another record reports an unnamed nurse who committed suicide and was buried at night "in Hogg Lane" on May 25, 1598.[17] When Thomas Maule hanged himself from a tree during a drunken "fitte" on April 3, a coroner's inquest was held two days later, which adjudged him to be a willful suicide, without benefit of insanity, and he was "at midnight buried in the nearest crossroads with a stake in him, [observed by] many people from Manesfield."[18] Obviously drunkenness (itself a subspecies of the sin of gluttony) was not regarded as excusing him from the sin of suicide.

At the other extreme, deranged persons who committed suicide while incapable of rational choice were buried in holy ground with the full rites of the church. An explicit case of the detailing of insanity as a reason for suicide, and for granting the full rites of burial, occurs in July, 1624, with John Blackman, who "died of a wound which he gave himself in his sickness being as it were distraught and lightheaded," so much so that the coroner's inquest decided that because "the sick man could not be held responsible for taking his life while irrational and neglected by his attendant—if he had one—his body should not be denied the last rites."[19] We should also cite the case of a certain Frederick John who apparently died much as did Ophelia, and for him the coroner's jury meeting at St. Martin's Vestry Hall adjudged "suffocation by drowning and temporary insanity."[20] Such distraught suicides included several mad women who died by drowning, and who were accorded Christian burial. Three such cases occur within as many years before Shakespeare's *Hamlet*. In 1597 it is recorded in the parish register of Drypole in the East Riding of Yorkshire that "a single woman" named Anne Ruter "drowned herself and was buried the fourth day on July on the north side of the church." Christian burial was also accorded to Isabell Taylor who "drowned herself in a well and was buried 7 April" in 1600 at Chesterfield, and for the suicide by drowning of Isbell Border at Chesham, Bucks, on July 11, 1600.[21]

Between the two extremes of Christian burial and *felo de se* degradation there may have been some middle treatment, but this cannot be firmly demonstrated. The canons do not provide for it, and such hints as come in the records of the disposition of corpses are so often incomplete that what can perhaps appear to be a halfway rite may be just a halfway report. Yet we may occasionally find a hint.[22] On June 6, 1562, Henry Machyn noted the elimination of singing in a funeral for the wife of one Crane in Basyng Lane, London, who "took a knife and thrust herself between the small ribs, and she died the morrow after, and the seventh day at afternoon was the same woman buried and certain clerks were at her burying, and Vernon the Frenchman did preach for her, and moreover he would not the clerks to bring her to the church"— by which Machyn means that the officiating clergyman would not allow the body to be brought to burial with the usual singing of the clerks.[23] Unfortunately, this halfway measure is merely mentioned, not explained, and we are left to assume that Mrs. Crane was *compos mentis*. The evidence is simply not sufficient to allow us to postulate a consistent and recognized category of maimed rites. For our purposes the important point remains that there was no justification in historical church law and typical practice for denying the mad Ophelia a full Christian burial.

## IV. *The Anomalous Funeral and the Churlish Priest*

Let us return now to Ophelia's funeral and the reaction to it which Shakespeare could reasonably have expected from his original audiences. On the basis of what we have seen it is clear that ancient tradition and contemporary practice support Laertes as against the churlish priest. But what explanation can be given for the priest's attitude? Surely there is no theological justification, whether in the Roman, the Anglican, or the Reformed traditions, nor can I find any faction within those churches which would have sanctioned acting as this clergyman does.[24]

He is a very strange figure here. For so obviously notable a funeral, one would expect to see a bishop or at least a dean in attendance, as when the Bishop of Peterborough conducted the funeral of Lady Jane Seymour in 1561 or the Bishop of London that of Lady Lumley in 1578, and Shakespeare could as easily have had an actor play a bishop as a priest.[25] But he chose instead to introduce a simple clergyman, referred to by Laertes as "priest" and by the stage direction as "doctor." According to Dover Wilson, the word "doctor" designated a Protestant minister, whereas John Draper interprets it as the title of a doctor of canon law.[26] But on neither count did such a clergyman have the legal right to set aside the verdict of a coroner's inquest and to deny the

"Christian burial" it established. And what does this "doctor" mean in his assertion that there would have been no Christian ceremony at all "but that great command o'ersways the order?" (5.1.215). Presumably he refers to the normal "order" for burial of sane suicides, which he then proceeds to describe in grisly detail, but is the "great command" from Claudius? So it is generally interpreted, but the only command necessary here would be from the coroner's inquest which had already found for Christian burial—and the priest does not obey that. If Claudius did indeed intervene, he had little effect in mollifying the arrogant will of a local minister. We are thus faced with a situation in which a simple parish priest has set aside laws in salutary effect over many centuries, and who still has the effrontery to say that things would have been much worse "but that great command o'ersways the order"—and all of this in a funeral attended by the King, who should have been the guarantor both of justice and of ceremony in the society. Thus we once again see Claudius presented in the very light in which Hamlet had described him to Gertrude, as "a king of shreds and patches" (3.4.103). With characteristic cleverness, however, Claudius uses these maimed rites to inflame the resentment of Laertes, and to prepare him for the final encounter with Hamlet.

## V. The Denial of Song

The absence of song is explicitly signaled by the priest as one aspect of Ophelia's maimed rites. Shakespeare could have dramatized an interment without introducing song on the stage, allowing the audience either to overlook that fact in the fast movement of the action or to assume that singing took place offstage, but he is doing something quite different here. He draws attention to the absence of customary singing by having the priest spell out the injury and make it unmistakable:

> We should profane the service of the dead
> To sing a requiem and such rest to her
> As to peace-parted souls.                          (5.1.223-25)

Such a denial was traditionally part of the debasing burial prescribed for willful suicides. Gratian had declared "nor shall they be brought to burial with psalms,"[27] and we have already noted that a choir of clerks was excluded from the burial of a suicide in London in 1562.[28] Although willful and sane suicides had in effect excommunicated themselves from the mercy of God by their act of *felo de se* (which if successful would presumably shut off the possibility of later repentance), and although it was therefore thought inappropriate that the music of Christian hope and consolation should be sung for them, this was not Ophelia's case. Her derangement had been obvious to the whole court, and to the Globe audience, and to the coroner's jury, which had pronounced for normal Christian burial. That is what Laertes expects, and it is what Shakespeare has the churlish priest deny. In order to understand Laertes' bitterness, we need to reestablish the Elizabethan expectations for song in the burial of the dead, and their experience of what it contributed. But another question should be dealt with first, and this concerns the meaning of the phrase used by the priest when he refused "to sing a requiem." The word "requiem" is clear enough in modern usage, where it almost automatically refers to the words "requiem aeternam dono eis," which open the introit of the Latin eucharistic burial service of the Roman Catholic Church, and in recent centuries it has been applied to music especially composed for such a commemorative mass. Technically, no such music appears to have been available for requiem masses in this sense either in Anglicanism or Roman Catholicism at this period in England. That is the conclusion of the major scholar of requiem music, Alec Robertson, who writes that at least until 1600 in England "one must conclude that plainsong was invariably used" instead of the specifically composed music for a sung mass which was familiar on the Continent.[29] It seems most likely, under these circumstances, that the Globe audience would have interpreted the refusal "to sing a requiem" for Ophelia as a denial of the usual plainsong, which was the only musical accompaniment to funerals most of them knew.

One further technicality should be clarified, and this concerns the language which would have been used "to sing a requiem." Except for such clandestine Roman services as were still conducted in Elizabethan England, Church of England services would normally be conducted in the English of the Book of Common Prayer but could take advantage of a specially authorized Anglican service book in Latin. Eucharistic funerals did occur in the Church of England, and a Latin funeral mass was made available in 1560 in the *Liber Precum Publicarum*. This Latin service book was authorized for use under Queen Elizabeth by letters patent on April 6, 1560, and was never officially superseded or declared invalid. Attached to the services of commemoration in this volume "were propers for a requiem celebration of the Holy Communion," with the specific explanation that these were provided "if the friends and neighbors of the departed wished to communicate."[30] We know, for example, that the funeral service for Frances, Duchess of Suffolk, included a requiem communion, as did the Earl of Shrewsbury's funeral in 1560.[31] The *Liber Precum* continued to provide a form for Latin requiem funerals in all save one diocese during the reign of Elizabeth, when "the only explicit prohibition in an episcopal order came from Bishop Barnes of Durham who, in 1577, ordered 'That no Communion or Commemoration (as some call them) be said for the dead, or at the burials of the dead.' It is uncertain how long the actual practice of communions at burials continued in the Elizabethan church, but in spite of militant efforts no known legal barrier appeared except in this diocesan regulation."[32]

It is thus possible to think of a Latin requiem either in terms of Roman Catholic or of Protestant services, or of a sung English service. The important issue here is not denominational, whether Roman or Reformed, but is rather the emotional importance of the music of Christian consolation at a funeral. Laertes' reference to the clergyman as a priest could apply equally well to a Catholic or Anglican officiant. That Shakespeare elsewhere used requiem in an Anglican sense with Anglican liturgical vestments has been persuasively argued by J. Dover Wilson in conjunction with the eminent liturgiologist Percy Dearmer in their joint reading of these lines from Shakespeare's *The Phoenix and the Turtle*:

> Let the priest in surplice white,
> That defunctive music can,
> Be the death-divining swan,
> Lest the requiem lack his right. (13-16)

Wilson comments that "the words 'surplice white' in these lines prove that the 'priest' is not intended to be a Roman one, seeing that the Roman requiem mass would be celebrated in mass vestments, without surplice."[33]

These clarifications of "requiem" are only ancillary to the far more important issue of the contribution made by song in funeral services familiar to the Globe audiences. In Elizabethan England, the hymns of hope and comfort sung at funerals were called requiem, as in Henry Machyn's account of the funeral of Sir Thomas Pope on February 6, 1558/9, which included six songs, "two prick songs, and four of requiem."[34] Such music was one of the most conspicuous features of English burials. In 1598 it was observed that "it is a custom still in use with Christians, to attend the funeral of their deceased friends, with whole chantries of choice choir men singing solemnly before them."[35] Commenting upon the burial service of the Church of England, Dean Thomas Comber (1665-99) noted that the clergyman should meet the corpse at the entrance to the churchyard and go before it, using "those holy hymns, wherewith the deceased were brought to their graves."[36] According to the Book of Common Prayer of 1559, repeated in later editions throughout Elizabeth's reign, clergymen either "shall say" or "shall sing" (perhaps with attendant clerks) various passages of the burial order, and Dean Comber noted that this emphasis upon song continued a long established pre-Reformation tradition, whereby Christians in "pious antiquity carried out their dead with hymns of triumph, as conquerors that had gloriously finished their course, and were now going to receive their crown of victory. To this end again were those Hallelujahs sung of old, as they went to the grave; a custom still retained in many parts of this nation, where they divert the grief of the friends and mourners, by singing psalms from the house to the very 'entrance of the churchyard' . . . [and] then devoutly sing the anthems of holy psalms, which are on the same subject, and tend to the same purpose."[37] The purpose (and apparently the effect) of such singing was to overcome grief and bitterness and to invoke faith and hope among surviving family and friends—and it is the denial of all this by the priest which Laertes so passionately resents.

The customary use of singing which would "divert the grief of the friends and mourners" may be illustrated by numerous examples. In September, 1559, Sir John Raynford was buried at St. Katheryn's Church in London, while "the clarkes sang Te Deum in English"; in 1561, a merchant's body was carried in funeral procession led by the clergy till they came to St. Paul's churchyard, where the choir of St. Paul's met them and "they began to sing"; and in 1562 a popular preacher named Crom, the parson of Aldemare, was buried on 29 June "with priests and clerks singing" in procession into the church for burial.[38] When Bishop John Parkhurst of Norfolk officiated at the burial of Margaret, Duchess of Norfolk, in January, 1568, he reported in his letters to continental Protestants that he had maintained a strictly Protestant ceremony, without candles or other "papist" observances, but added that there was abundant singing.[39] The general custom for funerals of important citizens, gentry, and nobility, was to provide a large measure of singing in the service not merely by relying upon the voices of priest and people but by retaining the services of trained choirs. The typical procedure at Westminster Abbey was that "the ministers, clerks, and scholars met the body at the west door and said or sang words of burial rite as set down in the prayer book. The body was brought in procession to the hearse and the group continued to sing a number of songs."[40]

As for the Anglican prayer book liturgy, the earliest musical setting was composed by Thomas Morley (1551-1604?) in his "renowned Burial Service" (not including a memorial mass), which was apparently produced early in his career, although the precise date is not certain.[41] Whether by the use of Morley's music, or by following other plainsong music in the established service books, it is clear enough that a great deal of music would have been expected even if the funeral had been that of a commoner, and much more of course for the burial of a prominent court lady such as Ophelia, whose father had been principal minister to the crown, and whose own future had seemed to include marriage with the heir apparent. The kind of service customary under the circumstances may be summarized in the words of E.G.P. Wyatt in his study of the Anglican burial rite: "The Primer of 1559 contains a service called the Dirge, which was used on the occasion of several state funerals in Elizabeth's reign. It is a choir service, adapted from the ancient office of the dead. Although it is printed as one continuous service, its component parts are easily distinguishable, consisting of evensong, matins, and lauds."[42]

The significant point here is not just that Shakespeare omitted requiem songs from the funeral of Ophelia, but that he specifically called attention to that omission and signalized it as important. When the funeral cortege entered the graveyard at Elsinore, with King, Queen, and courtiers in attendance upon the corpse under the direction of a simple parish clergyman who forbade the lifting of a single voice in the traditional music of Christian assurance, the audience would surely have sympathized with Laertes' sense of outrage that his sister was deprived of the respect due to her, and that he and her other friends were denied the comfort of familiar and expected hymns.

In sum, Elizabethan audiences may be expected to have sympathized with Laertes' protests against the "churlish priest," as a response deeply ingrained in social instinct.

# Notes

*Chapter One. The Form and Pressure of the Time*

1. *Ham.* 3.2.15-23 in *William Shakespeare: The Complete Works*, ed. Alfred Harbage, Baltimore, Maryland, 1969. Unless otherwise noted, all future references are to this text.

2. *Great Writings of Goethe*, ed. Stephen Spender, New York, 1958, pp. 274ff.

3. Many distinguished critics of *Hamlet* have failed to find a unity in the play or in its title character. Thus L. C. Knights at one point maintained that "this play contains within itself widely different levels of experience" which "cannot be assimilated into a whole" ("Prince Hamlet," reprinted in *Discussion of Hamlet*, ed. J. C. Levenson, Boston, 1960, p. 82, from *Explorations; Essays in Criticism*, London, 1946). A.J.A. Waldock holds that "an old plot is wrenched to new significances, significances, in places, that to the end it refuses to take. It was, perhaps, inevitable that the play should show signs, in fissures and strain, of all this forceful bending" (*Hamlet: A Study in Critical Method*, Cambridge, 1931, p. 97). As for the title character, Robert Speight declares that "he will never be an integrated person. He remains a catalogue of qualities which have never been added up" (*Nature in Shakespearian Tragedy*, London, 1955, p. 38), and Dame Edith Sitwell sees the play as "a hunting story—that of a man who is hunting his own soul, or the truth of his own soul, and never finds it" (*A Notebook on William Shakespeare*, London, 1948, p. 82). Finally, A. L. French concludes that "Hamlet is an astonishingly rich play . . . but its richness is the result of its incoherence. The various points of view are never comprehended from one central synoptic point of view" (*Shakespeare and the Critics*, Cambridge, 1972, p. 76). Intelligent members of Shakespeare's Globe audiences would not have agreed to such modern critical judgments, as will become apparent.

4. C. H. Herford, "Shakespeare and the Arts," *Bulletin of the John Rylands Library*, vol. 11 (1927), pp. 280-81, and *Variorum Hamlet*, ed. Horace Howard Furness, New York, 1963, vol. 1, p. 228.

5. But J. Dover Wilson holds that, in Hamlet, Shakespeare "attempted a really detailed reflection of the inner Essex" and declares that "the more one studies the character of the ill-starred Essex, the more remarkable Shakespeare's portraiture becomes. Everything is there. . . ." (*The Essential Shakespeare: A Biographical Adventure*, Cambridge, 1952, pp. 104f.). Such identification of Shakespeare's dramatic characters with his influential British contemporaries has never been carried further than by Lilian Winstanley, who argues that "Claudius is the two Bothwells," while Hamlet is both (or in part both) the Earl of Essex and King James—see her *Hamlet and the Scottish Succession*, Freeport, New York, 1970 (reprinting the 1921 ed.), pp. 179-80. The contention that Hamlet was patterned upon the Earl of Essex is given a balanced discussion by John Buxton, who counters with the equally plausible (and in some ways more plausible) possibility that he was based on Sir Charles Blunt, Lord Mountjoy, and the beloved of "Stella." Buxton is appraising affinities, rather than suggesting some sort of copying, and his discussion is useful for providing balance. (See John Buxton, *Elizabethan Taste*, London, 1963, pp. 308-10.) Buxton's point is not to identify a prototype for Hamlet, but to show that he represents the Elizabethan courtly ideal in circumstances where he "is suddenly confronted with

a primitive and loathsome task"—p. 311. Thus Buxton points to the tremendous affection showered upon Essex, and the high visibility of his character and of his weaknesses. He says that "when Hamlet was first acted Essex was the most vivid personality in the mind of every man in London, and all were as subject to his charm as we are to Hamlet's. . . . But Hamlet, who is no historical portrait of Essex but rather an ideal presentation of the sort of man Essex then seemed to be, can make us briefly rediscover what it felt like, in the winter of 1600, to be a spectator of that high tragedy of his fall"—p. 314. That is a more useful approach to the question than the one-for-one identifications posited by Wilson and Winstanley which seem to me to oversimplify history, literary history, and literature. Shakespeare's creativity did not operate on the basis of such mechanical equations between individuals among his contemporaries and his dramatic characters. Furthermore, the crown's censorship of the theater through the Master of the Revels would have made such explicitly topical characterizations dangerous, and would have made difficulties for Shakespeare and his company.

6. W. J. Lawrence, *Pre-Restoration Stage Studies*, Cambridge, Mass., 1927, p. 103.

7. T. S. Eliot, "Hamlet and his Problems," in *Essays*, New York, 1950, p. 121.

8. Wilbur Sanders, *The Dramatist and the Received Idea: Studies in the Plays of Marlowe and Shakespeare*, Cambridge, 1968, p. 320.

*Chapter Two. Problems, Challenges, and Ambiguities*

1. E.M.W. Tillyard, *The Elizabethan World Picture*, London, 1948.

2. *Certain Sermons or Homilies Appointed to be Read in Churches in the Time of Queen Elizabeth*, Oxford, 1822, pp. 104-16 and 506-51; hereafter referred to as *Homilies*.

3. *Homilies*, pp. 507 and 511.

4. Thomas Becon, *Early Works*, ed. John Ayre, Cambridge, 1843, p. 456, from his *The Governance of Virtue*.

5. John E. E. Dalberg-Acton, *Lectures on Modern History*, London, 1950, p. 156.

6. Robert H. West, *Shakespeare and the Outer Mystery*, Lexington, Kentucky, 1968, p. 67, discusses this response as well as others. West's study remains fundamental for Shakespeare. For the broad social context of sixteenth- and seventeenth-century English attitudes, see Keith Thomas, *Religion and the Decline of Magic*, Harmondsworth, 1980, pp. 700-24.

7. Lewes Lavater, *Of Ghosts and Spirits Walking by Night* (1572), eds. J. Dover Wilson and May Yardley, Oxford, 1929, p. 89.

8. Thomas Lodge, *The Devil Conjured*, 1596, sig. D1, p. 23 in facsimile reprint of Hunterian Club ed., *The Complete Works*, 5 vols., Glasgow, 1875-88, vol. 3.

9. The skepticism about ghosts which Horatio first holds was rare in Shakespeare's time, and was most notably expressed by Reginald Scot in his *Discovery of Witchcraft* of 1584, and in the *Discourse upon Devils and Spirits* appended to it, for which see the edition by Brinsley Nicholson, London, 1886. Scot's position is treated by J. Dover Wilson, *What Happens in Hamlet*, Cambridge, 1959, pp. 62-65, and also in Robert H. West, "Elizabethan Belief in Spirits and Witchcraft," in *Studies in Shakespeare*, Miami, 1952, pp. 65-73, esp. 69-73.

10. For scholars who have studied the problem of the Ghost extensively and recognize its ambiguity, see primarily the basic conclusions reached by West, *Shakespeare and the Outer Mystery*, pp. 56-68 (and especially pp. 62-63); note also that J. Dover Wilson, *What Happens in Hamlet*, p. 84, concluded that "it paid [Shakespeare] dramatically to let all three schools of thought have their views considered." In *Shakespeare's Use of Learning: An Inquiry into the Growth of his Mind and Art*, San Marino, Cal., 1953, p. 257, Virgil Whitaker interpreted the Ghost as "no stage convention but either an angel or a devil, almost certainly the latter," but later he apparently came to a different conclusion, maintaining that "what kind of ghost it was

Shakespeare never tells us" in his *The Mirror up to Nature: The Technique of Shakespeare's Tragedies*, San Marino, Cal., 1965, p. 193; Nigel Alexander, *Poison, Play, and Duel: A Study in Hamlet*, Lincoln, Nebraska, 1971, pp. 32-33, observed that because Shakespeare can always make evil unmistakable in its identification, his neglect of doing so here indicates purpose. To these judgments I shall add reinforcing evidence along the same lines, and one major new piece of evidence in the ambiguous response of a Protestant bishop to the appearance of a ghost in his diocese.

11. For a contrary view, see Roy W. Battenhouse, "The Ghost in *Hamlet*: A Catholic 'Linchpin'?" *Studies in Philology*, vol. 48 (1951), pp. 161-92, who presents a case for the pagan interpretation. Note particularly his argument that "the Ghost is not from a genuinely Catholic Purgatory. However, he has all the marks of being from one of several regions popularly confused with it in the Renaissance—the purgatory of the Ancients, or their hell, or their vague afterworld, hades. Just which is of little consequence, since all are Hell from a Christian point of view: an inhabitant of any one of them is a 'damned' spirit in authentic Christian vision, since he is outside Faith, Hope, and Charity"—p. 190. Other major interpretations will be identified as this chapter proceeds.

12. Roy W. Battenhouse, *Shakespearean Tragedy: Its Art and Its Christian Premises*, Bloomington, Indiana, 1969, p. 232, strangely ignores all this, plus Hamlet's repeated association with Wittenberg, and criticizes the Prince for not praying for his father's soul in a Purgatory in which he manifestly does not believe.

13. The major arguments for interpreting the Ghost as an evil spirit or demon have been carefully and learnedly marshaled by Eleanor Prosser, *Hamlet and Revenge*, Stanford, California, 1967, especially pp. 97-142. She is certainly correct in observing that for Hamlet to distrust the apparition was a sign of prudence (p. 108), but her own assurance as to the Ghost's essential identity is symptomatic of what I take to be an over–doctrinaire reading of the play as a whole.

14. Thomas Cranmer, *Miscellaneous Writings and Letters*, ed. John E. Cox, Cambridge, 1846, p. 41. Other early Protestant leaders warned to the same effect. For a brief capitulation of the standard Protestant view of ghosts as "mere delusions of Satan," see Sir John Davies, *Nosce Teipsum*, in *The Poems of Sir John Davies*, ed. Clare Howard, New York, 1941, pp. 187-88.

15. James Calfhill, *An Answer to John Martiall's Treatise*, ed. Richard Gibbings, Cambridge, 1846, p. 318.

16. Henry Bullinger, *Decades*, ed. Thomas Harding, 4 vols. in 3, Cambridge, 1849-52, vol. 4, p. 404.

17. *Ibid.*, p. 403.

18. Other relevant comments may be found in Archbishop Cranmer, *Miscellaneous Writings*, p. 45; Bishop John Hooper, *Early Writings*, ed. Samuel Carr, Cambridge, 1843, pp. 326 and 329; Bishop James Pilkington, *Works*, ed. James Scholefield, Cambridge, 1842, p. 25; Archbishop Edwin Sandys, *Sermons*, ed. John Ayre, Cambridge, 1841, pp. 17 and 129; and Richmond Noble, *Shakespeare's Biblical Knowledge*, London, 1935, p. 203.

19. Report from Bishop Pilkington in Matthew Parker, *Correspondence*, ed. John Bruce, Cambridge, 1853, p. 222. For other similar examples of Protestant attitudes toward ghosts, see Thomas, *Religion and the Decline of Magic*, pp. 706-08.

20. One could argue, of course, that a demonic ghost knew that Gertrude was in a state of mortal sin, and was attempting to divert Hamlet's attention from that fact. In such an interpretation, "leave her to heaven" was mere subterfuge, designed to prevent Hamlet from the attempt he later makes to bring his mother to repentance and a state of grace. Even so, the argument would remain inconclusive without the introduction of much stronger evidence than I know.

21. The Ghost is thus interpreted as a legitimate spirit returning from purgatory by Sister Miriam Joseph, "Discerning the Ghost in *Hamlet*," *PMLA*, vol. 76 (1961), pp. 493-502, and by Father I. J. Semper, "The Ghost in *Hamlet*: Pagan or Christian?" *The Month*, vol. 195 (1953), pp. 222-34, and *Hamlet without Tears*, Dubuque, Iowa, 1946, pp. 14-29. But see Battenhouse's "The Ghost in *Hamlet*," already cited (n. 11 above) for arguments that the purgatory cited by the Ghost is non-Catholic.

22. Latimer, *Sermons*, ed. G. E. Corrie, Cambridge, 1844, p. 212.

23. Bullinger, *Decades*, vol. 4, pp. 400, 402, and 404; see also Lavater, p. 200, and John E. Hankins, *The Character of Hamlet*, Chapel Hill, N.C., 1941, pp. 163f. and 166f. for other examples of the same view.

24. Lewes Lavater, *Of Ghosts and Spirits*, p. 173. See also Hankins, *The Character of Hamlet*, pp. 167-71 for Catholic suspicions of ghosts.

25. Thomas Becon, *The Catechism with Other Pieces*, ed. John Ayre, Cambridge, 1844, pp. 627-28. See also William Tyndale, *Doctrinal Treatises*, ed. Henry Walter, Cambridge, 1848, p. 413.

26. Translated by Thomas Cranmer in *Miscellaneous Writings*, p. 44.

27. Lavater, *Of Ghosts and Spirits*, p. 140, and Noel Taillepied, *A Treatise of Ghosts* (1588), trans. Montague Summers, London, n.d. [1933], p. 160.

28. Quoted by J. Dover Wilson, *What Happens in Hamlet*, p. 83 (and see p. 63) from *IIII Livres des Spectres ou Apparitions et Visions d'Esprits, Anges et Demons se monstrans sensiblement aux hommes*.

29. See Robert H. West, *The Invisible World: A Study of Pneumatology in Elizabethan Drama*, Athens, Georgia, 1939, p. 261, n. 58.

30. West, *Shakespeare and the Outer Mystery*, p. 57; see also his *The Invisible World*, Chapter IX, especially pp. 181ff. Battenhouse agrees that there was no orthodox Catholic account of a spirit from purgatory commanding the execution of revenge (*Shakespearean Tragedy*, pp. 239-40).

31. Latimer, *Sermons*, p. 439. The words of the Lord are quoted from the Vulgate text of Rom. 12:19 and Deut. 32:35 which Latimer then paraphrases in English. Recall too that both Laertes and Hamlet refer to revenge in connection with hell—4.5.130-36 and 2.2.568-89.

32. Sir Thomas Browne, *Religio Medici*, I.xxxvii, in *The Prose of Sir Thomas Browne*, ed. Norman J. Endicott, New York, 1968, p. 45.

33. Lily B. Campbell, *Shakespeare's Tragic Heroes: Slaves of Passion*, New York, 1930, p. 126.

34. I Kings 2.1-6 and 28-35. An analysis of interesting similarities between Hamlet and David may be found in Gene Edward Veith, Jr., " 'Wait upon the Lord': David, Hamlet, and the Problem of Revenge," in *The David Myth in Western Literature*, ed. Raymond-Jean Frontain and Jan Wojcik, West Lafayette, Ind., 1980, pp. 70-83.

35. William Gouge, *Of Domestical Duties*, London, 1622, Treatise 5, paragraph 51, p. 481.

36. John W. Draper, *The Hamlet of Shakespeare's Audience*, Durham, N.C., 1938, p. 103. Although *thou* was not always degrading (it was used in addressing both God and intimate friends), its use was frequently insulting, or at least belittling. For fuller studies of the implications of pronouns of address, see Sister St. Geraldine Byrne, *Shakespeare's Use of the Pronoun of Address; its Significance in Characterization and Motivation*, Washington, 1936, pp. xxxii-xxxv and 101-05; and E. A. Abbott, *A Shakespearean Grammar*, New York, 1966, sections 231 through 235. More will be said of these pronouns of address as we proceed.

37. From *A Warning for Fair Women*, as quoted by G. R. Hibbard in his "*Henry IV* and *Hamlet*," *Shakespeare Survey*, vol. 30 (1977), pp. 10-11, citing the 1912 ed. by J. S. Farmer,

"Induction," 48-51. William J. Lawrence argues that stage armor in the eighteenth century was made of a silvered leather "pilch," but that is surely a more dignified use than is described for the "filthy whining ghost" in *A Warning for Fair Women*—see W. J. Lawrence, *Pre-Restoration Stage Studies*, p. 109. Allardyce Nicoll (*Stuart Masques and the Renaissance Stage*, London, 1937, pp. 203-05) cites Angelo Ingegnieri advising on Italian stage practice in 1598 that a ghost should appear behind a dark veil, should be entirely dressed in black silk or similar material, that "it ought to look like some shapeless thing, moving rather on small wheels than taking formal steps and walking like a human being," and that at the "moment of disappearance the veil must be consumed by fire"—none of which seems to accord with the majestic appearance and stately movement of the Ghost in *Hamlet*. Not only is this ghost given a more attractive physical presence than was apparently customary on Elizabethan stages, but he was given a decidedly more moral concern, as Paul Gottschalk argues in his impressive essay "Hamlet and the Scanning of Revenge," *SQ* vol. 24 (1973), pp. 155-70, esp. 165f.

38. E. K. Chambers, *The Elizabethan Stage*, Oxford, 1951, vol. II, pp. 204 and 434.

39. Stephen Bateman, *The Doom Warning All Men to Judgment*, 1581, p. 420 (Sig. DD5 verso). The picture illustrates the story of an event in Bohemia in which "a ghost appeared to one that was asleep," led him to an open field, and showed him a vision of a coming battle. Bateman, although strongly Protestant, does not identify this ghost as demonic and indeed provides no judgment of the moral state of this ghost, but merely recounts the brief tale.

40. Bullinger, *Decades*, vol. 4, p. 361; *Lear* 4.6.69-72; Cranmer, *Miscellaneous Writings*, p. 50.

41. William Tyndale, *An Answer to Sir Thomas More's "Dialogue,"* ed. Henry Walter, Cambridge, 1850, p. 58; see also Thomas Becon's prayer "For the Help of God's Holy Angels" in *Prayers and Other Pieces*, ed. John Ayre, Cambridge, 1844, p. 84.

42. G. L. Kittredge, ed., *Hamlet*, New York, 1939, note to 1.4.39ff., p. 164. See also Virgil Whitaker, *The Mirror up to Nature*, pp. 191-92.

43. Kenneth Myrick, "Kittredge on Hamlet," *Shakespeare Quarterly*, vol. 15 (1964), p. 224 and n. 32.

44. Lavater, *Of Ghosts and Spirits*, p. 106.

45. For pronoun of address, see above n. 36. The critical debate as to the meaning of "old mole" has been extensive, largely as to whether or not a mole signified the devil: see, for example, R. W. Dent, *N&Q*, n.s. vol. 215 (1970), pp. 128f.; R. W. Battenhouse, *N&Q*, n.s. vol. 216 (1971), pp. 145f.; J. R. Rus, *ELN*, vol. 12 (1975), pp. 163-68; and J. A. Drake-Brockman, *Explicator*, vol. 32 (1973), no. 31. In itself, this debate testifies to the ambiguity of the Ghost as presented in *Hamlet*.

46. *The Interpreter's Dictionary of the Bible*, ed. George A. Buttrick, New York, 1962, vol. IV, p. 748, s.v. "Vengeance" by W. J. Harrelson.

47. See Numbers, chapter 35.

48. Deut. 32:25, Lev. 19:17-18; Rom. 12:19, and Heb. 10:30; see also Luke 18:7-8, and 21:22.

49. Rom. 13:1, 4.

50. Matt. 5:38-39.

51. William Tyndale, *Expositions and Notes on Sundry Portions of the Holy Scriptures*, ed. Henry Walter, Cambridge, 1849, p. 59.

52. *Ibid.*, p. 58.

53. *Ibid.*, p. 61.

54. Vincent of Beauvais, *Speculum Doctrinale*, VII, 77, quoted in Thomas Gilby, *The Political Thought of Thomas Aquinas*, Chicago, 1958, p. 218.

55. Aquinas, *de Regimine Principium*, i, 7, in *St. Thomas Aquinas Theological Texts*, ed.

Thomas Gilby, London and New York, 1955, entry 436, and *Summa Theologica* (II-II, qu. 108 art. 1) ed. by Fathers of the English Dominican Province, New York, 1947, vol. 2, p. 1656.

56. The oil painting is preserved in two contemporary versions, the royal copy now at Holyroodhouse and the other at Goodwood. The royal copy descended through the English branch of the Stewart family, the Dukes of Richmond and Lennox, but the verbal inscriptions on this version were altered to present a less condemnatory view of Mary Queen of Scots—presumably as part of royal efforts to rehabilitate Mary's reputation in the seventeenth century. The Goodwood version fortunately preserves the original sixteenth-century texts, which are followed here. In the mid-eighteenth century (presumably in reaction against the last Stuart effort to reclaim the throne), George Vertue executed an engraving of the whole and also of the insert at the lower left, known as *The Battle Array at Carberry*, to which reference may be made for greater clarity than is possible by photographic reproductions of the oil paintings. The earliest twentieth-century scholarly report is James L. Caw, *Scottish Portraits with an Historical and Critical Introduction and Notes*, London and Boston, n.d. [1903], pp. 29-34. The most authoritative analysis is by Sir Oliver Millar, *The Tudor, Stuart, and Early Georgian Pictures in the Collection of her Majesty the Queen*, London, 1963, Text Volume, pp. 75-77. See also the interesting treatment in Duncan Thomson's *Painting in Scotland 1570-1650*, Edinburgh, 1975, pp. 18-19.

57. Thomson, *Painting in Scotland*, p. 18.

58. Antonia Fraser, *Mary Queen of Scots*, London, 1969, pp. 448-49.

59. See Robert Keith, *History of the Affairs of Church and State in Scotland from the Beginning of the Reformation to the Year 1568*, Edinburgh, 1844-50, vol. 3, pp. 300-03, with copy of Bothwell's declaration pp. 305ff., and also vol. 2, pp. 551ff. for comments on the authenticity of the same.

60. R. B. Wernham, *Before the Armada: The Growth of English Foreign Policy 1485-1588*, London, 1966, p. 353.

61. It has been argued, for these and other reasons, that Shakespeare patterned *Hamlet* upon the situation of James in Scotland, but that is not my argument here: see Lilian Winstanley, *Hamlet and the Scottish Succession*, Freeport, N.Y., 1970 reprint of original 1921 edition.

62. The speech assigned to King James is reminiscent of many Old Testament passages, but I can find no single source in the Latin text of the Vulgate. Calls on God to defend or to avenge are common, as are calls upon the right hand of God, and so too are references to innocent blood, while the *exurge domine* occurs in six psalms in the Vulgate (3:7, 7:7, 9:20, [10:12], 16:13, and 73:22), and has an almost equally famous use as the title of the papal bull leveled against Martin Luther on June 15, 1520. Those who are curious about that bull (which has no relevance to *Hamlet*) may find a translation in Roland H. Bainton's *Here I Stand: A Life of Martin Luther*, New York, 1950, p. 147.

63. Fraser, *Mary Queen of Scots*, p. 221.

64. Thomson, *Painting in Scotland*, pp. 12, 34, and 39. The genre of revenge painting seems not to have appeared in England, just as the genre of revenge plays did not develop in Scotland, although they flowered in the same general period. The date on the Moray Memorial is 1591, which I have modernized to 1592 in my text.

65. *The Zurich Letters: 1558-79*, ed. Hastings Robinson, Cambridge, 1842, pp. 195-96.

66. Fredson Bowers, *Elizabethan Revenge Tragedy: 1587-1642*, Princeton, 1940, provides a brilliant study of the revenge tradition on the stage; for differing attitudes toward revenge in England at the time, Bowers also provides a brief but suggestive sketch—pp. 34ff.

67. The Belleforest source for the Hamlet story has the Prince say about killing the King that "it will neither be felony nor treason, he being neither my king nor my lord, but I shall justly punish him as my subject that hath disloyally behaved himself against his lord and sovereign

prince." The quotation is from the anonymous 1608 English version of Belleforest, *The History of Hamlet*, reprinted in vol. 7 of Geoffrey Bullough, *Narrative and Dramatic Sources of Shakespeare*, London and New York, 1973, p. 100. In contrast to Belleforest, Shakespeare's treatment capitalizes upon having the Prince debate these issues.

68. Wilbur Sanders, *The Dramatist and the Received Idea: Studies in the Plays of Marlowe and Shakespeare*, p. 155, cites a well-recognized distinction between method of entry into kingship and the method of administration, of which neither, either, or both, may be tyrannical.

69. George Buchanan, *De Jure Regni Apud Scotos*, trans. Charles F. Arrowood, Austin, Texas, 1949, p. 88.

70. The extent to which the presence of these Switzers was used to prevent Hamlet from killing Claudius is not entirely clear, except in the third scene of the fourth act in which Hamlet appears before the King as a prisoner and guarded, a scene which we will consider in Chapter Five. Aside from that scene, I suspect that the principal stage use of the Swiss guards was for establishing the impression of tyranny. Virgil Whitaker (*Shakespeare's Use of Learning*, p. 274) rightly observes that "Shakespeare changed the conflict from eluding the King's guards to the struggle of a human soul." My point is that the nature of that struggle in *Hamlet* and of the audience's response to it is illuminated by the fact that Shakespeare has presented so many recognizable signs of the tyrant in Claudius—including the readily dramatizable presence of Swiss mercenary guards. For a somewhat different interpretation, but one which seems unaware of the traditional significance attached to foreign mercenaries from the age of Aristotle through the age of Shakespeare, see John W. Draper, *The "Hamlet" of Shakespeare's Audience*, pp. 82-84.

71. Erasmus, *The Education of a Christian Prince*, ed. Lester K. Born, New York, 1936, p. 163. Philippe du Plessis-Mornay notes how a tyrant makes himself formidable with guards of strangers (*Vindiciae contra tyrannos*, 1579, translated in *Constitutionalism and Resistance in the Sixteenth Century: Three Treatises by Hotman, Bèza, and Mornay*, ed. Julian H. Franklin, New York, 1969, p. 186), while François Hotman, *Francogallia*, 1573, ed. Ralph E. Giesey and J.H.M. Salmon, Cambridge, 1972, p. 60, writes to the same effect.

72. Keith, *History of the Affairs*, vol. 2, pp. 679f.

73. Aristotle, *Politics*, V.10.1311a and III.14.1285a, ed. Benjamin Jowett, Oxford, 1885.

74. Aristotle, *Politics*, V.11.1314a and IV.4.1292a.

75. Erasmus, *Christian Prince*, p. 164.

76. Jeffrey Whitney, *A Choice of Emblems*, 1586, p. 151. Although I thought that I had discovered this visual analogue, I was in fact preceded by Joan Larsen Klein's "Hamlet, 4.2.12-21 and Whitney's *A Choice of Emblemes*," *N&Q*, vol. 23 (1976), pp. 158-61, and perhaps by others unknown to Klein and to me. Underlying Whitney's emblem and Shakespeare's image is an ancient and widely known conception that tyrants did use favorites as a sponge in just this sense. My quotation from Du Mornay's great Huguenot republican treatise *Vindiciae contra tyrannos*, first published in 1579, is from the anonymous translation of 1689, ed. Harold J. Laski, New York: Burt Franklin, 1972, p. 187. The conception goes back at least as far as Suetonius' *Lives of the Caesars*, where we are told that Vespasian "used these men as sponges, because he, so to speak, soaked them when they were dry and squeezed them when they were wet" (*Suetonius*, ed. for Loeb Classical Library by J. C. Rolfe, Cambridge, Mass., 1970, vol. 2, pp. 308-11, "The Deified Vespasian," XVI).

77. Aristotle, *Politics*, V.11.1313b.

78. For spying in *Hamlet*, see 2.2.15f., 3.1.32, and 3.3.32.

79. Johannes Althusius, *The Politics*, trans. Frederick S. Carney, Boston, 1964, pp. 185 and 186.

80. This is not to say that historical criticism offers the only valid approach to a literary

work, but rather that it cannot be ignored without running the risks of subjectivism, whether by an individual or a coterie of critics.

81. E. W. Talbert (*The Problem of Order: Elizabethan Political Commonplaces and An Example of Shakespeare's Art*, Chapel Hill, N.C., 1962) presented some valuable caveats to modify the unilateral view, and he may be said to have opened up the discussion even though he did not avail himself of much highly pertinent data which can make the need for revision overwhelmingly convincing. Half a dozen years later, Wilbur Sanders' *The Dramatist and the Received Idea: Studies in the Plays of Marlowe and Shakespeare*, took his lead from Talbert (see Sanders, p. 369 n. 44) and presented a critical re–analysis which argues against an oversimple reading of Tudor attitudes, while also warning sensibly against allowing even a fuller and more adequate historical reconstruction to dominate and displace our literary sensibilities. But he did not carry the historical investigation beyond Talbert to the point of filling in the spectrum of the major alternative views among Shakespeare's contemporaries. For the work of Robert Ornstein, see below, n. 94.

82. *Sixteenth-Century Journal*, vol. 11 (1980), pp. 63-64.

83. John Milton, *Complete Prose Works*, New Haven, 1962, vol. 3, p. 212.

84. For the development of the Christian approval of tyrannicide see Oscar Jászi and John D. Lewis, *Against the Tyrant: The Tradition and Theory of Tyrannicide*, Glencoe, Ill., 1957, pp. 13-15.

85. Clement C. J. Webb, *John of Salisbury*, New York, 1971, p. 66.

86. *Summa Theologica*, Secunda Secundae, qu. 42, art. 2, in Aquinas, *Selected Political Writings*, ed. A. P. d'Entrèves, Oxford, 1948, p. 161. The teachings of John and Thomas are compared in Thomas Gilby, *The Political Thought of Thomas Aquinas*, pp. 175 and 289. See also Jászi and Lewis, *Against the Tyrant*, pp. 26-27.

87. Jászi and Lewis, *Against the Tyrant*, pp. 29-30.

88. *Ibid.*, pp. 33 and 35.

89. More did refer to assassination as an instrument of policy when he wrote that the Utopians "promise great rewards to him that will kill their enemy's prince" in order that "the lives of a great number of innocents [soldiers and civilians on both sides or a war] . . . be ransomed and saved, which in fighting should have been slain"—Thomas More, *Utopia*, ed. J. Rawson Lumby, Cambridge, 1935, pp. 134-35. That stratagem was not directed against an internal usurper or tyrant, and even within its own limitations it suggests a whimsical or sardonic humor (killing off the leader who starts a war so as to save the lives of the warring soldiers).

90. Richard Hooker, *Of The Laws of Ecclesiastical Polity*, 8.1.7, in *Works*, ed. John Keble, New York, 1849.

91. E.M.W. Tillyard, *The Elizabethan World Picture* cited in n.1 of this chapter, and the same author's *Shakespeare's History Plays*, London, 1944; and Lily B. Campbell, *Shakespeare's "Histories": Mirrors of Elizabethan Policy*, San Marino, Cal., 1968. Following this line without significant awareness of other modifying and contradicting influences in sixteenth-century thought, Irving Ribner (see for example *The English History Play*, Princeton, 1957) is typical of many who take the *Homilies*, with their pervasive insistence on passive resistance, as virtually the sole criterion for judging actions on the stage and in the history of the period. It is only with the development of scholarly studies of the history and political theory of this period—studies largely carried out within the last two decades—that we can begin to move beyond such one-sided visions to recognize the full complexity of attitudes toward resistance in the age of Shakespeare.

92. This application is largely to the post-Roman plays.

93. Quentin Skinner, *The Foundations of Modern Political Thought*, Cambridge, 1978, vol. 1, pp. 239f.

94. Robert Ornstein objected to the imposition of "Tudor orthodoxies" upon Shakespeare's

plays, and his was a healthy and heuristic protest for which we should be grateful: "I would point out the inherent bias of the historical method toward what is conventional and orthodox in Elizabethan culture, because any search for the 'norms' of Elizabethan thought must lead to a consensus of truism and pieties," and he went on even more significantly to call not for a less historical approach, "but a more rigorous methodology for that approach" (*A Kingdom for a Stage: The Achievement of Shakespeare's History Plays*, Cambridge, Mass., 1972, p. 4). For his criticism of the univocal control of Tudor orthodoxy, see for example pp. 14-16 and 30-32. What Ornstein does not do is to adduce the history of monarchomachist developments which questioned and balanced the passive resistance ethos, and which would thus strengthen the case he makes. He does not show much awareness of the Calvinist and Jesuit proponents of resistance, or even of the significant shift in the Elizabethan doctrine which came with Thomas Bilson, but more will be said of these historical developments as our reconstruction proceeds.

95. G. E. Duffield, ed., *The Work of Thomas Cranmer*, Philadelphia, 1965, pp. 279-80; and see also Jasper Ridley, *Thomas Cranmer*, Oxford, 1962, pp. 343-48 and 356-59.

96. Ridley, *Cranmer*, p. 345.

97. Hooper, *Later Writings*, ed. Charles Nevinson, Cambridge, 1852, pp. 556-57.

98. *Ibid.*, p. xxii.

99. Hooper, *Early Writings*, p. 75.

100. *Ibid.*, pp. 75-76.

101. Elliot Rose, *Cases of Conscience: Alternatives open to Recusants and Puritans under Elizabeth I and James I*, Cambridge, 1975, p. 8. For another indication of important similarities of attitude between Protestant and Catholic "policy," see George L. Mosse, *The Holy Pretence: A Study in Christianity and Reason of State from William Perkins to John Winthrop*, Oxford, 1957, p. 47.

102. Rose, *Cases of Conscience*, p. 1.

103. See Jászi and Lewis, *Against the Tyrant*, p. 65, and Roland Mousnier, *The Assassination of Henry IV: The Tyrannicide Problem and the Consolidation of the French Absolute Monarchy in the Early Seventeenth Century*, trans. Joan Spencer, London, 1973, p. 97.

104. Arnold Pritchard, *Catholic Loyalism in Elizabethan England*, Chapel Hill, N.C., 1979, p. 197.

105. See Hugh R. Trevor-Roper, *Archbishop Laud: 1573-1645*, London, 1940, p. 70n.

106. Quentin Skinner, *The Foundations of Modern Political Thought*, vol. 2, p. 347.

107. See in Part E of this section.

108. Skinner proceeds to note that "the most important writers to adopt this stance were Jean Boucher (1548-1644), who published a defense of tyrannicide in 1589 entitled *The Just Renunciation of Henry III*, and Guillaume Rose (c. 1542-1611) who proclaimed the same theme even more stridently in the title of his enormous treatise of 1590 on *The Just Authority of A Christian Commonwealth Over Impious and Heretical Kings*"—Skinner, vol. 2, p. 345, and see also pp. 321 and 323.

109. E. I. Watkin, *Roman Catholicism in England from the Reformation*, London and New York, 1958, p. 27.

110. R. B. Wernham, *Before the Armada*, p. 339.

111. Arnold O. Meyer, *England and the Catholic Church under Queen Elizabeth*, London, 1967, pp. 135f.

112. Arnold Pritchard, *Catholic Loyalism in Elizabethan England*, pp. 52-54, and 56.

113. For a fine summary and overview of differing opinions among English Catholics as to resistance against Elizabeth, see J.H.M. Salmon, *The French Religious Wars in English Political Thought*, Oxford, 1959, pp. 34-36.

114. Thomas H. Clancy, S.J., *Papist Pamphleteers: The Allen-Persons Party and the Political Thought of the Counter-Reformation in England, 1572-1615*, Chicago, 1964, pp, 75f.

115. Meyer, *England and the Catholic Church under Queen Elizabeth*, in notes 111-20 gives references to Vatican archives.

116. Alison Plowden, *Danger to Elizabeth: The Catholics under Elizabeth I*, London, 1973, pp. 206f., and for another related event, pp. 198f.

117. Meyer, *England and the Catholic Church under Queen Elizabeth*, p. 267.

118. *Ibid.*, pp. 269-70.

119. *Ibid.*, p. 273, and for the Latin texts of both letters, pp. 490f. This episode is puzzling. Apart from the Vatican records published by Meyer (which establish the official attitude under Gregory XIII), we have little to go on, and it is not clear why Humphrey Ely would at this time have been an emissary for any unnamed group of recusant lords. In 1602, twenty years later, Ely wrote to Robert Cecil offering to protect "Her Majesty my Prince's person"; see T. G. Law, *The Archpriest Controversy*, Camden Society, 1898, vol. 2, pp. 195-200. The curious aspects of the case do not, however, impinge upon its usefulness to us here, which rests upon the moral sanction of tyrannicide under certain clearly defined conditions.

120. Meyer, *England and the Catholic Church*, pp. 272 and 271.

121. The major spokesmen for English Catholicism in the Elizabethan period displayed conflicting attitudes toward tyrannicide. There are some indications that Cardinal William Allen was involved in 1582-83 in a decision to hire an assassin to murder Queen Elizabeth, and Allen has been accused by a modern historian of seeking to mitigate or obscure his involvement in these and other plots with a "lack of frankness" and of withholding "an important part of the truth from his statements"—see Robert M. Kingdon, ed., *The Execution of Justice in England* by William Cecil and *A True, Sincere, and Modest Defense of English Catholics* by William Allen, Ithaca, New York, and Washington, 1965, pp. xxxiii-xxxiv. The only English Catholic who published a full analysis and advocacy of tyrannicide was William Rainolds, recusant brother of the Puritan John Rainolds, who called Jacques Clément, the assassin of King Henry III of France in 1589, "a special instrument in the hands of God." On the other hand, most of the major leaders of the English Catholic mission repudiated such tactics, according to Thomas Clancy, *Papist Pamphleteers*, pp. 73, and 97-99.

122. Garrett Mattingly, *The Armada*, Boston, 1959, p. 345.

123. Plowden, *Danger to Elizabeth*, p. 239.

124. Mousnier, *The Assassination of Henry IV*, p. 105.

125. George Albert Moore has provided an English translation under the title *The King and the Education of the King*, Washington, D.C., 1948, and a useful study may be found in Guenter Lewy, *A Study of the Political Philosophy of Juan de Mariana, S.J.*, Geneva, 1960.

126. This and the following quotations of Mariana are from G. A. Moore's translation, pp. 143-44.

127. Jászi and Lewis, *Against the Tyrant*, pp. 65-66.

128. All quotations are from G. A. Moore's translation, *The King and the Education of the King*, pp. 143-44.

129. Lewy, *Mariana*, p. 141.

130. Lewy, *Mariana*, p. 167.

131. *Ibid.*, pp. 146-47.

132. For a fair and balanced analysis of the tyrannicide arguments and responses pro and con within Catholicism (and to a lesser extent Protestantism) at the time and later, see Lewy, *Mariana*, pp. 66-81 and 133-51.

133. See J. W. Allen, *A History of Political Thought in the Sixteenth Century*, New York, 1957, pp. 103-06.

134. Allen, *Political Thought in the Sixteenth Century*, p. 113.

135. Quoted from Knox's *Appellation* in Allen, *Political Thought in the Sixteenth Century*, p. 112.

136. *Ibid.*, p. 120.

137. Bullinger, *Decades*, vols. 1 and 2, p. 318.

138. See Fredson Bowers, "Hamlet as Minister and Scourge," *PMLA*, vol. 70 (1955), pp. 740-49.

139. Théodore de Bèze, *Right of Magistrates* in Franklin, *Constitutionalism and Resistance*, p. 106.

140. J. E. Neale, *Queen Elizabeth I: A. Biography*, Garden City, N.Y., 1957, p. 288.

141. Jászi and Lewis, *Against the Tyrant*, p. 54.

142. Skinner, *Foundations*, vol. 2, pp. 339-43; Allen, *Political Thought in the Sixteenth Century*, p. 338; Jászi and Lewis, *Against the Tyrant*, p. 53; and Harold J. Laski, *A Defense of Liberty Against Tyrants*, New York, 1972, p. 5.

143. John Calvin, *The Institution of the Christian Religion*, 4.20.31, trans. Thomas Norton, London, 1611. The Norton translation of the *Institutes* was first published in England in 1561, and had gone through ten editions by 1611.

144. Calvin's attitude and the developing response in Geneva has been most authoritatively analyzed by Robert M. Kingdon, *Geneva and the Coming of the Wars of Religion in France: 1555-63*, Geneva, 1956; with regard to the effect of the Condé involvement, see p. 69. For Calvin's position, also see Nancy Lyman Roelker, *Queen of Navarre; Jeanne d'Albret 1528-72*, Cambridge, Mass., 1968, p. 428.

145. Michael Walzer, *The Revolution of the Saints: A Study in the Origins of Radical Politics*, Cambridge, Mass., 1965, p. 61. In addition, see Henri Naef, *La Conjuration d'Amboise et Geneva*, Geneva, 1922, especially pp. 462-63, 482, and 520, and also Marc-Edouard Chenevière, *La Pensée Politique de Calvin*, Geneva and Paris, 1937, pp. 340-47.

146. Clancy, *Papist Pamphleteers*, p. 104.

147. The important phrase "princes of the blood" referred to the blood relatives of the king who stood in the line of succession or, as the French had it, were "capables de la couronne"— see Ralph E. Giesey, "The Juristic Basis of Dynastic Right to the French Throne," *Transactions of the American Philosophical Society*, n.s. vol. 51, part 5, 1961, pp. 38-40.

148. Roland Mousnier, *The Assassination of Henry IV*, p. 135.

149. See Philippe Erlanger, *St. Bartholomew's Night*, trans. Patrick O'Brian, London, 1960; Henri Noguères, *The Massacre of St. Bartholomew*, trans. Claire E. Engel, New York, 1962; and N. M. Sutherland, *The Massacre of St. Bartholomew and the European Conflict 1559-72*, New York, 1973.

150. See J.H.M. Salmon, *Society in Crisis: France in the Sixteenth Century*, New York, 1975, esp. pp. 117-31.

151. Salmon, *French Religious Wars in English Political Thought*, p. 15.

152. *Ibid.*, pp. 16-17 and 181-85.

153. Donald R. Kelley, *François Hotman: A Revolutionary's Ordeal*, Princeton, 1973, p. 92.

154. Franklin, *Constitutionalism and Resistance*, pp. 22 and 29. See also François Hotman, *Francogallia*, and Donald R. Kelley, *op. cit.* For the argument that the "political Calvinism" of Hotman and his successors was directly contrary to Calvin's own position, see Chenevière, *La Pensée Politique de Calvin*. On the other hand, the last section of Calvin's *Institutes* offers strong

evidence that Calvin himself laid the groundwork for the future development of Calvinist resistance theory and practice, as has been noted above.

155. Franklin, *Constitutionalism and Resistance*, pp. 36f., and 111f. For the full French text, see Théodore de Bèze, *Du Droit des Magistrats*, ed. Robert M. Kingdon, Geneva, 1970.

156. Franklin, *Constitutionalism and Resistance*, p. 39; for a translation of the complete work, see *A Defense of Liberty Against Tyrants*, ed. Harold J. Laski, New York, 1972.

157. Skinner, *Foundations*, vol. 2, p. 317.

158. Skinner, *Foundations*, vol. 2, p. 322.

159. *Ibid.*, p. 335.

160. Giesey, "The Juristic Basis of Dynastic Right, pp. 30ff. In the same connection, see also Kelley, *François Hotman: A Revolutionary's Ordeal*, pp. 292-97 (especially 294) and 301.

161. J.H.M. Salmon, *Society in Crisis*, p. 237.

162. For Hotman's arguments in 1585, see Kelley, *François Hotman: A Revolutionary's Ordeal*, p. 295. The confusions inherent in tracing shifts in Hotman's arguments through successive published editions of his works are noted by Giesey, "The Juristic Basis of Dynastic Right," pp. 31 and 36.

163. For the arguments and issues, see Giesey, "The Juristic Basis," pp. 32-42.

164. Kelley, *François Hotman: A Revolutionary's Ordeal*, p. 301.

165. *The Memoirs of Philippe de Mornay*, trans. Lucy Crump, London, n.d. [c. 1926], pp. 240f.

166. *Ibid.*, pp. 243f.

167. Conyers Read, *The Tudors: Personalities and Practical Politics in Sixteenth Century England*, New York, 1936, p. 184.

168. *Dictionary of National Biography*, ed. Leslie Stephen, London, 1886, s.v. "Bilson," vol. 5, p. 44.

169. Anthony à Wood, *Athenae Oxoniensis*, ed. Philip Bliss, London, 1813-20, vol. 2, col. 170.

170. Thomas Bilson, *The True Difference between Christian Subjection and Unchristian Rebellion*, 1585, p. 521.

171. *Ibid.*, pp. 514f.

172. *Ibid.*, pp. 513 and 517.

173. *Ibid.*, pp. 517-18.

174. *Ibid.*, p. 513 These understandings as expressed by Bilson continued to influence opinion in England. In a 1682 edition of a work first published in 1649, Thomas Bayly wrote that "kings by election are always kings upon condition," and may be made "a *Jack-a-Lent* for apprentices to throw their cudgels at. . . . They are not actual kings, they do but act the part of a king: and I hold him that acts the part of a king an hour upon the stage to be as real a king for his time and territories as the best king by election, who is chosen but for his life. Herein consists the difference: as the one must act his part as the poets please, so the other must act his part as the people please; they must have their parts given them, they must act it accordingly; they must not so much as tread the stage awry; their subjects are both spectators and judges. . . ."— *The Royal Charter Granted unto Kings by God Himself: And Collected out of His Holy Word in both Testaments*, 1682, pp. 6f. In Chapter Six, Bayly considers the problem of deposing and murdering a king.

175. Franklin, *Constitutionalism and Resistance*, pp. 189f., 191f., and 193.

176. *Ibid.*, p. 195.

177. In Chapter V below, I shall analyze these examinations in terms of Christian and classical casuistry.

178. Quentin Skinner thus summarizes the Huguenot arguments in his *Foundations of Modern Political Thought*, vol. 2, p. 309.

*Chapter Three. The Court and the Prince*

1. T. S. Eliot, "Hamlet and His Problems," pp. 121-26. In the sixty years since its introduction, Eliot's "objective correlative" phrase has been much analyzed and much discussed, and it seems likely to have been more productive as a stimulant to critical discussion than as a precisely designed critical tool. For our purposes, however, the important thing is that Eliot found Hamlet's responses to be excessive and inadequately justified. It is thus possible to summarize under Eliot's rubric a broad array of interpretations which should be corrected in view of Elizabethan responses—that is, unless we are content to mire ourselves down into a twentieth-century provincialism.

2. From the canon law of the Church of Rome (which had legal as well as sacramental jurisdiction over marriage prior to the Reformation), Old Testament prohibitions entered the English statute books in the twenty-fifth year of the reign of Henry VIII. The future history of such enactments is traced in James T. Hammick, *The Marriage Law of England: A Practical Treatise*, London, 1887, pp. 30-43, a useful treatise published twenty years before the final repeal in 1907 of the last prohibition of marriage between brothers- and sisters-in-law—see F. G. Emmison, *Elizabethan Life: Morals and the Church Courts Mainly from Essex Archidiaconal Records*, Chelmsford, Essex, 1973, p. 42.

3. The full implication of all the Levitical definitions of incest according to degrees of consanguinity and affinity may be found in the official Elizabethan table of 1563 by consulting Hammick, *Marriage Law*, pp. 35-37, whereas Lord Coke's later formulation (for our purposes identical) is given in Richard Burn's *Ecclesiastical Law*, ed. Simon Fraser, 7th ed., London, 1809, vol. 2, pp. 441-45, and discussed pp. 439-50.

4. For the authoritative treatment of these issues (including the whole business of Henry VIII), against their biblical, theological, and Tudor legal backgrounds, see Jason P. Rosenblatt, "Aspects of the Incest Problem in *Hamlet*," *Shakespeare Quarterly*, vol. 29 (1978), pp. 349-64.

5. The legal technicalities are thus clarified by Sir Lewis Dibdin: "Once formed under the guise of a ceremony of marriage, the most lawless and even disgusting connection (e.g., between brother and sister) needed a suit for its effective annulment. This was required not to *make* such a marriage void, for it was void *ab initio*, but in order that its invalidity might be *acted on* it was necessary that there should be a sentence *declaring* it void"—see Sir Lewis Dibdin and Sir Charles E. H. Chadwyck Healey, *English Church Law and Divorce*, London, 1912, p. 74. Reference to the relations between Claudius and Gertrude as adulterous—"that incestuous that adulterate . . ." [1.5.42]—does not necessarily imply that they had fornicated before their marriage, but merely indicates that no putative marriage could legitimatize incest: even if whitewashed by ceremony, it remained adultery.

6. Thomas Becon, *Prayers and Other Pieces*, p. 611.

7. Tyndale, *Expositions and Notes on Sundry Portions of the Holy Scriptures*, p. 329.

8. That observation was made by Lawrence Rosinger after citing the passage from the *Homilies*: "One wonders whether Shakespeare, perhaps subconsciously, used the Herod image partly because it relates to a king's action in marrying his brother's wife. For in marrying Gertrude after murdering his brother, Claudius did indeed out-herod Herod, who merely married the divorced wife of a half-brother. Moreover, like John, Hamlet risks death to rebuke a king and would be 'more than twice mad' to do so for a trifle." See his "Hamlet and the Homilies," *SQ*, vol. 26 (1975), p. 300.

9. J. Dover Wilson, *What Happens in Hamlet*, the quotations being from pp. 39 and 43, with the analysis running through p. 44. The reference to Rosenblatt occurs in n. 4, above. Roy W. Battenhouse, *Shakespearean Tragedy: Its Art and Its Christian Premises*, pp. 253-54 and elsewhere, appears unaware of the biblical, Catholic, and Protestant background for incest in Gertrude's marriage, which is remarkably strange in a book purporting to read Shakespearean tragedy in connection with its Christian premises. The only problem with incest which he treats as important in *Hamlet* he ascribes to the Prince—p. 231; and see below, n. 31.

10. Edmund Grindal, *Remains*, ed. William Nicholson, Cambridge, 1843, pp. 455-57, and John Bradford, *Writings: Sermons*, ed. Aubrey Townsend, Cambridge, 1848, p. 50, n. 3.

11. F. G. Emmison, *Elizabethan Life: Morals*, pp. 41-42. These are the only cases of such marriage Emmison reported in his survey of Elizabethan records in Essex. For an account of the enactment of public penance for incest in the diocese of St. Albans, see Robert Peters, *Oculus Episcopi: Administration in the Archidiaconry of St. Albans 1580 1625*, Manchester, 1963, p. 75.

12. *The Diary of Henry Machyn . . . from A.D. 1550 to A.D. 1563*, ed. John Gough Nichols, London: Camden Society no. 42, 1848, pp. 227 and 238.

13. Paul Hair, ed., *Before the Bawdy Court*, New York, 1972, pp. 80-81; no record is given of any different sentence upon the woman. No pertinent cases appear in E.R.C. Brinkworth's *Shakespeare and the Bawdy Court of Stratford*, London, 1972.

14. J. Charles Cox, *The Parish Registers of England*, London, 1910, p. 218.

15. To assume that Gertrude married Claudius "in the midst of grief and perplexity to save the royal House of Denmark" as John W. Draper writes (*The "Hamlet" of Shakespeare's Audience*, pp. 137 and 208) not only introduces a threat to Denmark which Shakespeare did not mention, but minimizes the repulsiveness of incestuous unions in Elizabethan eyes, even though Draper is aware of it (pp. 114-15).

16. For a brilliant psychological essay on Hamlet as displaying the shame of a child over a parent, see F. L. Lucas, *Literature and Psychology*, Ann Arbor, Michigan, 1957, pp. 45-58.

17. For English kings and queens between the death of Edward VI in 1553 and of James I in 1625, the extensiveness of ceremony and display at funerals was such as to require at least one month of frenzied preparation between the demise of the monarch and his or her burial. Thirty-three days were required for Edward VI in 1553; thirty days for Mary I in 1558; six months for Mary Queen of Scots in 1587, a disproportionately long time because of diplomatic and political complications; thirty-six days for Queen Elizabeth I in 1603; one month for the funeral of Prince Henry in 1612, under the pressure of the planned marriage of the Princess Royal and the Elector Palatine; two months and twelve days for Queen Anne in 1619, the delay in good part a result of contests for precedence at the funeral; and one month and ten days for James I in 1625. Peers of the realm required similar preparation—six weeks for the burial of Edward, Earl of Derby, in 1572, and four months for that of the third Earl of Huntington in 1595/96, whereas the burial of William Cecil, Lord Burleigh, Elizabeth's principal minister, required almost a month in 1598. Much the same situation was found on the Continent. In France, the word *quarantaine* referred to the forty-day period between the death and burial of a French king, as one sixteenth-century French chronicler wrote: "it is the custom to celebrate the funerals of our Kings only forty days after their death. This time is employed to make the preparations for the funeral pomp" (Ralph E. Giesey, *The Royal Funeral Ceremony in Renaissance France*, Geneva, 1960, p. 163). In the case of Henry Stewart, Lord Darnley, consort to Mary Queen of Scots, the burial at night by pioners, without proper ceremony, within a week of the assassination was one of the more scandalous incidents in that sequence of events which cost Mary her throne. For the time lapse see David Hay Fleming, *Mary Queen of Scots from her Birth to her Flight to England*, London, 1898, pp. 152 and 441, n. 34.

18. Giesey, *Royal Funeral Ceremony*, p. 6.

19. Myra Lee Rifkin, *Burial, Funeral and Mourning Customs in England: 1558-1662* (Bryn Mawr doctoral dissertation), Ann Arbor, Mich., 1977, p. 119, quoting from British Library Add. MS 6309, fol. 4v.

20. John Brand, *Observations on Popular Antiquities* (arr. and rev. by Henry Ellis), London, 1813, vol. 2, p. 188.

21. Phyllis Cunnington and Catherine Lucas, *Costume for Births, Marriages, and Deaths*, New York, 1972, p. 264 and *passim*.

22. Rifkin, *Burial*, p. 88.

23. *The Letters of John Chamberlain*, ed. Norman E. McClure, Philadelphia, 1939, vol. 2 (June 5, 1619), p. 242.

24. In one sense, of course, Hamlet's black was unseemly, because "when anyone is at a wedding in black it is bad luck for the bride and bridegroom"—Cunnington and Lucas, *Costume*, p. 148, quoting from *Folklore*, vol. 36 (1926), p. 253. This was probably a popular superstition, but I am not certain how fully it would have applied in *Hamlet*. After all, King James wore "a most sumptuous black suit" at the wedding of his daughter to the Prince Palatine in 1613. It would surely have pleased Hamlet to think that his black clothing would bring bad luck for the bride and groom, but in view of that royal wedding in 1613, I am less sure of this old critical saw than I once was.

25. Bertram S. Puckle, *Funeral Customs: Their Origins and Developments*, New York, 1926, p. 98.

26. For the practice of the Russell family (Earls of Bedford) at Woburn Abbey, see Gladys Scott Thomson, *Life in a Noble Household 1641-1700*, London, 1937, p. 326, and for more general reference, Percy Macquoid, "The Home . . . Funerals," *Shakespeare's England*, Oxford, 1950, vol. 2, pp. 148-52. Lady Dorothy Unton's bed was hung with black velvet for at least five months after the death of her husband—Roy Strong, *The Cult of Elizabeth: Elizabethan Portraiture and Pageantry*, London, 1977, p. 106.

27. Cunnington and Lucas, *Costume*, p. 264.

28. See the portrait of her by Gerrit Honthorst dated 1650 in possession of the Earls of Craven at Hamstead Marshall.

29. For specifically royal mourning in England, our closest approximation in time is to a portrait of Queen Anne in 1613, when she was still grieving for Prince Henry who had died in the previous year, although mourning for a child (even an elder son) was less rigorous than for a husband. With a black cap on her head, a black lace fan-shaped ruff, black veil, and black dress edged with black lace about her neckline, and even black jewelry, she is a picture of proper mourning for a queen (National Portrait Gallery, London). Some variations in color were allowed, but these were within understood limits. Purple could be worn as a mourning color by royalty, and an inventory of Queen Elizabeth's wardrobe in 1600 records a number of mourning garments in that color—Cunnington and Lucas, *Costume*, p. 147.

30. Richard Burn, *Ecclesiastical Law*, vol. 2, p. 451.

31. As has already been suggested in n. 9, above, a strange focus of attention is found in Roy Battenhouse, *Shakespearean Tragedy*, pp. 253-54: Battenhouse seems to be principally concerned to show that there was no Christian prohibition against second marriages—which is so obviously true as scarcely to require demonstration—but he gives little attention to incest and indecent haste, which are the fundamental problems. Whether this rather curious focus helps to explain Battenhouse's general denigration of the Prince, or vice versa, I do not know. Carroll Camden, *The Elizabethan Woman*, New York, 1952, p. 102, summarizes Elizabethan attitudes: "If the widow remarries, she should wait for at least a year of mourning," and quotes contem-

porary opinion that if she marries sooner she is "by the law also adjudged unworthy of matrimonial dignity."

32. Henry VIII's eldest sister, Queen Margaret of Scotland, was widowed when her husband King James IV was killed in the Battle of Flodden on September 9, 1513. Eleven months later she was privately married to Archibald Douglas, Earl of Angus, thus aborting concurrent negotiations for her marriage either to King Louis XII of France or to the Emperor Maximilian I. For this and other reasons that remarriage alienated large segments of the Scottish nobility, and yielded much internecine conflict in Scotland, while bringing little contentment between the wedded couple. It ended in divorce in 1527, and Margaret next married Henry Stewart, Lord Methuen, with the consequent stirring of other conflicts both domestic and national. Within ten years she attempted to obtain a divorce from Methuen, but without success. Throughout her lifetime, Scotland was kept in a continual broil through the vacillating alliances, marital and otherwise, of this least admirable and least stable of the Tudor rulers. It was apparent to all that when a widowed queen remarried in haste and without discretion, the violation of decorum was accompanied by the even more basic violation of the nation's tranquility and well-being—a lesson even more conspicious in the case of Queen Margaret's granddaugher Mary.

33. Sumptuous and even elegant costumes were available to the principal Elizabethan companies for their stage presentations, and considerable money was expended by the companies for such costumes, as ample evidence indicates throughout the professional lifetime of Shakespeare [E. K. Chambers, *The Elizabethan Stage*, vol. 1, pp. 371-72, and vol. 2, pp. 215, 228, 243, 248, 254, and 256]. Moralistic critics of stage plays objected to the spectacular attire worn by actors (*ibid.*, vol. 4, pp. 204, 217, and 304), whereas hack writers such as Greene commented on the richness of the costuming on stage, reflecting what was apparently a topic of London conversation (*ibid.*, pp. 237, 240-41). Sometimes these costumes were bought directly from mercers and tailors, sometimes from the sale of wardrobes belonging to deceased noblemen, and on some occasions were taken in from pawnbroking (*ibid.*, vol. 2, pp. 184-85, and vol. 4, p. 237). There is even some evidence that actors, accustomed to playing roles on stage in fine Elizabethan costumes, would wear these costumes in the streets as well (*ibid.*, vol. 1, p. 348), but how typical this was we can only surmise. Sir Henry Wotton, writing to his nephew Sir Edmund Bacon on July 2, 1613, about the production at the Globe of Shakespeare's *Henry VIII* reported that it "was set forth with many extraordinary circumstances of pomp and majesty, even to the matting of the stage, the Knights of the Order with their Georges and Garters, the Guards with their embroidered coats, and the like: sufficient in truth within a while to make greatness very familiar, if not ridiculous" (*ibid.*, vol. 2, p. 419). With only the simplest items of furniture placed on a bare stage, the Elizabethan theaters relied heavily upon the visual effects of costumes worn by the actors, and these costumes were broadly representative of contemporary English fashions.

34. Cunnington and Lucas, *Costume*, pp. 92-94 and 99.

35. Roy Strong, *The Cult of Elizabeth*, pp. 17-55, and especially pp. 17, 23, 39, 46, and 54. In a style typical of the visual idiom of the late sixteenth century in England, Worcester had himself cast in the role of successor to the disgraced and executed Earl of Essex, attending the triumphal figure of Elizabeth, and surrounded by his family and relations.

36. John Chamberlain, *Letters*, Nov. 19, 1612, vol. 1, p. 391.

37. *Ibid.*

38. John Nichols, *The Progresses, Processions and Magnificent Festivities of King James I*, 4 vols., London, 1928, vol. 2, pp. 493-526, 541-49, esp. 512f.

39. *Ibid.*, and vol. 2, p. 513.

40. John Leland, *De Rebus Britannicis Collectanea*, London, 1774, vol. 5, pp. 331-35, and Chamberlain, *Letters*, February 18, 1613, vol. 1, pp. 423-24.

41. Chamberlain, *Letters*, February 18, and 23, 1613, vol. 1, pp. 424-29.

42. In Princess Elizabeth's "cloth of silver" wedding dress, we see an illustration of Roy Strong's point that "no Elizabethan bride would dress in black on her wedding day"—see *The Cult of Elizabeth*, p. 104. In Scotland, however, when Mary Queen of Scots wed Lord Darnley in 1565, she wore for the last time the great mourning gown (but this was the white widow's dress of France, and not black) which marked her distinction as Dowager Queen of France, but between the ceremony itself and the wedding dinner she changed into more festive attire suitable for the dancing, feasting, and general rejoicing of a court in celebration. See Fraser, *Mary Queen of Scots*, pp. 230-31.

43. See G. I. Duthie, *The "Bad" Quarto of Hamlet: A Critical Study*, Cambridge, 1941, passim.

44. *New Variorum Hamlet*, ed. Horace Howard Furness, New York, 1963, reprinting the 1877 edition, vol. 2, p. 126. For interesting comments by a modern scholar on the appearance of Osric, see Maurice Charney, *Style in Hamlet*, Princeton, 1969, p. 191.

45. A broad range of examples may be cited. In or about 1520, Sebastiano del Piombo painted an unnamed *Humanist*, whose scholarly bent is in part suggested by his dark clothing, and a dozen years later Hans Holbein the Younger painted the serious-minded German merchant Derich Born, who at the time was making his fortune in international commerce at the Steelyard in London; in the middle years of the century, Christof Amberger portrayed the great banker Hans Jacob Fugger in similar dress (National Gallery of Art, Washington; Royal Collection, London; Los Angeles County Museum). Color symbolism of this kind was equally employed by royal and noble figures, as when King Philip II of Spain indicated his seriousness of mind and purpose by wearing black armor (National Portrait Gallery, London, and many replicas elsewhere). Even famous warriors who aspired to be recognized as men of serious mind would have themselves portrayed in black, as we see both in the portrait of Sir Francis Drake and in a superb Hilliard miniature portrait of Robert Dudley, the Earl of Leicester (National Maritime Museum, Greenwich, and National Portrait Gallery, London). Sir Henry Unton is a similar case in point. A courageous soldier who was knighted for prowess at the Battle of Zutphen, he was also a diplomat so distinguished as to be held in particular esteem and affection by King Henry IV of France, to whom he was sent by Elizabeth. In addition, he was a notable student and a patron of learning (National Portrait Gallery and see the essay on Unton in Roy Strong's *The Cult of Elizabeth*, pp. 84-110). It is not surprising, given the tradition I have traced, that when the famous Unton panel was painted as a visual history of his life, Sir Henry was presented throughout as dressed in solemn black. Nor is it surprising that those elder statesmen whose devotion to the civil service of Queen Elizabeth made her reign so notable also affected such "serious" clothing, as we can often observe in portraits of William Cecil, Lord Burleigh, and of Sir Francis Walsingham.

46. Bertram S. Puckle, *Funeral Customs*, p. 87.

47. Whereas King Philip II served as chief mourner for his father Charles V in 1559, at the funeral of King Francis I of France a dozen years before, his son and successor Henry II never appeared in the public ceremonies of the procession. This apparently represented a rather late development in France, which subverted the ancient tradition of the son and successor following the father to his final resting-place. By the sixteenth century that innovation was firmly established in France, and as Jacques de La Guesle, *Avocat du roi*, said in 1594, "it is not fitting to their [kings'] sacred persons to associate themselves with things funereal" (Giesey, *Royal Funeral Ceremony*, p. 7). Although English royal practice in the sixteenth century would appear to have accorded with the French custom, this may have resulted from the very peculiar circumstances in England at the time rather than from conscious ceremonial choice. At the burial of Henry VIII in 1547, the young King Edward VI was still but a child, too young and perhaps too sickly

to have accompanied the elaborate cortege. For religious and other reasons, it would have been inappropriate for Mary to walk in procession after her brother Edward, or for Elizabeth to do so at Mary's funeral. The next royal English funeral did not occur until 1603; because Elizabeth had no child, and James had not yet arrived in London, there was no successor available to follow her bier. Under the Stuarts, the heir followed his predecessor, first in the funeral of 1612 when Prince Charles was chief mourner for his elder brother Henry, and again when he served as chief mourner for his father James I in 1625. We are thus left with the circumstances in which there had been no apposite royal funerals in England for almost half a century prior to 1600, and such models as we have must be taken from the great state funerals of prominent members of the nobility and gentry. Here the evidence is unmistakable that the son and/or heir followed his predecessor, as Henry, Earl of Darby, followed his deceased father in 1572, and as Sir Robert Sidney followed his elder brother Sir Philip in the cortege of 1587. In the elaborate funeral of 1624 for Ludowick, the Duke of Richmond and Lennox, his next younger brother and successor was also chief mourner. As for *Hamlet*, since Shakespeare does not tell us whether Claudius or the Prince served as chief mourner, it is patently unnecessary for us to know. In either case, as we shall see, Hamlet as a principal mourner would have worn at the funeral the inky cloak in which we first see him.

48. As I have been unable to obtain access to the original, I rely upon the reproduction printed in Richard Davey, *A History of Mourning*, London, n.d., fig. 41 on p. 60. The procession shows Philip preceded by the Herald of the Order of the Golden Fleece, and accompanied to the left and right by the Duke of Brunswick and the Duke of Arcos. The long train of Philip's inky cloak is borne by the Count of Milito, and Duke Emmanuel Philibert of Savoy brings up the rear.

49. Illustration from T. Lant, *Funeral Procession of Sir Philip Sidney*, London, 1587, p. 17, courtesy the Folger Shakespeare Library. Because Sir Philip died without a son, the family succession reverted to Sir Robert.

50. The picture of Worcester is taken from a late eighteenth-century reproductive printing of William Camden's *Funeral Procession of Queen Elizabeth*, published at London in 1791, which appears as figure 24 in the third volume of Henry E. Huntington role 122394.

51. Title page of George Wither, *Prince Henry's Obsequies*, London, 1612, courtesy of the Folger Shakespeare Library.

52. John Milton, "Il Penseroso," line 16. Here we may question Harley Granville-Barker's assurance that at Hamlet's reappearance before the court over the bier of Ophelia "they will hardly know him in his rough 'sea-gown' and travelling gear"—*Preface to Hamlet*, New York, 1957, p. 149. By that point in act five, however, the audience has heard nothing about the sea-gown which Hamlet only later tells Horatio that he had "scarfed about me in the dark" when he groped to find the grand commission given to Rosencrantz and Guildenstern, and we may well doubt that he either wore that sea-gown or carried it along with him when he leapt impetuously aboard the pirate vessel during the encounter. But the question is not subject to conclusive answer.

53. Fraser, *Mary Queen of Scots*, p. 230.

54. Fraser, *Mary Queen of Scots*, pp. 227f., 230, 241, and *Ham.* 1.2.143-45.

55. George Buchanan, quoted by Lilian Winstanley, *Hamlet and the Scottish Succession*, pp. 51-53. There had been another interesting rumor about Mary's first husband, King Francis II of France, that a barber attempted to kill him by pouring poison in his ear. Winstanley appears to assume that Mary was thought to have been involved in that rumored attempt, but she does not document this point and I have been able to find no contemporary charge that Mary was involved. Fraser, *Mary Queen of Scots*, p. 105, reports that the ear infection from which Francis

died in 1560 was related to ear troubles from which he had suffered since childhood, and which caused unsightly splotches on his skin, like eczema. Winstanley makes much of the relation between the assassination of the elder Hamlet and these reports about Francis.

56. Gordon Donaldson, *Mary Queen of Scots*, London, 1974, p. 112.

57. Fleming, *Mary Queen of Scots*, pp. 152 and 441-42.

58. George Buchanan, *Detection of the Doings of Mary Queen of Scots Touching the Murder of her Husband*, St. Andrews, 1572, Elv. I have modernized Buchanan's broad Scots dialect.

59. Fleming, *Mary Queen of Scots*, p. 152.

60. For comparison with the proper ceremonies of courtly mourning, see the account of the "lugubrious form" observed after the death of King Francis I, earlier in this chapter.

61. The ancient custom of spending forty days in darkened rooms is probably an instance of the French influence ("the Auld Alliance") in Scotland. The English customs called for only thirty days closeted "in blacks," as when Queen Anne remained for a month in such an apartment after the death of Prince Henry—see Rifkin, *Burial*, p. 88. For the development of these divergent traditions of *tricenarium* and *quadragesima*, see Giesey, pp. 159-64.

62. John Knox, *History of the Reformation in Scotland*, ed. William Croft Dickinson, London and Edinburgh, 1950, vol. 2, pp. 202-03. For a more favorable twentieth-century interpretation of Mary's conduct, see Fraser, *Mary Queen of Scots*, pp. 306 and 311.

63. The reference in *A Midsummer Night's Dream* to a mermaid on a dolphin's back and to singing such that "certain stars shot madly from their spheres" (2.1.149-54) was interpreted by many major critics of the eighteenth and nineteenth centuries as a reference to Mary Queen of Scots, according to Horace Howard Furness, *A New Variorum Edition of "Midsummer Night's Dream,"* pp. 75-91.

64. Robert Keith, *History of the Affairs*, vol. 2, pp. 583-84n.

65. Ian B. Cowan, *Enigma of Mary Stuart*, New York, 1971, p. 144, reprinting *Froude's History of England*.

66. See J. E. Neale, *Elizabeth I and her Parliaments 1559-81*, New York, 1953, pp. 247-90, 303-12.

67. Fleming, *Mary Queen of Scots*, pp. 151f.

68. *Ibid.*, p. 440, n. 29.

69. Peter Hume Brown, *George Buchanan*, Edinburgh, 1890, pp. 205-06 and note.

70. Fleming, *Mary Queen of Scots*, p. 440, n. 27.

71. Fraser, *Mary Queen of Scots*, p. 76.

72. Plowden, *Danger to Elizabeth*, p. 78.

73. George Buchanan, *The Tyrannous Reign of Mary Stuart: George Buchanan's Account*, trans. and ed. W. A. Gatherer, Edinburgh, 1958, p. 131 and, of course, *passim*.

74. James Anderson, *Collections Relating to Mary Queen of Scots*, Edinburgh, 1727-8, vol. 2, pp. 280-81; John Knox, *The Reformation in Scotland*, vol. 2, pp. 203 and 206-07; Fleming, pp. 162 and 454, n. 78.

75. Fleming, *Mary Queen of Scots*, p. 459. See also other judgments to the same effect in Cowan, *The Enigma of Mary Stuart*, pp. 130 and 153.

76. Gordon Donaldson, *Scotland: James V to James VII*, New York, 1966, p. 129. See also William Croft Dickinson, *Scotland from the Earliest Times to 1603*, ed. A.A.M. Duncan, Oxford, 1977, p. 358.

77. Cowan, *The Enigma of Mary Stuart*, p. 145.

78. Fraser, *Mary Queen of Scots*, pp. 331-32.

79. Donaldson, *Mary Queen of Scots*, pp. 111-12.

80. *Satirical Poems of the Time of the Reformation*, ed. James Cranstoun, Edinburgh, 1891-93, vol. 1, p. 30. Here and elsewhere I have at points silently modernized the spelling in these ballads.

81. *Ibid.*, p. 45.

82. *Ibid.*, pp. 31-38, and 43. She had in earlier years been described as Helen in beauty, Lucrece in chastity, Pallas in wisdom, Ceres in riches, Juno in power—Fraser, *Mary Queen of Scots*, p. 68.

83. *Satirical Poems*, pp. 59, 64 and 89.

84. *Ibid.*, p. 42. The Oxford English Dictionary cites "burrio" (also "burio" and "bourreau" with other variants) as a common Scottish word for hangman, executioner, or torturer. To preserve the contemptuous alliteration with "bridegroom," I suggest paraphrase as "butcher."

85. *Ibid.*, p. 59.

86. Fraser, *Mary Queen of Scots*, pp. 311-25.

87. Bothwell first fled from the mainland to the outer islands, pursued by the Confederate Lords, whom he escaped by sailing to Scandinavia as leader of a group of pirates. For several years he appears to have prospered by one stratagem or another, but in June, 1573, he was imprisoned by the king of Denmark for crimes real and reputed. In solitary confinement at the castle of Dragsholm or Adelersborg in Denmark, he declined into insanity and died on April 4, 1578. Efforts to bring him back to justice in Scotland had all failed. A succinct but fascinating account of those critical early months of 1567 may be found in William McElwee, *The Wisest Fool in Christendom: The Reign of King James I and VI*, London, 1958, pp. 25-31.

88. Fraser, *Mary Queen of Scots*, pp. 331-32.

89. With only one brief interlude of escape and freedom thereafter, she spent the rest of her life under guard of one kind or another, whether in Scotland or in England, until her execution at Fotheringay Castle on February 8, 1587—almost twenty years to the day after the murder of her "precedent lord" at Kirk o' Fields.

90. John Jewel, *Works*, ed. John Ayre, Cambridge, 1848, vol. 3, p. 174.

91. James E. Phillips, *Images of a Queen: Mary Stuart in Sixteenth-Century Literature*, Berkeley, California, 1964, pp. 43 and 44.

92. My approach is radically different from that of Lilian Winstanley who recounts and compares the stories of Mary Queen of Scots and of *Hamlet* (with a number of unfortunate scholarly solecisms) and flatly declares that "an Elizabethan audience would almost certainly have thought Denmark a real country, and they would have believed it to be contemporary Scotland"—*Hamlet and the Scottish Succession*, p. 7.

93. *Zurich Letters: 1558-79*, ed. H. Robinson, p. 193.


*Chapter Four. Choosing Sides*

1. For convenience, I follow what appears to be the usual presumption that Rosencrantz and Guildenstern as Hamlet's "schoolfellows" (3.4.203) are from Wittenberg, but that is not made explicit in the text.

2. We misread the tensions of the play if we assume that "Hamlet must become like Horatio," as we are invited to do by Irving Ribner, *Patterns in Shakespearian Tragedy*, New York, 1960, pp. 68-69.

3. For tyrannicide and the monarchomachs, see above Chapter Two, and especially n. 76.

4. For a fine analysis, see Camille Wells Slights, *The Casuistical Tradition in Shakespeare, Donne, Herbert, and Milton*, Princeton, 1981, p. 94 and pertinent earlier evidence on pp. 35 and 93.

5. Michael Long maintains that we can only understand the "complex and lucid unity" of the play "when we give Denmark, as well as its Prince, the same sustained attention as did its author. *Hamlet* without the Prince of Denmark would still be a very great play indeed." Long's analysis of the populace of Denmark is especially interesting: see *The Unnatural Scene: A Study in Shakespearean Tragedy*, London, 1976, pp. 123-45. See also the brief and telling analysis by L. C. Knights:

"The ethos of the place—so we are told, or directly shown—is made up of coarse pleasures—

This heavy-headed revel east and west
Makes us traduced and tax'd of other nations;
They clepe us drunkards, and with swinish phrase
Soil our addition;

it is made up of moral obtuseness (Polonius), sycophancy (Rosencrantz and Guilden-stern), base and treacherous plotting (Laertes) and—since Shakespeare didn't introduce Osric at the climax of the tragedy for the sake of a little harmless fun—brainless triviality. This is the world that revolves round the middle-aged sensuality of Claudius and Gertrude." (L. C. Knights, *An Approach to "Hamlet,"* London, 1960, p. 42.)

6. He adds that it is Fortune who "sends" them to Denmark (2.2.224-39).

7. Another version by Luca della Robbia is to be seen in the Chapel of the Cardinal of Portugal at the Church of San Miniato in Florence. See also the example in the Tarocchi E series of cards published at Ferrara c. 1465 and illustrated in *Early Italian Engravings from the National Gallery of Art*, ed. Jill Levenson, Konrad Oberhuber, and Jacquelyn L. Sheehan, Washington, 1973, fig. 48 and pp. 130-31. As an indication of the overlapping ambiences of this *topos*, that series uses the same image for Theology, *ibid.*, fig. 43 and p. 123. The engraving by Master IB with the Bird verbalizes this conception of Prudence with a Latin inscription which translates as "I weigh the present and link the future with the past"—Heinrich Schwarz, "The Mirror in Art," *Art Quarterly*, vol. 15 (1952), p. 104 and fig. 7. That this icon of Prudence had a long life may be noted from its inclusion in the 1758-60 Hertel edition of Cesare Ripa, reprinted as *Baroque and Rococo Pictorial Imagery*, ed. Edward A. Maser, New York, 1971, p. 179.

8. Erasmus, *Christian Prince*, p. 188, and Whitney, *Choice of Emblems*, p. 108.

9. For other representations of Prudence, see John B. Knipping, *Iconography of the Counter-Reformation in the Netherlands*, Leiden, 1974, vol. 1, p. 27. The famous *Allegory of Prudence* at the National Gallery in London, ascribed variously to Cesare Vecelli and to Titian, expands the bifrontal to a trifrontal image; it is treated in Edgar Wind, *Pagan Mysteries in the Renaissance*, London, 1968, pp. 259-62; in Erwin Panofsky, *Meaning in the Visual Arts*, New York, 1955, pp. 146-68; and in connection with Hamlet in Nigel Alexander, *Poison, Play, and Duel*, pp. 104-05. A fine verbal treatment of past, present, and future concerns of "Prudence or Wisdom (for I will here take them both for one)" may be found in Thomas Wilson's *Elizabethan Art of Rhetoric*, ed. G. H. Mair, Oxford, 1909, pp. 31-32. George Wither's *A Collection of Emblems*, 1635, Book 3, illus. 4, p. 138, features another emblem of Janus, with comments appropriate to Hamlet. The motto above the picture of Janus informs us that "He, that concealed things will find,/ Must look before him and behind," which accords with Hamlet's tactics of "looking before and after." The long explanatory verse makes the point that only God can do this perfectly in his Providence (recall here Hamlet's reliance upon Providence in the final act), but goes on to say that "in a moral sense, we may apply/ This double face, that man to signify,/ Who (whatsoever he undertakes to do)/ Looks before him, and behind him, too." Such concerns were ready at hand for Shakespeare to evoke.

10. For another familiar opposition in Renaissance culture also pertinent to *Hamlet*, that

between Fortune and Providence, see Ivor Morris, *Shakespeare's God: The Role of Religion in the Tragedies*, London, 1972, pp. 427ff., and my *Shakespeare and Christian Doctrine*, Princeton, 1963, p. 233.

11. For the earlier history of Fortune, see Howard R. Patch, *The Goddess Fortuna in Mediaeval Literature*, Cambridge, Mass., 1927.

12. William Warner, *Pan his Syrinx or Pipe*, 1584, sig. B2. The literary tradition is briefly traced by Samuel C. Chew, *The Pilgrimage of Life*, Port Washington, N.Y., 1973, pp. 48-49.

13. Jean Cousin, *El Libro de la Fortuna*, facsimile volume, Buenos Aires, 1947, fig. 27, referred to in my text as the *Book of Fortune*.

14. *Ibid.*, fig. 25. We have here a fine example of a polysemous image and the ambiguity as to switches or straw should not be resolved because it allows two readings, each appropriate to the context, but in different ways. In Chapter V, the meanings associated with straw or hay will be developed.

15. Knipping, *Iconography*, vol. 1, p. 35n.

16. Seneca, important here as elsewhere, speaks of Fortune as though she assaulted a person with "many engines" and "every weapon," but was confident that philosophy protected the wise person with "an impregnable wall"—see *Ad Lucilium Epistulae Morales*, trans. Richard Gummere, London, 1920, Epistle 82, vol. 2, p. 243. S. E. Sprott, *The English Debate on Suicide from Donne to Hume*, La Salle, Ill., 1961, pp. 7 and 9, cites John Case's teaching at Oxford after 1585 (*nullis ictibus fulminibusque adversae fortunae*), but the suggestion is not entirely clear and lacks necessary documentation.

17. For a similar treatment dating about 1590, see Bartolomaeus Spranger's painting *Fortune* in the Dayton Art Institute, and the discussion in the Vassar College Art Gallery, *Dutch Mannerism: Apogee and Epilogue*, Poughkeepsie, New York, 1970, entry 87, and Plate 1.

18. *Ham.* 3.2.63 and Castiglione's *Book of the Courtier*, trans. Sir Thomas Hoby, New York, 1967, p. 31.

19. De Bry, *Emblematum Liber*, Frankfurt am Main, 1593, pp. 118-19.

20. *Ant.* 3.13.79-81; and 3.*HVI*, 4.3.45f.

21. See Phyllis Dearborn Massar, *Presenting Stefano della Bella, Seventeenth-century Printmaker*, New York, 1971, p. 16; and Mitelli in Bartsch Photographic Archives XIX 292.67-116, University of Pennsylvania Libraries.

22. Guillaume de la Perrière, *Morosophie*, Lyons, 1553, emblem 91.

23. For an argument (with which I disagree) that these passages ironically imply that Hamlet is a pipe for Fortune's finger, see John Holloway, *The Story of the Night: Studies in Shakespeare's Major Tragedies*, London, 1961, pp. 34-35.

24. Seneca, "Of Providence," in *Moral Essays*, 3 vols., trans. John W. Basore, London, New York, and Cambridge, Mass., 1928-51, vol. 1, pp. 39-41. See also Kenneth Muir, "Arthur Brooke and the Imagery of *Romeo and Juliet*," *N&Q* n.s. 3 (1956), pp. 241-43. In Cousin's *El Libro de la Fortuna*, fig. 63 illustrates *Fortuna Naufraga*, or Fortune causing shipwrecks.

25. See Frances A. Yates, "The Allegorical Portraits of Sir John Luttrell," in *Essays in the History of Art Presented to Rudolf Wittkower*, ed. Douglas Fraser, London, 1969, pp. 149-60, with reproductions grouped at end for essay XXI.

26. Cousin, *El Libro de la Fortuna*, fig. 67.

27. Otto Vaenius (Otho van Veen), *Amorum Emblematum*, Antwerp, 1608, pp. 156-57; see also Erwin Panofsky, *Studies in Iconology*, New York, 1962, p. 124, and Wind, *Pagan Mysteries*, pp. 104-05. The role of Fortune with blindfolded Love in these emblems illustrates part of a broad imagistic background which Hamlet extends when he demands of his mother, "What devil was 't/ That thus hath cozened you at hoodman-blind" (3.4.77-78), substituting a devil for the more conventional Fortuna.

28. Cousin, *El Libro de la Fortuna*, fig. 69.

29. More may be implied by Claudius' words. He has already had ample evidence of how time qualified the spark and fire of Gertrude's love for her former husband. He could possibly be reflecting here on how her once passionate love for him as her second husband may grow to a pleurisy and so die in its own "too-muchness." All would depend on how the roles were acted and particularly upon whether Gertrude has shown herself cooler to Claudius since her private interview with Hamlet. The first or bad quarto makes it explicit that Gertrude recognized Claudius as a villain after that interview: see *Var. Ham.*, vol. 2, p. 77, lines 1756-60.

30. Soji Iwasaki, *The Sword and the Word: Shakespeare's Tragic Sense of Time*, Tokyo, 1973, fig. 15, reproduces such a drawing by Bronzino.

31. See Raymond Chapman, "The Wheel of Fortune in Shakespeare's Historical Plays," *RES* n.s. vol. 1 (1950), pp. 1-7.

32. Georg Hirth, *Picture Book of the Graphic Arts: 1500-1800*, 6 vols., New York, 1972, vol. 1, fig. 356.

33. Hirth, vol. 1, fig. 354.

34. *Lucr.*, 952. In Samuel Chew, *Pilgrimage of Life*, figs. 52-68 provide a wealth of visual material for Fortune's wheel, with a variant in the wheel of Death in fig. 145; and see also his pp. 37-59. Numerous versions were extant in England into the eighteenth and nineteenth centuries.

35. Samuel C. Chew, *The Virtues Reconciled: An Iconographic Study*, Toronto, 1947, pp. 8-9.

36. Chew, *Pilgrimage of Life*, p. 53, citing the third satire.

37. The embroidery has been lost, but a description survives in a letter dated July 1, 1619, from Drummond of Hawthornden to Ben Jonson in *Ben Jonson*, ed. C. H. Herford and Percy Simpson, Oxford, 1925, vol. 1, p. 209, lines 57-59. See Strong and Julia Trevelyan Oman, *Mary Queen of Scots*, London, 1972, p. 68. The print of Fortune's Castle is from the Bartsch Photographic Archives, s.v. "Fortuna," Passavant VI 239.79, University of Pennsylvania Libraries. For the relation of this tower to the Tabula Cebetis tradition, see Knipping, *Iconography*, vol. 1, pp. 73-75. The basic Renaissance texts and some illustrations are provided in *Cebes' Tablet*, ed. Sandra Sider, New York, 1979.

38. There are other references to Fortune in *Hamlet*—eighteen in all—but of less central importance. See Frank McCombie, "*Hamlet* and the *Moriae Encomium*," *Shakespeare Survey*, vol. 27 (1974), p. 66. Two extensive studies are also in the works, one by Frederick Kiefer and another by Rolf Soellner, both of which should provide further light on the general subject of Fortune in the Renaissance.

39. Xenophon, *Apology* [or *Socrates' Defense*] 24, ed. O. J. Todd, London and Cambridge, Mass., 1948, p. 657.

40. Alexander Schmidt, *Shakespeare Lexicon*, revised and enlarged by Gregor Sarrazin, New York, 1971, vol. 2, p. 905 s.v. "proclaim," and p. 895 s.v. "presently."

41. Early seventeenth-century anecdotes supportive of Hamlet's view may be found in *Variorum Hamlet*, vol. 1, p. 198, and in Gerald Eades Bentley, *The Jacobean and Caroline Stage: Plays and Playwrights*, vol. 5, Oxford, 1956, pp. 1345ff. Alan C. Dessen provides an interesting discussion in *Elizabethan Drama and the Viewer's Eye*, Chapel Hill, N.C., 1977, pp. 5-7.

42. The historical event occurred in 1564, and was recounted by the Spanish Ambassador De Silva, as reprinted in E. K. Chambers, *Elizabethan Stage*, vol. 1, p. 128.

43. For background material in addition to that given here, see my *Shakespeare and Christian Doctrine*, pp. 173-77, 223-25, and 239-42.

44. Latimer, *Sermons*, p. 507.

45. A. C. Bradley, *Shakespearean Tragedy*, London, 1964, p. 171.

46. Thomas Sackville, "Induction," lines 219-31, to "The Complaint of Henry Duke of Buckingham," in *A Mirrour for Magistrates*, ed. Lily B. Campbell, Cambridge, 1938.

47. Henry Bullinger, *Decades*, vol. 4, p. 111.

48. Translated and quoted from Epistle LIX (cliii) by Robert Some, *A Godly Treatise against the Foul and Gross Sin of Oppression*, 1562, published entire in James Pilkington, *Works*, p. 471.

49. See Thomas Becon, *Early Works*, ed. John Ayre, Cambridge, 1843, p. 90: John Bradford, *Writings*, p. 50; Miles Coverdale, *Remains*, ed. George Pearson, Cambridge, 1846, p. 98; Hugh Latimer, *Sermons*, pp. 404f., 414, 452-54, and *Sermons and Remains*, ed. G. E. Corrie, Cambridge, 1845, pp. 13, 41 and 63; Pilkington, *Works*, pp. 468-70; and William Tyndale, *An Answer to Sir Thomas More's "Dialogue,"* p. 23.

50. Thomas Becon, *Prayers and Other Pieces*, p. 613.

51. Tyndale, *Expositions and Notes on Sundry Portions of the Holy Scriptures*, p. 80.

52. John Norden, *A Progress of Piety*, Cambridge, 1847, pp. 16-17.

53. Plutarch, "On Tranquility of Mind" 476, in *Moralia*, ed. W. C. Helmbold, London and Cambridge, Mass., 1962, vol. 6, pp. 235-37, with quotation from *Orestes*, 396. Here recall also the Ghost's words to Hamlet that he leave his mother to heaven "And to those thorns that in her bosom lodge/ To prick and sting her" (1.5.86-88).

54. Seneca, Epistle CV, *Ad Lucilium Epistolae Morales*, ed. Richard M. Gummere, vol. III, p. 217.

55. A reference similar to "the painting of a sorrow," but in a different context and with a different meaning, is found when Hieronimo asks the Painter whether he can paint "a tear, or a wound, a groan, or a sigh" and even "a doleful cry," but these qualities do not refer to well-known artifacts as do the words of Claudius (Thomas Kyd, *The Spanish Tragedy*, ed. Andrew S. Cairncross, Lincoln, Neb., 1967, pp. 138-39, being part of the fourth addition incorporated in Pavier's edition of 1602 [appearing in Regents Renaissance Drama Series as III.XII A.107-23]). In another play, and this time in a humorous vein, Balurdo asks a painter whether he can paint a belch, or make a picture sing, in Marston's *Antonio and Mellida, The Plays of John Marston*, ed. H. Harvey Wood, Edinburgh and London, 1934, vol. 1, pp. 52f. I am indebted to Hallett Smith for these citations.

56. For an historical analysis of this convention, see Eric Mercer, *English Art 1553-1625*, Oxford, 1962, pp. 217-52 and for illustrations figures 75b, 77a and b, 78, 81b, 83a, 84a and b, 86b. Further illustrations may be consulted in Margaret Dickens Whinney, *Sculpture in Britain: 1530-1830*, Harmondsworth, Middlesex, 1964, figures 2B, 3B, 8A, and 8B.

57. The major English breakthrough in the representation of credible grief came when Epiphanius Evesham returned home from his Continental apprenticeship sometime between 1614 and 1618: see Mercer, pp. 242f.; Whinney, p. 18 and figure 11b.

58. Laertes does not pick up the telltale clue here to Claudius' own artifice, perhaps because he is not over-bright, or perhaps because he takes the "living monument" as a veiled allusion to the coming death of Hamlet as a monument to his sister's memory. The former seems to me the more persuasive reading.

59. In analyzing Polonius' funeral, I rely upon the words of Claudius and of Laertes, but not upon those of Ophelia, because as the Gentleman says of her madness, she "speaks things in doubt/ That carry but half sense" (4.5.6-7). Shakespeare gives us no way to judge how much (if anything) of what she says of her father's burial is to be taken literally. It is nonetheless interesting that he has her refer to her father's burial in connection with "a grass-green turf," and to their laying him in "th' cold ground," both implying a burial in the churchyard rather than within the church itself, as would have been proper for so prominent an official (4.5.31-

32 and 69-73). When she re-enters the court after the arrival of her brother, the first line she sings is "they bore him barefaced on the bier," and I think we can assume that this line would have elicited a strong reaction of shock from the stage Laertes, for it indicates or at least suggests that Polonius was not even buried in a coffin (4.5.163). Immediately Laertes comments, as though in reponse, "hadst thou thy wits, and didst persuade revenge,/ It could not move thus" (4.5.168-69). But we know enough about Polonius' funeral without relying upon Ophelia's confused comments.

60. Sir Philip Sidney's funeral in 1587 required four months of preparation; the third Earl of Huntington's in 1595/96 also required four months; that for William Cecil, Lord Burleigh, in 1598 required almost four weeks; and that for Ludowick Stewart, Duke of Richmond and Lennox, took two months in 1624. (See Chapter Three, especially n. 17). These times are cited here not because of their direct bearing upon the Polonius funeral (for which Shakespeare has no need to cite the time of preparation), but because of what they show of the elaborateness expected. For heraldic funerals, see Rifkin, *Burial*, pp. 104-28.

61. For the complete record and Elizabethan account, see John Nichols, *Illustrations of the Manners and Expenses of Ancient Times*, London, 1797, pp. 65-71. A brief summary is found in Cunnington and Lucas, *Costume*, p. 219, with a table organizing the funeral cavalcade on p. 284. As for funerals generally, Henry Machyn's business as a merchant tailor made him a supplier for many funerals, so *The Diary of Henry Machyn . . . 1550-1563*, London, 1848, supplies many useful insights. These are summarized by the editor, John Gough Nichols, along with supporting references, in his prefatory "Note upon Funerals," pp. xxi-xxxii.

62. Cunnington and Lucas, *Costume*, p. 129, indicate how "hatchment" later developed from that inclusive reference to the more modern usage meaning "a painting of the arms of the deceased on a black background, hung up over his doorway."

63. Explained, that is, by contemporary Elizabethan accounts.

64. *The Funeral Procession of Sir Christopher Hatton*, 1591, preserved as Folger manuscript 2.Z.3 provides another example, full of fine sketches; the British Library has several manuscripts with similar drawings of funeral processions: MS Add. 35324 includes the funerals of Anne of Cleves, of Lady Lumley, and of Queen Elizabeth I, whereas MS Add. 2408 has further details of the latter. I have not investigated the manuscript holdings of the Herald's Office.

65. A. L. Rowse, *The Elizabethan Renaissance: The Life of the Society*, London, 1971, p. 75. How many mourners were involved in the funeral of Queen Elizabeth, I do not know, but eight or nine thousand participated in the splendid ceremony for King James I, as noted in Nichols, *Progresses of King James I*, vol. 4, pp. 1040n and 1049. *The Fugger Newsletter* of July 20, 1596, reports the magnificent funeral procession at Innsbruck for Ferdinand, Archduke of Austria and Tyrol, which lasted for five hours, and which gives a vivid impression of such a funeral shortly before the first appearance of *Hamlet*—see George T. Matthews, ed., *News and Rumor in Renaissance Europe: The Fugger Newsletters*, New York, 1959, pp. 218-20.

66. Richard Hooker, *Ecclesiastical Polity*, Keble ed., 5.75.2-3.

67. Further evidence of the importance attached to such forms is shown by the intervention of Lord Burleigh, Elizabeth's principal minister, who saw to it that the hearse of a mere knight was altered to show the correct hierarchal design: Rifkin, *Burial*, pp. 128-29.

68. Nichols, *The Progresses of James I*, vol. 3, p. 100.

69. *Shakespeare's Plutarch*, ed. Walter W. Skeat, London, 1875, p. 121. Antony's oration of course creates an even greater crisis than might have ensued upon such a hugger-mugger burial.

70. George Buchanan, *Detection of the doings of Mary Queen of Scots*, sig. Elv., and John Knox, *The Reformation in Scotland*, vol. 2, p. 202.

71. Eramus, *Christian Prince*, p. 161.

72. See Appendix C on Ophelia's Funeral, and also the treatment in Chapter Six of the encounter between Laertes and Hamlet at the funeral.

73. The repeated distortion of funeral observances in Denmark under Claudius is one of the obvious corruptions of his reign. John Holloway, *The Story of the Night*, p. 32, puts the burials performed under Claudius in proper perspective: "that most rigorous and solemn of duties in an early society, the fitting burial of the dead, begins to be no longer performed."

74. Roy W. Battenhouse appears baffled by Hamlet's tactics in Gertrude's chamber, and unaccountably overlooks both the Mosaic law and immemorial custom (Catholic and Protestant) concerning such a marriage: see my treatment above, Chapter Two, notes 9 and 31.

75. Fredson Bowers correctly points out that, in Hamlet's view, his mother's "fate depends wholly (so far as he can see) upon his forcing her to a recognition of her sin," and that her fate is "at least as important as his revenge on Claudius"—"Hamlet's Fifth Soliloquy, 3.2.406-17," *Essays on Shakespeare and Elizabethan Drama*, ed. Richard Hosley, Columbia, Missouri, 1962, p. 221. A. C. Bradley judges that Hamlet's "whole heart" is never so engaged by revenge as "in his horror at his mother's fall and in his longing to raise her"—*Shakespearean Tragedy*, p. 138.

76. Shaw, "Preface" to *The Dark Lady of the Sonnets*, in *Bernard Shaw: Selected Plays*, New York, 1948, vol. 3, p. 843.

77. For the similar pertinence of several such meanings to Richard II holding the mirror, see Chew, *The Virtues Reconciled*, pp. 14-15.

78. Paraphrase by Sister Rita Mary Bradley, "Backgrounds of the Title *Speculum* in Medieval Literature," *Speculum*, vol. 29 (1954), p. 113.

79. Heinrich Schwarz, "The Mirror in Art," pp. 98f.

80. Guillaume de la Perrière, *Le Théâtre des Bons Engins . . . Cent Emblèmes Moraulx*, 1539, facs. ed., Gainesville, Florida, 1964, emblem 37, pp. 84-85.

81. *The Theater of Fine Devises*, trans. Thomas Combe, emblem 37.

82. George Wither, *A Collection of Emblems, Ancient and Modern*, 1635, Book IV, illus. 41, p. 249.

83. On the other hand, the mirror of society's judgment of a person is specifically cited by Cassius in his persuasion of Brutus in *Caes.* 1.2.51-70. An extensive use of the mirror for self-examination occurs in *RII* 4.1.264ff., for which see Peter Ure, "The Looking-Glass of *Richard II*," *PQ*, vol. 34 (1955), pp. 219-24.

84. The mirror was also importantly associated with confession in visual representations: see John B. Knipping, *Iconography*, vol. 1, pp. 39, 86, and 97. For the Protestant use, see Calvin, *Institution*, 2.7.7.

85. Thomas Trevelyon, *Pictorial Commonplace Book*, 1608, Folger Shakespeare Library, Ms. V.b. 232, p. 156v.

86. For Harding, see the long extract quoted in John Jewel, *Works*, ed. John Ayre, Cambridge, 1845-50, vol. 3, p. 355, and Jewel's citations from Lombard and Gregory on p. 357.

87. *Liturgies and Occasional Forms of Prayer set forth in the Reign of Queen Elizabeth*, ed. William Keatinge Clay, Cambridge, 1847, p. 251.

88. Post-Tridentine Catholicism introduced "the Borromean and 'Jansenist' method of deferring absolution until repentance had been proved by a period of amendment" which might provide a Roman parallel to Hamlet's postponement of reassuring his mother until she has shown a new life, but of course the parallel is inexact because "absolution" could scarcely be used in Protestantism as in that Catholic sense; for the latter see John Bossy, *The English Catholic Community: 1570-1850*, London, 1975, p. 270.

89. Bishop John Jewel, *Works*, vol. 2, 1847, p. 1133.

90. For Luther's views on this subject, see *What Luther Says: An Anthology*, ed. Ewald M. Plass, 3 vols., St. Louis, Missouri, 1956, items 974 (vol. 1), 2591-92 (vol. 2), and 4264 (vol. 3).

John E. Hankins' analysis of Hamlet's effort to bring his mother to repentance is useful so far as it goes, but it is founded upon too narrow a base of evidence: the only theologians consistently quoted are Aquinas and Hooker. Further, Hankins assumes a nineteenth- or twentieth-century High Church Anglicanism anachronistic in Elizabethan England: "Hamlet performs the duty of a priest, according to the Anglican conception, by seeking to help a sinful soul turn to God" (*The Character of Hamlet*, p. 207, and pp. 193-221 *passim*; see also footnote 113 below).

91. Thomas Cranmer, *Miscellaneous Writings*, p. 117. William Perkins, himself inclined toward Puritanism, strongly recommended that people in their own confession to God seek the help of experienced and discreet Christian advisors; see *The Whole Treatise of Cases of Conscience*, Cambridge, 1608, Bk. 1, cap. 1, sect. 1.

92. William Fulke, *A Defense of the Sincere and True Translations of the Holy Scriptures into the English Tongue*, ed. Charles H. Hartshorne, Cambridge, 1843, pp. 458-59.

93. In addition to earlier citations, see Thomas Becon, *Early Works*, p. 145; Latimer, *Sermons and Remains*, p. 9; Tyndale, *Expositions and Notes*, p. 62.

94. Tyndale, *Doctrinal Treatises*, p. 478, and *Expositions and Notes*, p. 47.

95. Bullinger, *Decades*, vol. 4, p. 75.

96. Sister Miriam Joseph interprets Hamlet's behavior toward Gertrude as violating the Ghost's admonition not to contrive against his mother ("*Hamlet*, a Christian Tragedy," *SP*, vol. 59 (1962), pp. 129, and 134f.), whereas Ruth Levitsky, in "Rightly to be Great," *Shakespeare Studies*, vol. 1 (1965), p. 166, n. 75, observes that "surely Hamlet is not here contriving against his mother: he is doing his best to save her. The Ghost goes on to say, 'leave her to heaven' and her conscience, but it seems pretty obvious that Gertrude's conscience needs stirring up." A. C. Bradley wrote of Hamlet's treatment of Gertrude that "no father-confessor could be more selflessly set upon his end of redeeming a fellow-creature from degradation, more stern or pitiless in denouncing the sin, or more eager to welcome the first token of repentance," *Shakespearean Tragedy*, p. 138.

97. Pilkington, *Works*, p. 49; see also Tyndale, *Doctrinal Treatises*, p. 452 for those who are beyond the "power to repent." Similarly, Hooker, Keble ed., *Eccl. Pol.* 1.12.2 refers to human proneness "to fawn upon ourselves, and to be ignorant as much as may be of our own deformities, without the feeling sense whereof we are most wretched."

98. See also Isa. 6:9f.; John 12:40; Acts 28:27; and 2 Cor. 4:4.

99. Hooper, *Early Writings*, pp. 87-88. A comparison is relevant here to the Elizabethan satirist who viewed his role as that of a surgeon "who burns, probes, cuts, and purges," according to Alvin B. Kernan, *The Cankered Muse*, New Haven, Connecticut, 1959, p. 93.

100. Nicholas Ridley, *Works*, ed. Henry Christmas, Cambridge, 1841, p. 67.

101. Tyndale, *Expositions and Notes*, pp. 45 and 62.

102. Tyndale, *Expositions and Notes*, p. 284.

103. Luther, Exp. Gal. 4.16 in *Werke*, Weimar, 1883, vol. 2, p. 546.

104. Bradford, *Writings*, p. 55.

105. Alexander Nowell, *A Catechism*, ed. G. E. Corrie, Cambridge, 1853, p. 141; Latimer, *Sermons and Remains*, p. 10; John Calvin, *Institution*, 2.7.7: see also Hooper, *Early Writings*, pp. 88-89, and *Homilies*, p. 63.

106. "Sermon for Easter Day, 1628," in *The Works of John Donne*, ed. H. Alford, London, 1839, vol. 1, p. 415. The reference is to the laver made from mirrors which Moses placed at the entrance to the Tabernacle.

107. Becon, *Early Works*, pp. 97f.

108. Becon, *Prayers and Other Pieces*, pp. 618f.; see also Bradford, *Writings*, pp. 51f.

109. Luther similarly declared that "forgiveness of sin demands that sin be both confessed

and renounced"—"Sermon on Luke 23:32-43," *Sermons on the Passion of Christ* (trans. E. Smid and J. T. Isensee), Rock Island, Ill., 1956, p. 182.

110. Bradford, *Writings*, vol. 1, p. 80. Ivor Morris, *Shakespeare's God*, pp. 393-95, places Hamlet's appeal to custom and habit in its Elizabethan context. Hamlet's concern to convert "that monster custom . . . , of habits devil" into an "angel" (3.4.162f.) reflects an approach to moral education through "habituation" which can be traced through Luther, Erasmus, Aquinas, and many others, back to Aristotle. Gerald Strauss, *Luther's House of Learning: Indoctrination of the Young in the German Reformation*, Baltimore, 1978, gives the Reformation background, and the same author's "Capturing Hearts and Minds in the German Reformation," *History Today*, vol. 31 (June, 1981), pp. 21-25 provides a brief but fascinating overview of the reliance upon habituation from classical Greece to sixteenth-century Europe.

111. We do not see Hamlet specifically claim that blessing from his mother after his return from captivity, but events then move with such breathtaking rapidity that his failure to claim it proves nothing one way or another about whether she is in a position to give it upon the conditions he had laid down. The first or bad quarto does give Gertrude a speech which unequivocally recognizes the treasonous villainy of Claudius—see *Var. Ham.*, vol. 2, p. 77, lines 1756-60. How Gertrude behaves toward Claudius is left more ambiguous in the received texts of the play, but it is clear that she recognizes her guilt as she never had before Hamlet's efforts to bring her to repentance (4.5.18-20).

112. Alexander Schmidt, *Shakespeare Lexicon*, vol. 2, p. 1399, *s.v.* "wretched."

113. Fredson Bowers maintains that Gertrude's "partly sacrificial death in Act V, and her warning to Hamlet of the cup, confirms her repentance in Act III" ("Hamlet's Fifth Soliloquy," p. 220). Ruth Levitsky agrees that Hamlet "is—so far as we can see—successful in his efforts to save his mother. He can now 'leave her to heaven'—as he departs for England." ("Rightly to be Great," p. 157). There are other critics who disagree, of course, as for example John Hankins who holds that Gertrude stopped short of the final step in repentance, and indeed that "by the canons of Christian theology" Gertrude would be "forever damned"—*The Character of Hamlet*, pp. 209 and 220. Two weaknesses appear in Hankins' argument: he has drawn his theological evidence almost entirely from three writers—Aquinas, Dante, and Hooker—an interesting group, but not sufficiently broad if one wishes to establish English religious attitudes in 1600. Futhermore, it is literarily dangerous to argue for the salvation or damnation of characters in plays just as though they were characters in real life and we were a panel of judicial angels, as I argue in my *Shakespeare and Christian Doctrine, passim*.

114. Hamlet's strategy of beginning with severe correction so as to engender sorrow which will lead to repentance and a clear life ensuing may be helpfully compared with a similar progression in Saint Paul's two epistles to the Corinthians. The first letter was devoted to "smiting" the Christian community at Corinth for various sins, including fornication. Arguing that the body is the temple of the Lord, Paul declares that "the body is not for fornication, but for the Lord, and the Lord for the body," and goes on to add that "he that commiteth fornication sinneth against his own body" (1 Cor. 6:13, 18). In his second letter, Paul looked back to the effects of the first, and wrote that "I perceive that the same epistle hath made you sorry, though it were but for a season. Now I rejoice, not that you were made sorry, but that ye sorrowed to repentance: for ye were made sorry after a godly manner, that ye might receive damage by us in nothing. For godly sorrow worketh repentance to salvation not to be repented of: but the sorrow of the world worketh death. For behold this selfsame thing, that ye sorrowed after a godly sort, what carefulness it wrought in you, yea, what clearing of yourselves, yea, what indignation, yea, what fear, yea, what vehement desire, yea, what zeal, yea, what revenge! In all things ye have approved yourselves to be clear in this matter." Paul's tactics apparently succeeded, and he was able to declare that "I rejoice therefore that I have confidence in you in

all things" (2 Cor. 7:8-16). Paul's attempt to correct the Christian community in Corinth is roughly approximated by Hamlet's attempt to correct Gertrude in the privacy of her chamber: that she may sorrow to repentance, "for godly sorrow worketh repentance to salvation."

*Chapter Five. The Deliberate Prince*

1. Those uncertainties apply not only to plot but also to the character of the protagonist. Michael Long finely expresses the "doubleness" of our reactions to the Prince: "If we follow through the development of Hamlet's traumatic reaction to Elsinore we shall see that at every point our attitude to him needs to be created out of doubleness. We recoil and are drawn back, we move close and are held away, while all the time the ambiguities remain alive. . . ." (*The Unnatural Scene*, p. 145). The ambiguities an Elizabethan audience would perceive are somewhat different from those which occur to twentieth-century readers, and so the "doubleness" will differ, but there is much to commend Long's view in both terms. As will become clear, however, I find that a resolution is achieved in the fifth act.

2. Helen Gardner makes the point with elegant precision: "In trying to set *Hamlet* back in its own age, I seem to have found in it an image of my own time. The Elizabethan Hamlet assumes the look of the Hamlet of the twentieth century"—*The Business of Criticism*, Oxford, 1959, p. 51.

3. The moral fable appears to have been introduced by Prodocus, a contemporary of Socrates and Plato, and is preserved in Xenophon's *Memorabilia* (2.1.21ff.), ed. E. C. Marchant, London and Cambridge, Mass., 1948, pp. 94-103. Francis Bond, *Wood Carving in English Churches: Stalls . . . and Chancel Chairs*, London and New York, 1910, p. 111, notes that the ninth-century ivory panels on the back of the chair of St. Peter in Rome show the labors of Hercules—a representative example of the Christian allegorizing of the Hercules story. The fullest study of this *topos* in the visual arts is Erwin Panofsky's *Hercules am Scheidewege*, Berlin and Leipzig, 1930, but see also A. Richard Turner, *Vision of Landscape in Renaissance Italy*, Princeton, 1966, pp. 32-33 and 112-16, and Henry V. S. and Margaret Ogden, *English Taste in Landscape in the Seventeenth Century*, Ann Arbor, Michigan, 1955, pp. 49-53. For the literary traditions, see Theodor E. Mommsen, "Petrarch and the Story of the Choice of Hercules," *JWCI*, vol. 16 (1953), pp. 178-92, and for broader treatments of Hercules, G. Karl Galinsky, *The Herakles Theme*, Oxford, 1972, and Eugene M. Waith, *The Herculean Hero in Marlowe, Chapman, Shakespeare and Dryden*, New York, 1962. When Hamlet contrasts himself with Hercules at 1.2.153, this whole tradition is somewhere in the ambience of his allusion.

4. John Doebler, *Shakespeare's Speaking Pictures: Studies in Iconic Imagery*, Albuquerque, N.M., 1974, p. 98 (and Plate 19) develops the parallel to the woodcut. For the same *topos* in the Low Countries, see John B. Knipping, *Iconography*, vol. 1, pp. 75-78 and Plates 69-71. Panofsky, *Hercules*, figs. 30-42, illustrates variants on the theme.

5. John Holloway observes that Hamlet's soliloquies, "are, after all, easily foremost in bringing the idea of his delay to notice. It is meaningless to see a delay, in a fiction, merely because something that requires doing is not done at once. The story is of its doing. Naturally it will be done at the end of the story, if it is what will end it"—*The Story of the Night*, p. 28. We cannot ignore the factor of delay, but we should keep it in proper context.

6. Maurice Charney, *Style in "Hamlet,"* Princeton, 1969, p. xvii.

7. Giovanni Botero, *The Reason of State*, trans. P. J. and D. P. Waley, New Haven, 1956, p. 57.

8. Philip Hughes, *The Reformation in England, III: "True Religion Now Established,"* London, 1954, p. 378.

9. Ophelia's admiring description of Hamlet recalls the particular kind of regard which virtually all Elizabethans had for Sir Philip Sidney, as for no other Englishman of the time. Others among Shakespeare's contemporaries aspired to emulate him and some were occasionally hailed by their own coteries as being similarly universal men, but all of England and much of Europe united in bestowing such an accolade upon Sidney. A hero at once of the Reformed Church and of the English state, a gallant soldier, a charming courtier, a wise counsellor, a distinguished man of learning, a fine poet, this brilliant young gentleman was the paragon of his age. It was not just valor, charm, and learning which made Sidney so admired, but the combination of these with a conscientious and considered rationality. Although he reached beyond others of his age, there was nothing of the Marlovian "overreacher" about him. Indeed, as one recent critic observes, he replaced "the ideal of the proud, self-centered hero with a ruler, burdened with the responsibilities of judgment" (Josephine A. Roberts, *Architectonic Knowledge in the "New Arcadia" (1590), Sidney's Use of the Heroic Journey*, Salzburg, Austria, 1978, p. 279). That emphasis on "the responsibilities of judgment" could be traced back to the Reformers' teachings about self-examination and also to the classical conception of conscience. Such were Sidney's roots, as well as Hamlet's. When Sidney wrote to the young Edward Denny about "what it is we desire to know," he concluded that "the knowledge of ourselves no doubt ought to be most precious unto us." (James M. Osborn, *Young Philip Sidney*, New Haven, 1972, p. 538). That tradition is at the farthest remove from the thoughtless impetuosity of Laertes and the superficial *machismo* of Fortinbras, and it is directly pertinent to what we find in Hamlet. This is not to suggest that Hamlet was modeled on Sidney, nor that Shakespeare created him to be or to represent Sidney—he is and he represents only himself, the fictional Prince of Denmark—but the example of Sidney helps us today to recognize something of what Ophelia's words would have suggested to Elizabethans. It is important in this connection to recall what Sidney meant to the Elizabethans, not what he means to certain moderns, as may be illustrated in T. S. Eliot's tongue-in-cheek reference to the heroic ideal in his line "Sir Philip Sidney/ . . . And other heroes of that kidney" from "A Cooking Egg," *Poems 1920*, in *Selected Poems*, New York, 1934, p. 38.

10. *The Mirror of Majesty or The Badges of Honor*, 1618, reprinted in facsimile by Holbein Society, 1870, emblems 13 and 30 on pp. 27 and 59.

11. See Gascoigne's *The Glass of Government* (and other works), ed. John W. Cunliffe, Cambridge, 1910, where the motto appears under the engraved portrait of the frontispiece, and elsewhere on various title pages. I am indebted to William R. Ringler, Jr., for this citation.

12. Charles Fitz-Geffrey, *Sir Francis Drake*, 1596, sig. Flv.

13. Wither, *Emblems*, Book I, emblem 32, p. 32. Mars and Mercury also appear on the facade of the triumphal arch erected for the entry of the emperor Maximilian II into Vienna on March 16, 1563; the arch is pictured in *The German Single-Leaf Woodcut*, ed. Walter L. Strauss, New York, 1975, vol. 1; p. 443.

14. Ruth Levitsky interprets this foiling in other interesting classical terms: "If Horatio served to remind Hamlet of the Stoic way rightly to be great, Fortinbras exemplifies the Aristotelian way. . . . The two faculties which set man apart from the beasts—namely, Reason and a sense of honor—operate in opposition to each other, the former causing man to think too precisely on the event and let action go, the latter causing man to think too little and act rashly." See Levitsky, "Rightly to be Great," p. 157.

15. See Harry Levin, *The Question of Hamlet*, New York, 1959, p. 43.

16. Hamlet's emphasis upon reason was in keeping with the Christian epistemology of the sixteenth century as it helped to form the English Renaissance and Reformation. Even Luther (who surely did not regard human reason as an infallible guide) wrote that "God certainly did

not give us our reason and the advice and aid which it supplies in order to have us contemptuously disregard them"—"Exp. Gen. 32:6-8" in *What Luther Says: An Anthology*, ed. Ewald M. Plass, St. Louis, 1959, vol. 2, item 2437. For Hooker on the "discourse of natural Reason," see *Eccl. Pol.* 1.8.8. Similarly, where Hamlet characterized one who uses his time only "to sleep and feed" as "a beast, no more," Calvin wrote that men have life not only "so that they can eat and drink," but that they also have "understanding and reason" (quoted in Thomas Torrance, *Calvin's Doctrine of Man*, London, 1949, p. 69), and that when "alienated from right reason, man is almost like the cattle of the field" (p. 102, and see also *Institution*, 2.2.12). Reason, so understood, also ties in with conscience: William Perkins thus wrote that "brute beasts ... because they want true reason, they want conscience also" (*William Perkins, 1558-1602, English Puritanist: His Pioneer Works on Casuistry*, ed. Thomas F. Merrill, Niewkoop, The Netherlands, 1966, p. 6). These attitudes were basic and virtually universal in 1600, and I do not mention them to suggest particular sources for Hamlet's words, but only to fill in the spectrum of our understanding, because Reformation thought is so often misunderstood or ignored. Even so helpful an introductory study as Robert Hoopes' *Right Reason in the English Renaissance* (Cambridge, Mass., 1962) minimizes that background.

17. *The Book of Common Prayer with Notes Explanatory, Practical, and Historical*, ed. Richard Mant, Oxford, 1820, pp. 8-9.

18. *What Luther Says*, vol. 1, item 966.

19. Luther, Exposition on Seventh Commandment in the *Greater Catechism, Luther's Primary Works*, eds. Henry Wace and C. A. Buchheim, London, 1896, p. 72. Compare *Macb.* 4.2.43-57.

20. Quoted by Calvin, *Institutes*, 2.5.2, ed. John T. McNeill, trans. Ford Lewis Battles, Philadelphia, 1960.

21. Slights, *The Casuistical Tradition*, p. 99. Yet, as Slights observes p. 35, Protestants held that "full intellectual assent was a necessary prerequisite for virtuous action." Hamlet achieves such assent only after he has worked out his doubts through his interior debates.

22. Romans 2:14-15.

23. Clancy, *Papist Pamphleteers*, p. 144.

24. Michael G. Baylor, *Action and Person in Late Scholasticism and the Young Luther*, Leiden, 1977, pp. 261 and 267. Such a position as that taken by More and Luther developed out of basic attitudes toward conscience held by medieval scholasticism and by the somewhat disparate *devotio moderna*, according to Clancy, *Papist Pamphleteers*, p. 144.

25. Baylor, *Action and Person ... The Young Luther*, p. 261.

26. Slights' judicious study balances the widely held view that "Protestant casuists insisted that the individual is supreme" (because, as she knows, "supreme" can only apply to the truly supreme will of God) by the crucial qualifications that "they also held that authority is divinely sanctioned and that just law is morally obligatory"—*The Casuistical Tradition*, p. 65.

27. Xavier G. Colavechio, *Erroneous Conscience and Obligations*, Washington, 1961, pp. 35 and 37.

28. *William Perkins*, pp. 41-42, from *A Discourse of Conscience*, 1596. At a later point Perkins added that "the error of the judgment cannot take away the nature of that which is simply evil. Sin is sin, and so remaineth notwithstanding any contrary persuasion of the conscience"—p. 100. For Richard Baxter's similar view, see Slights, *Casuistical Tradition*, p. 65.

29. Arthur Golding's translation of Jacques Hurault's *Politic, Moral and Martial Discourses*, 1595, p. 75, contains a pertinent observation linking fear, prudence, and ethics: "honorable is that fear that restraineth a man from doing evil."

30. See above, n. 16.

31. *William Perkins*, pp. 5, 38, and 41.

32. *William Perkins*, p. 38. For the consensus on this issue by Protestant casuists, see Slights, *Casuistical Tradition*, p. 40.

33. For a helpful differentiation between natural melancholy and the melancholy of an afflicted conscience, see Ivor Morris, *Shakespeare's God*, pp. 408-11, followed by pp. 413-16 on self-judgment.

34. *William Perkins*, pp. 39-40.

35. Nor is it to deny the long-recognized influence of Montaigne, which may for our purposes be summarized by the words of Harry Levin, *The Question of Hamlet*, p. 72: "In introspection, his mentor is Montaigne; the soliloquies are like the *Essays* in balancing arguments with counter-arguments, in pursuing wayward ideas and unmasking stubborn illusions, in scholarly illustrations and homely afterthoughts which range from the soul of Nero to John-a-dreams."

36. See the analyses by W. D. Davies in *Interpreter's Dictionary of the Bible*, ed. George A. Buttrick, New York, 1962, vol. 1, s.v. "Conscience," pp. 674-76, and the twentieth-century John Knox's exegesis of Romans, *Interpreter's Bible*, ed. George A. Buttrick, New York, 1954, vol. 9, p. 411, although the latter was written just a little too early to take advantage of C. A. Pierce's broadening reappraisal, *Conscience in the New Testament* (Studies in Biblical Theology, No. 15), London, 1958, especially pp. 13-20.

37. Horace, Epistle I.60-61, in *Satires, Epistles and Ars Poetica*, ed. H. Rushton Fairclough, London and Cambridge, Mass., 1941, p. 255.

38. Seneca, *De Clementia*, in *Moral Essays*, ed. John W. Basore, vol. 1, p. 357.

39. Seneca, Epistle 28, *Ad Lucilium Epistolae Morales*, ed. Richard M. Gummere, vol. 1, p. 203.

40. *What Luther Says*, vol. 2, item 2086.

41. For Horace, see above, and n. 37; also *William Perkins*, p. 43. Slights also emphasizes that English casuists held "that full intellectual assent was a necessary prerequisite for virtuous action"—*The Casuistical Tradition*, p. 35. There are obviously major differences between the Roman Stoic and the Elizabethan theologian (the Stoic depending primarily upon himself, the Christian primarily upon divine grace), but for our present purposes, the similarities are of greater interest. The similarities between Stoic and Christian conceptions are also observed by Virgil Whitaker, *Shakespeare's Use of Learning*, p. 269. For Hamlet's unstoic qualities, see above and below, Chapter Six.

42. See above, Chapter Two, Part III.

43. Robert Cawdrey, *A Table Alphabetical of English Words*, 1604, p. 9. Opinions on the meaning of "old mole" are treated above, Chapter II, n. 45.

44. J. A. Cuddon, *A Dictionary of Literary Terms*, Garden City, New York, 1977, *s.v.* "morology," where the term is defined as "deliberate foolishness or nonsense for effect."

45. 1 Samuel 21:11-22:1.

46. See Chapter Three, Part III.

47. R. R., *Questions concerning Cony-hood and the Nature of the Cony*, 1595, sigs. A4. and B2. This little pamphlet was said by the translator (in a dedication dated June 4, 1595) to have recorded a university performance while he was studying at Wittenberg. I suggest no necessary significance for Hamlet of the geographical origin of this skit.

48. We may also be sure that both Shakespeare and Burbage would not have allowed Hamlet's defensive pose of madness to appear too convincing, because true madness also evoked laughter in this period.

49. Ophelia at 3.2.122 notes that the Mousetrap play, which Hamlet planned in this second act soliloquy, took place four months after the death of the elder Hamlet, which in turn was

two months before the Prince saw the Ghost, as we find at 1.2.138. The Mousetrap was performed the day after it was planned and that soliloquy spoken: see 2.2.521, 525, and 3.1.21.

50. Slights, *The Casuistical Tradition*, pp. 61 and 62.

51. For the critical advantage of seeing a broader turning radius rather than a single turning point, see my *Shakespeare: The Art of the Dramatist*, London and Boston, 1982, pp. 147f.

52. Fraunce, *The Lawyer's Logic*, 1588, p. 86v. The relevance of this work to *Hamlet* was called to my attention by Leon Howard's *The Logic of Hamlet's Soliloquies*, Lone Pine, Cal., 1964.

53. *A Discourse of Conscience* in *William Perkins*, p. 6.

54. S. E. Sprott, *The English Debate on Suicide*, pp. 9-10, citing *Theses quaedam*, Edinburgh, 1607; *Theses philosophicae*, Edinburgh, 1612 and 1615, without page reference; and the same title published at Aberdeen, 1630, with a reference to p. 10; and other references to the same question in Augustine, Piccolomini, Barlow, Capel, and Sym. See also the suggestion by Yngve B. Olsson, "In Search of Yorick's Skull: Notes on the Background of Hamlet," *Shakespeare Studies*, vol. 4 (1969), p. 212.

55. Girolamo Cardano's *Comfort* in the English translation published in 1573 and again in 1576, has perhaps most frequently been cited as a source for or at least parallel to this soliloquy: Burton Pollin, "Hamlet, A Successful Suicide," *Shakespeare Studies*, vol. 1 (1965), pp. 243 and 256, n. 12 lists citations ranging from Francis Douce in 1839, through Hardin Craig in 1934, to Lily B. Campbell in 1952. Whether Hamlet reads part of his soliloquy from *Comfort* or another book, looking up from his reading to add comments of his own, may be left as indeterminate as the soliloquy itself.

56. In my judgment, we have here another instance in which critics of *Hamlet* have often required a univocal meaning from a passage Shakespeare designed as constructively ambiguous: the soliloquy considers questions both of life and death and of action and passivity, but an extensive debate has focused upon which one is intended. In his survey of a large body of critical opinion, M. B. Allen in 1938 reported that most regarded the question of suicide as predominant ("Hamlet's 'To be or not to be' Soliloquy," *SAB*, vol. 13 (1938), pp. 195-207), whereas in 1965 Ruth Levitsky noted that "the currently popular interpretation . . . is 'to act or not to act' rather than 'to exist or not to exist,'" the latter being the one which she cogently advances ("Rightly to be Great," *Shakespeare Studies*, vol. 1, pp. 165-66 and 155). For the general background of despair, see the copiously documented article by Susan Snyder, "The Left Hand of God: Despair in Medieval and Renaissance Tradition," *Studies in the Renaissance*, vol. 12 (1965), pp. 18-59.

57. See Charlton T. Lewis and Charles Short, *A Latin Dictionary*, Oxford, 1975, pp. 101f.

58. John Donne, Satyre III, lines 77-84 in *The Poems of John Donne*, ed. Herbert J. C. Grierson, London, 1945, p. 139.

59. Mousnier, *The Assassination of Henry IV*, pp. 291-92. The halting English couplets are from Joseph Sylvester's 1600 translation of du Bartas. The French poem was dedicated to Marguerite of Navarre.

60. Similarly, a new pope, Gregory XIII, found that Mary had developed a new virtue, making possible a different attitude from the condemnatory judgments of his predecessor in 1567: see Fraser, *Mary Queen of Scots*, pp. 484-85.

61. Elizabeth was like Hamlet in expressing concern that his (and her) actions might "damn me" (2.2.589). In rejecting one urgent appeal (this one unrelated to the Scottish Queen) from Parliament, she replied: "For I know that this matter toucheth me much nearer than it doth you all, who, if the worst happen, can lose but your bodies; but if I take not that convenient care that it behooveth me to have therein, I hazard to lose both body and soul"—John E. Neale, *Elizabeth I and Her Parliaments 1559-81*, New York, 1953, p. 108.

62. William Camden, *Annals, or The History of the Most Renowned and Virtuous Princess Elizabeth, Late Queen of England*, 1635, pp. 326-28.

63. Camden, *Annals*, p. 338.

64. Camden, *Annals*, p. 340.

65. Of some ancillary interest are two book illustrations which feature Mors striking at a man as he kneels in prayer: see ornament to first paragraph of Bishop John Fisher, *Sermon [at] . . . St. Paul's*, 1509, sig. A2, and title page of T. Nelson, *Blessed State of England*, 1591. There were somewhat comparable scenes enacted in the late morality play, for which see Alan C. Dessen, *Elizabethan Drama and the Viewer's Eye*, p. 37f.

66. *William Perkins*, p. 73. Perkins later goes on to say that the evildoer's own self-destructive conscience plays the part of such a nemesis.

67. In sixteenth-century terms, he acts out the personification of Revenge who, in Anthony Copley's *A Fig for Fortune*, 1596, p. 18, declares " 'Tis heaven's attain to send thy foes to hell." Paul N. Siegel, *Shakespearean Tragedy and the Elizabethan Compromise*, New York, 1957, pp. 105-06 appositely cites Gentillet's horror over Machiavellian avengers who "seek in slaying the body to damn the soul." The conception that revenge is inadequate unless it exceeds the original wrong has been traced back to Seneca's "*Scelera non ulciseris, nisi vincis*" in *Thyestes*: see S. P. Zitner, "Hamlet, Duellist," pp. 2f., and Paul Gottschalk, "Hamlet and the Scanning of Revenge," pp. 165f. In twentieth-century terms, Hamlet has here fallen victim to "the occupational disease of avengers" and so has become "the deed's creature," if I may apply the fine phrases used by Kenneth Muir in his *Shakespeare's Tragic Sequence*, London, 1972, pp. 57 and 92. But Muir maintains, as I also will, that at the end we do not reject a favorable judgment of the Prince.

68. Hardin Craig has observed (what few scholars would dispute) that "to have killed the King while he was purging his soul would have defeated the recognized principles of justice"— "Hamlet as a Man of Action," *Huntington Library Quarterly*, vol. 27 (1964), p. 235. Kittredge declared that "this is the one moment when it is impossible for anyone but an assassin to strike"—Myrick, "Kittredge on Hamlet," p. 227, and Kittredge's introduction to his edition of *Hamlet*, p. xiv. Helen Gardner (*The Business of Criticism*, p. 46) observes that "this 'opportunity' is no opportunity at all; the enemy is within touching distance, but out of reach." It also seems pertinent to add, in reference to Aristotelian theory, that if Hamlet had killed Claudius at prayer (or anywhere else in the frame of mind the Prince shows here), he would have escalated himself beyond the kind of *hamartia* or error which Oedipus showed when he unknowingly killed his father and married his mother or which Hamlet himself showed when he killed Polonius by mistake, and would consequently have put himself in the company of hubristic protagonists like Creon in the *Antigone* of Sophocles or Clytemnestra in the *Oresteia* of Aeschylus. In classical Greek thought, *hubris* is a far more serious fault than *hamartia*. For an interesting analysis of the Old Testament parallel when David has similar opportunities to strike down a defenseless and unexpecting Saul (I Sam. 24:1-15 and 26:6-20), see Gene Edward Veith, Jr., " 'Wait upon the Lord': David, *Hamlet*, and the Problem of Revenge," pp. 71, 75-80.

69. Kenneth Muir argues that the reasons Hamlet gives for not killing his uncle at prayer are not to be accepted, and that we must read between the lines to discover "the real reason"— *Shakespeare: Hamlet*, Great Neck, N.Y., 1963, pp. 40 and 58-59. Contentions that Hamlet's statements over the praying Claudius are false have been traced back to Richardson in 1784 by A.J.A. Waldock, *Hamlet: A Study in Critical Method*, p. 5, and what Waldock says at another point (p. 98) is perhaps worth noting here: "A play is not a mine of secret motives. We persist in digging for them; what happens usually is that our spade goes through the other side of the drama." Herbert R. Coursen, Jr., maintains that Hamlet "believes what he says," *Christian Ritual and the World of Shakespeare's Tragedies*, Lewisburg, Pa., 1976, p. 129.

70. T. S. Eliot, *Murder in the Cathedral*, New York, 1935, p. 44.

71. Thomas Aquinas, *Sumna Theologica*, II-II, qu. 108, art. 1, vol. 2, p. 1656.

72. Calvin, *Institution*, 4.20.12.

73. *Christian Morals* III, Sect. 12, in *The Prose of Sir Thomas Browne*, ed. Norman Endicott, p. 409.

74. Tyndale, *Expositions and Notes*, p. 62.

75. *William Perkins*, p. 182.

76. Myles Coverdale, trans., *Enchiridion*, in *Writings and Translations*, ed. George Pearson, Cambridge, 1844, p. 527.

77. In his brilliant article "Hamlet and the Scanning of Revenge," Paul Gottschalk argues that in the prayer scene Hamlet "nearly lost his soul—not in the afterlife by espousing the wrong doctrine, but on the stage and before our eyes" (p. 170). Maurice Charney, *Style in "Hamlet,"* p. 240, observes that here Claudius has noticeably taken over the "passionate, reflective style" of Hamlet's soliloquies, whereas Hamlet adopts Claudius' "brusque and menacing style."

78. John Downame, *Spiritual Physicke*, 1600, p. 54.

79. The significance of killing Polonius has been so perceptively analyzed and is so widely recognized that no more need be said of it here, but see especially Fredson T. Bower's brilliant "Hamlet as Minister and Scourge," already cited; John E. Seaman, "The Blind Curtain and Hamlet's Guilt," *Western Humanities Review*, vol. 19 (1965), pp. 345-53, is also worth reading. For a recent treatment of Hamlet's attitude toward the slaying of Polonius, and a comparison of the Prince with Claudius on the subject of repentance, see Robert G. Hunter, *Shakespeare and the Mystery of God's Judgment*, Athens, Ga., 1976, pp. 118-19.

80. See also above, Chapter II.

81. For the cogent analyses of G. L. Kittredge, see Kenneth Myrick, "Kittredge on Hamlet," p. 234.

82. Terence Hawkes describes Hamlet as "a confessed contemplative forced unwillingly to cope with a 'man's' world of action for which circumstances make him temperamentally unsuited"—*Shakespeare and the Reason: A Study of the Tragedies and the Problem Plays*, London, 1964, p. 35.

83. That Hamlet in effect endorses Fortinbras as king has caused understandable modern apprehensions, but these can be overstressed. Shakespeare's tragic closure always requires an announced continuity of leadership. And Hamlet's choices are limited, within the world of the play. Indeed, even in the far more populous worlds of British and American democracies, where one would expect a great wealth of desirable candidates for the chief leadership, we often find our options far less than ideal. For a fuller analysis, see Chapter Seven.

84. Aelian, *A Register of Histories*, trans. Abraham Fleming, 1576, pp. 22f.

85. The ideal epitomized in Sir Philip Sidney may again be cited as relevant. Languet's successful tutelage of the young Philip Sidney criticized what may be called the "Fortinbras model" of nobility in much the same way as Hamlet does: "most men of high birth are possessed with this madness, that they long after a reputation founded on bloodshed, and believe there is no glory for them except that which is connected with the destruction of mankind. . . . And yet, let them be never so strong, in this respect they are inferior to many of the brutes"—see *The Correspondence of Philip Sidney and Hubert Languet*, ed. W. A. Bradley, Boston, Mass., 1912, p. 165, letter dated May 2, 1578; see also pp. 172-73, letter of October 22, 1578. For the similar views of Erasmus, see Roland Bainton, *Erasmus of Christendom*, New York, 1969, pp. 120 and 123f. Luther should also be cited for his similar judgment: "The world regards this terrible vice as the highest virtue" he writes of princely pride and "honor" such as that displayed by men like Fortinbras. "For all heathen books are poisoned through and through with this striving after praise and honor; in them men are taught by blind reason, that they would not nor could

be men of power and worth who are not moved by praise and honor; but those are counted the best who disregard body and life, friend and property and everything in the effort to win praise and honor" ("A Treatise on Good Works," in *Works*, Philadelphia, 1915, vol. 1, pp. 208f.).

86. See above, Chapter Four, fig. 5.

87. Walter S. Gibson, *Hieronymus Bosch*, London, 1973, pp. 70 and 73.

88. Morris P. Tilley, *A Dictionary of the Proverbs in England in the Sixteenth and Seventeeth Centuries*, Ann Arbor, Michigan, 1950, S917-18 and 925, and note also Herbert's "Frailtie," *The English Poems of George Herbert*, ed. C. A. Patrides, London, 1974, p. 88. St. Thomas Aquinas, toward the end of his life, similarly declared "mihi videtur ut palea"—Jacques Maritain, *Art and Scholasticism*, New York, 1962, p. 36. For the most recent treatment, see R. W. Dent, *Shakespeare's Proverbial Language: An Index*, Berkeley and Los Angeles, California, 1981.

89. Tilley, *Proverbs* H235; Shakespeare, *3 HVI* 4.8.61.

90. *The Book of Common Prayer*, ed. Richard Mant, p. 492, presenting Ps. 90:5-6 in Coverdale's translation.

91. Wither, *Emblems*, London, 1635, Book IV, illus. 48, p. 256.

92. See Gibson, *Bosch*, pp. 69-77.

93. See Otto Kurz, "Four Tapestries after Hieronymus Bosch," *JWCI*, vol. 30. (1967), pp. 150-62.

94. Gibson, *Bosch*, p. 70. For the processional float, see Sheila Williams and Jean Jacquot, "Ommegangs anversois du temps de Bruegel et de van Heemskerk," in Jean Jacquot, ed., *Les Fêtes de la Renaissance, II: Fêtes et cérémonies au Temps de Charles Quint*, Paris, 1960, pp. 377-82, and J. Grauls, "Taalkundige tochlichting bij her Hooi en den Hooiwagen," *Gentsche Bijdragen*, vol. 5 (1938), pp. 156-75.

95. For the prints of 1559 and 1608, see L. Lebeer, "Het hooi en de hooiwagen in de beeldende Kunsten," *Gentsche Bijdragen*, vol. 5 (1938), pp. 141-55; the anonymous *Allegory*, at the Rijksmuseum in Amsterdam, is reproduced with scant documentation in *Life's Picture History of Western Man*, New York, 1951, pp. 152 and 294n. The Sibrechts painting is in the Museum of Fine Arts in Lille.

96. See Knipping, *Iconography*, vol. 1, pp. 42f., and also F.W.H. Hollstein, *Dutch and Flemish Etchings, Engravings, and Woodcuts c. 1450-1700*, 19 vols., Amsterdam, 1949-69, vol. 1, p. 83.

*Chapter Six. The Prince amid the Tombs*

1. Seneca, Epistles 120 and 82, *Ad Lucilium Epistulae Morales*, ed. Richard Gummere, vol. 3, pp. 389-91, and vol. 2; p. 253.

2. *Old Arcadia*, p. 357, according to Josephine Roberts' *Architectonic Knowledge in the New Arcadia*, p. 277. Philippe Ariès, *The Hour of Our Death*, New York, 1981, p. 300, quotes a similar reflection by Sidney's friend du Plessis-Mornay.

3. Within a few years of Shakespeare's introduction of the scene, Dekker used it in the first part of *The Honest Whore* (1604), which H. C. Hart ascribes to Shakespeare's influence. In 1606, John Raynolds makes similar use in his versified *Passionate Hermit*, while Thomas Randolph's *The Jealous Lovers: A Comedie* (1632) brought it back into the dramatic context. See C. M. Ingleby et al., *The Shakespere Allusion-Book*, London, 1909, vol. I, pp. 65, 160-61, and 361-62.

4. C. Hofstede de Groot, *A Catalogue Raisonné of the Works of the Most Eminent Dutch Painters of the Seventeenth Century*, 10 vols. of 1908-28 Paris ed. reprinted, London, 1976, vol. 3, col. 28, n. 102 confidently identified the painting with Hamlet. Wilhelm Reinhold Val-

entiner, *Frans Hals* (Stuttgart and Berlin, 1921), p. 214, merely refers to the painting as "the so-called Hamlet." Seymour Slive, *Frans Hals*, (3 vols., London, 1970-74), vol. 1, pp. 88-89, rejects the identification with Hamlet outright; see also vol. 1, p. 24 and vol. 3, pp. 37-38. The National Gallery's exhibition catalogue *Art in Seventeenth Century Holland*, London, 1976, no. 49, acknowledges the possibility that Hamlet is represented, but still regards this identification as "fanciful."

5. Although the backgrounds in visual iconography have hitherto been largely ignored, the homiletic and literary backgrounds have received very helpful attention. The most specialized of recent studies are Harry Morris, "*Hamlet* as a *Memento Mori* Poem," *PMLA* 85 (1970), pp. 1035-40, and Bridget Gellert [Lyons], "The Iconography of Melancholy in the Graveyard Scene of *Hamlet*," *SP* 67 (1970), pp. 57-66, which appears in expanded form in her *Voices of Melancholy: Studies in Literary Treatments of Melancholy in Renaissance England*, New York, 1971, pp. 77-112. Theodore Spencer, *Death in Elizabethan Tragedy*, Cambridge, Mass., 1936, pp. 50-52 discusses meditations upon death and notes that "some of the German pictures of the time, showing heads and bodies with all the details of corruption, are horrible—so disgusting that one can hardly bear to look at them"—but this is to miss the contemporary reaction to such works. When we can see such representations with their full implications, we will better understand both Prince Hamlet and his play. Louis L. Martz finds striking similarities between Hamlet's reflections in the graveyard and the meditations of Fray Luis de Granada; see *The Poetry of Meditation*, New Haven, 1954, pp. 137-38. For a more general treatment of the iconography here analyzed in particular connection with *Hamlet*, see Clifford Davidson, "Death in his Court: Iconography in Shakespeare's Tragedies," *Studies in Iconography*, vol. 1 (1977), pp. 74-86.

6. Even when similar images appeared in pagan art, their meaning was different. For an example from classical Rome, see Otto Brendel, "Untersuchungen zur Allegorie des Pompejanischen Totenkopf-Mosaiks," *Mitteilungen des deutschen archaeologischen Instituts, Roemische Abteilung*, Band 49 (1934), 157-71 and Tafel 10. Emily Townsend Vermeule, *Aspects of Death in Early Greek Art and Poetry*, Berkeley and Los Angeles, 1979, and Jocelyn M. C. Toynbee, *Death and Burial in the Roman World*, Ithaca, New York, 1971, provide comprehensive analyses. For a brief and convincing summary view of differences between classical and Christian *memento mori* sculpture, we can turn to Henriette s' Jacob, *Idealism and Realism: A Study of Sepulchral Symbolism*, Leiden, 1954, p. 65: "The antique effigies of corpses, no less than those of the Middle Ages, were intended as a 'memento mori'. Naturally every period is conscious of the shortness of life and ever-menacing hour of death. It must be peremptorily rejected, however, that the antique skeletons should reflect the same ideas of warning and repentance [as do the Christian works]. On the contrary, they sprang essentially from a sensuous view of life: the frailty of earthly existence was depicted only to stress the necessity of enjoying life to the full: 'Carpe diem!' The 'larvae' of the monuments were connected with the custom of passing round little skeletons of bronze, etc., during banquets as a culmination of the entertainment." The usual classical point was often that we should eat, drink, and be merry, although the Stoic treatment was closer to the Christian in ways which I note in this chapter.

7. Louis Réau, "Escatalogy," vol. 4, col. 822, in *Encyclopedia of World Art*, 15 vols., New York and London, 1959-68, and Horst W. Janson, "The Putto with a Death's Head," *Art Bulletin*, vol. 19 (1937), pp. 423-49.

8. Katharine A. Esdaile, *English Church Monuments 1510-1840*, New York, 1946, pp, 113-14, Samuel Schoenbaum, *William Shakespeare: A Documentary Life*, New York, 1975, pp. 252-56.

9. Erwin Panofsky, *The Life and Art of Albrecht Dürer*, Princeton, 1971, p. 212.

10. Panofsky, *Dürer*, pp. 211-13; see also John B. Knipping, *Iconography*, vol. 1, pp. 90-91.

11. Frederick P. Weber, *Aspects of Death and Correlated Aspects of Life in Art, Epigram, and Poetry*, New York, 1920, pp. 713-14 and 500.

12. John B. Knipping, *Inconography*, vol. 1, p. 80n.

13. *AYLI*, 2.7.26-27.

14. Weber, *Aspects of Death*, pp. 722-24, and F. J. Britten, *Old Clocks and Watches*, London and New York, 1911, pp. 127-38. Prosser, *Hamlet and Revenge*, p. 220, refers to such a watch.

15. Another version of Tuke by Holbein may be seen at the National Gallery of Art in Washington, without the skeleton, but with the same *memento mori* verse from Job.

16. Roy Strong, *The English Icon*, London, 1969, p. 39. Ariès, *The Hour of Our Death*, pp. 328-33 treats Continental portraits with skulls.

17. See Maria Fossi Todorow, *Mostra delle Incisioni di Luca di Leida*, Florence, 1963, fig. 11 (p. 27), comments pp. 22-24, and catalogue no. 66.

18. *Rich. II* 2.2.18ff. See also *Rom.* 1.2.88f.; *H V* 5.2.307; *TN* 5.1.209; *AW* 5.3.48; *Ant.* 2.5.116f., Arthur Fairchild, *Shakespeare and the Arts of Design*, in *The University of Missouri Studies*, vol. 12 (1937), Columbia, Missouri, pp. 126-27, is correct when he interprets the line "And perspective it is best painter's art" (Sonnet XXIV) in a far broader context than that of anamorphic art. For the Holbein, see John Pope-Hennessy, *The Portrait in the Renaissance*, New York and Washington, 1966, pp. 245-52.

19. For the popularity of skull-jewels in the sixteenth-century, see Kathleen Cohen, *Metamorphosis of a Death Symbol: The Transi Tomb in the Late Middle Ages and the Renaissance*, Berkeley, 1973, p. 85, n2, and Ariès, *The Hour of Our Death*, p. 330f.

20. Roy Strong, *Tudor and Jacobean Portraits*, London, 1969, vol. 1, 129-31. For the contemporary developments of this tradition in the Low Countries, see Martin Davies, *National Gallery Catalogue of Early Netherlandish School*, London, 1968, pp. 137 and 157.

21. See Antonia McLean, *Humanism and the Rise of Science in Tudor England*, New York, 1972, pp. 201-04. The skull, like the urinal, could be used as a visual attribute of the physician. In the Clowes portrait, it suggests both associations—professional and religious.

22. Roy Strong, *The English Icon*, fig. 196, reproduces a 1590 portrait of Sir Edward Grimston at age sixty-one, holding a skull. Here of course the ambience lacks the dashing qualities shown by Gresham and Clowes, although the confidence remains quite similar.

23. A. M. Hind et al., *Engraving in England in the Sixteenth and Seventeenth Centuries*, 3 vols., Cambridge, 1952-64, vol. 1, plate 36c and p. 75. Hind, *ibid.*, p. 314, places Hogenberg's English activities as ca. 1572-87. In conjunction with this motto, it might be apt to recall Hamlet's earlier words: "I do not set my life at a pin's fee,/ And for my soul, what can it do to that,/ Being a thing immortal as itself"—1.4.65-67.

24. See Hind, *op. cit.*, I, pl. 59 and pp. 126-27. At this time, De Bry was sixty-nine years old, the only old man whom I illustrate in this section of this chapter.

25. E. Carleton Williams, "Mural Paintings of the Three Living and the Three Dead in England," *The Journal of the British Archaeological Association*, 3rd ser., vol. 7 (1942), pp. 31-40, and W. F. Storch, "Aspects of Death in English Art and Poetry," *Burlington Magazine*, vol. 21 (1912), pp. 249-56 and 314-19.

26. Cohen, *Metamorphosis*, p. 89 and fig. 35, although there is some confusion in her text.

27. Richard Gough, *Sepulchral Monuments in Great Britain*, London, 1786, vol. 5, plate LXXII with commentary on pp. 187-89. Gough postulates that this mural was probably copied

from one scene in "The Dance of Death" cycle which adorned the walls of St. Paul's Cathedral before it burned in 1666.

28. Stephen Bateman, *The Travayled Pilgrime*, 1568, sig. L3.

29. Theodor de Bry, *Emblemata Nobilitatis*, Frankfurt am Main, 1592, p. 70. For a reverse image of this print, see also "Life's Swiftness" by Saenredam after Goltzius, also dated 1592. In both these versions, the rose is in the gallant's hand, but in a mural from about 1520 in the Markham Chantry at the Church of St. Mary Magdalene in Newark, Notts., the rose is held by Mors and handed to the gallant.

30. Hollstein, *Dutch and Flemish Etchings, Engravings, and Woodcuts*, vol. 18, p. 58 for account and vol. 19, p. 104 plate B109 for a reproduction.

31. Max Sander, *Le Livre à figures italien depuis 1467 jusqu'à 1530*, 6 vols. plus supplement. Milan, 1942-69, vol. 6, no. 630.

32. See Gereth Spriggs, "A Dog in the Pew," *Country Life* (Feb. 12, 1976), pp. 338-39; *Peterborough Cathedral*, London, 1975, p. 4. I am grateful to the Rev. Arthur S. Gribble, Chancellor of Peterborough, for supplying further information.

33. Cohen, *Metamorphosis*, p. 81 and figs. 28-30.

34. In 1597, William Warner's *Syrinx*, sig. D3 contained the similar reflection: "how beit man that so often devoureth death in other creatures, is himself at length by death devoured." It is well to note such parallels, but we must be careful to recognize the widespread network of such allusions which lies behind specific references. John E. Hankins (*Shakespeare's Derived Imagery*, New York, 1977, p. 145) too often ignores that broad cultural nexus, as when he writes that the line "we fat ourselves for maggots" "unmistakably echoes Palingenius' account of the voluptuary who [died] 'that so the worms may have more food to eat.'"

35. In emblem and device books, a king's scepter and a poor man's mattock were sometimes crossed, and the two placed under a skull to indicate this ultimate equality, as in Claude Paradin, *The Heroical Devices*, 1591, p. 273, and Wither, *Emblems*, Book One, illus. 48, p. 48, where the motto runs "In death no difference is made/ Between the scepter and the spade."

36. 3 *H VI* 5.2.26, and see also *R II* 3.2.152-54; and John Calvin, *Sermons upon the Book of Job*, trans. Arthur Golding, 1574, p. 33b, lines 21ff., on Job 1:20-22.

37. These doggerel rhymes sound like the verses which typically accompanied Dance of Death and other emblem illustrations, and so prosodically reinforce the allusion. So far as I know, no one has found a source for them, and none is needed. In a broader sense, they fit with what Ariès has called the antiepitaph, and with the *ubi sunt* traditions in literature—see *The Hour of Our Death*, pp. 111, and 228f. There are also overtones of the *ubi sunt* theme, which can be traced back to old English verse.

38. Henriette s' Jacob, *Idealism and Realism: A Study of Sepulchral Symbolism*, pp. 46-47. See also Eric Mercer, *English Art*, pp. 244-45.

39. For an inscription identifying these stages, see the tomb of Archbishop Chichele (d. 1443) in Canterbury Cathedral, or Weber, *Aspects of Death*, p. 102. That emphasis on the *caro vilis* continued long after the time when English Christianity broke away from Rome may be illustrated by words written by the great New England Puritan minister Increase Mather in 1721, and quoted by Ariès, *The Hour of Our Death*, p. 342.

40. Cohen, *Metamorphosis*, pp. 35, 37f.

41. *Ibid.*, p. 16, as translated in n. 9.

42. *Ibid.*, p. 45.

43. Similar episcopal tombs may be found in Lincoln for Richard Fleming (d. 1431) and in Wells for Thomas Beckington (1466). The latter is illustrated and analyzed in Gough, *Sepulchral Monuments*, vol. 5, part 2, plate LXXX and p. 209.

44. M. D. Anderson, *History and Imagery in British Churches*, Edinburgh, 1971, p. 148, and see also Katharine Esdaile, *English Church Monuments*, p. 4.

45. The Pilon sculpture is now in the Louvre. See Anthony Blunt, *Art and Architecture in France 1500-1700*, Harmondsworth, Middlesex, 1973, pp. 149-51, and Cohen, *Metamorphosis*, p. 174 and figs. 111-12.

46. Francis Steer, "Arundel Castle and its Owners 1067-1660," *The Connoisseur*, vol. 197 (1978), p. 156, and illustration on p. 157.

47. Cohen, *Metamorphosis*, pp. 192-94; and Gough, *Sepulchral Monuments*, vol. 1; pp. cx-cxii.

48. See William Dugdale, *History of St. Paul's Cathedral*, 1658, pp. 64-67.

49. Cohen, *Metamorphosis*, pp. 125-28.

50. *Ibid.*, p. 123.

51. David Cecil, *The Cecils of Hatfield House*, Boston, 1973, p. 158; see also Margaret Whinney, *Sculpture in Britain 1530-1830*, pp. 20-21 and 236 n. 42, and John Buxton, *Elizabethan Taste*, p. 166.

52. The Ligozzi paintings, in a private collection in Britain, are illustrated as figs. 4a and b (plate 9) and 5a and b (plate 10) and discussed on pp. 26f. of *La natura morta Italiana. Catalogo della mostra, Napoli, Zurigo, Rotterdam*, Milan, 1964.

53. Margaret M. Beck. "The Dance of Death in Shakespeare," *MLN*, vol. 37 (1922), pp. 372-74, makes the proposal that Hamlet is "playing the part of the 'Auctor' who points the melancholy moral to the 'Lector,' Horatio," but when she writes that "the very structure is reminiscent" (p. 373) of the *danse macabre* cycles, she ignores the fact that Holbein's structure began with the highest ranks and moved toward the lowest, whereas Shakespeare has generally reversed that order, so as to reach his climax with Emperor and King—Claudius. For the history of the tradition, see E. Carleton Williams, "The Dance of Death in Painting and Sculpture in the Middle Ages," *The Journal of the British Archaeological Association*, 3rd ser., vol. 1 (1937), pp. 229-57; J. M. Clark, *The Dance of Death in the Middle Ages and the Renaissance*, Glasgow, 1950; and the edition of Holbein's *Dance* by Werner L. Gundersheimer, cited n. 55 below. Ivor Morris (*Shakespeare's God*, pp. 420-23) compares Hamlet's words with those of John Donne on death and decay.

54. See Samuel C. Chew, *The Pilgrimage of Life*, pp. 227, 229, and 381. English Dance of Death poems are printed in William Dugdale, *Monastici Anglicani*, London, 1673, vol. 3, pp. 367-74.

55. Werner L. Gundersheimer, ed., *The Dance of Death by Hans Holbein the Younger*, New York, 1971, pp. ix-xi, with quotations from xi and xiii.

56. Jean Wirth, *La jeune fille et la mort*, Geneva, 1979. One of the most gruesome treatments of Death and the Woman is spoken by Constance in Shakespeare's *King John* 3.4.23-36. As for Death disguised as a fool, other graphic examples are cited by Samuel C. Chew, *The Pilgrimage of Life*, p. 234. If we are unaware of this tradition of Death as the Fool, we may miss the point here, and as one critic puts it "we might wonder by what curious turn of thought Shakespeare should have chosen to make the gruesome illustration of humanistic reflection the skull of a court jester": see Frank McCombie's useful article "*Hamlet* and the *Moriae Encomium*," pp. 62-63. The three Holbein woodcuts appear in Gundersheimer's ed. on pp. 26, 49, and 51 (repeated 116, 139, and 141 with English translations).

57. Louis Réau, *Iconographie de l'art chrétien*, 3 vols. in 6, Paris, 1955-59, vol. 2, part ii, 658. This Ligozzi panel is tandem to that of the young man already treated, for which see n. 52 above.

58. Bruegel's *Triumph of Death* at the Prado varies these themes somewhat by representing

in one detail a hooded Mors who presents a lady seated at table with a death's-head on a platter. That painting as a whole is also relevant to *Hamlet* because it represents Death as a universal hunter of life, the tradition evoked by Fortinbras at the end of the play when he comments that "this quarry cries on havoc," where "proud Death . . . so many princes at a shot/ So bloodily hath struck" [5.2.353-56].

59. Samuel C. Chew, *The Virtues Reconciled*, pp. 10 and 131n.

60. Nigel Alexander expresses the contrast in interesting and somewhat different terms (*Poison, Play, and Duel*, p. 164): "The certainty of human mortality, and even the acceptance of the general considerations set out so fully in Hamlet's conversation with the Clown, cannot eliminate grief or pain. . . . Death is an absolute condition that is the natural end of mankind. Yet the death of any individual becomes a particular case that alters irrevocably the balance of love and harmony of spirit of those who knew the living being. . . . Ophelia carries with her to destruction a large part of the play's treasure of human affection."

61. The direction reads "Enter King, Queen, Laertes and the corse." Because textual scholars assure us of their "near certainty" that this basic quarto text was printed from Shakespeare's own handwritten manuscript, we accept it as showing Shakespeare's original intention. The later substitution of coffin for corpse in the stage direction of the folio text may indicate changing theatrical practice, or merely what G. B. Evans has called the "already ambiguous authority" of the folio *Hamlet*—see Textual Notes, *The Riverside Shakespeare*, ed. G. B. Evans, Boston, 1974, p. 1186. See also below n. 66.

62. To visualize the effect of the shroud slightly parted to show the face, we may recall the famous statue of John Donne in his shroud, now in St. Paul's Cathedral. He ordered it made during his last illness, and posed for it himself. English churches sometimes contain recumbent stone figures in such shrouds, but usually on a lesser aesthetic level than Donne's image. Furthermore, the slight parting of the shroud to reveal the face appears only in this memorial statue, so far as I can ascertain. Ariès, *The Hour of Our Death*, pp. 127f., 168-72, and 607 discusses the historical process in which the corpse, face and all, came to be concealed.

63. The distinction between interments in coffins and merely in shrouds may be variously documented, the latter being far more frequent. "The wording of the Burial Service in the Book of Common Prayer clearly anticipates uncoffined burial. The word coffin is not used; it is always 'the corpse' or 'the body,' as in the rubric, 'the earth shall be cast upon the body.' In Wheatley's book on the Common Prayer, first issued in 1710, occurs the comment—'When the body is stripped of all but its grave clothes, and is just going to be put into the grave,' etc."—J. Charles Cox, *Parish Registers*, p. 120. Cox also reports that "it was the custom for each parish to provide a shell or coffin to rest on the bier for the carrying of the corpse to the edge of the grave, when it was lifted out and lowered into the grave in its shroud"—p. 121. For burial only in winding sheet or shroud, see Myra Rifkin's doctoral dissertation at Bryn Mawr, *Burial*, pp. 40-41 and 169-70, and Percy Macquoid, "The Home . . . Funerals," p. 151. Burials within the body of the church were apparently regulated to require the use of coffins, for obvious sanitary reasons—Rifkin, pp. 41, 44 and 55.

64. For English monarchs, a recumbent effigy representing the deceased was prepared for use in the funeral, but it was never shown in a shroud. Clothed and startlingly lifelike effigies of kings and queens were exposed to full view atop the royal coffins, and were carried in funeral processions, but such effigies were not used for members of the nobility until a quarter century after the appearance of *Hamlet*. The first such instance was for Lodowick Stewart, Duke of Richmond and Lennox, in 1624, and he was related to the royal family. For these practices, see W. H. St. John Hope, "On the Funeral Effigies of the Kings and Queens of England," *Archaeologia*, vol. 60 (1907), pp. 517-70, and R. P. Howgrave-Graham, "Royal Portraits in Effigy: Some New Discoveries in Westminster Abbey," *Journal of the Royal Society of Arts*, London, vol.

101 (1953), pp. 465-74. For an account of the identification of the head of Queen Elizabeth preserved from her funeral effigy, see the *Times*, April 10, 1959, p. 7. A number of these royal funeral effigies are preserved in the small museum at Westminster Abbey. They were never interred, so far as I can ascertain.

65. For the class distinctions of the place of burial, within the church and in the churchyard, see for example Margaret Spufford, *Contrasting Communities: English Villagers in the Sixteenth and Seventeenth Centuries*, Cambridge, 1974, pp. 108-09. See also n. 63, above, and Ariès, *The Hour of Our Death*, pp. 82f., 271, and 338, but Ariès' evidence for England is quite fragmentary. A century after Shakespeare's death, a French traveler provided an account of middle-class English funerals—see Henri Misson, *Memoirs and Observations in his Travels*, London, 1719, pp. 89-101.

66. The stage direction in the 1623 folio changed "corse" to "coffin" for reasons which we can now only surmise. Of course the change to coffin may merely be a loose reference to a bier, not a closed box, and the coffins or "shells" available for temporary transportation were obviously shallow enough to make the corpse easily accessible for lifting out; or it may represent a change made by the compositor in the printing house, and not actual theatrical usage. Another directorial problem may have relevance to this one. We have firm evidence from a few years after Shakespeare's death that when Burbage as Hamlet came forward at the funeral, he not only interrupted Laertes but leapt into the grave with him. Harley Granville-Barker has persuaded most scholars, however, that this was not Shakespeare's original intention. On the contrary, he argues from the good quarto text that Laertes, who is already in the grave, leaps out of it to hurl himself at Hamlet's throat. The ensuing struggle would thus have originated and been conducted on the open stage. As Granville-Barker explains, "the scene is played to this day in a muddle of excitement which confuses its dramatic intentions, when these are fairly plainly to be read in the text itself." At some later date (and we cannot fix the time) we know from a funeral elegy on Burbage in 1618 that Burbage did leap into the grave. Granville-Barker argues that this was just what an actor, "carried away by his own emotion, his mind anticipating the verbal onslaught, might do: it would prove startlingly effective," and he concludes "that we may have here a little history of Shakespeare's betrayal by his actors."—Harley Granville-Barker, *Preface to Hamlet*, New York, 1957, p. 150n. By the time of the first folio's publication nine years after Shakespeare's death, it was not only an established part of the stage business of *Hamlet*, but it could perhaps have led to the replacement of "corse" by "coffin" in the stage direction, for the following reason: A violent struggle between Hamlet and Laertes in the narrow grave (rather than on the open stage, as Granville-Barker holds) might have endangered the boy-actor who played Ophelia and subjected him to considerable harm. It may have been for this reason that corpse was replaced by coffin in the folio, or it may have been for one of the other reasons noted above. But I reduce these speculations to a footnote because they are not crucial to my interpretation.

67. Richard Gough, *Sepulchral Monuments*, Part II, p. cliii. For less massive corpses, six bearers would suffice for lowering the coffin, as in the 1559 funeral of Sir John Raynford of Essex, reported in *The Diary of Henry Machyn*, pp. 211-12. John Milton's second poem "On the University Carrier" entitled "Another on the Same," line 20, also refers to "six bearers." These pallbearers apparently made their livelihood by such work: H. M[ill], *Poems*, 1639, sig. N2 verso, records such bearers saying "that is all the means we have/ To live." The situation may have been different north of the Tweed. For an unusually detailed account of the traditional Scottish practice of the lowering of the coffin "by mourning cords" in the hands of the immediate family, see John Brand, *Observations on Popular Antiquities*, London, 1813, vol. 2, pp. 179-80.

68. Georg Hirth, *Picture Book of the Graphic Arts*, vol. 1, fig. 468. For the late fifteenth-

century illumination also reproduced in fig. VI.23 in my text, I am indebted to Mr. and Mrs. Eugene B. Power's manuscript *Book of Hours*, executed by a follower of Maître François about 1470, in the University of Michigan Library, discussed in the University of Michigan Museum of Art exhibition catalogue prepared by William R. Levin, *Images of Love and Death in Late Medieval and Renaissance Art*, Ann Arbor, 1975, plate LXII and pp. 50-51.

69. *The Journal of Nicholas Assheton*, ed. the Rev. F. R. Raines, Manchester: Chetham Society, 1848, vol. 14, pp. 81-82, and for a related incident, p. 52; Assheton's wife was still recovering from a very difficult and dangerous labor, so could not even attend the funeral. Earlier accounts with which I am familiar are more cryptic, but records of a burial in 1588 in a parish without a resident clergyman indicate that the corpse was "laid in" by friends or relatives—see Emmison, *Elizabethan Life: Morals*, p. 173.

70. *The Diary of Ralph Josselin, 1616-83*, ed. Alan MacFarlane, London, 1976, p. 203.

71. Geoffrey Rowell, *The Liturgy of Christian Burial*, London, 1977, p. 29. That "final kiss" is still a part of Russo-Greek-Orthodox funerals, I am told.

72. With or without reference to funerals, fracases growing out of personal rivalry or personal grudges recur again and again in sixteenth-century records as having occurred on hallowed ground, which was the common meeting place for the whole community. One such was a scandalous brawl in Glasgow Cathedral in 1545. Quite unrelated to a burial, but indicating the proclivity to violence even within sacred precincts, it involved the rivalry between Archbishop Dunbar and Cardinal Beaton: "Their respective processions became locked in combat, with the two rival crossbearers battering one another with their processional crosses"—certainly a striking scene, if not an edifying one: see Bruce Lenman and Geoffrey Parker, "Crime and Control in Scotland 1500-1800," *History Today*, vol. 30 (January, 1980), p. 13. In England there were so many violent disorders that legal prohibitions were carefully drawn up. The Act of 5 Edward VI c. 4 (1551) forbade the drawing of swords or other weapons in a church or on church grounds. The preamble to that act decried the practice of "quarrelling, brawling, fraying and fighting openly in churches and churchyards," and court records confirm this unruly state of affairs. To discourage such "fraying," the penalty of greater excommunication could be imposed, as well as "either cutting off an ear or branding a cheek"—see F. G. Emmison, *Elizabethan Life: Disorder*, Chelmsford, Essex, 1970, pp. 184 and 194; and *Elizabethan Life: Morals*, pp. 112-13. The gathering of a whole community for church services on Sundays and holy days provided an opportunity for settling personal grudges, large and small. These went far beyond mere mischief or petty malice of the kind evidenced in 1593 when Dorothy Richmond at Great Holland Church "thrust a pin in Edy Alefounder's buttocks in divine service," thereby causing notable "dis-quietness" in the church. Beyond childish pranks, men passed major insults back and forth, cursing, railing and brawling. Local church records show many verbal quarrels leading to actual bloodshed, with fists, staves, stools, swords, and daggers. See Emmison, *Elizabethan Life: Morals*, pp. 118, and 114-21 *passim*.

73. Giesey, *Royal Funeral Ceremony*, p. 9.

74. *Ibid.*, pp. 122-24.

75. Rifkin, *Burial*, pp. 116-17 and 191. See also *The Letters of John Chamberlain*, vol. 2, April 24, 1619, pp. 232-33.

76. Emmison, *Elizabethan Life: Morals*, p. 174.

77. The infuriated Prince, having just thrashed Laertes for what (in the Prince's eyes) seems an unjustified attack, now gives him a thorough verbal working over. The repeated, sarcastic questions beginning with "woo't" represent Elizabethan baby talk, ridiculing Laertes for acting like a child. Excessive verbal protestations of grief offended Elizabethan and Jacobean taste, which associated these with the Irish Catholics who "howled" over their dead, and with children who (as Hamlet charges Laertes) "come here to whine." Thus Jean Veron (*The Hunting of*

*Purgatory to Death*, 1561, fol. 37b) ridicules the "unseemly howling that your Papists use for the salvation of their dead," whereas Barnaby Rich (*The Irish Hubbub*, 1619, p. 2) defines the proverbial phrase "to weep Irish" as burial with "barbarous outcries" when you can see "their howling and their hallowing, but never see them to shed any tears." Such customs also were noted among English mourners in *Meditations and Resolutions*, 1612, by Anthony Stafford, which Percy Macquoid ("Marriage . . . Funerals," p. 151) quotes as follows: "It is a wonder to see the childish whining we nowadays use at the funerals of our friends. If we could howl them back again, our lamentations were to some purpose; but as they are, they are vain and in vain"— p. 16. James Brand, *Popular Antiquities*, vol. 2, pp. 174-77 discusses such objections to excessive expressions of grief. See also Jeremy Taylor, *Holy Dying*, in *The Whole Works*, London, 1880, vol. 1, pp. 605-06. For Continental attitudes, see Ariès, *The Hour of Our Death*, pp. 326f. For a recent treatment of the "disturbance" over Ophelia's body, see Lynda E. Boose, "The Father and the Bride in Shakespeare," *PMLA*, vol. 97 (1982), pp. 330f.

78. "The dog will have his day" was apparently a common conception, proverbial in the sixteenth century as it has been subsequently. The future Queen Elizabeth used it in a slightly different form from Hamlet's in writing to her brother King Edward VI on May 15, 1550, that "I shall never be ashamed to present [my mind]," which would always display faithfulness and integrity: "Of this also yet the proof could not be great, because the occasions have been so small; notwithstanding, as a dog hath a day, so many I perchance have time to declare it in deeds which now I do write them but in words"—quoted in John Strype, *Ecclesiastical Memorials of the Church of England*, Oxford, 1822, vol. 2, part 1, chapter XXVIII, p. 367.

79. *Caes.*, 4.3.190-92. The problems raised for the characterization of Brutus by the two references to Portia's death (4.3.144-59 and 179-95) do not directly concern us here, although I take them to imply Shakespeare's deep suspicion of Stoic *apatheia*. What counts here is that the speech quoted from Brutus epitomizes the quintessential Stoic response to learning of a loved one's death.

80. As early as 1952, Maynard Mack argued for a similar reading of the Prince in act five, where "Hamlet accepts his world and we discover a different man," but he adds that "I know there can be differences on this point"—"The World of *Hamlet*," reprinted from *The Yale Review*, vol. 41 (1952), in *Shakespeare: The Tragedies: A Collection of Critical Essays*, ed. Alfred Harbage, Englewood Cliffs, N.J., 1964, p. 57. Such differences have indeed existed, as when Gilbert Highet interpreted Hamlet's "ranting" as another indication of his "intermittent madness" in *The Powers of Poetry*, New York, 1960, pp. 286-90. I hope that the evidence presented here may make those difference less severe in future discussions.

*Chapter Seven. Finale*

1. John Calvin, *Institution*, 1.16.2.

2. Richard Hooker, *Ecclesiastical Polity*, 1.3.4 in *Works*, ed. John Keble.

3. Lancelot Andrewes, "A Sermon Preached at Chiswick in the Time of Pestilence, August 21, 1603," published in *Certain Sermons Preached at Sundry Times*, bound with *XCVI Sermons*, 1631. Bertram Joseph treats the role of Providence in a generally knowledgeable and helpful way, *Conscience and the King*, pp. 136-46.

4. *Liturgies and Occasional Forms of Prayer*, p. 254, with reference on p. 246 n. 1 to these "Godly Prayers" as originating in the Prayer Book of 1552. The reliance upon divine Providence, rather than upon one's own *virtus*, is one of the characteristic Christian rather than Stoic views. Ruth Levitsky ("Rightly to be Great," p. 159) observes of Hamlet's new mood that "the consequence of his wonderful experience is a calm acceptance of whatever is in store for him. This acceptance is stated in terms which, though sometimes reminiscent of Stoic resignation, never

theless indicate a reliance upon a wise and benevolent God rather than a submission to the unjust and capricious ways of Fortuna."

5. Bradford's "A Godly Meditation and Instruction of the Providence of God" appeared in so many Elizabethan collections after 1562 that they are difficult to trace adequately, but I quoted from John Bradford, *The Writings, Containing Sermons, Meditations, Examinations, etc.*, ed. Aubrey Townsend, Cambridge, 1848, p. 191; and see also p. 190n. In the good quarto text of *Hamlet* the reference to knowledge is primary ("since no man of aught he leaves knows"), but the folio version ("Since no man ha 's aught of what he leaves") might best be considered in connection with I Timothy 6:7: "We brought nothing into this world, neither may we carry anything out of this world," as read in the burial service in Shakespeare's England. See Richmond Noble, *Shakespeare's Biblical Knowledge*, New York, 1977, pp. 208-09.

6. Ruth Nevo correctly observes that "of all Shakespeare's tragic heroes, he [Hamlet] is the only one for whom a specifically Christian insight is the burden of his painfully acquired wisdom"—*Tragic Form in Shakespeare*, Princeton, 1972, p. 174. In a similar vein, Fredson Bowers declared that Hamlet "is confident because, like Samson, he feels himself once more reconciled to divine Providence," and he adds that "Hamlet dies in a victory that is the age-old demonstration of God's unchanging purposes as well as the symbol of a personal reconciliation and acceptance. This is a true Christian catharsis, superior to any possible for the Greeks, and it is important that we should not overlook its significance"—"Dramatic Structure and Criticism: Plot in *Hamlet*," *Shakespeare Quarterly*, vol. 15 (1964), p. 217.

7. Calvin's commentary on Matthew 10:29 interprets the sparrow's fall in terms of tyrants and the cruelty of men, whom we are not to fear: see John Calvin, *Commentaries*, 22 vols. (often with two in each bound volume), Grand Rapids, Michigan, 1981, vol. 16A, pp. 464f.

8. For the differences which I suspect lie between Hamlet's "readiness is all" and Edgar's "ripeness is all" (*Lear* 5.2.11), see my *Shakespeare and Christian Doctrine*, pp. 137-40, where I argue that Edgar's remark may be more aptly interpreted as Stoic and Hamlet's as Christian. See also J. V. Cunningham, *Woe or Wonder: The Emotional Effect of Shakespearean Tragedy*, Denver, Col., 1951, pp. 10-14; Bertram Joseph, *Conscience and the King*, pp. 140-42; and Lewis D. Levang, " 'Ripeness is all': A Semantic Approach to a *Lear* Question" *Etc.: A Review of General Semantics*, vol. 27 (1970), pp. 91-98.

9. Francis de Sales, *Letters to Persons in the World*, 3.4, in *The Book of Catholic Quotations*, ed. John Capin, New York, 1956, p. 248; I have been unable to find this sentence in the works of St. Francis.

10. Luther quoted in Heinrich Quistorp, *Calvin's Doctrine of the Last Things*, Richmond, Virginia, 1955, p. 107n.; Calvin, *Commentaries: Commentary on I Corinthians* (7:29), trans. John Pringle, p. 257, and Exposition on Romans 14:7-9, in *Calvin: Commentaries*, trans. Joseph Haroutunian, Philadelphia, 1958, p. 318.

11. Hooker, *Ecclesiastical Polity* 5.46.3 in *Works*, ed. Keble.

12. Coverdale, *Remains*, p. 96, and Latimer, *Sermons*, p. 416.

13. Edmund Grindal, *Remains*, pp. 6-7, and Edwin Sandys, *Sermons*, pp. 171, 175-76. Emblematic expressions of the thought may be found in Wither, *Emblems*, Book III, illus. 34 and Book IV, illus. 27, pp. 168 and 235.

14. Thus Harry Levin, in his admirable *The Question of Hamlet*, pp. 98f., misses this Elizabethan significance when he comments that "for Hamlet, welcoming death when it comes unsought, felicity seems to loom ahead in the prospect of nonexistence rather than the relish of salvation." If we consider *Hamlet* within a more or less naturalistic modern context, that interpretation may appear persuasive, but it misses the point within the context of 1600.

15. See Richmond Noble, *Shakespeare's Biblical Knowledge*, p. 209.

16. *Homilies*, p. 103.

17. Calvin, *Commentaries*, vol. 8A, p. 178.

18. Calvin, *Commentaries*, vol. 6A, p. 27, and vol. 4B, p. 494; and also vol. 6A, p. 356, on Psalms 115:17.

19. William Perkins had associated the recognition that all "honors, riches, and pleasures ... ye must leave behind you" with the final resolution of conscience—see *William Perkins*, p. 73.

20. See 3.4.173f.; 5.2.75-80 and 215-32. In the apology to Laertes, he relies upon the camouflage of madness which has thus far proved useful to him in a situation where he was essentially alone among enemies; to expect him to abandon that camouflage at this point is unrealistic.

21. See James L. Donovan, "A Note on Hamlet's 'Not Shriving Time Allow'd'," *Notes and Queries*, vol. 201 (Nov., 1956), pp. 467-69.

22. See above, Chapter Two, n. 127.

23. Modern readers really should not be disturbed by it either. Peter Alexander, *Hamlet, Father and Son*, Oxford, 1955, pp. 183-85, is worth pondering on these questions, as on many others: "The play dramatizes the struggle to which all civilization that is genuine is doomed," that is, the need "to be humane without a loss of toughness." I recognize the force at this point of Robert Ornstein's position that "what is not near Hamlet's conscience is not near our own because he is our moral interpreter"—*The Moral Vision of Jacobean Tragedy*, Madison, Wisconsin, 1960, p. 235. The issue of Hamlet's callousness may continue to arise, but it can be greatly clarified when placed in a Renaissance context.

24. For John of Salisbury, see above, Chapter Two, n. 85, and Althusius, *The Politics*, p. 187.

25. Thus, as Perkins wrote, after full and proper self-analysis and even self-accusation, "the Lord will send down his spirit into the conscience by a sweet and heavenly testimony to assure us that we are at peace with God"—*William Perkins*, p. 73.

26. See above, Chapter Two, n. 99 and n. 100.

27. See above, Chapter Two, n. 79 and n. 141.

28. See above, Chapter Two, n. 175.

29. Calvin, *Institution*, 4.20.10.

30. Shakespeare's sources supplied him with the information that Denmark was an elective monarchy, although J. Dover Wilson, *What Happens in Hamlet*, p. 36, argues very strangely that Shakespeare, in using the word "election," "was quite unconscious that it denoted any procedure different from that which determined the succession in England." See E.A.J. Honigmann, "The Politics in *Hamlet* and 'The World of the Play,'" *Stratford-upon-Avon Studies*, vol. 5 (1964), pp. 129-47, and A. P. Stabler, "Elective Monarchy in the Sources of Hamlet," *SP*, vol. 62 (1965), pp. 654-61.

31. Bilson, *True Difference*, pp. 513-15, 517-18, and see above, Chapter Two, notes 170-72. Bishop Bilson's argument on elected as distinguished from hereditary tyrants may strike us as a bit casuistic, but it was the authoritative view in England when Shakespeare wrote *Hamlet*.

32. The earliest substantial English treatment of the Danish monarchy I have been able to discover is the *Account of Denmark* by Robert, first Viscount Molesworth, which was apparently written in 1692 and was published in London in 1694. This account points out that the King of Denmark was "chosen by people of all sorts" (p. 43) and that if they found "that they had advanced a cruel, vicious, tyrannical, covetous, or wasteful person, they frequently deposed him, sometimes banished, sometimes destroyed him," whereas sometimes "they dispatched him without any more ceremony the best way they could" (pp. 44f.). Queen Elizabeth's Bishop Bilson, who would not have accepted the other Whig principles of Molesworth, would at least have concurred on the proper dispatch of an elected tyrant. And so, of course, did Prince Hamlet.

33. G. B. Harrison, *Elizabethan Plays and Players*, Ann Arbor, Michigan, 1956, pp. 238-39.

34. The elective monarch was of course specified in Shakespeare's sources (see n. 30 above), as well as still operative in Denmark, but I doubt that many theatergoers would have known or remembered this. For a late seventeenth-century English account of the elective Danish monarchy and the Danish practice of removing tyrannous kings, see n. 32 above.

35. In the order quoted, see Chapter Two, notes 86, 3, and 137.

36. Pertinent here is the comment of Nigel Alexander—*Poison, Play, and Duel*, p. 198: "the final entry of Fortinbras emphasizes the necessity, in the delicate balance of human existence, of the military virtues."

37. Franklin, *Constitutionalism and Resistance*, pp. 189f.

38. For Claudius, then, as for Rosencrantz and Guildenstern, there is a rational symmetry in the retribution Hamlet exacts, an exact balance appropriate to a just and judicious prince. For a radically different interpretation, see Roy Battenhouse (*Shakespearean Tragedy*, p. 256), who follows what seems to me to be an extraordinary line in explaining the poisoned cup as evoking "the added background of a Black Mass complete with the chalice of poison—an ultra-Italianate situation in which Hamlet can 'conscientiously' both kill and help administer a devilish communion, thus sealing his priesthood as a Scourge of God as the play ends." That of course fits with Battenhouse's consistent inversion of the play's obvious meanings which I have consistently questioned, but as a secondary point I am curious about when and where deadly poison was a part of Black Mass libations. I have never heard of such, and as a matter of common sense doubt that even the most deranged warlocks and witches would knowingly drink mortal poison during their demonic parodies of the Eucharist. At certain points in these matters, of course, the criteria of common sense seem strangely irrelevant. As for the mood of Hamlet at the end, Peter Ure has perceptively commented that "submission to Providence seems to take precedence over dedication to revenge"—"Character and Role from *Richard III* to *Hamlet*," *Stratford-upon-Avon Studies*, vol. 5 (1964), p. 27.

39. I do not understand it to be our function as critics to assign fictive characters to heaven and hell where the author has not made the matter explicit, as I have argued at length in my *Shakespeare and Christian Doctrine*. Shakespeare does not typically introduce the issue, but here he does do so through the words of Horatio. Those words accord with the previous development of the Prince's character, when understood within the principal frames of reference of Shakespeare's original audiences. Thus I cannot agree with Virgil Whitaker's point (*The Mirror up to Nature*, p. 199) that "Horatio's hope is not necessarily unfounded, but it is not founded on the action of the play." Throughout, the play seems to me far more integrated than it does to Whitaker. I must say, however, that I remain perplexed by Hamlet's reference to Horatio's attempted suicide in terms of "felicity" (5.2.336), for which perplexity some background is provided in my *Shakespeare and Christian Doctrine*, pp. 24-31. But that reference to Horatio is principally intended to keep him alive so that an orderly succession can be secured, and it has no other overriding significance in the play at this point.

40. Brother Baldwin Peter, F.S.C., in his "*Hamlet* and *In Paradisum*," *Shakespeare Quarterly*, 3 (1952), pp. 279-80, argues that the particular form of Horatio's phrasing links it with "*In Paradisum*." For similar arguments, see I. J. Semper, *Hamlet Without Tears*, p. 99, and Christopher Devlin, *Hamlet's Divinity*, London, 1963, p. 26. Philippe Ariès, *The Hour of Our Death*, pp. 247-50, provides a survey of Catholic thought and art on this angelic transference.

41. Martin Luther, *What Luther Says*, vol. 1, item 71; John Calvin, Comm. on Luke 16:22 in vol. 16B, p. 186, of *Commentaries*; Henry Bullinger, *Decades*, vol. 4, pp. 388-89.

42. See Geoffrey Rowell, *The Liturgy of Christian Burial*, pp. 16, 42, 44f., and 62.

43. Robert Hill, *The Pathway to Prayer and Piety*, 1613, p. 176; Matthew Griffith, *Bethel*

or a Form for Families, 1634, p. 525; and Richard Brathwait, A Spiritual Spicery, 1638, pp. 465-66.

44. Philip Stubbes, A Christal Glass for Christian Women, 1600, sig. C3v.-C4, and G. B. Harrison, The Life and Death of Robert Devereux, Earl of Essex, New York, 1937, p. 324.

45. H. P.[etowe], Elizabetha quasi Vivens, 1603, sig. B1; and John Lane, An Elegy upon the Death of Elizabeth, 1603, sig. B1v.

46. For Italian representations, see George Kaftal, Iconography of the Saints in Tuscan Painting, Florence, 1952, cols. 1075-77.

47. Richard Gough, Sepulchral Monuments, vol. 1, p. clv.

48. Gough, Sepulchral Monuments, vol. 1, p. cxi.

49. Thomas S. R. Boase, Death in the Middle Ages, London, 1972, p. 97.

50. Cohen, Metamorphosis, p. 123.

51. Gough, Sepulchral Monuments, vol. 5, pp. 310-12, and plates CX and CXI. See also vol. 1, p. 85 and plate CXII.

52. Ernst and Johanna Lehner, Devils, Demons, Death and Damnation, New York, 1971, fig. 182.

53. Richard Day, Book of Christian Prayers, 1578, sigs. Q2 and Q2v, and repeated elsewhere.

54. See Edward Hodnett, Francis Barlow: First Master of English Book Illustration, Ilkley, Yorkshire, 1978, p. 126.

55. See the engraving by James Caldwall and S. Smith after G. Carter in Sarah Stevenson, A Face for Any Occasion: Some Aspects of Portrait Engraving, Edinburgh, 1976, p. 110 and fig. 175.

56. Ellis Waterhouse, Anthony Van Dyck, "Suffer Little Children to Come Unto Me," Ottawa, Canada, 1978, p. 15.

57. For a short analysis, see Roy Strong, English Icon, p. 40.

58. Of the two last tributes to Hamlet, Nigel Alexander (Poison, Play, and Duel, p. 200) writes that "both tributes are true, but since Horatio and Fortinbras both see Hamlet in their own terms, neither contains the whole truth."


*Appendix A*

1. In the cumulative lineation of the Folio text, it commences at line 1849 out of a total of 3904 lines; see Charlton Hinman, ed., The Norton Facsimile: The First Folio of Shakespeare, New York, 1968, pp. 774 and 790.

2. For a study of the mirror in art, see Gustav F. Hartlaub, Zauber des Spiegels: Geschichte und Bedeutung des Spiegels in der Kunst, Munich, 1951.

3. Virgil K. Whitaker, The Mirror Up to Nature, p. 90.

4. John Pope-Hennessy, The Portrait in the Renaissance, New York, 1966, pp. 126-28. The first picture illustrating the painting of a self-portrait by use of a convex mirror appears in a French illuminated manuscript of Boccaccio's De claris mulieribus, which was completed in 1402 (Le Livre des femmes nobles et renommées, Bibliothèque Nationale Ms. Fr. 12420, Paris). It is reproduced as fig. 9 by Heinrich Schwarz, "The Mirror in Art," with comments on p. 110, and shows Marcia, a nun, looking into a small convex mirror and painting her own image on a flat panel. She corrects the distortions of the mirror, whereas Parmigianino later reproduced them faithfully.

5. Wolfgang M. Zucker, "Reflections on Reflections," Journal of Aesthetics and Art Criticism, vol. 20 (1962), p. 244. For the use of small pieces of mirror placed next to each other to

make a larger reflecting surface, the matter of expense went hand in hand with the limits of technology in the later seventeenth century and in the eighteenth, for which see Herbert Cescinsky and Ernest R. Gribble, *Early English Furniture and Woodwork*, London, 1922, vol. 1, p. 2 (the pieces of glass were "rarely larger than about six inches by four"), and R. W. Symonds, "English Looking-Glass Plates and their Manufacture—III," *Connoisseur*, vol. 98 (1936), pp. 11-12.

6. James R. Newman, ed., *The Harper Encyclopedia of Science*, New York, 1963, vol. 3, p. 788, reports that "mirrors of glass backed with an amalgam of tin mercury were first manufactured commercially by the Venetians in the sixteenth century."

7. For British glass-making in general, see Henry J. Powell, *Glass-Making in England*, Cambridge, 1923, and William A. Thorpe, *English Glass*, London, 1949. After some limited efforts at glass manufacture under Elizabeth, the British processes were put on a new footing in 1615 by a "proclamation touching glasses," but the major developments came only after the Restoration under the patronage of the Duke of Buckingham at Lambeth about 1670—see Charles Singer *et al.*, *A History of Technology*, Oxford, 1957, vol. 3, pp. 216-17, 220, and 238. An archaeological exploration of a sixteenth-century glass manufacturing site at Bishop's Wood in northwest Staffordshire reports no sign of mirror making there—see T. Pape, "An Elizabethan Glass Furnace," *The Connoisseur*, vol. 92 (1933), pp. 172-77. Insofar as we can now determine, "the first English factory for the making of looking-glass plates was set up in the reign of James I by Sir Robert Mansell" in 1618, but the best commendation which Inigo Jones could make for Mansell's mirrors in 1620 was to certify that "Mansell's glass is mixed good and bad, and very thin in the middle"—R. W. Symonds, "Early English Mirrors," *Connoisseur*, vol. 96 (1935), p. 315, and Powell, *Glass-Making in England*, p. 36. For further reports on Mansell's operations, see Thorpe, *English Glass*, pp. 115-27. For later developments, see Symonds' sequential articles in *Connoisseur*, vol. 97 (1936), pp. 243-49, and vol. 98 (1936), pp. 9-15. It is clear that in Shakespeare's time, the glass mirrors available in England would have been imported, small, and often distorted in their reflections. And Richard III's remark about being "at charges for a looking-glass" reminds us once again that they were expensive (*RIII* 1.2.255).

8. Even in the late decades of the seventeenth century, the market value of one Venetian mirror was greater than for an oil painting by Raphael. The eminent French statesman Colbert had led in the establishment of the French manufacture of mirrors, and had a fine collection, but when his estate was settled after his death in 1683, a Venetian mirror measuring 46 by 26 inches was valued at over eight thousand livres, while a painting by Raphael was put down at only three thousand. It is true that this remarkably large mirror was framed in silver, whereas the Raphael was not, but that fact too may be significant—see *Encyclopedia Britannica*, 11th ed., vol. 18, p. 576.

9. *WT*, 4.4.591. In the Victoria and Albert Museum (#W101-1921) there is a lovely French mirror frame of carved boxwood dating from about 1575; the mirror itself would have measured about one and a half inches across, but of course the silvering has been lost. This is the kind of mirror which might have been suspended from a girdle. The British Museum has a seventeenth-century gold and enameled locket (Waddeston Collection #170) containing a mirror of no more than two or three inches across. Such mirrors would of course have been too expensive for the pack of Autolycus, but they indicate something of the size carried by wealthy ladies. For the suspension of mirrors from a lady's girdle, see Carroll Camden, *The Elizabethan Woman*, Houston and New York, 1952, p. 230.

10. Mirrors from the sixteenth century have not often survived, but a fine example of the type of stand mirror which I illustrate from Guillaume de la Perrière, *Morosophie*, 1539, emblem 37, may be seen in Dresden, and is illustrated as fig. 247 in the catalogue, *Splendour of Dresden: Five Centuries of Collecting, An Exhbition*, n.p.: Metropolitan Museum of Art, 1978.

11. *The Works of Plato*, trans. and ed. Benjamin Jowett, New York, n.d., vol. IV, p. 24.

12. Based upon the quality of the images produced by the mirrors he knew, "Plato goes on to evoke several unflattering consequences about the character and value of art," as M. H. Abrams has put it in his *The Mirror and the Lamp: Romantic Theory and the Critical Tradition*, New York, 1958, p. 30. For differences between Platonism and Neo-Platonism, see Herbert Grabes, *Speculum, Mirror und Looking-Glass*, Tübingen, 1973, pp. 111-12.

13. Quoted from Heinrich Schwarz, "The Mirror in Art," p. 110.

14. For sixteenth- and seventeenth-century representations of Diogenes Laertius' story in art, see A. Pigler, *Barockthemen*, Budapest and Berlin, 1956, vol. 2, pp. 410-11.

15. See Sister Rita Mary Bradley, "Backgrounds of the Title *Speculum* in Medieval Literature," *Speculum*, vol. 29 (1954), pp. 102-04 and 108 for Augustine, and pp. 100-15 for a survey from the period of the early church into the eighteenth century.

16. For the theological affirmation of secular literature as a kind of natural revelation, see my *Shakespeare and Christian Doctrine*, pp. 63-110.

17. Quoted from the translation provided by A. J. Gossage, "Plutarch," in *Latin Biography*, ed. T. A. Dorey, London, 1967, p. 49. The passage appears in the first chapter of Plutarch's *Aemelius Paulus*, but in the Loeb Classical Library and in some other editions it precedes the *Timoleon*, as prefatory to both lives.

18. J. E. Spingarn, *A History of Literary Criticism in the Renaissance*, New York, 1954, pp. 104-05, with further references to Robortelli, B. Tasso, and Cervantes.

19. For a general survey see Herbert Grabes, *Speculum, Mirror und Looking-Glass*, especially pp. 108-11 for the drama. Grabes has provided the most thorough study to date of mirror imagery and symbolism in medieval and Renaissance literature. For an earlier and briefer treatment, see G. G. Smith, ed., *Elizabethan Critical Essays*, Oxford, 1904, vol. I, pp. 369-70. Citing Ben Jonson's conception of the court masques as "the mirrors of man's life," Roy Strong explains that Jonson uses mirror to mean "a spectacle in which the king and court see their true selves as in a looking glass. When Jonson presents members of the royal family as gods and goddesses, or as abstract virtues defeating wicked vices or banishing the forces of evil, he is showing the court its real self, its 'idea' in the Platonic sense"; see Strong's "Inigo Jones and the Stuart Court," *The Times*, July 7, 1977, p. 7.

20. *Publii Terentii Comoediae Sex*, Leiden, 1644, reproduced in Grabes, *Speculum*, as Abb. 13, and discussed pp. 110-11.

21. This proliferation reached its height between 1500 and 1700, but it is ultimately traceable to the thirteenth century when glass mirrors began to replace those made of polished steel, and so provided a less clouded image. See Hartlaub, *Zauber des Spiegels*, p. 159 and Schwarz, "The Mirror in Art," p. 103.

22. Grabes, *Speculum*, pp. 288-351; Louis B. Wright, *Middle-Class Culture in Elizabethan England*, Ithaca, New York, 1958, provides interesting comments on representative examples—pp. 105-06, 137-38, 190, 193-94, 212, 293, 334-35, 378-79, 424-25, and 552. Today, the most famous example is probably the *Mirror for Magistrates*, but there were many others.

23. See Sister Rita Mary Bradley, "Backgrounds of the Title *Speculum* in Medieval Literature," p. 112.

24. Leon Battista Alberti, *On Painting and on Sculpture*, ed. Cecil Grayson, London, 1972, p. 89, par. 46, and see also Schwarz, "The Mirror in Art," p. 111.

25. Hartlaub, *Zauber des Spiegels*, pp. 13-14, and *Leonardo da Vinci's Notebooks*, ed. Edward McCurdy, New York, 1923, pp. 163, 165, 167-69.

26. For the *Mona Lisa*, see Pope-Hennessy, *The Portrait in the Renaissance*, p. 108, who points out the contradictory visual elements; see also my "'Ut Pictura Poesis': Shared Principles of Organization in Painting and in Shakespearean Drama," in *Shakespeare's Art from a Com-*

*parative Perspective*, ed. Wendell M. Aycock, Lubbock, Texas, 1981, pp. 119-29, which compares *Hamlet* and the *Mona Lisa*. For Michelangelo's references to the mirror, see *A Documentary History of Art: Volume One: The Middle Ages and the Renaissance*, ed. Elizabeth Gilmore Holt, Garden City, N.Y., 1957, p. 284.

27. Seventeenth-century English poets associated painting with a mirror or glass, and typically within a moral context, as when Abraham Cowley declared of Van Dyck that he "did out-pass/ The mimic imag'ry of Looking-glass" in his memorial poem "On the Death of Sir Anthony Vandike, The famous Painter," in *The Complete Works in Verse and Prose of Abraham Cowley*, 2 vols., ed. Alexander B. Grosart, Edinburgh, 1881, vol. 1, p. 138. Similarly, William Strode reflected on the magnificent stained glass of Fairford Church that "you may think each picture was/ Some visage in a looking-glass," in his poem "On Fayrford Windowes," in *The Poetical Works of William Strode (1600-1645)*, ed. Bertram Dobell, London, 1907, pp. 25-27. Late in the century, Matthew Prior praised a group portrait which "as in some glass is well discry'd," but without the same didactic emphasis, in "To the Right Honourable the Countess Dowager of Devonshire, On a Piece of Wissin's; Whereon were all her Grandsons Painted," in *The Literary Works of Matthew Prior*, ed. H. Bunker Wright and Monrow K. Spears, Oxford, 1959, vol. 1, pp. 79-80.

28. Erwin Panofsky, "Van Eyck's Arnolfini Portrait," *Burlington Magazine*, vol. 64 (1934), pp. 117-27, and reprinted in Creighton Gilbert, ed., *Renaissance Art*, New York, 1970, pp. 1-20, from which it is cited here.

29. *Ibid.*, p. 12.

30. The interior mirror did not always reflect significantly upon the central concerns of a painting, as it did in the *Arnolfini Marriage*. Fifteen years after Van Eyck's painting, Petrus Christus executed his *Legend of St. Elegius* (in the Lehman Collection, Metropolitan Museum) which shows that goldsmith-saint in his workshop, visited by a young couple. The mirror on the shop counter is spherical, and directed outward beyond the shop which the artist takes as his primary focus to reveal the larger world. The function of the mirror here, as Wolfgang Zucker put it, is to expand "the space of the room to the outside," and it is in this one way (and in it alone) comparable to the function of the play-within-the-play in *Hamlet*, except that the outward-turned mirror in the Christus painting seems "totally unrelated to the content of the painting."— Zucker, "Reflections on Reflections," p. 242, and Schwarz, "The Mirror in Art," p. 103. In *Hamlet*, on the other hand, the mirror reflects the outside world so as to provide insight into the primary world of the play itself. Shakespeare's use of the mirror-metaphor thus corresponds more closely to the pattern of Jan Van Eyck than to that of Petrus Christus: the mirror is employed to provide insight into the interior world of the play or painting, and not just to expand it.

31. Zucker, "Reflections on Reflections," p. 241.

32. Panofsky, "Van Eyck's Arnolfini Portrait," pp. 18f.

*Appendix B*

1. The Danes' reputation as topers clearly distresses Hamlet, whereas Iago only found it amusing (*Oth.* 2.3.73-77).

2. The reference to Tchaikovsky is anachronistic, but it makes a valid point. As a character, Claudius is obsessed with artillery and gunfire. His speech is peppered with logistical similes— "as level as the cannon to his blank," "like to a murd'ring piece," "send thee hence with fiery quickness," and of course the festive noise when "the great cannon to the clouds shall tell" (4.1.42; 4.3.42; 4.5.95; 1.2.125).

*Appendix C*

1. See *The Annotated Book of Common Prayer*, ed. John Henry Blunt, New York, 1891, p. 477. For a thorough history and coverage of the canons, see Charles Moore, *A Full Inquiry into the Subject of Suicide*, 2 vols., London, 1790, vol. 1, pp. 286-322.

2. See *Decretum Gratiani*, ed. A. Friedberg, Leipzig, 1879, col. 935—Pars Secunda, causa 23, Q.5, Cap. 12.

3. Henry de Bracton, *Bracton de Legibus et Consuetudinibus Angliae*, trans. Samuel E. Thorne, ed. George E. Woodbine, Cambridge, Mass., 1968, p. 424.

4. Quoted in Richard Burn, *Ecclesiastical Law*, vol. 3, p. 378, and vol. 1, p. 266.

5. Edgar I. Fripp, *Shakespeare Man and Artist*, London, 1964, vol. 1, pp. 146f. cites the case of a specific charge given to a coroner's inquest in Stratford-upon-Avon in February 1617, to decide about a traveler, who drowned in the Avon, whether he did "willfully drown himself, yes or no." In another case of a drowning death, adjudged an accident by the court, Fripp assumes that burial would have been by "maimèd rites," but he provides no evidence for this assumption, which does not accord with general practice of allowing full rites to those who died an accidental death and not from chosen suicide. Although it is historically demonstrable that sane and willful suicides were denied Christian burial, no reference to such denial appeared in any edition of the Book of Common Prayer before 1662, and to that the standard exception for insanity also applied. H. Mutschmann and K. Wentersdorf, *Shakespeare and Catholicism* (New York, 1952, pp. 238-39, and 282-83) demonstrate the superficiality of their knowledge of Church of England practice and doctrine on this as on other matters, but what is most remarkable is their unawareness of the full Catholic tradition according Christian burial to insane suicides. A superficial awareness of the tradition, laws, and actual practices in cases of *non compos mentis* suicides also mars Draper's treatment in *The "Hamlet" of Shakespeare's Audience*, pp. 89-93.

6. Robert Burton, *The Anatomy of Melancholy*, ed. Floyd Dell and Paul Jordan-Smith, New York, 1948, Part III, Section IV, Number 2, Subsection 5, p. 949.

7. Moore, *Suicide*, vol. 1, pp. 318-19.

8. Thomas Rogers Forbes, "London Coroner's Inquests for 1590," *Journal of the History of Medicine and Allied Sciences*, vol. 28 (1973), p. 378.

9. The differences may be due to increased care in reporting and recording instances, rather than an increase in absolute numbers. *That* problem is, fortunately, one we do not need to investigate here.

10. E. K. Chambers, *William Shakespeare*, Oxford, 1930, vol. 2, p. 356. Edgar I. Fripp, *Shakespeare Man and Artist*, vol. 1, p. 4, posits an ancestral connection between the dramatist's family and land granted to earlier Shakespeares at Balsall by Henry VII, and finds evidence of some acquaintanceship between the Balsall and Stratford Shakespeares during William's childhood.

11. I am deeply indebted to Professor Terence R. Murphy of American University for sharing with me some of his yet unpublished results, which yield the statistics I have cited above. When Professor Murphy has completed his collection and analysis of this data, his published work will contribute to our understanding in very basic ways.

12. There is an account of the 1657 burial of suicide Miles Sindercome in the anonymous pamphlet, *The Whole Business of Sindercome*, 1657, pp. 15-16. The burial of suicides at a crossroad with the stake through the heart was not legally abolished until 1823—see S. E. Sprott, *The English Debate on Suicide*, p. 157, and Keith Thomas, *Religion and the Decline of Magic*, Harmondsworth, Middlesex, 1980, p. 711.

13. The verdict of willful suicide had the effect not only of degrading Hales' funeral but also of alienating his property from his family, and it passed first to the crown, and thence (I

presume by sale but perhaps as patronage) to others. We thus have here a notable exception to the gravedigger's rule "that great folk . . . have count'nance in this world to drown or hang themselves more than their even-Christen" (5.1.25f.).

14. For a Protestant view of this matter, see John Hooper, "A Brief Treatise Respecting Judge Hales" in *Later Writings*, pp. 374-80, and 592.

15. The quotation is from p. 105 of *Shakespeare's Legal Acquirements Considered*, New York, 1859, by John, Lord Campbell, Chief Justice under Queen Victoria. The case of Hales vz. Petit is reported at length in Edmund Plowden, *Commentaries*, London, 1761, pp. 253-64. The legal arguments were intricate and of that chop-logic variety which is easy to parody. Indeed, it has been said that the First Gravedigger's speeches do parody those arguments: see *New Variorum Hamlet*, vol. 1, pp. 376-77. Edmond Malone maintains, however, that we cannot assume Shakespeare to have read the law records in Old French legalese, and points out that those records were not translated into English until long after his death: see Malone's ed., *Plays and Poems*, 10 vols., London, 1790, vol. 9, p. 386, note to *Ham.* 5.1.4. For a clarification of the legal issues and of the putative relation to Shakespeare, see Campbell, *op. cit.*, 106-09. Other responsible treatments may be found in Sir Dunbar Plunket Barton, *Links Between Shakespeare and the Law*, Boston, 1929, pp. 51-54, and in Cushman K. Davis, *The Law in Shakespeare*, St. Paul, Minn., 1884, reprinted by AMS Press, New York, 1972, pp. 260-66. On the other hand, R. S. Guernsey, *Ecclesiastical Law in Hamlet: The Burial of Ophelia*, first printed in the 1880's and imprudently reprinted in New York in 1971, is to be pervasively mistrusted as a remarkable interweaving of occasional fact with fiction taken as fact or of fact misunderstood and distorted.

16. Thomas Rogers Forbes, *Chronicle from Aldgate: Life and Death in Shakespeare's London*, New Haven, 1971, pp. 164-65 and 169.

17. *Ibid.*, pp. 164 and 170.

18. This entry from the parish register at Pleasley in Derbyshire is as explicit as one might find anywhere. In another case, a prisoner in custody of the law attempted to escape and was drowned when he leapt into a river on June 28, 1620, at St. Alkmund's, Derby; he was adjudged a sane and willful suicide and was buried by the highway near the foot of the bridge from which he plunged—J. Charles Cox, *Parish Registers*, pp. 114-15.

19. Forbes, *Chronicle from Aldgate*, p. 31.

20. This case, which is preserved in the James Halliwell-Phillipps' files, exemplifies the irresponsible way in which Halliwell-Phillipps would simply clip out printed passages from very early books, and paste them into his scrapbooks, often without any evidence of particular source, and with a flagrant disregard for anything else of value in the pillaged publication. The instance appears to be from the time of Shakespeare, when judged by its placing. Although the phrase "temporary insanity" seems rather later, it may represent a translation or paraphrase from an earlier account. The clipping may be found in the Halliwell-Phillipps file-box numbered E3 at the Folger Shakespeare Library in Washington.

21. Cox, *Parish Registers*, pp. 114-15.

22. Thus Cox's report of the burial of Anne Ruter on the north side of the church (mentioned above), may suggest a kind of discrimination. When Mary Play of East Smithsfield poisoned herself in the house of her master, she was interred in "our new churchyard without any burial service" by virtue of "a license from my Lord Bishop of London," according to Forbes, *Chronicles from Aldgate* p. 170. No date is given. Moore, *Suicide*, vol. 1, p. 308 records a case in 1578 when a bishop (Alymer?) investigated a suicide who had cut his own throat, found some last signs of repentance, and allowed Christian burial—perhaps a case of a bishop's upgrading of a coroner's disposition. But I have found no reference to any case of downgrading a coroner's verdict, or any hint of such.

23. *The Diary of Henry Machyn, Citizen and Merchant-Tailor of London, from A.D. 1550 to A.D. 1563*, ed. John Gough Nichols, London: Camden Society vol. 42, 1848, p. 284. For the more usual practice which Machyn reports of the clerks singing the body to burial, see p. 247.

24. Clergy of all churches were responsible for protecting graveyards in their care from *pollutio cimiterii*, but the "churlish priest" in *Hamlet* has explicit and official protection against that in the verdict of the coroner's court.

25. The funeral for Lady Jane Seymour exemplifies what was expected by a young lady of the court who died a natural death (I have found no record of such a person committing suicide). Held "in great favor" as one of Elizabeth's "maids," Lady Jane was buried at Westminster Abbey with great formality: all the choir of the Abbey was in attendance, along with scores of members of the Queen's court, "lords and ladies, and gentleman and gentlewomen, all in black, beside others of the Queen's Privy Chamber, and she [had] a great banner of arms borne, and Master Clarenceau was the Herald, and Master Skameler the new Bishop of Peterborough did preach." See account in *The Diary of Henry Machyn*, p. 254. A somewhat simpler Scottish funeral held on March 27, 1633, in Edinburgh for the seventeen-year-old Margaret Ross, Lady Keir, is described by a contemporary observer in William Fraser, *The Sterlings of Keir and Their Family Papers*, Edinburgh, 1858, pp. 51-54, which was the least that was expected in the natural course of things for someone of Ophelia's age and station in life. Shakespeare could not have reproduced in full such formal and heraldic rites on the Globe stage, and it was not his purpose to do so, but he never had difficulty suggesting even more elaborate ceremonies and inspiring his audience to imagine them. With Ophelia's funeral, however, he wished us to imagine nothing beyond the stark reality which appears before us. When Ophelia's brief cortege enters the Globe stage, Hamlet at once recognizes that these are "maimèd rites," and by his words he insures that the audience will be alert to the anomalies involved.

26. Wilson, *What Happens in "Hamlet,"* pp. 295-300, and Draper, *The "Hamlet" of Shakespeare's Audience*, pp. 88f.

27. *Decretum Gratiani*, loc. cit., n. 2 above.

28. *The Diary of Henry Machyn*, p. 284.

29. Alec Robertson, *Requiem: Music of Mourning and Consolation*, London, 1967, pp. 53-54. Requiem masses were frequently endowed to be said, of course, as Robertson notes.

30. Richmond Noble, *Shakespeare's Biblical Knowledge*, p. 85, misses the point of "sing a requiem" here, and is unaware of the provisions for Latin requiem masses in the Church of England; see Rifkin, *Burial*, pp. 9-10.

31. William P. Haugaard, *Elizabeth and the English Reformation: The Struggle for a Stable Settlement of Religion*, Cambridge, 1970, pp. 113 and 115.

32. *Ibid.*, p. 124.

33. Wilson, *What Happens in "Hamlet,"* p. 299. But it should be emphasized once again that the identification of the officiant as Protestant or Catholic is of relatively less importance, whereas his violation of established doctrine and practice in either and both contexts is immensely important.

34. *The Diary of Henry Machyn*, p. 188.

35. Macquoid, "The Home . . . Funerals" in Shakespeare's England, vol. 2, p. 150, quotes the passage without assigning a source. The same passage is quoted in James Brand, *Observations on Popular Antiquities*, ed. and rev. by Henry Ellis, London, 1813, vol. II, p. 173n, with a reference to *Greene in Conceipt*, London, 1598, p. 43.

36. *The Book of Common Prayer . . .* , ed. Richard Mant, p. 488.

37. *Ibid.*, p. 489, and see also "The Order for the Burial of the Dead," in *Liturgies and*

*Occasional Forms of Prayer Set Forth in the Reign of Queen Elizabeth*, pp. 233-34, and *The Annotated Book of Common Prayer*, ed. John Henry Blunt, pp. 480f.

38. *The Diary of Henry Machyn*, pp. 211-12, 188-90, and 286.

39. *The Zurich Letters: 1558-79*, ed. Hastings Robinson, p. 137.

40. Myra Rifkin, *Burial*, p. 56.

41. Horton Davies, *Worship and Theology in England from Cranmer to Hooker: 1534-1603*, Princeton, 1970, pp. 401-02; E. H. Fellowes, *English Cathedral Music*, rev. J. A. Westrup, London, 1969, p. 80; Peter Le Huray, *Music and the Reformation in England: 1549-1660*, London, 1967, p. 248.

42. E.G.P. Wyatt, *The Burial Service*, Oxford, 1918, p. 6.

# Bibliography

Unless otherwise specified, all entries with publishing dates prior to 1800 may be assumed to have been published in London. The spelling of titles has been modernized.

Abbott, E. A., *A Shakespearean Grammar*, New York, 1966.

Abrams, M. H., *The Mirror and the Lamp*, New York, 1958.

Acton, *see* Dalberg-Acton

Aelian, *A Register of Histories*, trans. Abraham Fleming, 1576.

Alberti, Leon Battista, *On Painting and on Sculpture*, ed. Cecil Grayson, London, 1972.

Alexander, Nigel, *Poison, Play, and Duel: A Study in Hamlet*, Lincoln, Nebraska, 1971.

Alexander, Peter, *Hamlet: Father and Son*, Oxford, 1955.

Allen, J. W., *A History of Political Thought in the Sixteenth Century*, New York, 1957.

Allen, M. B., "Hamlet's 'To be or not to be' Soliloquy," *SAB*, vol. 13 (1938), pp. 195-207.

Allen, William, *A True, Sincere, and Modest Defense of English Catholics*, ed. Robert M. Kingdon, Ithaca, New York and Washington, 1965.

Althusius, Johannes, *The Politics*, trans. Frederick S. Carney, Boston, 1964.

Anderson, James, *Collections Relating to Mary Queen of Scots*, Edinburgh, 1727-28.

Anderson, M. D., *History and Imagery in British Churches*, Edinburgh, 1971.

Andrewes, Lancelot, *XCVI Sermons*, 1629.

*The Annotated Book of Common Prayer*, ed. John Henry Blunt, New York, 1891.

Aquinas, Thomas, *Selected Political Writings*, ed. A. P. d'Entrèves, Oxford, 1948.

Aquinas, Thomas, *Summa Theologica*, ed. Fathers of the English Dominican Province, 3 vols., New York, 1947.

Aquinas, Thomas, *Theological Texts*, ed. Thomas Gilby, London and New York, 1955.

Ariès, Philippe, *The Hour of Our Death*, New York, 1981.

Aristotle, *Politics*, ed. Benjamin Jowett, 2 vols., Oxford, 1885.

Assheton, Nicholas, *The Journal of Nicholas Assheton*, ed. Reverend F. R. Raines, Manchester, 1848.

Bagly, Thomas, *The Royal Charter Granted unto Kings by God Himself: and collected out of His Holy Word in both Testaments*, 1682.

Bailey, Margery, "Shakespeare in Action," *College English*, vol. 15 (1954), pp. 307-15.

Bainton, Roland H., *Erasmus of Christendom*, New York, 1969.

Bainton, Roland H., *Here I Stand: A Life of Martin Luther*, New York, 1950.

Barasch, Moshe, *Gestures of Despair in Medieval and Early Renaissance Art*, New York, 1976.

Barton, Dunbar Plunket, *Links Between Shakespeare and the Law*, Boston, 1929.

Bateman, Stephen, *The Doom Warning All Men to Judgment*, 1581.

Bateman, Stephen, *The Travayled Pylgrime*, 1568.

Battenhouse, Roy W., "The Ghost in Hamlet: A Catholic 'Linchpin'?" *Studies in Philology*, vol. 48 (1951), pp. 161-92.

Battenhouse, Roy W., "The 'Old Mole' of Hamlet 1.5.162," *N&Q*, n.s., vol. 216 (1971), pp. 145-46.

Battenhouse, Roy W., *Shakespearean Tragedy:*

*Its Art and Its Christian Premises*, Bloomington, Indiana, 1969.

Baylor, Michael G., *Action and Person: Conscience in Late Scholasticism and the Young Luther*, Leiden, 1977.

Bebbington, W. G., "Soliloquy?" *TLS*, March 3, 1969, p. 289.

Beck, Margaret M., "The Dance of Death in Shakespeare," *MLN*, vol. 37 (1922), pp. 372-74.

Becon, Thomas, *The Catechism with Other Pieces*, ed. John Ayre, Cambridge, 1844.

Becon, Thomas, *Early Works*, ed. John Ayre, Cambridge, 1843.

Becon, Thomas, *Prayers and Other Pieces*, ed. John Ayre, Cambridge, 1844.

Bentley, Gerald Eades, *The Jacobean and Caroline Stage*, 7 vols., Oxford, 1941-68.

de Bèze, Théodore, *Du Droit des Magistrats*, ed. Robert Kingdon, Geneva, 1970.

de Bèze, Théodore, *Right of Magistrates*, trans. Henri-Louis Gonin, in *Constitutionalism and Resistance*, ed. Julian H. Franklin, New York, 1969, pp. 97-135.

Bible—*see Interpreter's Bible*.

Bilson, Thomas, *The True Difference between Christian Subjection and Unchristian Rebellion*, Oxford, 1585.

Blunt, Anthony, *Art and Architecture in France 1500-1700*, Harmondsworth, Middlesex, 1973.

Boase, Thomas S. R., *Death in the Middle Ages*, London, 1972.

Bond, Francis, *Wood Carving in English Churches: Bishops' Thrones and Chancel Chairs*, London and New York, 1910.

*The Book of Catholic Quotations*, ed. John Capin, New York, 1956.

Book of Common Prayer, see also *The Annotated Book of Common Prayer*, and *The Book of Common Prayer with Notes Explanatory . . .*

*The Book of Common Prayer with Notes Explanatory, Practical and Historical*, ed. Richard Mant, Oxford, 1820.

Boose, Lynda E., "The Father and the Bride," *PMLA*, vol. 97 (1982), pp. 325-47.

Bossy, John, *The English Catholic Community: 1570-1850*, London, 1975.

Botero, Giovanni, *The Reason of State*, trans. P. J. and D. P. Waley, New Haven, Connecticut, 1956.

Bowers, Fredson, "Dramatic Structure and Criticism: Plot in *Hamlet*," *SQ*, vol. 15 (1964), pp. 207-18.

Bowers, Fredson, *Elizabethan Revenge Tragedy: 1587-1642*, Princeton, 1940.

Bowers, Fredson, "Hamlet's Fifth Soliloquy, 3.2.406-17," in *Essays on Shakespeare and Elizabethan Drama in Honor of Hardin Craig*, ed. Richard Hosley, Columbia, Missouri, 1962, pp. 213-22.

Bowers, Fredson, "Hamlet as Minister and Scourge," *PMLA*, vol. 70 (1955), pp. 740-49.

de Bracton, Henry, *Bracton de Legibus et Consuetudinibus Angliae*, 2 vols., trans. Samuel E. Thorne, ed. George E. Woodbine, Cambridge, Massachusetts, 1968.

Bradford, John, *The Writings, Containing Sermons, Meditations, Examinations, etc.*, ed. Aubrey Townsend, Cambridge, 1848.

Bradford, John, *Writings: Sermons*, ed. Aubrey Townsend, Cambridge, 1848.

Bradley, A. C., *Shakespearean Tragedy*, London, 1964.

Bradley, Rita Mary, "Backgrounds of the Title *Speculum* in Medieval Literature," *Speculum*, vol. 29 (1954), pp. 100-15.

Brand, John, *Observations on Popular Antiquities* (arr. and rev. by Henry Ellis), 2 vols., London, 1813.

Brathwait, Richard, *A Spiritual Spicery*, 1638.

Brinkworth, E.R.C., *Shakespeare and the Bawdy Court of Stratford*, London, 1972.

Britten, F. J., *Old Clocks and Watches*, London and New York, 1911.

Brown, Peter Hume, *George Buchanan*, Edinburgh, 1890.

Browne, Thomas, *The Prose of Sir Thomas Browne*, ed. Norman Endicott, New York, 1967.

Buchanan, George, *De Jure Regni Apud Scotos*, trans. Charles F. Arrowood, Austin, Texas, 1949.

Buchanan, George, *Detection of the Doings of Mary Queen of Scots*, St. Andrews, 1572.

Buchanan, George, *The Tyrannous Reign of*

*Mary Stuart: George Buchanan's Account*, trans. and ed. W. A. Gatherer, Edinburgh, 1958.

Bullinger, Henry, *Decades*, ed. Thomas Harding, 4 vols. in 3, Cambridge, 1849-52.

Bullough, Geoffrey, *Narrative and Dramatic Sources of Shakespeare*, 8 vols., London and New York, 1957-75.

Burn, Richard, *The Ecclesiastical Law*, 4 vols., ed. Robert P. Tyrwhitt, London, 1824.

Burton, Robert, *The Anatomy of Melancholy*, ed. Floyd Dell and Paul Jordan-Smith, New York, 1948.

Buxton, John, *Elizabethan Taste*, London, 1963.

Byrne, St. Geraldine, *Shakespeare's Use of the Pronoun of Address; its Significance in Characterization and Motivation*, Washington, 1936.

Calfhill, James, *An Answer to John Martiall's Treatise*, ed. Richard Gibbings, Cambridge, 1846.

Calvin, John, *Calvin: Commentaries*, trans. Joseph Haroutunian and Louise Pettibone Smith, in *The Library of Christian Classics*, vol. 23, Philadelphia, 1948.

Calvin, John, *Commentaries*, 22 vols., Grand Rapids, Michigan, 1981.

Calvin, John, *Institutes of the Christian Religion*, 2 vols., ed. John T. McNeill, trans. Ford Lewis Battles, Philadelpia, 1960.

Calvin, John, *The Institution of the Christian Religion*, trans. Thomas Norton, 1611.

Calvin, John, *Sermons upon the Book of Job*, trans. Arthur Golding, 1574.

Camden, Carroll, *The Elizabethan Woman*, Houston and New York, 1952.

Camden, William, *Annals, or the History of the Most Renowned and Virtuous Princess Elizabeth, Late Queen of England*, 1635.

Camden, William, *The Funeral Procession of Queen Elizabeth*, London, 1791.

Campbell, Lord John, *Shakespeare's Legal Acquirements Considered*, New York, 1859.

Campbell, Lily B., *Shakespeare's "Histories:" Mirrors of Elizabethan Policy*, San Marino, California, 1968.

Campbell, Lily B., *Shakespeare's Tragic Heroes: Slaves of Passion*, New York, 1930.

Cardano, Girolano, *Cardanus' Comfort*, 1573 and 1576.

Castiglione, Baldassare, *The Book of the Courtier*, trans. Thomas Hoby, ed. Walter Raleigh, New York, 1967.

Caw, James L., *Scottish Portraits with an Historical and Critical Introduction and Notes*, London and Boston, 1903.

*Cebes' Tablet*, ed. Sandra Sider, New York, 1979.

Cecil, David, *The Cecils*, Boston, 1973.

Cecil, William, *"The Execution of Justice in England" by William Cecil and "A True, Sincere, and Modest Defense of English Catholics" by William Allen*, ed. Robert M. Kingdon, Ithaca, New York, and Washington, 1965.

Cescinsky, Herbert, and Gribble, Ernest R., *Early English Furniture and Woodwork*, 2 vols., London, 1922.

Chamberlain, John, *The Letters*, 2 vols., ed. Norman E. McClure, Philadelphia, 1939.

Chambers, E. K., *The Elizabethan Stage*, 4 vols., Oxford, 1951.

Chambers, E. K., *William Shakespeare*, 2 vols., Oxford, 1930.

Chapman, Raymond, "The Wheel of Fortune in Shakespeare's Historical Plays," *RES*, vol. 1 (1950), pp. 1-7.

Charney, Maurice, "The 'Now Could I Drink Hot Blood' Soliloquy and the Middle of Hamlet," *Mosaic*, vol. 10 (1977), pp. 77-86.

Charney, Maurice, *Style in "Hamlet,"* Princeton, 1969.

Chenevière, Marc-Edouard, *La Pensée Politique de Calvin*, Geneva and Paris, 1937.

Chew, Samuel C., *The Pilgrimage of Life*, Port Washington, New York, 1973.

Chew, Samuel C., *The Virtues Reconciled*, Toronto, 1947.

Clancy, Thomas H. S., S.J., *Papist Pamphleteers: The Allen-Persons Party and the Political Thought of the Counter-Reformation in England, 1572-1615*, Chicago, 1964.

Clark, J. M., *The Dance of Death in the Middle Ages and the Renaissance*, Glasgow, 1950.

Cohen, Kathleen, *Metamorphosis of a Death Symbol: The Transi Tomb in the Late Middle Ages and The Renaissance*, Berkeley, 1973.

Colavechio, Xavier G., *Erroneous Conscience and Obligations*, Washington, 1961.

Colie, Rosalie, *Shakespeare's Living Art*, Princeton, 1974.

Conklin, Paul S., *A History of "Hamlet" Criticism*, New York, 1968.

Copley, Anthony, *A Fig for Fortune*, 1596.

Council, Norman, *When Honour's at the Stake: Ideas of Honour in Shakespeare's Plays*, London, 1973.

Coursen, Herbert R., Jr., *Christian Ritual and the World of Shakespeare's Tragedies*, Lewisburg, Pennsylvania, 1976.

Cousin, Jean, *El Libro de la Fortuna*, Buenos Aires, 1947.

Coverdale, Miles, *Remains*, ed. George Pearson, Cambridge, 1846.

Cowan, Ian B., *The Enigma of Mary Stuart*, New York, 1971.

Cowley, Abraham, *The Complete Works in Verse and Prose of Abraham Cowley*, 2 vols., ed. Alexander B. Grosart, Edinburgh, 1881.

Cox, J. Charles, *The Parish Registers of England*, London, 1910.

Craig, Hardin, "Hamlet as a Man of Action," *HLQ*, vol. 27 (1964), pp. 229-37.

Cranmer, Thomas, *Miscellaneous Writings and Letters*, ed. John E. Cox, Cambridge, 1846.

Cranmer, Thomas, *The Work of Thomas Cranmer*, ed. G. E. Duffield, Philadelphia, 1965.

Cranstoun, James, ed., *Satirical Poems of the Time of the Reformation*, 2 vols., Edinburgh, 1891-93.

Cuddon, J. A., *A Dictionary of Literary Terms*, Garden City, New York, 1977.

Cunningham, J. V., *Woe or Wonder: The Emotional Effect of Shakespearean Tragedy*, Denver, Colorado, 1951.

Cunnington, Phyllis, and Lucas, Catherine, *Costume for Births, Marriages and Deaths*, New York, 1972.

Curtius, Ernst Robert, *European Literature and the Latin Middle Ages*, Princeton, 1953.

Dalberg-Acton, John E. E., *Lectures on Modern History*, London, 1950.

Davey, Richard, *A History of Mourning*, London, n.d.

Davidson, Clifford, "Death in his Court," *Studies in Iconography*, vol. 1 (1977), pp. 74-86.

Davies, Horton, *Worship and Theology in England: 1534-1608*, Princeton, 1970.

Davies, Sir John, *Nosce Teipsum* in *The Poems of Sir John Davies*, ed. Clare Howard, New York, 1941.

Davies, Martin, *National Gallery Catalogue of Early Netherlandish School*, London, 1968.

Davis, Cushman K., *The Law in Shakespeare*, New York, 1972.

Day, Richard, *A Book of Christian Prayers*, 1578.

Dent, R. W., "*Hamlet* 1.5.162: 'Well said, Old Mole,' " *N&Q*, vol. 215 (1970), pp. 128-29.

Dent, R. W., *Shakespeare's Proverbial Language: An Index*, Berkeley and Los Angeles, 1981.

Dessen, Alan C., *Elizabethan Drama and the Viewer's Eye*, Chapel Hill, North Carolina, 1977.

Devlin, Christopher, *Hamlet's Divinity*, London, 1963.

Dibdin, Lewis, and Healey, Charles, *English Church Law and Divorce*, London, 1912.

Dickinson, William Croft, *Scotland from the Earliest Times to 1603*, ed. A.A.M. Duncan, Oxford, 1977.

*Dictionary of National Biography*, ed. Leslie Stephen, Sidney Lee, s.v. "Bilson," London, 1886.

*Discussions of Hamlet*, ed. J. C. Levenson, Boston, 1960.

Doebler, John, *Shakespeare's Speaking Pictures: Studies in Iconic Imagery*, Albuquerque, New Mexico, 1974.

Donaldson, Gordon, *Mary Queen of Scots*, London, 1974.

Donaldson, Gordon, *Scotland: James V to James VII*, New York, 1966.

Donne, John, *The Poems of John Donne*, ed. Herbert J. C. Grierson, London, 1945.

Donne, John, *The Works of John Donne*, ed. H. Alford, 6 vols., London, 1839.

Donovan, James L., "A Note on Hamlet's 'Not Shriving Time Allow'd'," *Notes and Queries*, vol. 201 (November, 1956), pp. 467f.

Downame, John, *Spiritual Physick*, 1600.

Drake-Brockman, J. A., "Shakespeare's *Hamlet* 1.4.24," *Explicator*, vol. 32 (1973), no. 4.

Draper, John, *The "Hamlet" of Shakespeare's Audience*, Durham, North Carolina, 1938.

Dugdale, William, *History of St. Paul's Cathedral*, 1658.

Dugdale, William, *Monastici Anglicani*, London, 1673.

*Dutch Mannerism: Apogee and Epilogue*, Poughkeepsie, New York, 1970.

Duthie, G. I., *The "Bad" Quarto of "Hamlet": A Critical Study*, Cambridge, 1941.

*Early Italian Engravings from the National Gallery of Art*, ed. Jill Levenson, Konrad Oberhuber, and Jacquelyn L. Sheehan, Washington, 1973.

Eastman, Arthur M., *A Short History of Shakespearean Criticism*, New York, 1958.

Eliot, T. S., *Essays*, New York, 1950.

Eliot, T. S., *Murder in the Cathedral*, New York, 1935.

Eliot, T. S., *Selected Poems*, New York, 1934.

Emmison, F. G., *Elizabethan Life: Disorder*, Chelmsford, Essex, 1970.

Emmison, F. G., *Elizabethan Life: Morals and the Church Courts Mainly from Essex Archidiaconal Records*, Chelmsford, Essex, 1973.

*Encyclopedia Britannica*, 11th ed., 28 vols., New York, 1911.

*Encyclopedia of World Art*, 15 vols., New York and London, 1959-68.

Erasmus, Desiderius, *The Education of a Christian Prince*, ed. Lester K. Born, New York, 1936.

Erasmus, Desiderius, *Enchiridion*, trans. Miles Coverdale, in Coverdale's *Writings and Translations*, ed. George Pearson, Cambridge, 1844.

Erlanger, Philippe, *St. Bartholomew's Night*, trans. Patrick O'Brian, London, 1960.

Esdaile, Katherine A., *English Church Monuments 1510-1840*, New York, [1946].

Evans, G. B., "Textual Notes," *The Riverside Shakespeare*, ed. G. B. Evans, Boston, 1974.

Faber, Melvyn Donald, *Suicide in Shakespeare*, 1964 doctoral dissertation at University of California, Los Angeles.

Fairchild, Arthur, *Shakespeare and the Arts of Design*, Columbia, Missouri, 1937.

Fellowes, E. H., *English Cathedral Music*, rev. J. A. Westrup, London, 1969.

Fisher, John, *Sermon [at] . . . St. Paul's*, 1509.

Fitz-Geffrey, Charles, *Sir Francis Drake*, 1596.

Fleming, David Hay, *Mary Queen of Scots: from her Birth to her Flight into England*, London, 1898.

Forbes, Thomas, *Chronicle from Aldgate*, New Haven, 1971.

Forbes, Thomas, "London Coroner's Inquests for 1590," *Journal of the History of Medicine and Allied Sciences*, vol. 28 (1973), pp. 376-86.

Franklin, Julian H., ed., *Constitutionalism and Resistance in the Sixteenth Century: Three Treatises, Hotman, Bèze, and Mornay*, New York, 1969.

Fraser, Antonia, *Mary Queen of Scots*, London, 1969.

Fraser, William, *The Sterlings of Keir and Their Family Papers*, Edinburgh, 1858.

Fraunce, Abraham, *The Lawyer's Logic*, 1588.

French, A. L., *Shakespeare and the Critics*, Cambridge, 1972.

Fripp, Edgar I., *Shakespeare Man and Artist*, 2 vols., London, 1964.

Frye, Roland Mushat, *Shakespeare: The Art of the Dramatist*, London and Boston, 1982.

Frye, Roland Mushat, *Shakespeare and Christian Doctrine*, Princeton, 1963.

Frye, Roland Mushat, " 'Ut Pictura Poesis': Shared Principles of Organization in Painting and in Shakespearean Drama," *Shakespeare's Art From A Comparative Perspective*, ed. Wendell M. Aycock, Lubbock, Texas, 1981, pp. 101-29.

Fulke, William, *A Defense of the Translations of the Holy Scriptures into English*, ed. Charles H. Hartshorne, Cambridge, 1843.

Galinsky, G. Karl, *The Herakles Theme*, Oxford, 1972.

Gardner, Helen, *The Business of Criticism*, Oxford, 1959.

Gascoigne, George, *The Glass of Government*, ed. John W. Cunliffe, Cambridge, 1910.

*The Geneva Bible: A Facsimile of the 1560 Edition*, intro. Lloyd E. Berry, Madison, Wisconsin, 1969.

Gibson, Walter S., *Hieronymus Bosch*, London, 1973.

Giesey, Ralph E., "The Juristic Basis of Dynastic Right to the French Throne," *Transactions of the American Philosophical Society*, N.S., vol. 51, part 5, 1961, pp. 1-47.

Giesey, Ralph E., *Royal Funeral Ceremony in Renaissance France*, Geneva, 1960.

Gilby, Thomas, *The Political Thought of Thomas Aquinas*, Chicago, 1958.

Goethe, Johann Wolfgang von, *Great Writings of Goethe*, ed. Stephen Spender, New York, 1958.

Gossage, A. J., "Plutarch," *Latin Biography*, ed. T. A. Dorey, New York and London, 1967, pp. 45-78.

Gottschalk, Paul, "Hamlet and the Scanning of Revenge," *SQ*, vol. 24 (1973), pp. 155-70.

Gottschalk, Paul, *The Meanings of Hamlet: Modes of Literary Interpretations since Bradley*, Albuquerque, New Mexico, 1972.

Gouge, William, *Of Domestical Duties*, 1622.

Gough, Richard, *Sepulchral Monuments of Great Britain*, 5 vols., London, 1786.

Grabes, Herbert, *Speculum, Mirror und Looking-Glass*, Tübingen, 1973.

Granville-Barker, Harley, *Preface to Hamlet*, New York, 1957.

Gratian, *Decretum Magistri Gratiani*, ed. A. Friedberg, Leipzig, 1879.

Grauls, J., "Taalkundige tochlichting bij her Hooi en den Hooiwagen," *Gentsche Bijdragen*, vol. 5 (1938), pp. 156-75.

Grebanier, Bernard, *The Heart of Hamlet*, New York, 1960.

Greene, Richard Leighton, "Hamlet's Skimmington," from *Evidence in Literary Scholarship: Essays in Honor of James Marshall Osborn*, ed. René Wellek and Alvaro Ribeire, Oxford, 1979, pp. 1-11.

Greene, Thomas, "The Postures of Hamlet," *SQ*, vol. 11 (1960), pp. 352-66.

Griffith, Matthew, *Bethel, or a Form for Families*, 1633.

Grindal, Edmund, *Remains*, Cambridge, 1843.

Groot, C. Hofstede de, *A Catalogue Raisonné of the Works of the Most Eminent Dutch Painters of the Seventeenth Century*, 10 vols. of the 1908-28 ed. reprinted, London, 1976.

Guernsey, R. S., *Ecclesiastical Law in Hamlet: The Burial of Ophelia*, New York, 1971.

Hair, Paul, *Before the Bawdy Court*, New York, 1972.

*Hamlet: An Authoritative Text, Intellectual Backgrounds. Extracts from the Sources, Essays in Criticism*, ed. Cyrus Hoy, New York, 1963.

*Hamlet: Enter Critic*, ed. Claire Sacks and Edgar Whan, New York, 1960.

Hammick, James T., *The Marriage Law of England*, London, 1887.

Hanford, James Holly, "Suicide in the Plays of Shakespeare," *PMLA*, vol. 27 (1912), pp. 380-97.

Hankins, John E., *The Character of Hamlet and Other Essays*, Chapel Hill, North Carolina, 1941.

Hankins, John E., *Shakespeare's Derived Imagery*, New York, 1977.

Harbage, Alfred, *see* William Shakespeare, *The Complete Works*.

*The Harper Encyclopedia of Science*, ed. James R. Newman, New York, 1963.

Harrison, George Bagshawe, *Elizabethan Plays and Players*, Ann Arbor, 1956.

Harrison, George Bagshawe, *The Life and Death of Robert Devereux, Earl of Essex*, New York, 1937.

Hartlaub, Gustav F., *Zauber des Spiegels*, Munich, 1951.

Haugaard, William P., *Elizabeth and the English Reformation*, Cambridge, 1970.

Hawkes, Terence, *Shakespeare and the Reason: A Study of the Tragedies and the Problem Plays*, London, 1964.

Herbert, George, *The English Poems of George Herbert*, ed. C. A. Patrides, London, 1974.

Herford, C. H., "Shakespeare and the Arts," *Bulletin of the John Rylands Library*, vol. 11 (1927), pp. 273-85.

Hibbard, G. R., "*Henry IV* and *Hamlet*," *Shakespeare Survey*, vol. 30 (1977), pp. 1-12.

Highet, Gilbert, *The Powers of Poetry*, New York, 1960.

Hill, Robert, *The Pathway to Prayer and Piety*, 1613.

Hind, Arthur M., Marjorie Corbett, and Michael Norton, *Engraving in England in the Sixteenth and Seventeenth Centuries*, 3 vols., Cambridge, 1952-64.

Hinks, Roger, *Myth and Allegory in Ancient Art*, London, 1939.

Hinman, Charlton, ed., *The Norton Facsimile: The First Folio of Shakespeare*, New York, 1968.

Hirth, Georg, *Picture Book of the Graphic Arts: 1500-1800*, 6 vols., New York, 1972.

Hodnett, Edward, *Francis Barlow: First Master of English Book Illustration*, Ilkley, Yorkshire, 1978.

Holbein, Hans, the Younger, *The Dance of Death*, ed. Werner L. Gundersheimer, New York, 1971.

Holloway, John, *The Story of the Night: Studies in Shakespeare's Major Tragedies*, London, 1961.

Hollstein, F.W.H., *Dutch and Flemish Etchings, Engravings and Woodcuts, ca. 1450-1700*, 19 vols., Amsterdam, 1949-69.

Holt, Elizabeth G., ed., *A Documentary History of Art: Volume One: The Middle Ages and the Renaissance*, Garden City, New York, 1957.

Homilies: *Certain Sermons or Homilies Appointed to be Read in Churches in the Time of Queen Elizabeth*, Oxford, 1822.

Honigmann, E.A.J., "The Politics in *Hamlet* and 'The World of the Play'," *Stratford-upon-Avon Studies*, vol. 5 (1964), pp. 129-47.

Hooker, Richard, *Of the Laws of Ecclesiastical Polity*, ed. Georges Edelin and W. Speed Hill, Cambridge, Massachusetts, 1977—.

Hooker, Richard, *Works*, ed. John Keble, 2 vols., New York, 1849.

Hooper, John, *Early Writings*, ed. Samuel Carr, Cambridge, 1843.

Hooper, John, *Later Writings*, ed. Charles Nevinson, Cambridge, 1852.

Hoopes, Robert, *Right Reason in the English Renaissance*, Cambridge, Massachusetts, 1962.

Hope, W. H. St. John, "On the Funeral Effigies of the Kings and Queens of England," *Archaeologia*, vol. 60 (1907), pp. 517-70.

Horace, *Satires, Epistles and Ars Poetica*, ed. H. Rushton Fairclough, London and Cambridge, Massachusetts, 1941.

Hotman, François, *Francogallia*, ed. Ralph Giesey and J.H.M. Salmon, Cambridge, 1972.

Howard, Leon, *The Logic of Hamlet's Soliloquies*, Lone Pine, California, 1964.

Howgrave-Graham, R. P., "Royal Portraits in Effigy: Some New Discoveries in Westminster Abbey," *Journal of the Royal Society of Arts*, vol. 101 (1953), pp. 465-74.

Hughes, Philip, *The Reformation in England, III: "True Religion Now Established,"* London, 1954.

Hunter, G. K., "Hamlet Criticism," *Critical Quarterly*, vol. 1 (1959), pp. 27-32.

Hunter, Robert G., *Shakespeare and the Mystery of God's Judgments*, Athens, Georgia, 1976.

Hurault, Jacques, *Politic, Moral and Martial Discourses*, trans. Arthur Golding, 1595.

*Interpreter's Bible*, ed. George A. Buttrick, 12 vols., New York, 1954-57.

*The Interpreter's Dictionary of the Bible*, ed. George A. Buttrick, 4 vols., New York, 1962.

Iwasaki, Soji, *The Sword and the Word*, Tokyo, 1973.

Jacob, Henriette s', *Idealism and Realism: A Study of Sepulchral Symbolism*, Leiden, 1954.

Jacquot, Jean, ed., *Fêtes et Cérémonies au temps de Charles Quint*, Paris, 1960.

Janson, Horst W., "The Putto with a Death's Head," *Art Bulletin*, vol. 19 (1937), pp. 423-49.

Jászi, Oscar, and Lewis, John D., *Against the Tyrant: The Tradition and Theory of Tyrannicide*, Glencoe, Illinois, 1957.

Jewel, John, *Works*, 3 vols., Cambridge, 1847-48.

Jonson, Ben, *Ben Jonson*, ed. C. H. Herford

and Percy Simpson, 7 vols., Oxford, 1925-41.

Jones, Ernest, *Hamlet and Oedipus*, Garden City, New York, 1949.

Joseph, Bertram, *Conscience and the King: A Study of "Hamlet,"* London, 1953.

Joseph, Bertram, *Elizabethan Acting*, Oxford and London, 1951.

Joseph, Miriam, "Discerning the Ghost in *Hamlet*," *PMLA*, vol. 76 (1961), pp. 493-502.

Joseph, Miriam, "*Hamlet*, A Christian Tragedy," *SP*, 59 (1962), pp. 119-40.

Josselin, Ralph, *The Dairy of Ralph Josselin, 1616-83*, ed. Alan MacFarlane, London, 1976.

Kaftal, George, *Iconography of the Saints in Tuscan Painting*, Florence, 1952.

Keith, Robert, *History of the Affairs of Church and State in Scotland*, 3 vols., Edinburgh, 1844-50.

Kelley, Donald R., *François Hotman: A Revolutionary's Ordeal*, Princeton, 1973.

Kernan, Alvin B., *The Cankered Muse*, New Haven, Connecticut, 1959.

Kingdon, Robert, *Geneva and the Coming of the Wars of Religion in France: 1555-63*, Geneva, 1956.

Kittredge, G. L., ed., *Hamlet*, New York, 1939.

Klein, Joan Larsen, "Hamlet 4.2.12-21 and Whitney's *A Choice of Emblems*," *N&Q* 23 (1976), pp. 158-61.

Knights, L. C., *An Approach to Hamlet*, London, 1960.

Knights, L. C., "Prince Hamlet," *Discussion of Hamlet*, ed. J. C. Levenson, Boston, 1960, pp. 77-83, reprinted from *Explorations: Essays in Criticism*, London, 1946.

Knipping, John B., *Iconography of the Counter-Reformation in the Netherlands*, 2 vols., Leiden, 1974.

Knox, John, *History of the Reformation in Scotland*, ed. William Croft Dickinson, 2 vols., London and Edinburgh, 1950.

Kurz, Otto, "Four Tapestries after Hieronymous Bosch," *JWCI*, vol. 30 (1967), pp. 150-62.

Kyd, Thomas, *The Spanish Tragedy*, ed. Andrew S. Cairncross, Lincoln, Nebraska, 1967.

Lane, John, *An Elegy upon the Death of Elizabeth*, 1603.

Languet, Hubert, *The Correspondence of Philip Sidney and Hubert Languet*, ed. W. A. Bradley, Boston, 1912.

Latimer, Hugh, *Sermons*, ed. George E. Corrie, Cambridge, 1844.

Latimer, Hugh, *Sermons and Remains*, ed. George E. Corrie, Cambridge, 1845.

Lavater, Lewes, *Of Ghosts and Spirits Walking by Night*, ed. J. Dover Wilson and May Yardley, Oxford, 1929.

Law, T. G., *The Archpriest Controversy*, Westminster, 1898.

Lawrence, William J., *Pre-Restoration Stage Studies*, Cambridge, Massachusetts, 1927.

Lebeer, L., "Het Hooi en de Hooiwagen in de beeldende Kunsten," *Gentsche Bijdragen*, vol. 5 (1938), pp. 141-55.

Lehner, Ernst and Johanna, *Devils, Demons, Death and Damnation*, New York, 1971.

Le Huray, Peter, *Music and the Reformation in England: 1549-1660*, London, 1967.

Leland, John, *De Rebus Britannicis Collectanea*, 6 vols., London, 1774.

Lenman, Bruce, and Parker, Geoffrey, "Crime and Control in Scotland 1500-1800," *History Today*, vol. 30 (January, 1980), pp. 13-17.

Leonardo, *Leonardo da Vinci's Notebooks*, ed. Edward McCurdy, New York, 1923.

Levang, Lewis D., " 'Ripeness is all': A Semantic Approach to a *Lear* Question," *Etc.: A Review of General Semantics*, vol. 27 (1970), pp. 91-98.

Levin, Harry, *The Question of Hamlet*, New York, 1959.

Levin, William R., *Images of Love and Death in Late Medieval and Renaissance Art*, Ann Arbor, Michigan, 1975.

Levitsky, Ruth, "Rightly to be Great," *Shakespeare Studies*, vol. 1 (1965), pp. 142-67.

Lewis, Charlton T., and Short, Charles, *A Latin Dictionary*, Oxford, 1975.

Lewis, Clive S., "Hamlet: The Prince or the Poem?" *Proceedings of the British Academy*, vol. 28 (1942), pp. 3-18.

Lewy, Guenter, *The Political Philosophy of Juan de Mariana, S.J.*, Geneva, 1960.

Lidz, Theodore, *Hamlet's Enemy: Madness and Myth in "Hamlet,"* London, 1975.

*Life's Picture History of Western Man*, New York, 1951.

*Liturgies and Occasional Forms of Prayer set Forth in the Reign of Queen Elizabeth*, ed. William Keatinge Clay, Cambridge, 1847.

Lodge, Thomas, *Complete Works*, Hunterian Club edition, 5 vols., Glasgow, 1875-88.

Long, Michael, *The Unnatural Scene: A Study in Shakespearean Tragedy*, London, 1976.

Lucas, F. L., *Literature and Psychology*, Ann Arbor, Michigan, 1957.

Luther, Martin, *The Greater Catechism*, in *Luther's Primary Works*, ed. Henry Wace and C. A. Buchheim, London, 1896.

Luther, Martin, *Sermons on the Passion of Christ*, trans. E. Smid and J. T. Isensee, Rock Island, Illinois, 1956.

Luther, Martin, *Werke*, 57 vols., Weimar, 1883.

Luther, Martin, *What Luther Says: An Anthology*, ed. Ewald M. Plass, 3 vols., St. Louis, Missouri, 1956.

Luther, Martin, *Works*, 6 vols., Philadelphia, 1915-32.

Lyons, Bridget Gellert, "The Iconography of Melancholy in the Graveyard Scene of *Hamlet*," *SP*, vol. 67 (1970), pp. 57-66.

Lyons, Bridget Gellert, "The Iconography of Ophelia," *ELH*, vol. 40 (1977), pp. 60-73.

Lyons, Bridget Gellert, *Voices of Melancholy: Studies in Literary Treatments of Melancholy in Renaissance England*, New York, 1971.

Macquoid, Percy, "The Home . . . Funerals," *Shakespeare's England*, vol. 2, pp. 119-52, Oxford, 1950.

McCombie, Frank, "*Hamlet* and the *Moriae Encomium*," *Shakespeare Survey*, vol. 27 (1974), pp. 59-69.

McElwee, William, *The Wisest Fool in Christendom: The Reign of King James I and VI*, London, 1958.

McLean, Antonia, *Humanism and the Rise of Science in Tudor England*, New York, 1972.

Machyn, Henry, *The Diary of Henry Machyn . . . from A.D. 1550–A.D. 1563*, ed. John Gough Nichols, London, 1848.

Mack, Maynard, "The World of *Hamlet*," *The Yale Review*, vol. 41 (1952), pp. 502-23, reprinted in *Shakespeare, the Tragedies: A Collection of Critical Essays*, ed. Alfred Harbage, Englewood Cliffs, New Jersey, 1964, pp. 44-60.

Maguin, Jean-Marie, "Of Ghosts and Spirits Walking by Night," *Cahiers Elizabethains*, no. 1 (1972), pp. 25-40.

Malone, Edmond, *Plays and Poems of William Shakespeare*, 10 vols., London, 1790.

Mariana, Juan de, *The King and the Education of the King*, trans. George Albert Moore, Washington, 1948.

Maritain, Jacques, *Art and Scholasticism*, New York, 1962.

Marston, John, *Antonio and Mellida*, in *The Plays of John Marston*, ed. H. Harvey Wood, Edinburgh and London, 1934.

Martz, Louis, *The Poetry of Meditation*, New Haven, Connecticut, 1954.

Massar, Phyllis Dearborn, *Presenting Stefano della Bella, Seventeenth-Century Printmaker*, New York, 1971.

Matthews, George T., ed., *News and Rumor in Renaissance Europe: The Fugger Newsletters*, New York, 1959.

Mattingly, Garrett, *The Armada*, Boston, 1959.

Meagher, John C., "Vanity, Lear's Feather, and the Pathology of Editorial Annotation," *Shakespeare 1971*, ed. Clifford Leach and J.M.R. Margeson, Toronto, 1972, pp. 244-59.

*The Memoirs of Philippe de Mornay*, trans. Lucy Crump, London, n.d. [c. 1926?].

Mercer, Eric, *English Art 1553-1625*, Oxford, 1962.

Meyer, Arnold O., *England and the Catholic Church under Queen Elizabeth*, London, 1967.

M[ill], H., *Poems*, 1639.

Millar, Oliver, *The Tudor, Stuart, and Early Georgian Pictures in the Collection of Her Majesty the Queen*, 2 vols., London, 1963.

Milton, John, *Complete Poems and Major Prose*, ed. Merritt Y. Hughes, New York, 1957.

Milton, John, *The Tenure of Kings and Magistrates*, ed. Merritt Y. Hughes, in *Complete Prose Works*, vol. 3, New Haven, Connecticut, 1962.

*The Mirrour of Majestie, or The Badges of Honour*, 1618, in facsimile reprint of Holbein Society, n.p., 1870.

Misson, Henri, *Memoirs and Observations in his Travels*, London, 1719.

Molesworth, Robert, first Viscount, *Account of Denmark*, 1694.

Mommsen, Theodor E., "Petrarch and the Story of the Choice of Hercules," *JWCI*, vol. 16 (1953), 178-92.

Moore, Charles, *A Full Inquiry Into the Subject of Suicide*, London, 1790.

Moorman, F. W., "The Pre-Shakespearean Ghost," *MLR*, vol. 1 (1906), pp. 85-95.

Moorman, F. W., "Shakespeare's Ghosts," *MLR*, vol. 1 (1906), pp. 192-201.

More, Thomas, *Utopia*, ed. J. Rawson Lumby, Cambridge, 1935.

Mornay, Philippe de, *see The Memoirs of Philippe de Mornay.*

Mornay, Philippe du Plessis-Mornay, *Vindiciae Contra Tyrannos*, see Julian H. Franklin.

Morris, Harry, "*Hamlet* as a *Memento Mori* Poem," *PMLA*, 85 (1970), pp. 1035-40.

Morris, Ivor, *Shakespeare's God: The Role of Religion in the Tragedies*, New York, 1972.

Mosse, George L., *The Holy Pretense: A Study in Christianity and Reasons of State from William Perkins to John Winthrop*, Oxford, 1957.

Mousnier, Roland, *The Assassination of Henry IV: The Tyrannicide Problem and the Consolidation of the French Absolute Monarchy in the Early Seventeenth Century*, London, 1973.

Muir, Kenneth, "Arthur Brooke and the Imagery of *Romeo and Juliet*," *N&Q*, n.s. vol. 3 (1956), pp. 241-43.

Muir, Kenneth, *Shakespeare: Hamlet*, Great Neck, New York, 1963.

Muir, Kenneth, *Shakespeare's Tragic Sequence*, London, 1972.

Mutschmann, H., and Wentersdorf, K., *Shakespeare and Catholicism*, New York, 1969.

Myrick, Kenneth, "Kittredge on *Hamlet*," *SQ*, 15 (1964), pp. 218-34.

National Gallery, *Art in Seventeenth Century Holland*, London, 1976.

*La natura morta italiana. Catalogo della mostra, Napoli, Zurigo, Rotterdam*, Milan, 1964.

Neale, J. E., *Queen Elizabeth I: A Biography*, Garden City, New York, 1957.

Neale, J. E., *Elizabeth I and Her Parliaments 1559-81*, New York, 1953.

Nelson, Thomas, *Blessed State of England*, 1591.

Nevo, Ruth, *Tragic Form in Shakespeare*, Princeton, 1972.

Newell, Alex, "The Dramatic Context and Meaning of Hamlet's 'To Be or Not to Be' Soliloquy," *PMLA*, vol. 80 (1965), pp. 38-50.

Newman, James R., *see Harper Encyclopedia of Science.*

Nicoll, Allardyce, *Stuart Masques and the Renaissance Stage*, London, 1937.

Nichols, John, *Illustrations of the Manners and Expenses of Ancient Times*, London, 1797.

Nichols, John, *The Progresses, Processions, and Magnificent Festivities of King James I*, 4 vols., London, 1828.

Noble, Richmond, *Shakespeare's Biblical Knowledge*, New York, 1977.

Nogueres, Henri, *The Massacre of St. Bartholomew*, London, 1962.

Norden, John, *A Progress of Piety*, Cambridge, 1847.

Nowell, Alexander, *A Catechism*, ed. George E. Corrie, Cambridge, 1853.

Ogden, Henry V. S., and Margaret, *English Taste in Landscape in the Seventeenth Century*, Ann Arbor, Michigan, 1955.

Olsson, Yngve B., "In Search of Yorick's Skull: Notes on the Background of Hamlet," *Shakespeare Studies*, vol. 4 (1969), pp. 183-220.

Ornstein, Robert, *A Kingdom for a Stage: The Achievement of Shakespeare's History Plays*, Cambridge, Massachusetts, 1972.

Ornstein, Robert, *The Moral Vision of Jacobean Tragedy*, Madison, Wisconsin, 1960.

Osborn, James M., *Young Philip Sidney*, New Haven, Connecticut, 1972.

Panofsky, Erwin, *Hercules am Scheidewege*, Berlin and Leipzig, 1930.

Panofsky, Erwin, *The Life and Art of Albrecht Dürer*, Princeton, 1971.

Panofsky, Erwin, *Meaning in the Visual Arts*, New York, 1955.

Panofsky, Erwin, *Studies in Iconology*, New York, 1962.

Panofsky, Erwin, "Van Eyck's Arnolfini Portrait," reprinted in Creighton Gilbert, ed., *Renaissance Art*, New York, 1970, pp. 1-20.

Pape, T., "An Elizabethan Glass Furnace," *Connoisseur*, vol. 92 (1933), pp. 172-77.

Paradin, Claude, *The Heroical Devices*, 1591.

Parker, Geoffrey, see entry for Bruce Lenman.

Parker, Matthew, *Correspondence*, ed. John Bruce, Cambridge, 1853.

Patch, Howard, *The Goddess Fortuna in Medieval Literature*, Cambridge, Massachusetts, 1927.

Perkins, William, *The Whole Treatise of Cases of Conscience*, 1608.

Perkins, William, *William Perkins, 1558-1602, English Puritanist: His Pioneer Works on Casuistry*, ed. Thomas F. Merrill, Niewkoop, The Netherlands, 1966.

Perrière, Guillaume de la, *Morosophie*, Lyons, 1553.

Perrière, Guillaume de la, *Le Théâtre des Bons Engins . . . Cent Emblèmes Moraulx*, 1539, facsimile edition, Gainesville, Florida, 1964; and Thomas Combe, trans., *The Theater of Fine Devises*, 1614.

Peter, Baldwin, F.S.C., "*Hamlet* and *In Paradisum*," *SQ*, vol. 3 (1952), pp. 279f.

*Peterborough Cathedral*, London, 1975.

Peters, Robert, *Oculus Episcopi: Administration in the Archidiaconry of St. Albans 1580-1625*, Manchester, 1963.

P[etowe], H., *Elizabetha quasi Vivens, Eliza's Funeral*, 1603.

Phillips, James E., *Images of a Queen: Mary Stuart in Sixteenth-Century Literature*, Berkeley, 1964.

Pierce, C. A., *Conscience in the New Testament (Studies in Biblical Theology*, No. 15), London, 1958.

Pigler, A., *Barockthemen*, 2 vols., Budapest and Berlin, 1956.

Pigler, A., "Portraying the Dead," *Acta Historiae Artium Academiae Scientiarum Hungari*, vol. 4 (1956), pp. 1-74.

Pilkington, James, *Works*, ed. James Scholefield, Cambridge, 1842.

Plato, *The Works of Plato*, trans. and ed. Benjamin Jowett, New York, n.d.

Plowden, Alison, *Danger to Elizabeth: The Catholics under Elizabeth I*, London, 1973.

Plutarch, "On Tranquility of Mind," in *Moralia*, vol. 6, ed. W. C. Helmbold, London and Cambridge, Massachusetts, 1962.

Plutarch, *Shakespeare's Plutarch*, ed. Walter W. Skeat, London, 1875.

Pollin, Burton, "Hamlet, A Successful Suicide," *Shakespeare Studies*, vol. 1 (1965), pp. 240-60.

Pope-Hennessy, John, *The Portrait in the Renaissance*, New York and Washington, 1966.

Powell, Henry J., *Glass-Making in England*, Cambridge, 1923.

Prior, Matthew, *The Literary Works of Matthew Prior*, ed. H. Bunker Wright and Monroe K. Spears, Oxford, 1959.

Pritchard, Arnold, *Catholic Loyalism in Elizabethan England*, Chapel Hill, North Carolina, 1979.

Prosser, Eleanor, *Hamlet and Revenge*, Stanford, California, 1967.

Puckle, Bertram S., *Funeral Customs: Their Origins and Developments*, New York, 1926.

Quarles, Francis, *Emblems, Divine and Moral*, London, 1845.

Quistorp, Heinrich, *Calvin's Doctrine of the Last Things*, Richmond, Virginia, 1955.

R. R., *Questions concerning Cony-hood and the Nature of the Cony*, 1595.

Ralli, Augustus, *A History of Shakespearian Criticism*, 2 vols., New York, 1959.

Ranum, Orest, "The French Ritual of Tyrannicide in the Late Sixteenth Century," *Sixteenth Century Journal*, vol. 11 (1980), pp. 63-82.

Read, Conyers, *The Tudors: Personalities and Practical Politics in Sixteenth Century England*, New York, 1936.

Réau, Louis, "Eschatology," *Encyclopedia of World Art*, New York and London, 1959-68, vol. 4, col. 822.

Réau, Louis, *Iconographie de l'art chrétien*, 3 vols. in 6, Paris, 1955-59.

Reese, M. M., *The Cease of Majesty: A Study*

of *Shakespeare's History Plays*, London, 1961.

Ribner, Irving, *The English History Play*, Princeton, 1957.

Ribner, Irving, *Patterns in Shakespearian Tragedy*, New York, 1960.

Rich, Barnaby, *The Irish Hubbub*, 1619.

Ridley, Jasper, *Thomas Cranmer*, Oxford, 1962.

Ridley, Nicholas, *Works*, ed. Henry Christmas, Cambridge, 1841.

Rifkin, Myra Lee, *Burial, Funeral and Mourning Customs in England: 1558-1662*, 1977 doctoral dissertation at Bryn Mawr.

Ringler, William, "Hamlet's Defense of the Players," in *Essays on Shakespeare and Elizabethan Drama in Honor of Hardin Craig*, Columbia, Missouri, 1962, pp. 201-11.

Ripa, Cesare, *Baroque and Rococo Pictorial Imagery*, ed. Edward Maser, New York, 1971.

Roberts, Josephine, *Architectonic Knowledge in the New Arcadia (1590), Sidney's Use of the Heroic Journey*, Salzburg, Austria, 1979.

Robertson, Alec, *Requiem: Music of Mourning and Consolation*, London, 1967.

Robertson, D. W., Jr., *Essays in Medieval Culture*, Princeton, 1980.

Roelker, Nancy Lyman, *Queen of Navarre: Jeanne d'Albret 1528-72*, Cambridge, Massachusetts, 1968.

Rose, Elliott, *Cases of Conscience: Alternatives open to Recusants and Puritans under Elizabeth I and James I*, Cambridge, 1975.

Rosenblatt, Jason P., "Aspects of the Incest Problem in *Hamlet*," *SQ*, vol. 29 (1978), pp. 349-64.

Rosinger, Lawrence, "Hamlet and the Homilies," *SQ*, vol. 26 (1975), pp. 299-301.

Rowell, Geoffrey, *The Liturgy of Christian Burial: An Introductory Survey of the Historical Development of Christian Burial Rites*, London, 1977.

Rowse, A. L., *The Elizabethan Renaissance: The Life of the Society*, London, 1971.

Rus, J. R. "'Old Mole' in *Hamlet* 1.5.162," *ELN*, vol. 12 (1975), pp. 163-68.

Sackville, Thomas, "Induction: The Complaint of Henry Duke of Buckingham," in *A Mirrour for Magistrates*, ed. Lily B. Campbell, Cambridge, 1938.

Salmon, J.H.M., *The French Religious Wars in English Political Thought*, Oxford, 1959.

Salmon, J.H.M., *Society in Crisis: France in the Sixteenth Century*, New York, 1975.

Sander, Max, *Le Livre à figures italien depuis 1467 jusqu'à 1530*, 6 vols. plus supplement, Milan, 1942-59.

Sanders, Wilbur, *The Dramatist and the Received Idea: Studies in the Plays of Marlowe and Shakespeare*, Cambridge, 1968.

Sandys, Edwin, *Sermons*, ed. John Ayre, Cambridge, 1841.

Schmidt, Alexander, *Shakespeare Lexicon*, rev. Gregor Sarrazin, 2 vols., New York, 1971.

Schoenbaum, Samuel, *William Shakespeare: A Documentary Life*, New York, 1975.

Schwarz, Heinrich, "The Mirror in Art," *Art Quarterly*, vol. 15 (1952), pp. 97-118.

Scot, Reginald, *Discovery of Witchcraft and Discourse upon Devils and Spirits*, 1584, ed. Brinsley Nicholson, London, 1886.

Seaman, John E., "The Blind Curtain and Hamlet's Guilt," *Western Humanities Review*, vol. 19 (1965), pp. 345-53.

Semper, I. J., "The Ghost in *Hamlet*: Pagan or Christian?" *The Month*, vol. 9 (1953), pp. 222-34.

Semper, I. J., *Hamlet Without Tears*, Dubuque, Iowa, 1946.

Seneca, *Ad Lucilium Epistulae Morales*, trans. Richard M. Gummere, 3 vols., London and New York, 1920-25.

Seneca, *Moral Essays*, 3 vols., ed. John W. Basore, London, New York, and Cambridge, Massachusetts, 1928-51.

Shakespeare, William, *The Complete Works*, ed. Alfred Harbage, Baltimore, Maryland, 1969.

Shakespeare, William, *The First Folio*—see Charlton Hinman.

*Shakespeare's England: An Account of the Life and Manners of his Age*, 2 vols., Oxford, 1950.

Shaw, George Bernard, "Preface" to *The Dark Lady of the Sonnets*, in *Bernard Shaw: Selected Plays*, New York, 1948.

Siegel, Paul N., *Shakespearean Tragedy and the Elizabethan Compromise*, New York, 1957.

Singer, Charles, *et al.*, *A History of Technology*, 5 vols., Oxford, 1957.

Sisson, C. J., "The Mouse-Trap Again," *RES*, vol. 16 (1940), pp. 129-36.

Sitwell, Dame Edith, *A Notebook on William Shakespeare*, London, 1948.

Skinner, Quentin, *The Foundations of Modern Political Thought*, 2 vols., Cambridge, 1978.

Skulsky, Harold, " 'I Know my Course': Hamlet's Confidence," *PMLA*, vol. 89 (1974), pp. 477-85.

Slights, Camille Wells, *The Casuistical Tradition in Shakespeare, Donne, Herbert, and Milton*, Princeton, 1981.

Slive, Seymour, *Frans Hals*, 3 vols., London, 1970-74.

Smith, G. G., *Elizabethan Critical Essays*, 2 vols., Oxford, 1904.

Snyder, Susan, "The Left Hand of God: Despair in Medieval and Renaissance Tradition," *Studies in the Renaissance*, vol. 12 (1965), pp. 18-59.

Soellner, Rolf, *Shakespeare's Patterns of Self-Knowledge*, n.p.: Ohio State University Press, 1972.

Speight, Robert, *Nature in Shakespearian Tragedy*, London, 1955.

Spencer, Theodore, *Death in Elizabethan Tragedy*, Cambridge, Massachusetts, 1936.

Spingarn, J. E., *A History of Literary Criticism in the Renaissance*, New York, 1954.

Spriggs, Gereth, "A Dog in the Pew," *Country Life* (February 12, 1976), pp. 338f.

Sprott, S. E., *The English Debate on Suicide from Donne to Hume*, La Salle, Illinois, 1961.

Spufford, Margaret, *Contrasting Communities: English Villagers in the Sixteenth and Seventeenth Centuries*, Cambridge, 1974.

Stabler, A. P., "Elective Monarchy in the Sources of *Hamlet*," *SP*, vol. 62 (1965), pp. 654-61.

Stafford, Anthony, *Meditations and Resolutions*, 1612.

Stainer, David, "To Out-Herod Herod: The Development of a Dramatic Character," *Comparative Drama*, vol. 10 (1976), pp. 29-53.

Steer, Francis, "Arundel Castle and Its Owners 1067-1660," *The Connoisseur*, vol. 197 (1978), pp. 155-61.

Stevenson, Sarah, *A Face for any Occasion: Some Aspects of Portrait Engraving*, Edinburgh, 1976.

Strauss, Gerald, "Capturing Hearts and Minds in the German Reformation," *History Today*, vol. 31 (June, 1981), pp. 21-25.

Strauss, Gerald, *Luther's House of Learning*, Baltimore, Maryland, 1978.

Stroch, W. F., "Aspects of Death in English Art and Poetry," *Burlington Magazine*, vol. 21 (1912), pp. 249-56 and 314-19.

Strode, William, *The Poetical Works of William Strode*, ed. Bertram Dobell, London, 1907.

Strong, Roy, *The Cult of Elizabeth: Elizabethan Portraiture and Pageantry*, London, 1977.

Strong, Roy, *The English Icon: Elizabethan and Jacobean Portraiture*, London and New York, 1969.

Strong, Roy, "Inigo Jones and the Stuart Court," *The Times*, July 7, 1977.

Strong, Roy, and Oman, Julia Trevelyan, *Mary Queen of Scots*, London, 1972.

Strong, Roy, *Tudor and Jacobean Portraits*, 2 vols., London, 1969.

Strype, John, *Ecclesiastical Memorials of the Church of England*, 3 vols. in 6, Oxford, 1822.

Stubbes, Philip, *A Christal Glass for Christian Women*, 1608.

Suetonius, *Lives of the Caesars in Suetonius*, ed. J. C. Rolfe, Cambridge, Massachusetts, 1950.

Sutherland, N. M., *The Massacre of St. Bartholomew and the European Conflict 1559-72*, London, 1973.

Symonds, R. W., "Early English Mirrors," *Connoisseur*, vol. 96 (1935), pp. 315-21.

Symonds, R. W., "English Looking-Glass Plates and Their Manufacture," *Connoisseur*, vol. 97 (1936), pp. 243-49.

Symonds, R. W., "English Looking-Glass Plates and Their Manufacture—III," *Connoisseur*, vol. 98 (1936), pp. 9-15.

Taillepied, Noel, *A Treatise of Ghosts*, trans. Montague Summers, London, [1933].

Talbert, E. W., *The Problem of Order: Elizabethan Political Commonplaces and An Ex-*

*ample of Shakespeare's Art*, Chapel Hill, North Carolina, 1962.

Taylor, Jeremy, *Holy Dying* in *The Whole Works*, 3 vols., London, 1880.

Thomas, Keith, *Religion and the Decline of Magic: Studies in Popular Beliefs in Sixteenth- and Seventeenth-Century England*, Harmondsworth, Middlesex, 1980.

Thomson, Duncan, *Painting in Scotland, 1570-1650*, Edinburgh, 1975.

Thomson, Gladys Scott, *Life in a Noble Household, 1641-1700*, London, 1937.

Thorpe, William A., *English Glass*, London, 1949.

Tilley, Morris P., *A Dictionary of the Proverbs in England in the Sixteenth and Seventeenth Centuries*, Ann Arbor, Michigan, 1950.

Tillyard, E.M.W., *The Elizabethan World Picture*, New York, 1960.

Tillyard, E.M.W., *Shakespeare's History Plays*, London, 1944.

Todorow, Maria Fossi, *Mostra delle Incisioni di Luca di Leida*, Florence, 1963.

Torrance, Thomas, *Calvin's Doctrine of Man*, London, 1949.

Toynbee, Jocelyn M. C., *Death and Burial in the Roman World*, Ithaca, New York, 1971.

Trevor-Roper, Hugh R., *Archbishop Laud: 1573-1645*, London, 1940.

Turner, A. Richard, *Vision of Landscape in Renaissance Italy*, Princeton, 1966.

Tyndale, William, *An Answer to Sir Thomas More's "Dialogue,"* ed. Henry Walter, Cambridge, 1850.

Tyndale, William, *Doctrinal Treatises*, ed. Henry Walter, Cambridge, 1848.

Tyndale, William, *Expositions and Notes on Sundry Portions of the Holy Scriptures*, ed. Henry Walter, Cambridge, 1849.

Ure, Peter, "Character and Role from *Richard III* to *Hamlet*" *Stratford-upon-Avon Studies*, vol. 5 (1964), pp. 9-28.

Ure, Peter, "The Looking-Glass of Richard II," *PQ*, vol. 34 (1955), pp. 219-24.

Vaenius, Otto, *Amorum Emblematum*, Antwerp, 1608.

Valentiner, W[ilhelm], *Frans Hals*, Stuttgart and Berlin, 1921.

Vassar College Art Gallery, *see Dutch Mannerism, Apogee and Epilogue*.

Veith, Gene Edward, Jr., " 'Wait Upon the Lord': David, *Hamlet*, and the Problem of Revenge," in *The David Myth in Western Literature*, ed. Raymond-Jean Frontain and Jan Wojcik, West Lafayette, Indiana, 1980, pp. 70-83.

Vermeule, Emily Townsend, *Aspects of Death in Early Greek Art and Poetry*, Berkeley and Los Angeles, 1979.

Veron, Jean, *The Hunting of Purgatory to Death*, 1561.

Vickers, Brian, ed., *Shakespeare: The Critical Heritage, 1623-1801*, 6 vols., London and Boston, 1974-82.

Waith, Eugene M., *The Herculean Hero in Marlowe, Chapman, Shakespeare and Dryden*, New York, 1962.

Waldock, A.J.A., *Hamlet: A Study in Critical Method*, Cambridge, 1931.

Walker, Roy, *The Time is Out of Joint*, London, 1948.

Walzer, Michael, *The Revolution of the Saints: A Study in the Origins of Radical Politics*, Cambridge, Massachusetts, 1965.

Warhaft, Sidney, "The Mystery of *Hamlet*," *ELH*, vol. 30 (1963), pp. 193-208.

Warner, William, *Pan his Syrinx or Pipe*, 1584.

Warner, William, *Syrinx: A Sevenfold History*, 1597.

Waterhouse, Ellis, *Anthony Van Dyck, "Suffer Little Children to Come Unto Me,"* Ottawa, Canada, 1978.

Watkin, E. I., *Roman Catholicism in England from the Reformation*, London and New York, 1958.

Webb, Clement C. J., *John of Salisbury*, New York, 1971.

Weber, Frederick P., *Aspects of Death*, New York, 1920.

Weitz, Morris, *Hamlet and the Philosophy of Literary Criticism*, New York and Cleveland, 1966.

Wernham, R. B., *Before the Armada: The Growth of English Foreign Policy 1485-1588*, London, 1966.

West, Robert H., "Elizabethan Belief in Spirits

and Witchcraft," in *Studies in Shakespeare*, ed. Arthur D. Matthews and Clark M. Emery, Coral Gables, Florida, 1953, pp. 65-73.

West, Robert H., *The Invisible World: A Study of Pneumatology in Elizabethan Drama*, Athens, Georgia, 1939.

West, Robert H., *Shakespeare and the Outer Mystery*, Lexington, Kentucky, 1968.

Westfall, Alfred Van Rensselaer, *American Shakespearean Criticism: 1607-1865*, New York and London, 1968.

Whinney, Margaret, *Sculpture in Britain: 1530-1830*, Harmondsworth, Middlesex, 1964.

Whitaker, Virgil, *The Mirror Up to Nature*, San Marino, California, 1965.

Whitaker, Virgil, *Shakespeare's Use of Learning*, San Marino, California, 1953.

Whitney, Jeffrey, *A Choice of Emblems*, 1586.

*The Whole Business of Sindercome*, 1657.

Williams, E. Carleton, "The Dance of Death in Sculpture and Paintings in the Middle Ages," *The Journal of the British Archaeological Association*, 3rd series, vol. 1 (1937), · pp. 229-57.

Williams, E. Carleton, "Mural Paintings of the Three Living and the Three Dead in England," *The Journal of the British Archaeological Association*, 3rd series, vol. 7 (1942), pp. 31-40.

Williams, George Walton, "Another Line from the *Ur-Hamlet*?" *N&Q*, vol. 23 (1976), pp. 157-58.

Williamson, Claude C. H., *Readings on the Character of Hamlet*, London, 1950.

Wilson, J. Dover, *The Essential Shakespeare*, Cambridge, 1952.

Wilson, J. Dover, *What Happens in Hamlet*, Cambridge, 1959.

Wilson, Thomas, *Elizabethan Art of Rhetoric*, ed. G. H. Mair, Oxford, 1909.

Wind, Edgar, *Pagan Mysteries in the Renaissance*, London, 1968.

Winstanley, Lilian, *Hamlet and the Scottish Succession*, Freeport, New York, 1970.

Wirth, Jean, *La Jeune Fille et la Mort*, Geneva, 1979.

Wither, George, *A Collection of Emblems, Ancient and Modern*, 1635.

Wither, George, *Prince Henry's Obsequies*, London, 1612.

Wood, Anthony à, *Athenae Oxoniensis*, 5 vols., ed. Philip Bliss, London, 1813-20.

Wood, Edward J., *Curiosities of Clocks and Watches from the Earliest Times*, London, 1866.

Wright, Louis B., *Middle-Class Culture in Elizabethan England*, Ithaca, New York, 1958.

Wyatt, E.G.P., *The Burial Service*, London and Oxford, 1918.

Xenophon, *Memorabilia and Oeconomicus, Symposium and Apology*, ed. E. C. Marchant and O. J. Todd, London and Cambridge, Massachusetts, 1948.

Yates, Francis A., "The Allegorical Portraits of Sir John Luttrell," in *Essays in the History of Art Presented to Rudolf Wittkower*, ed. Douglas Fraser, London, 1969.

Zitner, S. P., "Hamlet, Duellist," *UTQ*, vol. 39 (1969), pp. 1-18.

Zucker, Wolfgang M., "Reflections on Reflections," *Journal of Aesthetics and Art Criticism*, vol. 20 (1962), pp. 239-50.

*The Zurich Letters 1558-79*, ed. Hastings Robinson, Cambridge, 1842.

381

# General Index

Shakespeare's plays, where quoted or cited, are included below by reference to title, act, scene and lines followed by dashes and page references to my text, prefaced in this case by *p* or *pp* to distinguish the numbers. Books of the Bible are similarly cited by chapter and verse, with *p* or *pp* references to my text. References to cited or quoted passages from *Hamlet* are provided in a separate index, following this one. All other references follow convention.

# *Hamlet* Index

*Library of Congress Cataloging in Publication Data*

Frye, Roland Mushat.

The Renaissance Hamlet.

Bibliography: p.

Includes index.

1. Shakespeare, William, 1564-1616. Hamlet.

2. Shakespeare, William, 1564-1616—Contemporary England.   I. Title.

PR2807.F79  1984      822.3′3      83-42555

ISBN 0-691-06579-9